Navigating Political Science

Professional Advancement & Success in the Discipline

KENT WORCESTER, EDITOR

apsa
AMERICAN
POLITICAL
SCIENCE
ASSOCIATION

Thanks to PS: Political Science & Politics, Perspectives on Politics, the Journal of Political Science Education, Cambridge University Press, and Taylor & Francis.

Designed by Nicholas Townsend

Cover image: *Ascend*
Generously provided by Robert Hauck
www.robhauck.com

ISBN (Soft Cover) 978-1-878147-59-2
ISBN (ePub Fixed Layout) 978-1-878147-60-8
ISBN (ePub Reflowable) 978-1-878147-61-5

Table of Contents

Introduction   1
Kent Worcester, editor

Tasks and Responsibilities   5

Doing a Literature Review   7
Jeffrey W. Knopf

How To Be a Peer Reviewer: A Guide for Recent and Soon-to-be PhDs   17
Beth Miller Vonnahme, Jon Pevehouse, Ron Rogowski, Dustin Tingley, and Rick Wilson

Publishing as a Graduate Student:
A Quick and (Hopefully) Painless Guide to Establishing Yourself as a Scholar   25
Timothy S. Rich

Women Also Know Stuff:
Meta-Level Mentoring to Battle Gender Bias in Political Science   31
Emily Beaulieu, Amber E. Boydstun, Nadia E. Brown, Kim Yi Dionne, Andra Gillespie,
Samara Klar, Yanna Krupnikov, Melissa R. Michelson, Kathleen Searles, and Christina Wolbrecht

Do Political Science Majors Succeed in the Labor Market?   39
Gregory B. Lewis

The Classroom   49

Fostering Scholarly Discussion and Critical Thinking in the Political Science Classroom   51
Michael P. Marks

Turning the Classroom Upside Down:
Experimenting with the Flipped Classroom in American Government   69
Wendy N. Whitman Cobb

Learning Through Discussions:
Comparing the Benefits of Small-Group and Large-Class Settings   85
Philip H. Pollock III, Kerstin Hamann, and Bruce M. Wilson

Born Digital: Integrating Media Technology in the Political Science Classroom   97
Linda K. Mancillas and Peter W. Brusoe

Conflict in the Classroom:
Considering the Effects of Partisan Difference on Political Education   109
April Kelly-Woessner and Matthew Woessner

Field Research

125

Fieldwork in Political Science: Introduction
127
Roselyn Hsueh, Francesca Refsum Jensenius, and Akasemi Newsome

Navigating Fieldwork as an Outsider:
Observations from Interviewing Police Officers in China
131
Suzanne E. Scoggins

Positionality, Personal Insecurity, and Female Empathy in Security Studies Research
137
Vasundhara Sirnate

The Fieldwork of Quantitative Data Collection
143
Francesca Refsum Jensenius

Data Collection, Opportunity Costs, and Problem Solving:
Lessons from Field Research on Teachers' Unions in Latin America
149
Christopher Chambers-Ju

Knowing When to Scale Back: Addressing Questions of Research Scope in the Field
157
Akasemi Newsome

Confronting a Crisis of Research Design
163
Jody LaPorte

The Profession and the Public

169

Political Science and the Public Sphere Today
171
Rogers M. Smith

Disenchanted Professionals:
The Politics of Faculty Governance in the Neoliberal Academy
185
Timothy Kaufman-Osborn

The Most Important Topic
Political Scientists Are Not Studying: Adapting to Climate Change
205
Debra Javeline

An Interesting Bias: Lessons from an Academic's Year as a Reporter
223
David Niven

The Political Scientist as a Blogger
233
John Sides

Complicating the Political Scientist as Blogger
241
Robert Farley

Self-Conceptions 247

Political Science as a Vocation 249
Robert O. Keohane

American Politics and Political Science
in an Era of Growing Racial Diversity and Economy Disparity 257
Rodney E. Hero

Left Pessimism and Political Science 275
Jennifer L. Hochschild

Restructuring the Social Sciences:
Reflections from Harvard's Institute for Quantitative Social Science 293
Gary King

Restructuring the Social Sciences?
A Reflection from the Editor of Perspectives on Politics 305
Jeffrey C. Isaac

Contributors 313

Introduction

KENT WORCESTER

Frank J. Goodnow delivered APSA's inaugural presidential address in 1903, the same year the association was founded.[1] In his remarks, Goodnow defined the discipline as "that science which treats the organization known as the State." It is the State, after all, that "causes the phenomena of the greatest practical concern to the individual." Goodnow acknowledged that political parties, judicial doctrines, and even "extralegal customs and extra-legal organizations" were each key features of "the actual political system of a country." But his primary focus was on what he characterized as the "expression," "content," and "execution of the State will." "Our new association," he explained, "has opened to it a field which ought to be cultivated and offers opportunities that ought to be availed of."

More than a century on, Goodnow's Progressive Era disquisition makes for interesting reading. Some of his formulations are starchy, and his fixation on two cases, the United States and Great Britain, seems purblind. The idea that the discipline should be organized around the study of the State has slipped in and out of fashion over the years, and will strike many readers as unduly constrictive. But Goodnow was onto something when he talked about "the work of a tangible and measurable sort" that a political science "association may do":

> Only by comparison of notes with our colleagues can we learn whether we can improve our methods. Only in this way can we rub away the prejudices and lose the narrowness resulting from our environment. Only in this way can we secure the inspiration which is consequent upon the comradeship and good fellowship of those engaged along the same lines of work. There is hardly one of us who is engaged in the work of instruction who does not feel a sense of loneliness, thrown, as we are, in our different intellectual homes in the companionship of those, who, in their enthusiasm for their own line of work, are prone to imagine we are engaged in the study of a vain thing. There are none of us, I am sure, who do not feel that the establishment of the American Political Science Association offered us an advantage which we have long envied the historian and economist. (Goodnow 1903)

Comparison of notes, lose the narrowness, secure the inspiration—these phrases may be a little idiosyncratic, but they nonetheless capture APSA's mission. As Goodnow and others of his generational cohort anticipated, there really *are* advantages in mutual association along disciplinary lines, even if our understanding of such terms as "politics," "science," and "state" have evolved since the *fin de siècle*. Certainly it is harder for colleagues in other disciplines to "imagine we are engaged in the study of a vain thing" if we feel a sense of shared excitement about our own "line of work." The association's scholarships, workshops, annual meetings, special events, reports and pamphlets, and teaching and research awards all promote the cause of "comradeship and good fellowship," which at some point was renamed professional collaboration and development. APSA may not be *quite* as long-lived as its counterparts in history and economics,[2] but the scope and range of its programs and initiatives compare favorably to those of its disciplinary correlatives.

Scholarly publications are especially significant in this context. Three years after Frank Goodnow gave his inaugural address, the association established what is now known as the *American Political Science Review* (*APSR*). In its early incarnation, *APSR* not only published research articles and book reviews, but notices about conferences and grants, committee reports, news about APSA, and obituaries. Recognizing that the "number of political scientists, the diversity of their interests, the research they do, the books they publish, their specialization, the money available, and the complexity of their professional environment have very greatly increased in recent years," APSA launched a second publication, *PS: Political Science & Politics*, in 1968—"a newsletter...conceived as a means of communicating to association members such relevant information" (Kirkpatrick 1968). *Perspectives on Politics* (*PoP*) followed suit in 2003, and the *Journal of Political Science Education* (*JPSE*) arrived in 2005 and became an APSA member-wide journal in 2017. In addition, APSA sponsors nearly 50 organized sections, 18 of which currently publish or partner to publish their own titles—the *Journal of Law and Courts*, *Politics & Religion*, *State Politics & Policy Quarterly*, the *Journal of Race, Ethnicity, and Politics*, the *Journal of Experimental Political Science*, and *Politics & Gender* among others.[3] APSA is not quite a publishing empire but it oversees a much larger ecosystem of print and electronic communication than many of its members probably realize.

APSR, JPSE, and the organized section journals offer peer-reviewed research, and sometimes review essays and book reviews, along with adverts, announcements, editorials, and letters columns. But some APSA publications—most notably *PS: Political Science & Politics*, and also *Perspectives on Politics*—make room for material that does not quite conform to the research journal model, from how-to pieces and personal essays to broadly framed debates and symposia, and, yes, presidential addresses.[4] These public interventions rarely make or break careers but they are popular with readers. A solid article on the day-to-day work of the profession—teaching, writing, editing, advising, field research, and so on—will generate hits if not necessarily citations. These kinds of texts are sometimes narrow in focus but they can also take aim at larger questions. They constitute a kind of intellectual space within which members of the discipline reflect on what we do, how we do it, and whether we could be doing things differently.

Navigating Political Science: Professional Advancement & Success in the Discipline brings together some of the most engaging and noteworthy of these discipline-focused contributions, with an emphasis on work that has appeared over the past decades or so. It builds on a "virtual special issue" of *PS*, titled "Navigating the Profession: Sage Advice from the Pages of *PS*," which was posted in early 2015 (Worcester 2015). When we talked about putting together a print version, Jon Gurstelle at APSA helpfully suggested that we expand our search to encompass other APSA journals. The result is a wide-ranging compendium of 28 chapters by 45 contributors, one that will hopefully prove relevant and interesting for political scientists across the board, from aspiring ABDs to seasoned PhDs.

The volume is divided into five sections—Tasks and Responsibilities, The Classroom, Field Research, The Profession and the Public, and Self-Conceptions. While in certain respects the book proceeds from pragmatic concerns to theoretical debates, the earlier sections address issues of intellectual substance, and the latter sections are attentive to the practical and institutional implications of various theoretical and methodological claims and positions.

The first section identifies specific areas of professional responsibility, from literature reviews, peer reviews, and getting started as a published author, to gender and mentoring, and the performance of political science majors in the labor market. This section may be of particular interest to colleagues who are entering or have recently entered the academic job market, as well as graduate student advisors.

The second section collects empirical studies on classroom teaching that were originally published in the *Journal of Political Science Education*. The topics under review include the challenge of fostering productive political debate and discussion, the pros and cons of delivering instructional content outside of the traditional classroom, the comparative benefits of small-group and large-class discussions, the connection between the increasing use of technology and student performance, and the question of how perceptions of professors' political orientations contribute to or inhibit student learning.

The third section reproduces a print symposium on the challenges of field research that first appeared in *PS* in April 2014. This section is aimed at graduate students who have embarked, or are about to embark, in field research outside the United States, as well as faculty who advise PhD students.

The fourth focuses on public engagement and the public sphere. It explores such matters as the contribution(s) that the profession can make to public debates, the future of faculty governance, the discipline's neglect of the issue of climate change, the nexus of scholarship and political journalism, and the ways which political scientists can contribute to new forms of online discourse.

The closing section presents a range of views about the discipline and where it should be heading. It features contributions from prominent members of the discipline.

As this brief summary makes clear, *Navigating Political Science* includes narrative essays, empirical studies, how-to essays, and reprinted speeches. Taken as a whole, the collection helps bring into focus the extent to which the achievements of the association and the discipline have become "tangible and measurable."

Notes

1. Frank Johnson Goodnow (1859–1939) attended Amherst College and Columbia Law School. He taught at Columbia from 1884 until 1914, when he became the third president of Johns Hopkins University. The Frank J. Goodnow Award for Distinguished Service was established by APSA in 1996.
2. The American Historical Association and the American Economic Association were founded in 1884 and 1885 respectively.
3. For more information, see http://www.apsanet.org/PUBLICATIONS/Journals/Organized-Section-Journals.
4. Presidential addresses from 1903–2001 were published in *APSR*, and from 2002 onwards have appeared in *PoP*. APSA maintains transcripts of presidential addresses from 1903 to the present: http://www.apsanet.org/ABOUT/Leadership-Governance/APSA-Presidents-1903-to-Present.

References

Goodnow, Frank J. 1903. "The Work of the American Political Science Association." Presidential Address. http://www.apsanet.org/Portals/54/PresidentialAddresses/190405AddrGOODNOW.pdf.

Kirkpatrick, Evron M. 1968. "Introducing PS." *PS: Political Science & Politics* 1(1). doi:10.1017/S1049096500058182.

Worcester, Kent, ed. 2015. "Navigating the Profession: Sage Advice from the Pages of PS." *PS: Political Science & Politics* 49 (S1).

Part One

Tasks and Responsibilities

Doing a Literature Review

1

Jeffrey W. Knopf

S tudents entering a graduate program often encounter a new type of assignment that differs from the papers they had to write in high school or as college undergraduates: the literature review (also known as a critical review essay). Put briefly, a literature review summarizes and evaluates a body of writings about a specific topic. The need to conduct such reviews is by no means limited to graduate students; scholarly researchers generally carry out literature reviews throughout their research careers. In a world where the internet has broadened the range of potentially relevant sources, however, doing a literature review can pose challenges even to an experienced researcher.

In recent years, I have taught a course designed to help students in a policy-oriented master's program draft thesis proposals. In looking for readings to assign to guide their literature reviews for these proposals, I discovered a paucity of appropriate published sources.[1] The vast majority of methods textbooks written for students in political science or public policy contain no discussion whatsoever of the literature review.[2] Some general methods texts contain sections on the literature review (for example, Cresswell 2003; Patten 2005), but these turned out not to be very helpful in meeting the needs of the student population I was teaching. Finally, there are a few books devoted solely to preparing a literature review (Fink 2005; Galvan 2005; Pan 2004), but these were too long to be a viable reading assignment for the course. In the end, I drafted my own "how to" handout on doing a literature review. In the hope that my observations might be helpful to others, I have adapted my handout for publication here.

In general, a literature review has two key elements. First, it should concisely summarize the findings or claims that have emerged from prior research efforts on a subject. Second, a literature review should reach a conclusion about how accurate and complete that knowledge is; it should present your considered judgments about what's right, what's wrong, what's inconclusive, and what's missing in the existing literature. In contrast to some other ways of surveying a body of literature, such as an annotated bibliography, the literature review is a work of synthesis. For this reason, it is important not to simply write a summary list of what each individual work says, but instead to focus on the body of work viewed as a whole.

Conducting a literature review can have several benefits:

1. It can give you a general overview of a body of research with which you are not familiar.

2. It can reveal what has already been done well, so that you do not waste time "reinventing the wheel."

3. It can give you new ideas you can use in your own research.

4. It can help you determine where there are problems or flaws in existing research.

5. It can enable you to place your research in a larger context, so that you can show what new conclusions might result from your research.

Three Contexts for Literature Reviews

In general, literature reviews are produced in one of three contexts: A literature review can be an end in and of itself; it can be a preliminary stage in a larger research project; and it can be a component of a finished research report. In any of these contexts, a literature review can address either theoretical or practical questions. In academic settings, review essays most often focus on the theories scholars have proposed to explain some phenomenon; sample topics might include the causes of terrorism or the preconditions for democratization. A literature review can also be used, however, to determine and assess the practical know-how available in regard to which measures are likely to be effective or not in dealing with a certain problem. In this context, one might focus, for example, on the "lessons learned" from previous efforts to deal with a certain problem (and those lessons learned might have been proposed by outside scholars or by practitioners themselves).

To return to the first context, reviewing existing knowledge can itself be the end goal if one simply wants to ascertain the current "state of the art" on a particular subject or problem. In this context (as well as the other two), it is important not to simply summarize the available research, but also to evaluate it critically. Such critical analysis should not be exclusively negative; it is also important to identify positive results to take away from the existing work.

Second, a review of existing knowledge can be a preliminary step in a larger research project. Such a literature review is often required for a thesis or dissertation proposal; it is also frequently an element in proposals for research grants. The most basic reason to undertake a literature review in this context is to make sure the proposed research question has not already been answered. If an existing study convincingly answers the question you want to address, it is better to find out before you get started than when you are in the middle of a research project.

Assuming no prior study has solved your problem of interest, then the purpose of your proposal's literature review is to situate your proposed project in relation to existing knowledge. This enables you to address the concept of a "contribution to knowledge," which is important because potential advisors and other people who might review a proposal generally ask of any research proposal "what is the expected contribution to knowledge?" or "what will be the value added of completing this research?" The goal here is to show that people who read the final research product are likely to learn some new or different information or argument compared to what they would find in existing studies. In short, a literature review in a research proposal provides an overview of existing scholarship and explains how your proposed research will add to or alter the existing body of knowledge.

Conducting a literature review at a preliminary stage of a research project can also be helpful in stimulating your own thinking. A broad review of existing literature might reveal new theoretical hypotheses, research methods, or policy recommendations that you want to incorporate in your own research.

Third, a literature review can be a component of a finished research report. This literature review will generally involve building on and/or revising the literature review completed at the proposal stage. Its purpose is to help show how your final conclusions relate to the prior wisdom about your subject.

Ways to Frame the Contribution to Knowledge

The literature review is an attempt to summarize the existing state of knowledge about a subject and, in research proposals, to frame the proposed research's expected contribution to knowledge. Knowledge, in this context, does not necessarily mean "Truth" with a capital T. Rather, knowledge refers to beliefs, in particular beliefs that some individuals have a degree of confidence in due to study or experience. In the social sciences and policy research, many hypotheses cannot be proven conclusively. When reviewing literature, therefore, it is common to refer to the "claims" or "arguments" advanced by a study or school of thought. Hence, a typical review of existing knowledge identifies the claims made in a literature and assesses the strength of the support offered for those claims.

It is helpful to think of knowledge as having two elements: what we believe and how strongly we believe it. Further research can affect either or both of those elements, either positively or negatively, and any of these results would be a contribution to knowledge. This is similar to the logic of Bayesian analysis in statistics. In Bayesian statistics, if one believes a statement has a certain probability of being true and then obtains additional pertinent data, one can revise the estimated probability the statement is true using a mathematical formula provided by Bayes theorem. Even where such precise quantification is not feasible, one can attempt an analogous qualitative assessment.[3]

This provides a framework for thinking about the possible consequences of new research. Further research could create a new belief in an area where people have no prior knowledge, it could alter an existing belief, or it could change how much certainty people feel about a current belief. Most obviously, something brand new is a potential contribution to knowledge; this might be new factual information, a new theoretical proposition, or a new policy proposal. In addition, information or reasoned argument that changes our degree of confidence in an existing belief is also a contribution to knowledge. This might be new evidence or analysis that corroborates and thereby strengthens a particular belief. It can also be evidence or analysis that challenges and thereby casts doubt on a particular point of view. If new information or analysis is powerful enough, it might convince people that their prior belief was wrong and lead them to embrace a different perspective. When using a literature review to indicate where proposed research might make a contribution to knowledge, therefore, it is helpful to think in terms of identifying the existing beliefs people have and the level of confidence with which they hold them. This facilitates the task of showing where additional research could make a difference.

Consider Casting Your Net Widely

The traditional literature review focuses on books published by academic presses and articles published in academic journals. For many purposes, these will continue to be the appropriate focus. However, on many questions, especially those involving a policy dimension, actors besides university-based academics might issue relevant reports. In addition, the development of the Internet has made it easier to disseminate research reports in formats other than in academic publications. This growth in alternative research producers and outlets for disseminating research makes it advisable to consider a wider range of sources when conducting a review. Indeed, because relevant information and analysis is increasingly found in sources other than traditional academic publications, it may be more accurate to think of your task as a "review of existing knowledge"[4] than as a review of literature *per se*.

Other entities that might produce research relevant to your topic include government agencies, international governmental organizations, non-governmental organizations, think tanks, and independent, freelance researchers. Some of their reports are still produced in print form and are available through any good library collection. Increasingly, though, many of their reports are released electronically and can be found through careful searching on the Internet. Traditional academics are also using the Internet as a vehicle for disseminating their work. Scholars are increasingly posting conference papers, working papers, and monographs on the Internet.[5]

These postings are often part of a work in progress that has not been published in a book or journal article; they represent these scholars' most current thinking. For this reason, it can be important to search for such work to keep a review of existing knowledge as up-to-date as possible.

At the same time, the Internet must be used with great caution. Most academic publications go through peer review, which in most cases helps ensure that the published work meets certain standards of scholarship. In contrast, anyone with access to the necessary equipment can post anything they want on the Internet. Many postings are based on little or no research, make no attempt to be unbiased, and contain factual claims that are questionable. If you use the Internet to broaden the range of sources consulted in a literature review, be sure to consider carefully whether the items that you find are credible and meet at least minimal standards of scholarly research. Look to see whether the authors have provided their credentials and consider whether these make them credible sources on the subject. Also examine whether an item contains documentation of its sources and whether these appear to be credible. If your interest is in existing policy proposals or practices, then academic credibility may matter less than other considerations, such as whether the source of information is in a position of authority or has inside knowledge; even in these cases, however, you need to screen Internet postings to weed out those that lack a valid basis for their assertions. Despite the risks, valuable sources of research exist beyond traditional academic books and journals, and it is worth using the Internet to seek these out. At the same time, be sure not to limit your search for sources to just the Internet as any college or university library will have many items on its shelves that are not available electronically.

Pointers on How to Create an Effective Review

First, especially if this is your first literature review, read some existing review essays to see how other researchers have carried out this task.[6]

Imitate what you think works well, and avoid those things that strike you as ineffective or unnecessary. Chances are that some review essays will have been assigned in some of your graduate classes; if so, begin by re-examining them. You can also ask your instructors or advisors to suggest literature reviews that they believe provide good models to follow.

Second, for each research study you read for your review, be sure you can succinctly summarize the study's main claim. You should be able to describe in a sentence or two the central argument of each item you read. It will not always be necessary to include this information, but having an awareness of each study's overarching thesis will help you compare different items as you write your review.

Third, your written review should be selective. When you write the literature review, it is often not necessary to discuss every item you read. The write-up should discuss only the studies that have a direct bearing on the central focus of your review or your proposed research. In addition, rather than summarizing the studies in their entirety, the review should focus only on the aspects of those studies that are relevant for your purposes.

Fourth, when you write a literature review, do not simply summarize, item by item, each publication you have read. A literature review should *not* have the following structure: paragraph 1 notes that book A says X; paragraph 2 notes that article B says Y; paragraph 3 notes that book C says Z; etc.

In general, a literature review should impose some intellectual order on the material. Therefore—as a fifth pointer—it often helps to think about grouping individual studies into larger "camps" or "schools of thought." One can do this in terms of different theories they propose or defend, different methodological approaches they take, or different policies they favor. Often, alternative views reflect differences in the disciplines or backgrounds of the authors—academics vs. government officials, psychologists vs. economists, etc. This can stand as another basis for categorizing schools of thought. If you group similar studies together, rather than discuss three like-minded authors separately in three successive paragraphs, you can mention all three together in a single sentence such as 'A, B, and C argue that policy X has been ineffective and propose policy Y instead.'

For any subject where there is already a substantial body of research, chances are that some scholars have already sought to classify the research into contrasting schools of thought. In such cases, it is a good idea to start by familiarizing yourself with existing summaries of the research. Many fields or sub-fields have encyclopedias or other reference works that contain short, introductory essays on the research on particular topics.[7]

If you were interested in learning about research on deterrence, for example, you could search for encyclopedias or handbooks of social science, of international relations, or of conflict and violence. If you cannot find a relevant source for your area of interest, consult a reference librarian or be creative in trying different combinations of keywords when searching an online library catalogue.

There are a couple of other likely sources for summaries of existing research that identify contrasting schools of thought. Academic journals often publish review essays that reflect upon one or more recently published books on a particular topic. Identify the journals that publish regularly on your topic of interest and peruse the tables of contents for the past few years to determine whether there are recent review essays that could help orient you to a body of research. In addition, theses and dissertations usually contain a literature review section or chapter. Many dissertations become the basis for books, so identifying books published by freshly minted PhDs is often a fruitful way to find recent surveys of a field. Many graduate schools also deposit copies of dissertations and theses completed by their students with UMI (formerly University Microfilms). It is now possible to search the UMI collection online, and you can buy copies of theses and dissertations that appear relevant.[8]

Sixth, while seeing how others have characterized a field of research is helpful, it is essential not to rely on others' summaries of existing studies. Review articles in specialized encyclopedias or academic journals are a good place to get started, but they cannot substitute for your own reading. Read for yourself the sources that are most critical for your own interests and draw your own conclusions.

A seventh and final pointer: Get into the habit of associating individual authors and major camps or points of view with each other. In academic writing, scholars often use the last name of the author of a study as a shorthand to refer to the theory or argument advanced by that author. For example, in International Relations Theory, Kenneth Waltz was one of the leading developers of a theory known as "neo-realism." In writing about this approach, other authors will switch back and forth between referring to Waltz, to the Waltzian approach, and to neo-realism. Since this has become standard practice in scholarly writing and conversation, it is a good idea to get used to thinking about each alternative camp both in terms of the generic label by which it is known as well as in terms of the authors identified with that camp.

The Nuts and Bolts:
What Questions Should the Literature Review Try to Answer?

A literature review summarizes and evaluates the state of knowledge or practice on a particular subject. To do this, most literature reviews must address four tasks or sets of questions. The first two steps are to determine what each individual study has examined and what each has concluded from its examination. The third step involves summarizing the collective results. To do this, sort the results into three categories: what the existing studies and reports have in common, what the studies disagree about, and what they overlook or ignore. Finally, the fourth step is to reach a judgment about the quality of the literature overall: what are the key findings that appear to be valid, and where is more work needed?

To elaborate, the first task is simply to be clear about what each item you are reviewing was trying to do. For example, was the work concerned with theory? If so, was the goal explanatory, or did it have some other objective? If the goal was explanation, what was the dependent variable for the study? How was it conceptualized and operationalized? Ascertaining this information before you compare studies will help you determine if they were even examining the same problem. Sometimes different studies reach different conclusions because they asked different questions or defined the phenomenon of interest in different ways.

The second step involves identifying the main argument in each work. Does it have a thesis?

If so, how strongly does the study say its findings support the thesis, and what qualifications or reservations does the author report?

The third task listed above—summarizing existing studies in terms of three categories—can be especially valuable in a research proposal. In short, any body of research can be usefully summarized in terms of the following:

1. Areas of consensus or near-consensus. On some issues nearly all of the relevant experts may agree. Such conclusions can be either positive or negative; i.e., they can involve beliefs about what is true or what works or what is false or does not work. Areas of consensus represent the "conventional wisdom" about a subject.

2. Areas of disagreement or debate. In many cases, there exists information and analysis about a topic but no consensus about what is correct. These areas of debate usually give rise to the alternative "camps" or "schools of thought" mentioned above.

3. Gaps. There may be aspects of a topic that have not been examined yet. These gaps in knowledge might involve questions no one has tried to answer, perspectives no one has considered, or bodies of information that no one has attempted to collect or to analyze.

Once you have identified where there is conventional wisdom, where there are debates, and where there are gaps, you can use the literature review to describe what will be the contribution to knowledge of the research you are proposing and why it will be of interest to your intended audience. Your contribution can address any or all of these. For example, you might believe there are reasons to doubt the conventional wisdom. In general, you should not accept areas of agreement uncritically. The fourth task noted above—assessing the quality of the literature— includes probing for areas where the existing wisdom is less than conclusive. The literature review can then be used to highlight potential flaws in the reasoning or evidence related to an area of consensus. This could be used to set up proposed research that might challenge the conventional wisdom.

Weighing in on an existing debate is another possibility. Here, one uses the literature review to show the likely value of research that could help judge the relative merits of conflicting points of view or that could help point the way to a useful synthesis.

Finally, proposing to fill a gap in existing knowledge is an obvious way to frame the useful-ness of a suggested piece of research. A gap may involve theory, if no scholar on a topic has yet considered an important theoretical question or a particular alternative theory (e.g., although there is a growing body of research on the causes of terrorism, perhaps no one has yet studied what influences terrorist decisions about whether to target agriculture versus people). Or a gap may be empirical, if there is a historical case or a source of data no one has analyzed (e.g., we know a lot about how local emergency responders acted on September 11, but are there useful lessons that could be learned from how emergency personnel dealt with an incident in some other locality, for example, an anthrax threat phoned in to a local Planned Parenthood clinic?).

The relevant gaps in knowledge can be broad or narrow. In some cases, a topic might essen-tially be virgin territory: no one has studied any aspect of it. In that case, it is easy to show that proposed research on the topic would make a contribution to knowledge. More often, however, the gap will be narrower than this. People will have studied some, but not all, aspects of a prob-lem, or they will have examined a problem using some theories or methodologies, but neglected others. In this situation, if your goal is to fill the gap you identify, your research proposal would state something like "researchers have studied a, b, and c, which are related to the problem of X, but they have not studied d, which is also relevant to understanding [or solving] X."

The fourth task in a review—evaluating the overall state of knowledge on a topic—requires a thorough examination of how the answers given by the literature have been produced. In examining how people have reached their conclusions, consider evaluating the following:

1. Their assumptions. If there are disagreements, can they be traced to different assumptions made by the conflicting studies? Are the key assumptions made by the most important studies a plausible basis for research, or are they so problematic that they call into question the rest of the analysis?

2. Their logic. If there are disagreements, can they be traced to different theoretical perspectives? Do the studies explain the reasoning that supports their key conclusions, or are important arguments made purely by assertion? Is the reasoning that is provided logically persuasive, or does it contain internal contradictions or make a giant leap at a key point in the analysis? What are the most plausible counterarguments or alternative explanations to the main thesis in each study, and does each study address these adequately?

3. Their evidence. If there are disagreements, can they be traced to the use of different bodies of evidence or to disagreements about the facts? Do the studies provide evidence to back up their main claims, or are important claims made purely by assertion? Is the evidence valid—i.e., is it factually accurate and on point? Has all the relevant evidence been considered, or have some obviously relevant cases or bodies of data been overlooked? Is the evidence that has been considered representative, or are the cases or data selected for study likely to have biased the results?[9]

4. Their methodology. If there are disagreements, can they be traced to the use of different methodologies? Do the studies make clear the methodology by which they have reached their conclusions, or are key claims made purely by assertion? Was the methodology used an appropriate choice for the question being researched, and was it applied correctly?

By identifying and comparing the assumptions, theories, data, and methods of the studies you review, you can pinpoint the underlying disagreements responsible for debates in the literature. You can then, if you wish, target your own research on one of the underlying disagreements, which could help resolve an existing debate. By evaluating each of these elements critically, you can also show where there are problems or flaws in existing studies and then, if you wish, target your own research on fixing one or more of these problems in the literature. Finally, as noted previously, you can also look for important issues that the existing research has overlooked and frame your research as an effort to fill this gap.

The Problem of Too Few Sources and the Problem of Too Many Sources

Students sometimes choose a research topic, such as how to address a new policy problem or what can be learned about a recent event, because they think no one has yet studied the issue. In such cases, students expect that there will not be any literature relevant to the question they want to research. It does not pay to be too skeptical on this score; you might be surprised at what you find once you start to search for resources. Even if you come up empty, however, this is not a wasted effort. If you can report that a serious search uncovered no examples of studies that examined your research question, then you have largely demonstrated that your research will fulfill the "contribution to knowledge" criterion for evaluating research proposals (I say "largely" because you still have to show that the proposed research could produce meaningful results).

This still leaves the problem of what to discuss in a literature review. The problem of too few sources can usually be solved by thinking in terms of two tiers (or circles) of literature. In the first tier (or inner circle), you are concerned with studies that directly address your own proposed research question. In the second tier (or outer circle), you broaden your review to consider publications that are relevant to or overlap some part of your own question, even though they do not directly address the same point. If there is a reasonable body of work in the first tier, in many cases this will be all that you discuss in the literature review. You would only go outside this inner circle if there was some specific other publication that proposed a theory, policy proposal, or research method that you want to apply in your own research project.

If there is nothing or very little that is directly on the same topic as yours, then your literature review will need to consider some items in the second tier. You might consider items that have a theoretical perspective you want to explore in your research. Even if no one has applied the theory to your specific question, it is still appropriate to discuss key works that have developed the theory so you can explain why it might provide a good perspective for analyzing your topic.

It can also be helpful to think in terms of analogies. In particular, are there situations or problems that are similar to the one you want to study, so that research on those other problems might contain relevant ideas? For example, if you were interested in identifying ways to protect crops from agro-terrorism and you could find no studies directly on this topic, you could consider looking for research on efforts to protect crops against natural disease outbreaks. If your literature review reveals findings about ways to address the latter problem, you could then propose research to consider whether these techniques could be adapted for your problem of interest.

Once you consider literature in this second tier or outer circle, you are likely to encounter the problem of too many sources. The number of potentially relevant publications, especially once you begin considering well-developed areas of theory, could be vast. Hence, you need a way to restrict your focus. It is important not to simply select a few books or articles that you find at random (for example, whatever happens to be on the library shelf or the first few "hits" returned by a Google search) and make them the basis for your review, because they might not reflect the current state of knowledge and debate. Instead, consider using one or more of the following rules of thumb:

1. Focus on the leading authorities. You may discover that certain authors or studies are cited quite frequently in the literature. These are probably considered key works, so it is a good idea to respond to what they have to say, even if it means ignoring some less-influential studies.

2. Focus on recent studies from high-prestige or high-visibility sources. You generally want to emphasize the most recent research in the field you are reviewing. Among recent studies, look especially for those that have been published in a high-prestige outlet: examples include books from the university press of a highly ranked university or articles in the leading journal in the field in question. Sources that garner a lot of attention are also important to evaluate: in some cases, for example, it might be relevant to assess a book on the best-seller list.

3. Focus on the studies that are most relevant and helpful for your question of interest. The more a study is directly on point for your research, or the more you are relying on a study for inspiration about how to approach your own research, the greater the role it should play in your literature review.

When there is a lot of literature, it is not necessary for a review to be comprehensive. The literature review should focus mainly on those parts of the literature that relate to and help advance your specific interests; edit out the rest.

The Bottom Line

A literature review should concisely summarize from a set of relevant sources the collective conclusions most pertinent to your own research interests. It should also evaluate the state of knowledge in terms of what's right, what's wrong, what's an area of uncertainty or debate that cannot be resolved using the existing research, and what's missing because no one has yet considered it carefully. To create such a review of existing knowledge, it helps to ask and answer the following questions:

1. What questions have the existing publications addressed? What issues have been neglected?

2. What are the main conclusions of existing research? What do the studies actually argue?

3. What are the points of convergence in the literature, and what are the main disagreements? Where disagreements exist, what are the bases of the disagreement?

4. What theories or policies or evidence has the literature looked at? What potentially relevant information and alternative theories or policies have not been examined?

5. How solid are the conclusions that have been reached? Are they based on sound reasoning, careful assessment of the evidence, and a well-executed methodology? Or are there good reasons to doubt some of the existing conclusions?

6. What is the overall quality of the literature? What have we learned to date?

7. What are the most important problems and gaps that require additional research?

These questions are relevant whether one is producing a stand-alone review essay, a literature review for a research proposal, or a literature review section in a finished report such as a thesis or dissertation. When one proceeds systematically and aims to reach a considered judgment about the state of knowledge on a given subject, the resulting literature review can itself make a useful contribution to knowledge.

Reprinted from Jeffrey W. Knopf. 2006. "Doing a Literature Review." PS: Political Science & Politics 39 (1). Cambridge University Press: 127–32. doi:10.1017/S1049096506060264.

Notes

1. In Internet searches, however, I have found several good items. Given the mutability of the Internet, rather than list URLs here, I suggest that researchers who want to supplement the information in this essay conduct their own search for web pages on doing a literature review.
2. The one exception I have found is Johnson and Reynolds (2004, ch. 5).
3. For an introduction to Bayesian statistics, see Wonnacott and Wonnacott (1985, 75–79 and 515–75). For a discussion of the relevance of Bayesian reasoning in qualitative research, see McKeown (1999, 179–83)
4. Paul Pitman first suggested to me this phrasing and the reasoning behind it, for which I thank him.
5. For example, many political science materials of this sort are available through Political Research Online (PROL); this includes papers presented at Annual Meetings of the American Political Science Association (APSA). See www.politicalscience.org.
6. This is the first suggestion on a short handout created by John Odell. It's a good place to start, so I have followed his lead and included it first in my own list of pointers.

7. For a list of handbooks and encyclopedias in many fields of study, see Booth, Colomb, and Williams (2003), "An Appendix on Finding Sources."
8. The electronic database of UMI dissertations and theses is now part of ProQuest Information and Learning, at www.il.proquest.com/umi/dissertations (accessed Jan. 24, 2005).
9. For a discussion of selection bias, see King, Keohane, and Verba (1994, 128–39).

References

Booth, Wayne C., Gregory G. Colomb, and Joseph M. Williams. 2003. *The Craft of Research*. 2nd ed. Chicago: University of Chicago Press.

Cresswell, John W. 2003. *Research Design: Qualitative, Quantitative, and Mixed Methods Approaches*. 2nd ed. Thousand Oaks, CA: SAGE Publications.

Fink, Arlene. 2005. *Conducting Research Literature Reviews: From the Internet to Paper*. 2nd ed. Thousand Oaks, CA: SAGE Publications.

Galvan, Jose L. 2005. *Writing Literature Reviews*. 3rd ed. Glendale, CA: Pyrczak Publishing.

Johnson, Janet Buttolph, and H. T. Reynolds. 2004. *Political Science Research Methods*. 5th ed. Washington, DC: CQ Press.

King, Gary, Robert O. Keohane, and Sidney Verba. 1994. *Designing Social Inquiry: Scientific Inference in Qualitative Research*. Princeton, NJ: Princeton University Press.

McKeown, Timothy J. 1999. "Case Studies and the Statistical Worldview." *International Organization* 53 (1): 161–90.

Pan, M. Ling. 2004. *Preparing Literature Reviews*. 2nd ed. Glendale, CA: Pyrczak Publishing.

Patten, Mildred L. 2005. *Understanding Research Methods: An Overview of the Essentials*. 5th ed. Glendale, CA: Pyrczak Publishing.

Wonnacott, Ronald J., and Thomas H. Wonnacott. 1985. *Introductory Statistics*. 4th ed. New York: John Wiley & Sons.

How To Be a Peer Reviewer: A Guide for Recent and Soon-to-be PhDs

2

Beth Miller Vonnahme
Jon Pevehouse
Ron Rogowski
Dustin Tingley
Rick Wilson

Scholarly peer review—the idea that the merits of academic work are best judged by subjecting them to the scrutiny of experts from within the relevant field—is central to the twin goals of maintaining standards and providing credibility to published material. Top academic journals in political science regularly receive more than 700 new submissions from graduate students and faculty. According to the most recent editorial reports available on the journal's websites, the *Journal of Politics* received 729 new submissions in 2010, the *American Journal of Political Science* received 798 new submissions in 2011, and the *American Political Science Review* received 685 new submissions in 2010–2011. The editors of these journals recruited, on average, 3,000 political scientists (professors and graduate students)[1] to assess anonymously these papers' suitability for publication in the specific journal. The completion rate for reviews over this period typically exceeds 50%. For example, *AJPS* requested 3,196 reviews and 1,770 completed reviews were returned.

Impartial peer review is central to the scientific endeavor that all of us are engaged in and requires a sizable community of expert volunteers to fulfill its promise. However, scholars able and willing to referee manuscripts incur undeniable opportunity costs—the most obvious of which is time that could be spent on research and teaching commitments (Niemi 2006). Although most researchers acknowledge the importance of the peer-review process, they often consider reviewing manuscripts to be a burden—an occupational hazard. As a result, completing reviews often ends up at the bottom of to-do lists.

There are, however, important benefits to consider, and it might be helpful to underscore such benefits before describing the basics of reviewing.

1. Refereeing allows you to keep up with cutting-edge research in your subfield, while also helping to keep your sights set more broadly;

2. Too often, we only see the final product, which can give us a false sense of elegance. Reviewing manuscripts in their early stages reminds us that everyone (and every published bit of research) has to go through a process of refinement;

3. By exposing you to diverse examples and writing styles, reviewing allows you develop an appreciation of effective writing and helps you improve as a writer;

4. Related, refereeing allows you to understand and apply the subtle differences between writing papers for seminars, conferences, and journals;

5. Finally, many academic journals allow reviewers to see the other reviews of the same manuscript, which allows you to assess your own review and compare your assessment of a manuscript to what other researchers think about it. It also allows you to see how much disagreement may prevail in evaluating even important manuscripts.

Despite the tangible benefits associated with refereeing manuscripts for publication, graduate programs do not typically advise students on the importance of contributing to the peer-review process or on how to effectively referee manuscripts. In line with recently published articles in other disciplines (Benos, Kirk, and Hall 2003; Drotar 2009; Lovejoy, Revenson, and France 2011; Neill 2009; Roediger 2007), this article outlines the benefits and responsibilities of peer reviewing for recent, and not so recent, political science researchers. The suggestions and advice provided here represents the collective ideas of the authors, who met as a panel at the 2011 American Political Science Association Annual Meeting. Recent interest in the peer-review process, evident by conference panels on the topic (e.g., APSA's 2011 panel on peer reviewing), articles on the topic (e.g., Niemi 2006) and its discussion on a number of blogs,[2] raises these questions: What makes a review effective and useful? How does one write such a review?

How Do Journals Select Referees?
What Should Editors Know About Their Referees?

Editorial staff at academic journals comb graduate program websites, other published work, and conference registration lists to maintain an ongoing database of potential referees. Each journal has its own policies and guidelines regarding how many reviews they require for each submission as well as whom they will invite to be referees; some journals, such as *International Organization* or the *American Political Science Review*, do not reach out to anyone without a PhD.

Within those parameters, when deciding whom they should ask to review a manuscript, journal editors generally try to cover their bases. In other words, a typical review panel will include experts in the field, scholars with general knowledge of the field, and scholars with specific methodological and substantive expertise. If, when an author resubmits a manuscript after making suggested revisions, editors decide the revisions need to be reviewed, they generally ask the same set of reviewers. In a few cases, however, editors do reach out to reviewers beyond the original panel (for instance, when the paper includes a methodological innovation that requires specific expertise, or when previous reviewers have noted their own lack of expert knowledge in some area).

As important as knowing who is asked to serve as a referee is knowing who *may not* review a manuscript. Most editors try to exclude discussants and chairs of panels where the paper previously has been presented. If their suggestions have been followed, they may be biased in favor; if their suggestions have been disregarded, they may react negatively. Similarly, scholars acknowledged by the author are generally excluded, as are those the author feels have a bias that would prevent an impartial review.

In theory, the review process is "double blind"; none of the reviewers should know who the authors of the manuscript are and the authors should not know who is reviewing their paper. In practice, this is a difficult standard to maintain, and some leading economics and psychology journals have turned to a "single-blind" process. Reviewers who want to identify the author(s) of the manuscript can easily turn to search engines (this is particularly true within more specialized fields). Nonetheless, it is critical that referees approach their review without any bias, or, if they feel they have a slight bias, to acknowledge this to the editor. In those instances where the bias is serious, potential referees should turn down the invitation to review the manuscript. Lastly, reviewers should explicitly note (whether as a part of their review or, separately, in a note to the editor) those cases/issues where they feel they do not have deep expertise (for example, procedural issues in papers about Congress) so that editors can assess their reviews fairly, and where necessary invite additional referees.

What Goes Into a Review?

In this section we discuss the different components of a "typical" review. Of course, reviewers have their own style and prioritize things differently. That said, making sure that several, if not most, of these elements are included in your review is the best way to insure that it is as helpful to the author(s) as it can be.

Your Judgment of the Quality of the Research/Analysis and the Broader Academic Merits of the Manuscript

When you say there is a strong case for a particular recommendation make a succinct argument as to why. If you think the manuscript has merit, make an argument for why you advocate publication. If you think the manuscript lacks merit, again say why you oppose publication. Editors engage with the submission but they also receive many submissions. Clear, direct, and actionable advice is typically preferred to vague suggestions.[3] This does not mean you have to be more definitive than you feel comfortable with, but in every case make your argument explicit rather than via a long laundry list followed up by "in summary."

1. Think about whether there is something in the manuscript—the kernel of an idea—which with some work can be brought out. Some editors refer to this as "the angel in the marble."

2. Is it suitable for the audience of the specific journal to which it was submitted? The paper might be salvageable, or even very good, but if the audience of this journal will not read it, then it should not be published there.

3. Give two or three foundational points to support your recommendation.

Brief Overview of Where the Manuscript Fits in the Literature or a Debate

Editors will not always know the nuances of the discussion the paper addresses. An extremely brief overview can help set the basis for your suggestions. Providing an overview of how the manuscript engages the literature can also give the author(s) a different perspective on the role of their manuscript.

1. Is the contribution empirical, theoretical, or both?

2. Compared to previous work, what is the key value-added component?

3. Be certain not to conflate new ideas with good, nor assume that revisiting earlier ideas is bad.

Distinguish between Major Deal-Breaking Reservations and Minor Quibbles That You Think Should be Addressed but Which Would Not Sink the Paper if Ignored

It is reasonable to make a broad variety of suggestions, but be clear about the importance of different types of suggestions.

1. Important but usually secondary suggestions include issues of formatting, readability, typos, and suggestions for extensions.

2. Do not hold a manuscript up with a suggested extension (e.g., further research or experiments) unless you see it as central to the contribution of the paper. Let the authors decide.

3. If there are missing citations that are not essential but desirable, probably raise them toward the end of the review.

How Should You Write a Good Review?

A good review—one that helps journal editors make an informed decision about whether to publish a paper—is not merely one that covers the various components from the previous section. Certainly being comprehensive is important, but it is not what separates a good review from a passable one. In what follows, we discuss ways that will help you write an effective and helpful review and earn the respect of editors, authors, and just might earn you a "Super Reviewer" badge at the next academic conference you attend.[4]

Take the Process Seriously

If a paper gets sent out for peer review, it has survived the editor's desk review and, therefore, has presumably at least *some* redeeming quality. Refereeing is a key part of your professional responsibility and not a chore toward which you dedicate minimal time and cognitive effort. And, as already noted, there is something in it for you, too.

Be Timely

If you know you will not be able to get to the review for the next several weeks, it is your responsibility to let the editor know. Tardy reviewers are the single most important bottleneck in the publication process, and without being too dramatic about it, you might be jeopardizing a colleague's career. Think about it. Your (negative) review, sent to the editor three months after you accepted the responsibility, means that the author will have had to wait four or five months to find out he or she will not get published in the journal and now will have to go through the same process with another journal.[5] And tenure review starts in six months.

Be Realistic

Often you are under a time crunch and may not be able to complete the review. If so, decline to do this particular review, but offer one or two suggestions about others who you feel may be well qualified. However, do not get into a habit of routinely declining to review. Editors have long memories.

Be Succinct, but Thorough

An average review should be a couple of pages long. Also, organize the review in some way, such as distinguishing between theoretical and empirical issues, and major and minor suggestions. If, exceptionally, you think the paper is completely unsuitable for the specific journal, be sure to specify why you believe this. If it is suitable for another journal, mention an example or two of a more appropriate venue.

Be Courteous and Gracious

There may be a place in life for snide comments; a review of a manuscript is definitely not it. Good scholarship is a process that often involves submitting imperfect ideas to scrutiny. It is easier to be critical than to be constructive. Acknowledge the author's effort and try to highlight the paper's strengths so that they can be showcased, even if you clearly recommend rejection. And remember, your own scholarship will also be subject to the same scrutiny.

Be Specific and Avoid Criticisms without Context
Broad generalizations—for instance, claiming an experimental research design "has no external validity" or merely stating "the literature review is incomplete"—are unhelpful. Take the time and effort to qualify and explain those statements. At the same time, remember that it is not your paper and, as a reviewer, it is not your job to fix it.

Appreciate the Evolutionary Nature of Research
Often tradeoffs exist between theoretical and analytical strengths (sound identification/causal analysis, etc.) and empirical strengths (good datasets/strong observational data, etc.). When deciding how to assess those tradeoffs, remember that we exist in a marketplace of ideas, and the scientific process is an evolutionary one that involves ongoing improvement (rather than first-time perfection). Often a good paper opens a useful debate rather than settling it once and for all.

What Else Should You Know About Refereeing Manuscripts For Academic Journals?
Academic journals frequently require referees to supplement their written review with a quantitative evaluation of the manuscript. This quantitative section might ask you to assess, for instance, the importance of the topic, the clarity of the argument, or the persuasiveness of the evidence. Each journal has a slightly different set of questions, and a different (often arbitrary) scale on which they should be assessed. In other words, if the responses seem subjective to you, it is because they are. Keep in mind that what is most important about this section is not the specific number you assign to each answer. Rather, editors ask these questions because they underscore the parameters—relevance, clarity, persuasiveness, originality, writing—that should frame your review. Therefore, rather than agonizing over whether the paper you are reviewing is a 3 or a 4 on any given question, make sure you cover all the questions in your written review.

When refereeing a manuscript, your main responsibility is to give the journal's editorial staff advice about whether it should be published in that specific journal, and why. In practice, what this implies is that you need to make a substantiated argument about the scholarly merits of the paper while keeping in mind the journal's purpose and audience. Also, to the extent that there are any tradeoffs between arguing the (de)merits of the paper versus general comments to improve it, remember that the paper is not yours to fix. The *specific* decision—accept, reject, or revise and resubmit—is also not yours to make, so whereas you should feel free to suggest a course of action, do not feel compelled to.

Along the same lines, it is always useful to visit the journal's website and educate yourself about its purpose, audience, and manuscript acceptance rate. This will clarify the journal's publication criteria, which in turn allows you, as a reviewer, to offer a more considered and effective opinion. Comparing your reviews to the journal's acceptance rate will also help you calibrate your own standards as a reviewer; for instance, if you have rejected all five articles you were asked to review for a journal that typically publishes 50% of its submissions, you are probably being too critical in your assessment. If you have recommended acceptance or minor revisions on all five articles sent to you by a journal that typically publishes only 10% of submissions, you are being too lenient (and will probably be invited less often).

Visiting journal websites will also help you assess more accurately which journals would be most receptive to publishing your own research, thereby saving you the anxiety of waiting several months only to find that the journal thinks that your paper does not fit or is not of high enough quality for its readership. In fact, of the 15% to 30% (depending on journal) of manuscripts that get "desk rejected" (in other words, the journal's editor does not even send them out to reviewers), many are simply deemed inappropriate for the journal's target audience. Manuscripts whose topics do not fall within the scope of the journal will never be published there, no matter how good they are *per se*.

Finally, to reiterate an earlier point—namely, to take the review process seriously—we would remind would-be referees of the following. Although you are not, strictly speaking, under review yourself, you have every incentive to do at least due diligence. On the one hand, a thorough, persuasive review will not only earn you respect and a reputation, you might even be invited to publish a formal response to the original article in the same journal. On the other hand, a particularly shoddy review will often elicit an apology on your behalf from the journal's editor to the manuscript's author, acknowledging that yours was a particularly superficial and unhelpful review. Further, the memo that is sent by the editor to the author is also sent to you and the other referees. The confidential nature of the review process means that you escape with your dignity somewhat intact, but only just!

Now What?

With those guidelines out of the way, that leaves one last question: "How do I sign up?" Some journals, especially subfield journals, encourage would-be reviewers to email the journal's managing editor to volunteer. Other journals, like *AJPS* and *APSR*, will approach you (subject to their specific policies), based on the work you have published or presented at conferences. The longer answer is that, although in general the journals will approach you (subject to their specific policies), you should always feel free to contact them directly if you are interested.

Reprinted from Beth Miller, Jon Pevehouse, Ron Rogowski, Dustin Tingley, and Rick Wilson. 2013. "How To Be a Peer Reviewer: A Guide for Recent and Soon-to-Be PhDs." PS: Political Science & Politics 46 (1). Cambridge University Press: 120–23. doi:10.1017/S104909651200128X.

Acknowledgements

Our thanks to Vinay Jawahar for editorial assistance and Sean Twombly for organizational assistance. This article came out of a 2011 APSA panel on refereeing organized by Dustin Tingley.

Notes

1. Some journals invite reviews only from scholars with a completed PhD or equivalent.
2. The issues of the validity of peer review and "best practices" have been discussed on blogs authored by individual political scientists (http://fparena.blogspot.com), department blogs (e.g., http://unlpsgs.wordpress.com), and anonymous blogs (e.g., www.poliscirumors.com).
3. The clear recommendation should usually be expressed by ticking a summary evaluation, e.g., "Reject" or "Minor Revision," not always in the body of your report—since editors prefer to retain some leeway. Consistency is key. You should avoid saying "Major Revision" when you really mean "Reject," or recommending "Reject" but writing a report that sounds entirely favorable.
4. At the Midwest Political Science Association in 2011, the American Journal of Political Science began awarding "Super Reviewer" badges to those reviewers the editor believes went above and beyond the call of duty. Other journals also reward their reviewers. For example, Political Psychology and Political Research Quarterly invite reviewers to a reception at the annual meetings of their affiliated organizations.
5. It usually takes a journal a couple of weeks to put a manuscript through technical check and invite referees and another week or two for a full complement of referees to accept their invitations. Referees are asked to report within a month, but if one is three months overdue, five months will have passed before all referees' reports go to the editor.

References

Benos, Dale J., Kevin L. Kirk, and John E. Hall. 2003. "How to Review a Paper." *Advances in Physiology Education* 27 (2): 47–52.

Drotar, Dennis. 2009. "Editorial: How to Write Effective Reviews for the Journal of Pediatric Psychology." *Journal of Pediatric Psychology* 34 (2): 113–17.

Lovejoy, Travis I., Tracey A. Revenson, and Christopher R. France. 2011. "Reviewing Manuscripts for Peer-Review Journals: A Primer for Novice and Seasoned Reviewers." *Annals of Behavioral Medicine* 42 (1): 1–13.

Neill, Ushma S. 2009. "How to Write an Effective Referee Report." *Journal of Clinical Investigation* 119 (5): 1058–60.

Niemi, Richard G. 2006. Reducing the Burden of Manuscript Reviewing." *PS: Political Science & Politics* 39(4): 887–89.

Roediger, Henry L., III. 2007. "Twelve Tips for Reviewers." *Observer* 20 (4).

Publishing as a Graduate Student: A Quick and (Hopefully) Painless Guide to Establishing Yourself as a Scholar

3

Timothy S. Rich

The mantra of "publish or perish" guides the decisions of many academics, yet graduate students seldom know how to navigate the publishing process. Juggling other commitments, graduate students still need to consider the process early in their program so that they can present a competitive publishing record when entering the job market. Whereas a decade ago publishing while in graduate school remained rare, today in most subfields of political science a peer-reviewed publication[1] is considered a prerequisite for success on the job market.[2] From large research-oriented universities to small liberal arts colleges, a growing expectation is that new hires are capable of immediately producing publishable research as well as teaching. Although a myriad of factors such as departmental reputation and teaching experience influence placement on a search committee's shortlist, publishing remains one of the clearest means for a candidate to positively influence this process. Considering trends in publishing and the current state of the job market, graduate students should plan early to take advantage of the opportunities to publish well before entering the job market.

What Should I Publish?

Starting a research project and following through to submitting results to a journal is time intensive, especially if you are not already immersed in the relevant literature or have relevant data at hand in a usable format. Scholars in other fields have already highlighted the importance of initiating research early in their graduate career (e.g., Hansen 1991). To ease this process, I recommend that, from the start of graduate school, you should keep notes on possible research topics of interest. Often these notes will be a question or, at most a paragraph or two. As you progress in graduate school, you will routinely see overlooked areas or unanswered questions that interest you. Although you are unlikely to develop all of these ideas into research projects, writing down these ideas prevents you from forgetting what may be a good idea, especially ones in which you may not have the requisite substantive or methodological background to address properly.

Converting seminar papers into articles is also a common first step, however, not all seminar papers are destined for publication and even those with promise will likely require considerable revision before submission. Replicating an existing publication, either with additional cases or additional variables, is often another potential route (King 2006). After a general paper idea has been chosen (whether from a class or from scratch), the most important question to address is how will this work contribute to the existing literature. One way to think about this is to ask this question: what is the take-home message of this paper and what is the value added to the general literature on this topic? Contributions could be theoretical (e.g., challenging existing theory or testing such theories in a new way), methodological (e.g., quantitative analysis of a topic largely only addressed through qualitative means), the use of original data or case selection (e.g., a least-likely case), or even a combination of these factors. Similarly, challenging the conventional wisdom has more appeal than reaffirming what is already accepted. If you cannot identify the "hook" in your paper, it is unlikely that reviewers will either. Thus, within the first or second paragraph, your contribution should be clear to potential readers.

Next, concentrate on one argument in the paper, rather than trying to address the vastness of a particular topic. You will be surprised how much can be written on what originally might appear to be a niche. Ask yourself what is the one point you want readers to remember and structure your paper so that both careful readers and casual skimmers can grasp this point. If sections of your paper distract from this main point, no matter how well written the section may be, remove them.

Because this should be original research, choose topics in which you already have a general understanding of the literature and a topic that sustains your interest. Ideally, you would like to enter the job market with a series of publications tightly related to your main research interest, as a group of unrelated publications may suggest a lack of focus and undermine any claims on your CV of a commitment to a main research interest. Connecting your first piece to a coherent research agenda is of some concern, but the larger concern should be the general time commitment of moving from research idea to published project. If you are not passionate about this project (e.g., an obscure seminar paper on a topic you are unlikely to revisit), investing the additional time prepping for publication is unwarranted.

After you have a potential research paper, follow the general format of published work in your subject area. Weingast (1995) is a good starting point. In general, papers should follow the structure of introduction, roadmap, literature review, research method, analysis, and conclusion. Some journals have an explicit format other than this one, yet following this format from the inception makes later edits for specific journals easier. Furthermore, not only does this formatting aid reading for those who are not immersed in your research topic (even if the reader is skimming the piece), but it forces you to remain on target. Subheadings should remain jargon-free. Because most journal articles follow the same pattern, following this basic format reduces the time needed to prepare the work for future publication.

Finally, before sending a paper to a journal for review, have colleagues and professors read it. Not only are they more likely to give it a thorough reading as they have a stake in your success, but the turnaround time from people who know you is usually much shorter than the months it takes to get reviewer comments. Some papers during this informal peer review fall apart at this point well before submission to a journal. Perhaps your article is laced with too much jargon, with only those readers in your narrow subfield able to decipher and evaluate the piece. Perhaps nearly identical work has already been published, which unfortunately commonly occurs. Worse yet, your paper could be a rambling mess. Regardless, find this out from colleagues or professors who will most likely give suggestions on how to rectify these problems early rather than external reviewers who, while usually professional, have little reason to sugarcoat critiques to a stranger. Furthermore, have a diverse mix of people read early works, from those intimately familiar with the topic to those who have no background in your topic. For example, as a specialist in East Asian electoral politics, I often asked those in other subfields (e.g., American politics, public policy) to read my drafts to identify if the work was decipherable to the broader field. Asking for comments from a methodologically diverse group exposes potential weak points and ambiguous language. This review stage should not only gauge the paper's potential appeal to a larger audience, but provide suggestions as to venues for publication.

Another common avenue to gain feedback is to present at a conference, however, the overall usefulness of comments vary widely. Conference participation is a crucial aspect in preparing for the job market, especially in terms of concisely presenting your work (usually in 15 minutes or less) and in networking. Generally conference papers should not exceed 30 pages double-spaced and should be sent to the discussant at least a week before the conference, yet unfortunately, scholars frequently violate both of these common courtesies. Conferences range in terms of the number of presenters, the subfields or topics represented, and the receptiveness to inter-disciplinary work. Unfortunately, feedback is often quite minimal; few in the audience (and unfortunately sometimes not even the discussant) have read the paper, relying primarily on the presentation itself. If you have presented a work with largely positive feedback, especially after multiple presentations, consider this a sign that your piece should be sent out for publication. Two additional points regarding conference presentations should be noted. First, presenting numerous conference papers that never result in publications potentially sends the undesired signal that you are unable to produce quality work (Van Cott 2005). In this regard, presenting the same paper multiple times with publication in mind is better than seeing conferences as the end goal (Cooper 2008). Second, often only after presenting a paper do you realize its major weaknesses, many of which may not be easy to fix. There is no shame in deserting a project after a conference presentation.

Where Should I Send My Work?

There is no perfect answer to this question, but consider journals in which you expect the largest number of people interested in your topic will potentially read the paper. In publishing, your goal is hopefully to have an impact on current debates, and publishing in a journal in which experts in your subfield read is the best means to make such an impact.

With the proliferation of journals, deciding the best venue can be an onerous task. Here are a few broad factors to consider. First, identify what sort of audience would be interested in your paper. If it deals with broad issues that would appeal to a large swath of the discipline or subfield, then shooting for one of the broader journals is not unreasonable. However, if the topic is a niche that admittedly only a small number of scholars would find interesting, then submitting to a journal known specifically for that niche makes more sense. Skimming articles from the past five years in a variety of journals should give you some sense of the expectations in terms of quality and style and thus a better gauge of which journals may be interested in your piece. If a journal has recently published something similar on your topic in the past few years, attempt to cite this work; many journals ask the recently published authors to review articles. After you choose a journal for submission, tailor the paper based on the journal's particular theoretical, methodological, or interdisciplinary focus to encourage positive reviews or at least minimize negative remarks.

Second, consider general reputation of the journals. In theory, you want your piece placed in the most highly regarded journal that would possibly accept it. Remember that even solid works are often rejected from first-tier journals because of the finite space for print, the large number of submissions, or what appears, from the author's perspective, as arbitrary or superficial reasons. In these cases, consider a second-tier journal. In addition, just because you have not heard of a journal before is not necessarily an accurate measure of its quality. Many newer journals, some with prominent editors, produce high-quality work but receive far fewer submissions. Remember that not all peer-reviewed journals are equal nor will these likely be evaluated equally on the job market.

Third, consider the turnaround time. Journals commonly post their average turnaround time from when papers are submitted to when they expect to have reviews to the author. Most target for about three months, but this can vary significantly and often independently from the reputation of the journal itself. For example, Yoder and Bramlett (2011) identify a range from 21 to 118 days as the average turnaround time of journals that responded to their survey. Other than desk rejects—where the editor declines to send out the paper for review based usually on its poor fit for the theme of the journal—having a decision on a paper in less than two months is rare. In contrast, horror stories abound of waiting six months or more, with the end result little more than a paragraph panning the work. For example, once I waited seven months to receive a rejection that included the especially helpful one-line reviewer critique of "he uses someone else's data" (in that case a publicly available dataset). On another occasion I waited 10 months for reviews which all pointed out flaws that had been rectified since submission (due to presenting at several conferences over that time).[3] If time is crucial (e.g., you are planning to go on the market within the year), finding a journal known for a faster response time is a wise move. Few search committees are impressed by a CV listing papers under review, even if your intention is to signal productivity.

Finally, be realistic. Although every graduate student would love to have an article in a top-tier journal, this is unrealistic unless you have something above and beyond simply an interesting idea. Thus, when colleagues and professors suggest a journal that is not in the upper echelon, this should not be interpreted as a mistake on their part ("Oh, they just didn't get it"), but most likely an accurate evaluation. After all, professors have not only published in these journals, but in many cases have been reviewers for these same journals. Newer journals generally receive fewer submissions and may be a good avenue for your first submission. That said, there is little cost other than time in sending out a paper to a top journal and hoping for the best, expecting in reality to get feedback that will allow a revised version to be published in a slightly less prestigious journal.

After choosing a journal, pay careful attention to the submission requirements. Most journals have an explanation of submission requirements in the journal or on their website. The requirements define a style for citation (e.g., *Chicago Manual of Style*) and often suggest limitations on the number of tables and figures. Specifications vary, but most journals also limit the length of submissions from 8,000 to 10,000 words or about 25 to 30 pages. Ignore these limitations at your own peril as you risk irritating both the editor and reviewers. Generally, shorter papers are both easier to review and to allocate limited space in journals. Use this to your advantage. Word limits, in particular, should encourage writers to develop a clear and concise style that ultimately results in a paper accessible to a wider audience. When in doubt, if a sentence or section is not crucial to the main argument of the paper, strongly consider cutting it.

I've Sent Off My Work, Now What?

Wait. And wait some more. If you are motivated, start on another paper. Assistant professors commonly have multiple articles under review at a time to meet tenure requirements. Often data collected for one paper in mind is amenable to additional projects. Similarly, many graduate students find that data that failed to be incorporated into their dissertation finds a second life through side papers. By starting an additional project within the same basic literature, the time for preparing a paper for submission is shortened. Although you might not be prepared for multiple submissions, the lag between submission and a decision provides time to focus on other endeavors, such as your dissertation and teaching. If after three or four months you have heard nothing, contact the editor to inquire about the status. Occasionally editors will tell you how many reviews have been received and even release these before a final decision has been made. Other journals may ask if you can recommend potential reviewers. Both of these practices remain rare but may become more commonplace. In the meantime, develop a thick skin. Everyone at some point receives highly critical reviews, constructive or otherwise, and learning to properly respond to these reviews is a skill. With each submission, you should get better at anticipating problem areas (which, not surprisingly, are often the same areas addressed by colleagues and conference discussants).

After reviews come in, your paper will likely fall in one of three categories: accept with minor revisions, reject, and revise/resubmit (R&R). Rejections are commonplace, even with relatively positive reviews. In fact, many good papers will be rejected multiple times before finding an appropriate outlet, taking a year or more before publication. If reviews are uniformly negative (and negative for the same reasons), it may indicate the end of the road for this paper. While papers are often submitted that are not developed to their full potential or would be more convincing with significant rewriting, not all papers are destined for publication. Realizing the sunk costs in dead-end papers is part of the process.

The category of revise and resubmit is the purgatory where often decent papers struggle to reach publication. Whereas in years past an R&R almost certainly indicated future publication in that journal (assuming that suggested revisions were addressed), increasingly R&Rs in top journals are an invitation to a second round of revision, albeit with a greater yet undefined chance of publication. If the revisions are workable, address these quickly and resubmit the paper (in under a month if possible). In contrast, if the revisions are extensive, withdrawing the paper and submitting elsewhere remains an option. Keep in mind that for papers in a niche research area, the likelihood of receiving one of the same reviewers again at a different journal is common, thus ignore reviewer suggestions at your own risk.

When making revisions, synthesize the reviewers' comments and address each point as clearly as possible in the revised paper. Presume that any misinterpretations by reviewers are because of your lack of clarity rather than their ignorance or inability to realize your brilliance. We commonly presume that everyone in the discipline understands our niche's jargon, only realizing our errors when others read our work. After careful revision, include a page to the editor detailing these points, so that the editor can easily identify what changes have been made. Not only does this make the editor's job easier, but also signals that you took the reviewers' comments seriously, even if you did not implement all of the suggested changes.

Other Suggestions

The demands for publishing in both time and effort may seem daunting, but several factors can be more manageable. First, considering eventual publication when initially writing seminar or conference papers simplifies the process. Second, consider coauthoring, although this does not necessarily reduce time commitments or frustrations. Coauthoring has long been the norm in the natural sciences and is increasingly common in the social sciences. This strategy potentially allows you to combine individual research strengths, and ideally this should be evident within the final work. However, be cautious in coauthoring when your main contribution consistently is only methodological rather than substantive, even if you are attempting to market yourself as a methodologist. Similarly, although coauthoring with an advisor certainly will aid in generating name recognition, there is a tendency to assume that the student contributed considerably less to the project regardless of whether this accurate. Another option is collaborating with fellow graduate students either at your home university or elsewhere as this overcomes some of the potential biases in coauthoring with faculty. Ultimately, producing at least one solo-authored publication signals your ability to independently conduct research, while coauthored pieces produces slightly different signals, namely the ability to collaborate.

Conclusion

Disseminating one's work is a crucial component for success in academia. As publishing demands increase, graduate students must prepare accordingly to be competitive on the job market. Although the venues for publication increase, and the path to acceptance is a stochastic process, the actual preparation for publication remains remarkably similar across outlets. With a thick skin and an appreciation for the standards of publication, graduate students can certainly find outlets for their work.

Reprinted from Timothy S. Rich. 2013. "Publishing as a Graduate Student: A Quick and (Hopefully) Painless Guide to Establishing Yourself as a Scholar." PS: Political Science & Politics *46 (2).* Cambridge University Press: 376–79. doi:10.1017/S104909651300005X.

Notes

1. This article focuses on peer-review publishing. Many other publishing options exist for graduate students, from book reviews and short articles in newsletters to journals in which the editor has sole discretion on publication. While the value of nonreview publications varies greatly by search committee (Polsky 2011), the same general rules apply.
2. In an analysis of the 2001–2002 job market, Lopez (2003) makes little mention of graduate publication as an indicator of market success. Within a decade, publications became increasingly important for an initial interview (see Jaschik 2009). From my own nonscientific survey of colleagues on the market in recent years, I knew of only a scant few who received a job offer without at least a coauthored publication. The importance of publishing in graduate school is not limited to the social sciences. Mangematin (2000) finds that among engineering graduate students that publications correlate with success in academia.
3. Several colleagues have suggested that in cases like this authors can ask the editor to reconsider the submission, especially if there is clear evidence of revision. There appears to be a fine line between politely requesting reconsideration and irritating what is commonly an overworked editor. In my case, I opted to send the paper elsewhere.

References

Cooper, Christopher A. 2008. "Reassessing Conference Goals and Outcomes: A Defense of Presenting Similar Papers and Multiple Conferences." *PS: Political Science & Politics* 41 (2): 293–95.

Hansen, W. Lee. 1991. "The Education and Training of Economics Doctorates: Major Findings of the Executive Secretary of the American Economic Association's Commission on Graduate Education in Economics." *Journal of Economic Literature* 29 (3): 1054–87.

Jaschik, Scott. 2009. "Job Market Realities." *Inside Higher Ed.* http://www.insidehighered.com/news/2009/09/08/market.

King, Gary. 2006. "Publication, Publication." *PS: Political Science & Politics* 39 (1): 119–25.

Lopez, Linda. 2003. "Placement Report: Political Science PhDs and ABDs on the Job Market in 2001–2002." *PS: Political Science & Politics* 36 (4): 835–41.

Mangematin, V. 2000. "PhD Job Market: Professional Trajectories and Incentives during the PhD." *Research Policy* 29: 741–56.

Polsky, Andrew J. 2011. "Preparing for an Academic Career: Some Suggestions for Graduate Students." Unpublished.

Van Cott, Donna Lee. 2005. "A Graduate Student's Guide to Publishing Scholarly Journal Articles." *PS: Political Science & Politics* 38 (4): 741–43.

Weingast, Barry R. 1995. "Structuring Your Papers (Caltech Rules)." Unpublished. www.stanford.edu/group/mapss/colloquium/papers/caltech.pdf.

Yoder, Stephen, and Brittany H. Bramlett. 2011. "What Happens at the Journal Office Stays at the Journal Office: Assessing Journal Transparency and Record-Keeping Practices." *PS: Political Science & Politics* 44 (2): 363–73.

Women Also Know Stuff: Meta-Level Mentoring to Battle Gender Bias in Political Science

4

EMILY BEAULIEU
AMBER E. BOYDSTUN
NADIA E. BROWN
KIM YI DIONNE
ANDRA GILLESPIE
SAMARA KLAR
YANNA KRUPNIKOV
MELISSA R. MICHELSON
KATHLEEN SEARLES
CHRISTINA WOLBRECHT

W e are political scientists. We are women. We know stuff. And we are deeply concerned about the implicit bias in our profession that minimizes and marginalizes the voices of women.

More than a decade ago, the American Political Science Association noted the problem of underrepresentation of women in the professoriate, created by (1) a leaking pipeline, (2) a chronological crunch, (3) a hostile institutional climate, and (4) insufficient opportunity and support in the culture of research (American Political Science Association 2004). That report highlighted the various factors contributing to the lack of gender parity in the profession, with the result that men outnumber women in political science, especially at higher rungs of the academic ladder. This problem is particularly true for women of color, who are even less well represented than women overall. Yet, even taking into account the imbalance in the number of men and women political scientists, men have *disproportionately* outpaced women in reaching prominence in the field (Masuoka, Grofman, and Feld 2007). Furthermore, women political scientists are *disproportionately* less likely to have their research cited (Maliniak, Powers, and Walter 2013; Mitchell, Lange, and Brus 2013); to be included in teams of coauthors (Teele and Thelen 2017); to appear on professional panels at conferences (Gruberg 2009); to be invited to contribute to edited volumes (Mathews and Andersen 2001); and (anecdotally, at least) to be invited to speak at university colloquia.

Is the problem one of simple math? Men certainly outnumber women in faculty positions: women hold only 29% of full-time faculty positions in political science (American Political Science Association 2011). This proportion is much smaller than the proportion of women who earn doctoral degrees: 42% of PhDs awarded in political science in 2013 went to women, which is—of course—still short of parity (National Science Foundation 2013). Nevertheless, men do not outnumber women enough to explain well-documented gender gaps in political science

(Mitchell, Lange, and Brus 2013; Teele and Thelen 2017). As Mershon and Walsh (2016, 463) noted, "research produced by women is read and cited less often than is research by men, which means that this research is 'systematically undervalued.'"

Implicit Bias

Women's underrepresentation is not a "men-versus-women" problem; many men champion their women colleagues. Moreover, although women generally are better about citing other women, women academics can be as guilty of underrepresenting other women in scholarly citations and conference/colloquia invitations. Rather, men and women alike hold implicit biases about gender that shape their attitudes and behavior, including the tendency to think of—and reference—men rather than women as experts (Jones and Box-Steffensmeier 2014; Leslie et al. 2015).

Implicit bias is an established phenomenon whereby subconscious attitudes and stereotypes influence a person's perceptions of others and can manifest in nondeliberate discriminatory behavior (Greenwald and Krieger 2006). Unlike explicit biases, which operate under conscious control, implicit biases can affect a person's behavior without that person even being aware.

Both men and women in academia and in the media often express their genuine concern regarding issues of equality. However, these people also are busy and, when a deadline looms, the most efficient strategy is to call or reference the experts that most quickly come to mind— who often tend to be men. Implicit biases have an especially strong tether in academia, where a person's perceived intellect is paramount. Indeed, across STEM fields, women's underrepresentation correlates with the degree to which researchers in each field view academic success as hinging on raw intellectual talent, or "innate genius" (Leslie et al. 2015).

When women political scientists are missing from academic discussions about politics, the profession loses out on the expertise and perspective they have to offer—some of it directly related to women's different experiences in life and some of it simply because roughly one third of the available expertise is missing. The absence of women also reinforces stereotypes about who is an expert. If we could increase the volume of voices of women in our discipline, we could diversify and strengthen our science.

The Launch of "Women Also Know Stuff"

Our witnessing of and experience with this implicit bias against women political scientists reached a tipping point in 2016. We launched a crowd-sourced website, WomenAlsoKnowStuff.com, to highlight the diversity of expertise among women in the profession and to make it easier for scholars who are writing papers; developing syllabi; and convening workshops, colloquia, and conference panels to find women experts. We also wanted our website to be a resource for journalists who aim to achieve greater gender balance in asking experts to comment on current political events.

Our editorial board consists of members with a wide range of scholarly expertise, racial and ethnic backgrounds, and institutional affiliations and ranks. We embody the fact that women have a range of skills and identities that further the production of knowledge in the discipline and the larger public discourse.

The women in our database encompass and expand on this diversity in experience and expertise. After only a few weeks, nearly 1,000 women political scientists with expertise in more than 80 topical areas added their names and profiles to our website, which—to date—has been viewed more than 80,000 times by more than 15,000 unique visitors. Our Twitter account has nearly 8,000 followers and has made nearly 57 million impressions.[1]

Much of the initial response to the "Women Also Know Stuff" initiative has come from media outlets, including the immediate use of our website by journalists who want to reach out to individual women political scientists for their expert commentary on events ranging from the 2016 US presidential campaign to the recent corruption scandal and subsequent presidential impeachment in Brazil. We are delighted that members of the media see the value of diversifying their rolodexes.

Impact on the Profession

We are excited about the initial engagement among women political scientists and the warm response from the media. However, our primary goal for the "Women Also Know Stuff" initiative is to have an impact on our profession. In short, we want the site and future related activities to counter implicit bias among political scientists, as evidenced through greater gender equity on syllabi, in book and journal-article bibliographies, on conference panels, and in invited talks. Drawing on the many anecdotes already relayed to us, we see important opportunities for impact.

As one example, after our website launched, we received the following email from APSA then President-Elect David A. Lake:

Thank you for putting together the website "Women Also Know Stuff." I just happily spent the afternoon going through your expert lists. On the penultimate draft of a paper where I needed to make sure I cited all the relevant materials, I just worked my way down your list of experts on civil conflict. Slapping my forehead numerous times, I kept repeating "of course I need to cite that." By the end, my reference list changed from 2/3 male to 50-50 male/female. I may have slighted my male colleagues in this process, but I take this to be fair retribution for years of past negligence. Fantastic resource, for which we are all in your debt.

We hope other political scientists will follow Dr. Lake's lead. We still need to explore the systematic ways that our profession and our institutions discount the achievements of women scholars. Yet, there are ways that "Women Also Know Stuff" can help scholars be individually proactive. We recommend the following first steps:

Check your syllabus for gender bias. We may be inadvertently giving our students—especially our graduate students—the impression that women are not making significant contributions to the field by omitting them from assigned readings. This form of representation is especially important because today's reading lists become the reference lists of tomorrow's scholars. (See the appendix for a web-based tool to help achieve this.)

Check the lists of references in your current research projects. Are you omitting relevant work from women? When we neglect to cite important work by women scholars, it has implications for their career trajectories and also negatively impacts the discipline in that we come to equate the canon with work written by men (see step #1). Moreover, these scholars bring important insights to bear that can enhance our work.

Think about your list of invited presenters for events or panels that you are organizing for an upcoming conference or department speaker series. Featuring only or mostly men in colloquia gives the impression that women are not doing important work. By disproportionately inviting men to give talks, we unnecessarily diminish the profiles of our women colleagues.

Recommend that your women colleagues join the website. There are almost 1,300 women currently listed, but we know that many more are out there. Do not keep the good news to yourself; recommend to all of your colleagues that they use the website when putting together their syllabi, bibliographies, conferences, and speaking events.

Reflecting on Our Experiences

Working on this project is both rewarding and frustrating. It is encouraging to see enthusiastic responses from those like Dr. Lake, who recognize the problem and are making our profession more inclusive. We also have our share of trolls. The amount of time and energy we invest is the stereotypical type of service that is unlikely either to be recognized by our institutions or to assist our individual ambitions for advancement and/or tenure. It also is the type of service that women are more likely to perform. We remain convinced that the work is both necessary and worthwhile.

Our founding board member, Samara Klar, launched the first version of the website when one day she simply had had enough, after seeing both a conference program with a nearly all-male lineup and a news article asking six (white male) political scientists for their views on the election. She created a bare-bones WordPress blog site and emailed her women political science friends to invite them to add their own information—and then to forward the email to other potentially interested women. The initial response was overwhelming; within a week, it was clear that the website would need more hands-on management. Eventually, nine other women agreed to become members of a founding editorial board. Initial goals included improvement of the website, increased visibility, and development of a grant proposal to provide support for ongoing efforts.

There were growing pains. Shifting to a centralized system of adding women to the site—rather than globally sharing the password—ensured that only women political scientists were added and that women were adding only themselves (rather than others without their consent). However, doing so also meant that we suddenly needed a way to process and post the massive influx of applications. After a few forays into possible solutions—such as simply investing hours of our own (or our research assistants') time adding names—we moved to a new website that includes a mechanism for women to add and edit their own listings.

Another challenge was facing our own implicit biases. However inadvertently, our initial board had limited racial and ethnic diversity. As soon as we noticed this oversight, existing board members enthusiastically and unanimously agreed to extend invitations to two women of color to join the board. Both accepted, and our work is much improved as a result. However, we remain cognizant of the need to be attentive to our own biases going forward.

With 10 women on board, the massive amount of work associated with the project's goals was more easily shared (although still representing a sizeable workload for each of us). Women with expertise in website programming took on that role; those with expertise in social media focused on developing a Twitter presence. Other women branched off to work on a proposal to the National Science Foundation; others refined the group's logo and branding (see figure 1). Individual board members conducted interviews with various media outlets and wrote blog posts for The Conversation, the *Washington Post*'s Monkey Cage, and the *Huffington Post*, to name only a few. After months of operating through mostly informal subcommittees and ad hoc conference calls, we now have a codified set of by-laws.

As the project began to bear fruit in the form of increased visibility and website hits, board members also received feedback from those hoping we would expand our scope, such as to nonpolitical scientists and to nonacademics, and to include other underrepresented groups in political science, such as people of color and members of the LGBT community. Although we wholeheartedly concur that implicit bias also negatively impacts members of these groups, we decided to retain our narrow focus on women in political science. At the same time, we hope eventually to produce a how-to manual for others that describes our project and

Figure 1. The "Women Also Know Stuff" Logo

allows them to launch similar initiatives to raise the visibility and inclusion of other underrepresented voices. We are thrilled to see that others have launched an effort to amplify the voices of people of color in the discipline: @POCalsoknow.

We also had to make difficult decisions. For example, although we were thrilled by the volume of women academics who expressed interest in participating in our initiative, we ultimately had to commit to restricting our database to only women in political science. Similarly, we are pleased that women in graduate school have enthusiastically embraced the site, although we decided to distinguish those experts who hold a PhD from those who do not. Regarding the website, we are constantly struggling to maximize its effectiveness and utility, all with limited technical expertise and no source of funding on which we can rely. Together, we developed a mission statement for our initiative that will allow this project to persist well into the future; we deliberated about the tone and purpose of our social media voice; and we even gave careful consideration to the design of our logo. Initial consensus on a stack of binders (thanks, Mitt Romney) soon gave way to a more nonpartisan visual incorporating a light bulb.

The development of our initiative has been fueled by—and has fueled—our internal discussions and ponderings about gender in academia. Our first (video) conference call was held the only time that we were all available—late at night, with nearly half of the editorial board sporting pajamas. This call was only one instance of the mix of dedication and honesty that buoys our efforts. Since that first call, we have had long discussions about how to move forward, such as how much effort we should put into responding to individual journalists' queries and which features should be included in the search function on the website. We also share stories about our experiences as women in this profession: the need to find a private space in which to pump breastmilk while traveling, the pressure to have a drink during an on-campus interview to demonstrate to prospective employers that we are not pregnant, and the degree of support (or lack thereof) from our respective institutions.

These latter discussions, which often incorporate considerable humor and flurries of hashtags, are part of what has made the project so fulfilling. Coming together as a group of strong, knowledgeable women to share our experiences of implicit bias, outright sexism, and bean-counting bureaucrats has relieved some of the stress of those challenges. This is yet another aim of the "Women Also Know Stuff" initiative: to bring women in the profession together in solidarity and strength.

Given the time commitments that this work has required, why are we doing it? Why, after so many months, have none of the 10 board members "cried uncle" and asked to cycle off? Why, as members of the "harmed" group (i.e., women in the discipline), are we the ones doing the work to fix that harm? Simply stated, we find this work to be one of the most rewarding projects that we have been part of as academics.

We are changing the profession into one in which we want to and feel like we belong: one that is inclusive and committed to diversity. This work reminds us that the state of our discipline is not static; with collective effort, it is changing for the better. It allows us to give back to those who paved the way and made our own careers possible (both men and women) and to pay it forward to the next generation of women political scientists. We are proud to be part of a group that is confronting head on those professional and popular biases, in a classically feminine fashion: by being helpful.

The work also has brought us personal rewards. The work nurtures our souls, providing us with support and inspiration to do our other professional work. We have formed bonds with one another as well as with other women in the discipline that we have met because of this project. We are building our networks and feeling more connected—building a community that makes us personally happier and more fulfilled.

Next Steps
"Women Also Know Stuff" board members are active in attending disciplinary conferences.

We continue to reach out to women political scientists who may want to add their names to our website as well as to all political scientists, with the aim of mitigating the ongoing issue of implicit gender bias. Within the next year, we plan to hold a series of focus groups with women political scientists to better understand their challenges in the profession and how the "Women Also Know Stuff" initiative can help.

We also plan to keep an eye on the profession, systematically measuring the presence of gender bias at conferences, in lists of references, and in syllabi. We urge all political scientists to make use of the expertise listed on our website and of women in political science more broadly.

In every instance in which you can make a difference, take personal responsibility to be inclusive and fight back against implicit gender bias. Remember, women also know stuff. You should ask them about it. Be like Dr. Lake: include women.

Reprinted from Emily Beaulieu, Amber E. Boydstun, Nadia E. Brown, Kim Yi Dionne, Andra Gillespie, Samara Klar, Yanna Krupnikov, Melissa R. Michelson, Kathleen Searles, and Christina Wolbrecht. 2017. "Women Also Know Stuff: Meta-Level Mentoring to Battle Gender Bias in Political Science." PS: Political Science & Politics *50 (3). Cambridge University Press: 779–83. doi:10.1017/S1049096517000580.*

Notes

1. An impression refers to the appearance of a tweet on an individual user's Twitter feed.

References

American Political Science Association. 2004. "Women's Advancement in Political Science: A Report of the APSA Workshop on the Advancement of Women in Academic Political Science in the United States." http://files.eric.ed.gov/fulltext/ED495970.pdf.

American Political Science Association. 2011. "Political Science in the 21st Century: Report of the Task Force on Political Science in the 21st Century." www.apsanet.org/portals/54/Files/Task%20Force%20 Reports/TF_21st%20Century_AllPgs_webres90.pdf.

Anthony G. Greenwald and Linda Hamilton Krieger. 2006. "Implicit Bias: Scientific Foundations." *California Law Review* 94 (4): 945–67.

Gruberg, Martin. 2008. "Participation by Women in the 2007 APSA Annual Meeting." *PS: Political Science & Politics* 41 (1): 171–72.

Jones, Hazel Morrow and Jan Box-Steffensmeier. 2014. "Implicit Bias and Why It Matters to the Field of Political Methodology." *The Political Methodologist.* http://thepoliticalmethodologist.com/2014/03/31/ implicit-bias-and-why-it-matters-to-the-field-of-political-methodology.

Leslie, Sarah-Jane, Andrei Cimpian, Meredith Meyer, and Edward Freeland. 2015. "Expectations of Brilliance Underlie Gender Distributions across Academic Disciplines." *Science* 347 (6219): 262–5.

Maliniak, Daniel, Ryan M. Powers, and Barbara F. Walter. 2013. "The Gender Citation Gap in International Relations." *International Organization* 67 (4): 889–922.

Masuoka, Natalie, Bernard Grofman, and Scott L. Feld. 2007. "The Political Science 400: A 20-Year Update." *PS: Political Science & Politics* 40 (1): 133–45.

Mathews, A. Lanethea and Kristi Andersen. 2001. "A Gender Gap in Publishing? Women's Representation in Edited Political Science Books." *PS: Political Science & Politics* 34 (1): 143–7.

Mershon, Carol and Denise Walsh. 2016. "Diversity in Political Science: Why It Matters and How to Get It." *Politics, Groups, and Identities* 4 (3): 462–6.

Mitchell, Sara McLaughlin, Samantha Lange, and Holly Brus. 2013. "Gendered Citation Patterns in International Relations Journals." *International Studies Perspectives* 14 (4): 485–92.

National Science Foundation. 2013. "Survey of Earned Doctorates." www.nsf.gov/statistics/sed/2013/ data/tab16.pdf.

Teele, Dawn and Kathleen Thelen. 2017. "Gender in the Journals: Methodology, Coauthorship, and Publication Patterns in Political Science's Flagship Journals." *PS: Political Science & Politics* 50 (2): 433–47.

Appendix

Following are additional resources for increasing women's visibility in the discipline:

1. VIMbot automatically sends out tweets to announce when Visions in Methodology participants publish a new article. See @PSci_VIMbot or http://shawnakmetzger.com/wp/vimbot for more information.
2. Check the gender (and race) balance in your syllabus with this online tool, available at https://jlsumner.shinyapps.io/syllabustool.
3. Get involved in the Women's Caucus for Political Science (WCPS); see the group's website for more information: https://womenscaucusforpoliticalscience.org. WCPS meets during the APSA Annual Meeting, publishes a quarterly newsletter, and hosts a listserv.
4. Visit the website hosted by the APSA Committee on the Status of Women in the Profession, available at http://web.apsanet.org/cswp. The website includes data, advice columns, graphs that make you gasp, and other valuable resources.

Do Political Science Majors Succeed in the Labor Market?

5

Gregory B. Lewis

Although most political science faculty probably hope students choose our major to think more deeply about really important things, many students and parents (and even a few faculty) worry that political science will not prepare graduates for careers. Responding to "jokes ... that political science majors ... have not acquired the necessary practical skills to make a living, let alone to acquire a lucrative career," Breuning, Parker, and Ishiyama (2001, 657) argue that political science departments need to be much more explicit about the tangible skills they are delivering. In the provocatively titled "Would You Like Fries with That?" Bobic (2005, 349–50) suggests eliminating the BA in political science altogether, because "the standard program of study in Political Science ... virtually guarantees that a student with a Bachelor's degree will be unable to find employment using those skills or interests." Although APSA's Task Force on the Political Science Major (Wahlke 1991) recommended restructuring the political science curriculum to prepare students for the world, Ishiyama, Breuning, and Lopez (2006) find that undergraduate political science education has changed very little over the past century, and that departments place little emphasis on career preparation (Ishiyama 2005; Collins, Knotts, and Schiff 2012).

Clearly, however, college graduates are more prepared for lucrative careers than are high school graduates. People with bachelor's degree earn 84% more over their lifetimes than people with high school diplomas (Carnevale, Rose, and Cheah 2011), though the payoff to a college diploma varies widely by major, by as much as a factor of four (e.g., Altonji, Arcidiacono, and Maurel 2015; Altonji, Blom, and Meghir 2012; Black, Sanders, and Taylor 2003; Carnevale, Strohl, and Melton 2011). Analysis of earnings by majors shows that economics majors, for instance, earn more than graduates of most other programs (exceptions include engineering and computer science), whether they stop with a bachelor's degree or earn an MBA or law degree (Black, Sanders, and Taylor 2003; Craft and Baker 2003; Winters 2015). Similarly, Chen and Johnson (2016) find that political science majors fare better than comparable graduates of other fields (collectively) in the federal civil service.

I look more broadly at the success of political science graduates in the labor market. Using recent census data, I follow labor economists' methodology to compare unemployment rates, educational attainment, and earnings of political science majors to graduates in other fields, controlling for sex, race/ethnicity, age, and educational attainment. The findings are mostly positive: although political science majors have above-average unemployment rates in their 20s, they are among the most likely to obtain graduate degrees and earn meaningfully more than those in most other social sciences and humanities.

Data and Method

Since 2001, the US Census Bureau has fielded the American Community Survey (ACS) to gather the detailed information on Americans' personal and work characteristics that was traditionally collected on the census long form. Since 2009, the ACS has asked college graduates the field of study for their undergraduate (but not subsequent) degrees. Combining ACS data for 2009–2014 yields information on a random sample of 3.4 million college graduates, including 86,000 political science majors. Samples are so large that almost all relationships are statistically significant, allowing a focus on the size of differences.

The key independent variables are 28 fields of study (listed in all tables). I use broad categories for most fields, but break out the social sciences—the most likely competitors for our students—into more detailed majors. Regression models use 27 dummy variables for field of study, with political science majors as the reference group; thus, coefficients represent differences from political science majors with similar characteristics on factors that influence career success.

The three dependent variables are unemployment, educational attainment, and annual earnings. The first is coded 1 for those who are unemployed and 0 for those with jobs. I restrict the sample to 21-to-30-year-olds (those with the highest unemployment rates), who are not in school and are in the labor force. I run a logit analysis and convert coefficients on the majors to expected differences in unemployment rates from political science majors, using Stata's *margins* command to calculate average partial effects (APEs).

Second, educational attainment has four values (bachelor's, master's, professional, and doctoral degrees). I restrict the sample to those aged 34 and above.[1] I use multinomial logit analysis, as the values do not have a clear order, and translate coefficients into probability differences using APEs.

Third, I run the earnings models on full-time, full-year employees aged 25 and above, who were not in school. The dependent variable is the natural logarithm of annual earnings, a coding that assumes that the independent variables have consistent percentage (rather than dollar) effects on earnings. I exponentiate the 27 major coefficients, subtract 1, and multiply by 100 to yield expected percentage differences in earnings from political science majors.

I control for a variety of factors that affect career success—age/experience, race/ethnicity/ gender, sexual orientation, education, time, and location—using dummy variables for each unique value of each independent variable. (See the online technical appendix for justification.)

To tease out how majors affect earnings, I enter variables into the model sequentially. The first only includes major to show average percentage differences in earnings. The second adds educational attainment to compare those with the same degrees. The third adds race/ethnicity/ gender, relationship status/sexual orientation, military service, age, and year to see how the type of people who choose each major affects the apparent earnings differences. The fourth includes state of employment and 69 dummy variables for hours worked per week, to examine the impact of where and how much one works. The fifth model repeats the fourth, but limited to people without graduate degrees.

I present the original regression analyses in the online appendix, but show only the percentage differences by major in the tables. In each table, I arrange the majors in order of their success on that measure and present differences from comparable political science majors.

Limitations

Students with different interests and abilities choose different majors, and ability has a substantial impact on earnings (Arcidiacono 2004; Webber 2014, 2015) and, presumably, educational attainment. Students in the highest-paying majors have the highest mean SAT-math scores (Altonji, Blom, and Meghir 2012), and math ability and classes have important impacts on earnings (Rendall and Rendall 2013). Because ACS data do not include any measures of ability, this research cannot test the possibility that differences in abilities among people choosing different majors explain all the differences in unemployment, educational attainment, and earnings. Political science graduates may not have earned more if they had majored in computer science, nor less if they had chosen English.

Findings

Unemployment

Unemployment rates are high for those in their 20s, but substantially lower for college graduates than for the less-educated (4.9% *versus* 11.7% in 2009–2014). Political science majors' unemployment rate of 6.6% was nearly the highest among college graduates, however (table 1), and a logit model controlling for individual characteristics did not substantially alter that picture (also see appendix table 1). The first column shows unemployment rates; the rate of 2.8% for health science majors, for instance, is 3.8 percentage points lower than for political science majors. The second column shows the differences in unemployment rates (relative to political science) after controlling for education, age, race/ethnicity, gender, relationship status, year, and state; this difference remained at 3.5 points. Graduates of half the majors—including business, social work, psychology, criminal justice, economics, sociology, and communications—were 1 to 3 percentage points less likely to be unemployed than comparable political science majors. No major had a significantly higher unemployment rate than political science.

Educational Attainment

This possible difficulty in starting a career may contribute to political science majors' decisions to pursue further education. Only 46% of political science majors stopped with a bachelor's degree; 5.5% earned doctorates, and the remaining 49% were split almost evenly between master's and professional degrees (table 2). The remainder of the table shows differences from political science in probabilities of each degree after a full set of controls (also see appendix tables 2 and 3). Only biology, philosophy, and physics majors are more likely to obtain graduate degrees, with the difference primarily in doctorates. Political science majors stand out for professional degrees: only biology majors are more likely to earn them, and only history majors are within 10 percentage points as likely as comparable political science majors to do so. One-fifth of political science graduates complete law school.

Occupations

Although career guidance for political science majors (e.g., American Political Science Association 2001; Clark 2004) typically emphasizes government careers, three-quarters of political science majors work in the private sector. The most common jobs of those with bachelor's degrees are in management and sales (table 3). Government jobs include public administrators, police officers, and primary school teachers. Those with master's degrees are most typically in management or education, and most of those with professional degrees or doctorates work as lawyers, though management is also common.

Earnings

Political science majors with bachelor's degrees earn, on average, 67% more than comparable high school graduates; those with master's, professional, and doctoral degrees earn 99%, 170%, and 128% more than high school graduates, respectively (not shown). Table 4 shows mean earnings by major, and model 1 of table 5 shows percentage differences from political science majors, controlling for year; only engineering, economics, biology, and physics majors earn more. Political science majors' mean salaries are slightly higher than those for computer science and business majors and are 20% to 30% higher than for those in English, communications, psychology, criminal justice, and sociology.

One reason is political science majors' high educational attainment. When model 2 controls for degree, most majors' pay rises by at least 10% relative to political science. Individual demographics also explain some of the pay advantage in the most lucrative majors. Engineering, computer science, and economics majors are disproportionately male, white, and Asian (appendix table 4), groups that tend to earn higher salaries overall; when those factors are controlled in model 3,

	Unemployed	Difference from Political Science After Controls
Health Sciences	2.8***	-3.5***
Agriculture	2.9***	-3.0***
Education	3.1***	-2.8***
Theology	3.7***	-1.8*
Physical Fitness	3.8***	-2.5***
Engineering	3.9***	-2.6***
Mathematics and Statistics	4.0***	-2.4***
Physical Sciences	4.2***	-2.2***
Computer Sciences	4.5***	-2.2***
Biology	4.5***	-1.9***
Social Work	4.6***	-1.6**
Business	4.6***	-2.0***
Psychology	5.4***	-1.0**
Criminal Justice	5.6*	-1.4***
Communcations	5.6**	-1.1**
Economics	5.8	-1.5***
Interdisciplinary Studies	5.9	-0.5
Environment	6.1	-0.2
Sociology	6.2	-0.8
History	6.4	-0.2
Languages	6.4	0.1
English	6.4	0.1
Philosophy and Religion	6.4	0.1
Political Science	6.6	-
Liberal Arts and Humanities	6.7	0.0
Fine Arts	6.8	0.0
Other Social Sciences	7.0	0.3
Architecture	7.5	1.1
Observations: 384,765		

Table 1. Probability of Unemployment for 21-to-30 Year Olds, by Major Differences from political science are significant at the ***.001, **.01, or *.05 level. Logit model for unemployment includes college graduates aged 21-30 living in the US and not currently attending school. Model uses dummy variables to control for age, educational attainment, race/ethnicity/gender, relationship type, year, and state of residence. Logit coefficients were converted to probability differences using Stata's margins command to calculate average partial effects.

the pay differential shrinks (see appendix table 5). The pay advantage to majoring in the health sciences jumps, however, because of their overrepresentation of women, blacks, and Latinos. [2]

Adding hours worked and state of employment also shifts political science majors downward (model 4), partly because they are among the four majors who work the longest hours and the three majors who work in the highest-paying states. (In particular, 5.4% of political science majors work in Washington, DC, 4.6 times the rate for college graduates overall and nearly

	Bachelor's Degree Only	Master's Degree	Professional Degree	Doctoral Degree
Percentage				
Political Science	45.7	24.9	23.9	5.5
Differences in Percentages after Controls				
Biology	-10.5	-2.3	3.7	9.1
Philosophy and Religion	-5.3	7.0	-7.2	5.5
Physical Sciences	-1.3	1.9	-10.3	9.8
Psychology	0.2 N.S	8.4	-12.9	4.4
Languages	0.5	8.7	-12.5	3.2
Mathematics	1.5	11.2	-16.3	3.6
History	1.9	4.7	-7.6	1.0
Education	3.5	15.6	-17.4	-1.7
English	4.2	6.1	-11.5	1.2
Social Work	5.8	14.7	-17.8	-2.7
Other Social Sciences	8.3	5.4*	-14.2	0.6*
Theology	8.7	5.8*	-16.8	2.3
Economics	9.4	3.9	-12.5	-0.8
Interdisciplinary Studies	10.2	0.8	-11.0	0.2*
Engineering	11.1	7.7	-18.2	-0.6
Sociology	12.9	2.6	-15.0	-0.5
Health Sciences	13.4	-2.8	-11.0	0.4
Architecture	15.1	3.9	-15.6	-3.4
Physical Fitness	16.9	-0.8	-15.9	-0.2
Environment	19.7	-1.1	-17.6	-1.0
Agriculture	20.6	-5.3	-16.1	0.7
Liberal Arts and Humanities	20.9	-4.0	-14.9	-2.0
Computer Science	21.3	1.2	-19.7	-2.8
Fine Arts	22.1	-2.2	-18.0	-1.9
Communications	25.8	-4.9	-18.0	-3.7
Business	26.6	-4.9	-18.0	-3.7
Criminal Justice	26.8	-6.9	-16.8	-3.2
Observations: 2,807,200				

Table 2. Educational Attainment of College Graduates Aged 34 and Above, by Major Differences from political science are significant at.0001, except *.05 or N.S. not significant. Multinomial logit model for educational includes college graduates aged 34 and over, living in the United States. Model uses dummy variables to control for age, race/ethnicity/gender, relationship type, year, and state of employment and for whether currently attending school. Logit coefficients were converted to average partial effects.

twice the rate even for economics and foreign language majors.) With all these variables in the model, political science majors earn 10% to 20% less than engineering, computer science, health science, economics, and math majors, but only 4% less than business majors and at least 10% more than those in other social sciences and the humanities.

		Mean Salary	% in Occupation
Bachelor's Degree Only	Managers and administrators, n.e.c	92,762	9.4
	Salespersons, n.e.c	92,203	4.8
	Supervisors and proprietors of sales jobs	79,341	4.3
	Managers and specialists in marketing	103,623	3.9
	Legal assistants, paralegals, legal support	47,196	3.8
	Chief executives and public administrators	155,730	2.6
	Police, detectives, and private investigators	76,551	2.5
	Computer systems analysts and computer scientists	68,499	2.3
	Other financial specialists	102,000	2.3
	Primary school teachers	41,145	2.3
	Retail sales clerks	54,840	2.3
	Secretaries	39,669	2.1
	Customer service reps, investigators and adjusters	45,600	2.0
	Management analysts	84,876	1.9
	Personnel, HR, training, and labor relations	69,482	1.8
	Financial managers	107,879	1.8
	Accountants and auditors	66,851	1.6
	Real estate sales occupations	63,108	1.6
	Office supervisors	67,311	1.6
	Military	62,835	1.5
Master's Degree	Managers and administrators, n.e.c	115,406	12.0
	Primary school teachers	55,084	7.0
	Managers in education and related field	82,875	3.8
	Chief executives and public administrators	171,816	3.8
	Management analysts	95,174	3.5
	Managers and specialists in marketing	119,866	3.4
	Salespersons, n.e.c	95,625	2.7
	Accountants and auditors	99,255	2.6
	Supervisors and proprietors of sales jobs	104,132	2.4
	Other financial specialists	134,739	2.4
	Financial managers	151,839	2.4
	Subject instructors (HS/college)	50,724	2.4
	Computer systems analysts and computer scientists	86,059	2.4
	Managers of service organizations, n.e.c.	77,911	2.3
	Military	91,331	2.2
	Secondary school teachers	56,091	1.9
	Lawyers	116,180	1.8
	Personnel, HR, training, and labor relations	93,602	1.6
	Social workers	50,806	1.5

Table 3. Top Occupations for College Graduates Who Majored in Political Science

		Mean Salary	% in Occupation
Profession-al Degree	Lawyers	133,225	72.9
	Managers and administrators, n.e.c	136,805	3.1
	Physicians	176,777	1.7
	Chief executives and public administrators	185,774	1.5
Doctoral Degree	Lawyers	118,819	33.9
	Subject instructors (HS/college)	85,514	24.9
	Managers in education and related field	115,863	4.8
	Managers and administrators, n.e.c	126,890	4.5
	Chief executives and public administrators	162,561	2.4
	Management analysts	112,858	1.9
	Physicians	161,025	1.6
	Primary school teachers	71,863	1.5

Table 3 (Continued). Top Occupations for College Graduates Who Majored in Political Science

Conclusion

Studying political science seems to have a positive impact on students' careers. Political science majors with bachelor's degrees earn two-thirds more than comparable high school graduates, and most obtain graduate degrees. Only engineering, economics, computer science, and health science majors make at least 10% more than demographically similar political science majors working the same number of hours in the same states. Our graduates make nearly as much as those who obtain far more career-oriented business degrees, and they earn 10% to 25% more than comparable majors in most other social sciences and humanities, even after controlling for our majors' higher probability of pursuing graduate degrees. That higher pay depends, in part, on working somewhat longer hours in high-wage, high-cost locations; but a 1-in-20 probability of a career in Washington, DC, may be an attraction to our majors.

Our majors' relative ranking in the economic hierarchy may have more to do with their innate abilities than with what they learn from us, of course. The ACS data do not include any ability measures to test that possibility, but Altonji, Blom, and Meghir (2012, supplementary table 2) find that political science majors' SAT-math scores are markedly lower than those in the highest-paying majors, somewhat lower than those in history and philosophy, and as high as or higher than those in psychology, English, business, other social sciences, and social work. If their findings hold more generally, we can probably claim some credit for our students earning more than history and philosophy majors and reject claims that majoring in business, the other social sciences, or the humanities offers better paths to good careers.

Two weaknesses do stand out. First, young political science graduates had fairly high unemployment rates in recent years. Efforts to smooth the transition to the labor market (e.g., internships, career counseling) could have high short-run payoffs. Second, our career advice should probably recognize more explicitly that political science is a generalist degree. Very few of our graduates go into politics, and only a quarter of them end up in government jobs, many of which are in schools. Substantial percentages work in sales. High unemployment rates in the 20s may partly reflect an unwillingness to accept that reality. Nonetheless, our majors are developing the writing and thinking skills that allow them to succeed in many venues, and many may be deciding to save their professional training for graduate school.

	Mean	Median	Sample Size
Economics	$116,271	85,000	42,026
Biology	107,541	75,000	95,349
Engineering	105,182	93,000	170,818
Physical Sciences	102,605	80,000	61,205
Political Science	99,651	75,000	53,889
Mathematics	98,892	80,000	28,135
Computer Science	88,695	64,061	80,000
History	88,302	62,000	42,333
Business	84,791	65,000	432,755
Total	81,450	62,000	1,889,755
Philosophy & Religion	81,347	57,000	13,192
Health Science	79,344	69,000	132,177
Architecture	76,554	65,000	15,383
Interdisciplinary Studies	74,778	55,000	14,914
English	74,677	56,000	55,010
Other Social Sciences	74,378	60,000	23,758
Languages	73,175	58,000	17,033
Communications	69,761	55,000	72,876
Liberal Arts & Humanities	69,581	53,000	24,654
Environment	69,553	58,000	13,669
Psychology	69,368	55,000	82,936
Sociology	66,049	52,000	29,561
Agriculture	65,954	50,000	27,768
Criminal Justice	64,839	55,000	35,226
Physical Fitness	59,856	50,000	15,412
Fine Arts	57,380	46,000	65,878
Education	55,790	50,000	196,957
Social Work	52,347	45,000	20,857
Theology	50,725	41,000	11,984

Table 4. Mean and Median Salaries by Major 2009–14

Reprinted from Gregory B. Lewis 2017. "Do Political Science Majors Succeed in the Labor Market?" PS: Political Science & Politics 50 (2). Cambridge University Press: 467–72. doi:10.1017/S1049096516003012.

Supplementary Material
To view the Appendix and data for this article, visit doi:10.1017/S1049096516003012.

Notes
1. Most people who are going to earn graduate degrees have done so by age 34. The percentage who had graduate degrees rose nearly a full point between ages 33 and 34, then fluctuated with a slight upward drift at higher ages.

	All Degree Levels				Bachelor's Degree Only
	Model 1	Model 2	Model 3	Model 4	Model 5
Engineering	13.5	26.5	16.3	20.1	19.7
Economics	11.1	20.2	15.4	13.1	10.8
Biology	4.0	-2.5	-0.5[N.S.]	4.9	-3.6
Physical Sciences	3.3	4.6	0.3N.S.	5.3	-0.5[N.S.]
Mathematics and Statistics	1.7	8.7	5.6	9.6	10.5
Political Science	0.0	0.0	0.0	0.0	0.0
Computer Science	-3.0	13.3	10.9	15.8	14.3
Business	13.3	1.8	0.3[N.S.]	3.6	2.1
History	-13.6	-10.7	-13.0	-10.4	-12.0
Health Sciences	-13.8	-4.8	3.1	14.1	16.3
Architecture	-15.7	-5.0	-8.8	-6.1	-3.3
Philosophy and Religion	-20.9	-21.0	-22.7	-19.5	-17.6
Other Social Sciences	-22.8	-15.6	-14.4	-9.9	-11.4
Environment	-23.9	-12.8	-18.0	-11.2	-12.0
English	-24.1	-19.0	-15.2	-12.0	-11.7
Interdisiplinary Studies	-24.1	-17.1	-10.9	-6.3	-8.1
Languages	-25.1	-21.0	-15.5	-12.5	-12.8
Agriculture	-26.7	-16.9	-22.3	-17.1	-19.2
Communications	-26.9	-14.1	-9.4	-6.2	-6.1
Psychology	-27.3	-22.5	-16.4	-11.3	-11.9
Liberal Arts and Humanities	-28.2	-17.9	-16.0	-12.4	-13.4
Criminal Justice	-29.5	-17.1	-15.4	-10.0	-9.9
Sociology	-29.9	-21.6	-15.8	-11.5	-11.5
Physical Fitness	-35.4	-26.3	-22.1	-15.7	-18.1
Education	-37.4	-30.9	-27.2	-21.1	-22.5
Fine Arts	-38.1	-27.8	-23.4	-19.5	-18.8
Social Work	-41.0	-34.3	-26.7	-19.2	-20.2
Theology	-45.3	-39.9	-44.6	-39.5	-36.1
Model controls for:					
Educational Attainment	No	Yes	Yes	Yes	Yes
Race, gender, age, veteran, year	No	No	Yes	Yes	Yes
Hours worked, state	No	No	No	Yes	Yes
Observations: 1,808,514 (1,102,644 for bachelor's only model)					

Table 5. Percent Difference in Expected Earnings Relative to Comparable PoliSci Majors, 2009–14 All differences from political science are significant at the.0001 level unless indicated by [N.S.]

2. Using a different subset of the ACS and different model specifications, Altonji, Blom, and Meghir (2012) also find political science pay lagging behind engineering, computer science, and economics (and slightly behind mathematics and chemistry) and leading communications, biology, English, history, sociology, and criminal justice (and barely ahead of business).

References

Altonji, Joseph G., Peter Arcidiacono, and Arnaud Maurel. 2015. "The Analysis of Field Choice in College and Graduate School: Determinants and Wage Effects." National Bureau of Economic Research.

Altonji, Joseph G., Erica Blom, and Costas Meghir. 2012. "Heterogeneity in Human Capital Investments: High School Curriculum, College Major, and Careers." *Annual Review of Economics* 4: 185–223.

American Political Science Association. 2001. *Careers and the Study of Political Science: A Guide for Undergraduates.* Rev. and expanded 6th ed. Washington, DC: American Political Science Association.

Arcidiacono, Peter. 2004. "Ability Sorting and the Returns to College Major." *Journal of Econometrics* 121 (1): 343–75.

Black, Dan A., Seth Sanders, and Lowell Taylor. 2003. "The Economic Reward for Studying Economics." *Economic Inquiry* 41 (3): 365–77.

Bobic, Michael P. 2005. ""Do You Want Fries with That?" A Review of the Bachelor's Program in Political Science." *Politics & Policy* 33 (2): 349–70.

Breuning, Marijke, Paul Parker, and John T. Ishiyama. 2001. "The Last Laugh: Skill Building Through a Liberal Arts Political Science Curriculum." *Political Science & Politics* 34 (3): 657–61.

Carnevale, Anthony P., Stephen J. Rose, and Ban Cheah. 2011. *The College Payoff: Education, Occupations, Lifetime Earnings.* Washington, DC: Georgetown University, McCourt School of Public Policy, Center on Education and the Workforce. https://cew.georgetown.edu/cew-reports/the-college-payoff/.

Carnevale, Anthony P., Jeff Strohl, and Michelle Melton. 2011. *What's it Worth?: The Economic Value of College Majors.* Washington, DC: Georgetown University, Center on Education and the Workforce.

Chen, Jowei and Tim Johnson. 2016. "Incentives for Political versus Technical Training in the US Federal Bureaucracy." American Political Science Association Annual Meeting. Philadelphia, PA.

Clark, Joel. 2004. *Careers in Political Science.* Pearson Longman: New York.

Collins, Todd A., H. Gibbs Knotts, and Jen Schiff. 2012. "Career Preparation and the Political Science Major: Evidence from Departments." *PS: Political Science & Politics* 45 (1): 87–92.

Craft, R. Kim and Joe G. Baker. 2003. "Do Economists Make Better Lawyers? Undergraduate Degree Field and Lawyer Earnings." *The Journal of Economic Education* 34 (3): 263–81.

Ishiyama, John. 2005. "Examining the Impact of the Wahlke Report: Surveying the Structure of the Political Science Curricula at Liberal Arts and Sciences Colleges and Universities in the Midwest." *Political Science and Politics* 38 (1): 71–75.

Ishiyama, John, Marijke Breuning, and Linda Lopez. 2006. "A Century of Continuity and (Little) Change in the Undergraduate Political Science Curriculum." *American Political Science Review* 100 (4): 659–65.

Rendall, Michelle and Andrew Rendall. 2013. "Math Matters: Student Ability, College Majors, and Wage Inequality." Society for Economic Dynamics Annual Meeting, Seoul, South Korea.

Wahlke, John C. 1991. "Liberal Learning and the Political Science Major: A Report to the Profession." *PS: Political Science & Politics* 24 (1): 48–60.

Webber, Douglas A. 2014. "The Lifetime Earnings Premia of Different Majors: Correcting for Selection based on Cognitive, Noncognitive, and Unobserved Factors." *Labour Economics* 28: 14–23.

Webber, Douglas A. 2015. Are College Costs Worth It? How Individual Ability, Major Choice, and Debt Affect Optimal Schooling Decisions. IZA Discussion Paper No. 8767. SSRN. https://papers.ssrn.com/sol3/papers.cfm?abstract_id=2554915.

Winters, John V. 2015. "Is Economics a Good Major for Future Lawyers? Evidence from Earnings Data." IZA Discussion Paper No. 9416. http://ftp.iza.org/dp9416.pdf.

Part Two

The Classroom

Fostering Scholarly Discussion and Critical Thinking in the Political Science Classroom

6

MICHAEL P. MARKS

This article advances the proposition that learning in the political science classroom can be enhanced by emphasizing scholarly discussion and critical thinking while reducing opportunities for students to personalize classroom discussion.[1] The subject matter of this essay is the phenomenon of students taking the occasion of classroom discussion in political science courses to needlessly inject personal partisan preferences into what instead should be opportunities for scholarly debate of analytical and empirical themes. Discussion in political science classes should not be drearily dull affairs centered on dry topics that put students to sleep and dampen their interest in politics. However, neither do they have to rely on appeals to personally held political convictions to spark students' interest. Exciting and lively classroom discussion can be had by emphasizing the dynamic theoretical debates and empirical investigations that are part of the discipline of political science.

The problem with a politicized classroom is that it gives students a false impression of what constitutes the study of politics and the discipline of political science. When scholars study politics they are engaged in an investigation into the dynamics of governance, not a debate over personal political beliefs. To illustrate that politics is about governance and not a debate over personal perspectives, one need only consider that among the themes that are studied by political scientists are abstract philosophical and theoretical principles, historical case studies, models, and comparative analyses. Political scientists know this, but it is not necessarily readily apparent to students, especially undergraduate students who are enthusiastic about knowing more about how they can interact with current events but may not be fully cognizant that what is in the news does not represent the full range of topics studied within the field of political science.

Additionally, political science is about methods of inquiry, not argument or debate. In this it is useful for students to distinguish political science classes from rhetoric and communication studies classes. Although the finer points of disciplinary distinctions may be lost on undergraduates, it is nonetheless useful and part of students' education to understand how academic disciplines are defined in part by their methods of inquiry and not just their empirical subject matter. When students are more concerned with "making a point" or winning a debate, they may erroneously equate the art of rhetoric with the social science skills that are part of the disciplinary practice of political science.[2]

This article will outline steps political science instructors can take to emphasize the benefits that can be realized by fostering scholarly discussion and critical thinking in the political science classroom. The purpose of a college education is to master the skills of scholarly inquiry, not to cling unquestioningly to personal beliefs.[3] It almost goes without saying that part of the goal of a college education is to get students to think beyond their own personal experiences. In 1970 Kenneth Boulding (105) wrote: "…it is the principal task of formal education in schools and colleges to expand the student's image of the world beyond his personal experience and to give him an image which encompasses the total system of the earth or even the universe." This can be difficult if students are permitted to make their own convictions the basis on which they commence their higher education. While college courses in any number of academic disciplines are susceptible to the problems that arise when students confuse their personal beliefs with scholarly analysis, political science classes are particularly prone to this problem given the immediacy of politics to students' lives and the ubiquity of politics in the news media. In the next section evidence related to the benefits of avoiding appeals to students' personal predilections from other academic disciplines is reviewed. This evidence suggests that students in the social sciences learn most effectively when the focus of classroom discussions is on analytical principles and tools, theoretical concepts, and hypothetical case studies. The remainder of the article then applies the lessons from other disciplines and suggests strategies instructors can use to encourage appropriate approaches to the study of politics in the political science classroom.

Evidence from Other Disciplines

There is little in the literature on political science education on the benefits of discouraging personal opinions in the classroom. Instead, indirect evidence comes from related social science disciplines as well as studies of the science of pedagogy in general. A review of this research is instructive for political scientists who surmise that student opinions expressed in terms of partisanship does not contribute meaningfully to the learning process but who find little written in the scholarly literature that supports this supposition.

Classroom Techniques in Sociology

Among other social science disciplines, sociology appears to be the field in which scholars have been most attentive to developing classroom strategies designed to discourage students from drawing on their preconceived preferences when studying societal relations.[4] A review of articles in the leading journal on pedagogy in the field—*Teaching Sociology*—reveals that virtually every issue within the last several years includes at least one article documenting the effectiveness of classroom exercises that emphasize hypothetical situations while downplaying real-world cases that draw on students' preconceived notions of the societal interactions. Some recent examples are discussed below.

A major area of sociology in which tensions in the classroom can run high is the study of social stratification and inequality. To counter this, sociology instructors have devised classroom techniques that emphasize experimental scenarios instead of real-world examples. For example, Renzulli, Aldrich, and Reynolds (2003) describe an exercise in which students engage in a series of coin-toss games designed to illustrate uneven statistical distributions. The purpose of the game is to show how results can be unequal despite best efforts to produce equality of outcomes. Obviously students can have strong beliefs when it comes to questions of equality. The instructors in this case were motivated to highlight the abstract nature of statistical inequality rather than real-world examples of societal inequality (50). The instructors concluded from the in-class exercise that the "coin toss provides a way to illustrate how the sociological imagination can increase a student's understanding of the social world better than individual explanations can" (57).

These kinds of exercises designed to illustrate social stratification are common in the teaching of sociology. For example, William Brislen and Clayton Peoples (2005) devised a classroom exercise involving hypothetical distribution of grades to introduce students to the concept of social stratification. Social stratification is also illustrated using the game Monopoly in a classroom exercise designed by Catherine Coghlan and Denise W. Huggins (2004) while Wynne Wright and Elizabeth Ranson (2005) have developed an exercise wherein students study the nature of restaurant menus as a way to examine economic class. Similarly, in order to teach about gender inequalities, Peggy Petrzelka (2005) developed an exercise in which students look not at their own situations but rather at those involving college faculty, specifically, faculty salaries. In each of these instances students' interest in social stratification is piqued by focusing the exercise on curious situations. But since students' own experiences are excluded there is less temptation for students to opine about lessons learned from their own life situations. By focusing on simulated examples of stratification rather than students' own grievances about social inequality, the instructors were able to convey important lessons about controversial topics without allowing the controversies themselves to take over the classroom discussion.

Classroom exercises that utilize simulated experiences can be used to illustrate other sociological phenomena as well. In one example Fletcher Winston (2003) developed a classroom exercise designed to elicit student perceptions about authority that would not be colored by students' personal beliefs about it. Rather than center the discussion on controversial real-world examples (e.g., why soldiers blindly follow officers into battle), Winston used his own authority as an instructor to require students to write what the students would otherwise see as a pointless in-class essay about everything they ever learned about math. In another instance, in order to give a concrete face to functional and conflict theory, Mellisa Holtzman (2005) uses an exercise in which students study irrigation in an ancient Sumerian village. Students' interest in the subject matter can be evoked, but since the setting is relatively alien to students' own lives, the temptation to ground their analysis in personal preferences is minimized.

A particularly interesting case from the sociology classroom with relevance for political science teaching is a collective action problem lesson described by Brian Obach (2003). When political scientists introduce the collective action concept to students there is the temptation to use real-world examples (e.g., taxation, free trade, or arms control) about which students may have a partisan preference. To avoid this Obach uses an exercise in which students must work as a group to solve a simple picture puzzle that requires most of the students to participate in order for the puzzle to be solved. Students are presented with two sets of rewards that entail bonus points on an upcoming quiz—two points that go to the entire group if the puzzle is solved and/or one point to individual students who refrain from providing their puzzle piece (which may result in the puzzle not being solved). Obviously students have a personal interest in receiving bonus points on an upcoming quiz, and in fact this is the primary motivating factor in how they respond to a collective action problem. Ironically, precisely because students are put into a situation in which they personalize the concept of collective action, they are less likely to frame their learning experience from a possibly ill-informed position reflective of their feelings about a *larger societal issue* such as taxation, free trade, or arms control (see also Pickhardt and Watts 2005 and Marks, Lehr, and Brastow 2006 for collective goods exercises from the field of economics). By removing controversy from the exercise the instructor can get students to think about the concept of collective action rather than their preexisting political beliefs about it.

Perhaps the best evidence from sociology of the benefits of minimizing students' reliance on their personal beliefs is provided by Pat António Goldsmith in the aptly titled article "Learning to Understand Inequality and Diversity: Getting Students Past Ideologies" (2006). Goldsmith devised two teaching strategies—Problem-Based Learning (PBL) and Exploratory Writing—designed to initiate students into the sociological method by leaving aside their impulse to bring their own ideological preferences. "PBL channels students' initiative, curiosity, and skills towards investigating content-related problems" while Exploratory Writing, meanwhile, encourages students to critically examine previously held ideas (Goldsmith 2006, 266). Goldsmith found that after employing the PBL and Exploratory Writing teaching strategies students were more likely to approach sociological problems using the tools of sociology than their ideological predispositions (Goldsmith 2006, 274–276). This study offers evidence that these strategies have tangible benefits for teaching social science concepts as opposed to a reinforcing of students' ill-formed beliefs.

The exercises summarized above only begin to scratch the surface of what sociologists have written about pedagogical tools that enable students to conceptualize sociological principles by devising exercises that deal with these principles in the abstract in ways that appeal to students' interest in the subject matter without necessarily invoking controversial real-world examples about which students may have preexisting preferences that might interfere in the learning process. It is commonplace in sociology teaching today to utilize methods that personalize issues to students but in ways that minimize the temptation to convert an examination of *sociology* into a *societal* debate.

Classroom Techniques in Economics

In economics, too, college and university educators have noted the benefits of encouraging students to think beyond their own personal experiences in formulating theories about social science phenomena. For example, Fryer, Goeree, and Holt describe a classroom exercise on employment discrimination in which students simulate such discrimination using hypothetical scenarios rather than real-world cases drawn from legal case law or the news. Because students' understanding of the issue is based on their experience with the classroom exercise rather than real-world controversies, the experiment "allows them to approach the emotionally charged issues of discrimination with more objectivity" while still being "eager to engage in policy-relevant discussions" (Fryer, Goeree, and Holt 2005, 161, 166).

The tightly controlled nature of classroom exercises in economics also demonstrates that students can be introduced to real-world problems but in a way that reduces their ability to use personal beliefs as a basis for their contributions to classroom discussions. For example, students can have strong views on economic policies that are formulated by governments to manage environmental resources. To avoid the invitation to students to inject their personal beliefs into the discussion James Murphy and Juan-Camilo Cardenas (2004) describe a classroom exercise that simulates different means for governments to approach environmental management. Since the exercise uses a simulated rather than a real-world example, students are constrained in their ability to rely on anything other than the exercise results to formulate their positions on a potentially controversial topic.

In one particularly interesting study from economics, two faculty members discuss the results of a teaching experiment in a money and banking course in which they hypothesized that students would come away with a deeper understanding of economics if they were encouraged to analyze real-world economic data as opposed to abstract models that are traditionally used in economic teaching. What is interesting in this study is that the authors of the study (Santos and Lavin 2004) expected to find that introducing real-world economic data would engage students in the subject more than the traditional models used in economics classes. Rather, the authors found no conclusive support for their hypothesis, suggesting perhaps that the traditional method of using abstract concepts in economics teaching, at least at the introductory level, remains the standard by which other economic pedagogies must be measured. It should also not be surprising that when it comes to matters of money management, students will learn better when it is not their own assets at risk (see, for example, Ewing, Kruse, and Thompson 2004, for a classroom exercise wherein students manage a hypothetical portfolio obviously not of their own).

Classroom Techniques in Psychology

Evidence from studies of pedagogy in the field of psychology also indicates that the inclusion of material tangential to the lesson at hand can impair student comprehension of concepts being taught. Shannon Harp and Amy Maslich (2005) report on the results of an experiment in which students were tested on their ability to learn about a scientific principle either with or without so-called "seductive details" injected into the lecture. Harp and Maslich found that while interesting and entertaining examples that illustrate a lecture's points have no ill effect on student learning, material that is tangential to the lecture can interfere with students' ability to learn the concepts covered. What constitutes tangential is of course relative to disciplines, topics, and classroom lessons, but the thrust of Harp and Maslich's research is that information that is interesting but nonetheless not purely illustrative of concepts at hand can stymie student learning. Whether or not discussion of partisan preferences in political sciences classes qualifies as "seductive details" is open to debate, but Harp and Maslich provide at least a cautionary note that it can have deleterious effects in the political science classroom.

This does not mean that teachers of psychology, or political science for that matter, should avoid introducing controversial themes into classroom lessons, but rather the evidence suggests that students learn better when such lessons avoid invitations to students to draw on their personal prejudices. Students are better aided in their learning when controversial topics are approached with pedagogical tools that emphasize hypothetical situations. For example, very little is more controversial in contemporary times than prejudice and discrimination. One would think that this is precisely the type of topic that would invite students to indulge their personal biases and distract from a scholarly classroom environment. However, Christopher et al. (2004) report that when students are introduced to these concepts through popular films, the temptation to respond in an uneducated fashion can be reduced. Likewise, the use of classroom simulations such as mock trials in psychology classes can situate controversial topics within a framework that allows controversies to be addressed via a pedagogical device rather than a free-form classroom discussion (see Werth et al. 2002).

Teaching with Hypotheticals

A common thread running through evidence from other social science disciplines is the importance of hypothetical scenarios for enhancing student learning. The effectiveness of hypotheticals has been chronicled in writings on pedagogy and learning styles. Much of the literature on the use of hypotheticals in classroom literature has come out of Australia based on research on improving learning at the secondary level. A good example of this literature is Barry Kentish's study (1995) of the use of hypotheticals in student learning about environmental issues. Kentish describes how hypothetical scenarios can engage students by encouraging them to see multiple sides of an issue. Kentish's research is based on scholarship on simulations, games, and hypothetical situations. For instance, Kentish cites Boehrer and Linsky (1990) who note that critical thinking skills are fostered in students through hypothetical case studies. Kentish (1995, 22) points out that in real-life cases students already know the resolution of the case, whereas in hypothetical case studies students can examine the full range of possible outcomes.

Much of the work of scholars in Australia on the utility of hypothetical scenarios is inspired by the popular Australian television series "Hypotheticals" hosted by Geoffrey Robertson (see, for example, Robertson 1986, 1987, 1991; Cook 1998). Robertson's program assembled experts from a variety of fields to whom the host posed a series of questions around a hypothetical situation involving a range of moral and ethical issues. Australian educators, inspired by Robertson's televised Socratic lessons, have adapted his approach to classroom teaching with positive effects. As Kentish (1995, 22) points out, "simulation and games...provide opportunities for personal reflection on experiences that can be tested within the 'safety' of the simulation."[5] Alan Cook, 34) echoes these sentiments, and further finds that hypothetical situations help students focus on the "big picture" of an issue rather than the facts of a single discrete case.

Summary

In sum, evidence from other social science disciplines, as well as research conducted in Australia on the utility of hypotheticals, indicates that getting across lessons about the real world does not necessarily have to entail drawing upon students' preferences about that real world and, in fact, may yield learning that is superior to that which appeals to students' personal preferences. We can extrapolate from the literature that simulated and hypothetical simulations have advantages over lessons that rely on events that have a direct immediacy in students' lives. Research shows that pedagogical techniques that foster student objectivity have beneficial effects on learning and the classroom experience. Therefore, while research on the effects of personal preferences in a political science setting is not directly available, the literature on related areas gives support for techniques that emphasize objective classroom methods and discourages methods that invite students to inject their partisan biases into the learning environment.

Strategies for the Political Science Classroom

Based on the evidence from other disciplines, political scientists can begin to assemble a toolkit for teaching about politics using methods that emphasize principles, concepts, and empirical applications without relying on students' preconceived notions or personal preferences about controversial topics of the day. The strategies outlined below offer ways to take partisanship and personal opinions out of the political science classroom while keeping the rigor of a political science education intact.

Use Historical Case Studies and Simulation Exercises

One of the main ways that students can inadvertently be invited to inject their personal political convictions into the classroom is through discussion that focuses on current events. While current events certainly spark students' interests, they also create a tempting opportunity for students to argue over their personal take on what is in the news. Rather than relying on current events, political science classes can use historical case studies to illustrate themes that come up in class. The obvious advantage of historical case studies over current events is that students are far less likely to have taken sides on history than they have on issues of immediate concern to them; yet historical case studies can still emphasize enduring concepts that are of interest in the study of politics.

A well-documented and much-studied historical case study that can stimulate student interest in politics is the Melian Debate in Thucydides' *History of the Peloponnesian War*. As Suresht Bald (1996) conveys, the Melian Debate provides opportunities for students to discuss issues they care about such as relationships of unequal power, moral precepts in war, and the interplay of domestic political debate with the imperatives of global security in the context of a historical event that took place centuries ago. Without the distractions of current events preoccupying their minds, students can focus on the abstract principles at play in cases such as the Melian Debate. This minimizes the temptation to "take sides" as students are more likely to do with current instances of foreign policy in which students have a far greater personal stake.

Simulation and role-playing exercises also can help minimize opportunities to rely on personally held political opinions in classroom discussions because students are busy adopting the personae of the characters they have been assigned in these exercises. The subfield of international relations is especially rich in the use of classroom simulation and role-playing exercises (see, for example, Marks 1998; Asal 2005; Chasek 2005; Asal and Blake 2006; Boyer, Trumbore, and Fricke 2006; Shellman and Turan 2006; Young 2006). One of the virtues of role-playing exercises and simulations in international relations courses is that students are encouraged to see the world from the perspective of individuals from a variety of political experiences. In role-playing exercises in my own American Foreign Policy course I frequently assign students to play the parts of political officials whose positions are different (so far as I can tell) from those held by the students who take on those roles. This helps students see beyond their own beliefs in approaching world affairs.

Using historical case studies to avoid the temptation to dramatize passions about current political circumstances also is useful in modeling for students the methods that political scientists use in their own research and scholarship. To avoid the perils of tautology, political scientists frequently conduct research on historical case studies to "get out of" the present. It is instructive for students to understand how historical case studies can be used for theory generation without relying on the facts of that which is being explained. As an added benefit, a historical detachment from contemporary politics encourages both scholars and students alike to apply more objective analysis than if one's focus were on current events. This objective analysis need not result in dry classroom discussions and in fact can appeal to students' desire to apply theoretical principles to real-world instances of politics (see, for example, Erskine 2006).

Use Hypothetical and Fictional Examples

As discussed above, certain other disciplines in the social sciences appear to do a better job at minimizing opportunities for students to inject their personal views into classroom discussions by relying on hypothetical situations rather than real-world examples. The field of economics seems to be especially adept at this. The ubiquitous "widgets" example is a good illustration of how a hypothetical commodity can be used to illustrate economic principles rather than a good or service in which students might have a personal stake.[6] There are many good opportunities in political science for analogs to the economics widget. For example, in American politics and government courses, in discussions of interest group politics, rather than invoking controversial interest groups such as the National Rifle Association or the National Organization for Women—groups about which students are likely to have very strong opinions—interest group politics could be illustrated with hypothetical organizations such as the National Association of Widget Manufacturers or the American Association for Economic Prosperity. The same principles of interest group politics can be studied as in examinations of real-life interest groups, but since the examples are hypothetical in nature students are not personally invested in the outcome.

Hypotheticals can also include fictionalized accounts of politics. For example, Kimberly Cowell-Meyers (2006, 347) discusses how Sophocles' *Antigone* can be used in political science classes to illuminate themes of "leadership and legitimacy, what good law looks like, how citizens should behave, and how they ought to live together." Popular television shows, movies, and music also offer myriad possibilities for fictional illustrations of political concepts. Paul Cantor (1999) astutely writes about how the popular animated television program *The Simpsons* illustrates a host of issues and concepts found in politics and political science.[7] Science fiction also provides a way to use imagined worlds to explore politics and governance without relying on contemporary real-world examples. Books such as *To Seek Out New Worlds* (Weldes 2003) and *Political Science Fiction* (Hassler and Wilcox 1997) can be used to draw out extended fictional "case studies" from the realm of science fiction, and it is even possible to construct entire classes about political science using science fiction to illustrate political concepts.[8] Hypothetical exercises need not necessarily avoid students' interest in current events. For example, Khristina Haddad (2005) outlines a writing exercise in political theory courses in which students are invited to channel their political fears and desires into imagining political utopias.

Metaphorical constructions also allow for examination of political concepts without reliance on current events or contemporary political circumstances to illustrate these concepts. As with historical case studies, metaphors are useful to scholars because they guard against tautology in generating theories to empirically test hypothetical propositions (because the source of observations and assumption from which hypothetical propositions are deduced are independent of the empirical case under examination). More importantly for classroom discussion, metaphorical representations of politics focus the mind away from controversial topics of contemporary politics and onto more abstract ways of conceptualizing politics and political activity. In international relations classes, for example, first-year college students are often taught to think of states as "billiard balls." Likewise, the concept of state sovereignty typically is introduced to students by having them think of states metaphorically as hard-shelled "containers" or "black boxes." Leaving aside the validity of the international relations paradigms that are supported by such metaphors, the larger point is that the more abstract the principle, the less likely students will find something in it that corresponds to their personal response to political issues of immediate concern. Metaphorical depictions of political phenomenon also invite students to be creative in their ability to imagine manifestations of politics that leave aside the actual practice of politics in the world around them. Students are less inclined to be advocates for a metaphorical representation of politics than an issue on which they have a personal stake.

Emphasize Theory, Methods, and Critical Thinking Skills

Another strategy to reduce students' preoccupation with their personal political views is to get them to focus on the disciplinary tools of the social sciences in general and political science in specific. Political science is, after all, a broad discipline that encompasses a wide range of theories and practices ranging throughout the discipline from political philosophy to comparative government to public policy analysis. Furthermore, the field of political science is as much about specific tools of investigation as it is the subject matter of politics, and students can only be enlightened by being made aware of this fact.

To assist in stressing the disciplinary tools of the social sciences and political science, many colleges and universities apply general education designations to those political science courses that emphasize social science methods and inquiry. At Willamette University, which is an interesting example, general education requirements categorize courses according to the "mode of inquiry" they employ as opposed to the usual cataloging of courses into traditional academic divisions. At Willamette, methodological considerations take precedence over empirical content of courses tagged with a mode of inquiry designation. Thus, for example, courses that are designated with the "Understanding Societies" mode of inquiry (the designation assigned to classes that employ the social science method), among other things, are designed to "develop models or theories to explain social phenomena and evaluate those through observation and the collection of data" (*College of Liberal Arts Catalog* 2005–2007, 32). The mandate of courses with the Understanding Societies mode of inquiry, then, is to place social science methods at the center of those courses while deemphasizing their empirical subject matter. This has the beneficial effect of keeping classroom discussion focused on relatively noncontroversial aspects of political science methods instead of contemporary politics that can invite students to indulge their personal biases.

The types of assignments students are given can also be used as an opportunity to encourage a more detached perspective on the subject matter of politics. For example, Jim Josefson (2005) suggests that students can gain by writing reflective essays as opposed to argumentative writing that stresses the taking of a position. Among its virtues, in reflective writing, students "are challenged to reflect explicitly on how [course] material calls into question their preconceptions about the topic" (Josefson 2005, 763). Including writing assignments that involve literature reviews (see, for example, Knopf 2006; McMenamin 2006) can also focus students' attention on matters wider than pressing current events.

Emphasizing critical thinking skills can also discourage students from relying on their personal political beliefs as a basis for approaching topics in political science classes. It is widely accepted among scholars of education that critical thinking skills require individuals to leave their own personal perspectives and biases behind.[9] Critical thinking skills are essential for embracing accepted standards of scholarly inquiry that are frustrated when personal beliefs come into play. James Wilkinson and Heather Dubrow (1991, 258) astutely observe that "[s] ome students confuse proof with intensity of belief. They preface statements with 'I feel very strongly that…' and trust that their sincerity will carry the day. Like students who think that grades should be based on effort alone, the partisans of personal conviction must learn to test their ideas against a more stringent standard." Critical thinking skills discourage students from putting blinders on and work in favor of methods of inquiry that keep all options open; a skill that is important given the relative unfamiliarity students initially have with the terminology of traditional academic disciplines (see, for example, McPeck 1990, 40).

The teaching of critical thinking skills also is important for encouraging students to think more as social scientists than as partisans with a "dog in the fight." When students do master critical thinking, then they are better equipped to solve real-world political problems when they choose to do so (see Olsen and Statham 2005). In this way appeals can still be made to students' interest in politics and public policy, but students can be made to see the advantages of holding their own political preferences in abeyance if the goal is to arrive at the best possible solution to problems of governance they are facing.

Use Political Philosophy and Political Theory Classes as a Model

Some solutions to the problem of a politicized classroom are specific to certain subfields in the discipline. Political theory classes are to some extent (although not entirely) immune to students' temptation to inject partisan opinions since the subject matter of these courses typically emphasizes analytical concepts over empirical examples. A similar approach can be useful in the remaining subfields of political science that tend to be more empirical in their focus. Despite the factual subject matter of these subfields, students can be encouraged to focus on the abstract concepts of governance that are at stake.

All of the major subfields in political science lend themselves to this type of approach. In American politics classes emphasis can be placed, for example, on the concepts of separation of powers, federalism, pluralism, and interest representation, among other things. Comparative politics classes can focus on variations in government structures, policy formulation, and practices such as corporatism. In international relations courses stress can be placed on the competing paradigms utilized in international relations theory. By keeping the discussion focused on abstract concepts rather than current events students can train their minds on the principles of governance rather than on things in which they have a personal stake. Part of the strategy in this area is to choose course texts that emphasize concepts over empirical formulations that lend themselves to "debate."

The virtue of political philosophy courses as a model is that while students certainly have opinions about the themes studied in these courses—themes such as justice, democracy, leadership, the good life, power, constitutionalism, law, sovereignty, legitimacy, and citizenship—they tend to be approached as abstractions rather than in terms of their empirical manifestations. While courses in subfields such as American politics, comparative politics, and international relations clearly cannot eschew investigation of empirical subject matter, if the concrete manifestations of politics are preceded by a discussion of the abstract concepts to which they pertain, students are more prone to weigh various sides of a debate instead of relying on their personal preferences that are likely to be influenced by their own experiences and that which they read in the news. To a certain extent all political science classes are political philosophy courses in that they proceed from the abstract to the concrete. Stressing the philosophical roots of empirical problems can be useful in discouraging overpoliticized perspectives on the factual subject matter at hand.

Additional Suggestions

In comparative politics and international relations classes the opportunities for students to indulge their personal political proclivities can be reduced by minimizing references to the United States and American politics or foreign policy to illustrate course themes. It can be rather tempting to rely on examples drawn from the US experience since students likely are more familiar with American politics and foreign policy than with the politics and foreign policy of other countries. However, discussions that focus on the United States, its politics, and foreign policies can provide opportunities for students to make their personal opinions about politics the center of classroom activity. The opportunity for politicized discussion to break out among students is lessened when the United States is not the center of attention.

Another thing instructors can do to discourage students from politicizing classroom discussions is to avoid the so-called "we" problem that consists of the dangers to classroom objectivity when students adopt the first-person plural (we, us, our, ours) in discussions of the United States and American politics (Marks 2002). It can be tempting, almost second-nature, for students to talk about how "we" are approaching a certain issue or how something in politics affects "us." Thus, for example, the "we" problem exists in discussions of US politics when students identify with certain segments of the electorate, interest groups, regional political entities, or other particularistic groups, while in foreign policy discussions the "we" problem exists when students speak of the United States in terms of such things as "our foreign policy." The problem with these formulations is that they literally invite students to see politics from their own personal perspectives rather than the object of scholarly inquiry. Encouraging students to adopt a more neutral third-person perspective is a useful way to minimize this temptation.

Perhaps the most obvious strategy for reducing opportunities for students to fall back on partisan convictions is to minimize current events in classroom discussions. Discussion of current events and topical themes easily invites students to draw on their own political preferences, especially when classroom discussion is presented as a type of "debate." It is not surprising that students typically enjoy current events discussions in political science classes and frequently request them. In my own introductory classes I have found that many students who have never taken a political science class are under the mistaken impression that the study of political science places current events at its core. As I discuss above, discussion of historical cases instead of current events causes less polarization among students because there is less immediately at stake. When students are familiarized with the historical breadth of politics their own personal preferences about issues of pressing yet fleeting immediate concern can be put into the proper perspective.

Evaluation

Evaluations of the classroom strategies described in this article can be found in the studies that have been conducted in related social science disciplines such as sociology and economics summarized above as well as systematic and anecdotal evidence from the political science classroom. Evidence from my own teaching comes from a paired comparison of two classes I have taught in recent years that deal with the common subject matter of international conflict. The first class, a course entitled "International Security and Cooperation," is a straightforward undergraduate political science class that focuses on theories of international security and analyses of international cooperation and organization. The second course, "War and Its Alternatives," was a freshman seminar required of all first-year students that was part of a college-wide freshman experience known as "World Views."[10] These two classes were distinct in their organization and in their classroom settings yet covered many of the same topics of international conflict and cooperation. The results, as illustrated in student assessments of the courses, indicate that a classroom environment that encourages the airing of student opinions yields less learning and more frustration than a classroom setting that emphasizes analytical inquiry and directed discussion.

The syllabus for the political science class "International Security and Cooperation" lays out a standard set of expectations for how students should approach the subject matter in the course: "This course is designed to introduce students to important theoretical approaches to the study of international security and cooperation. It also applies these approaches to empirical cases and concrete issues of international harmony and discord.... Among the theories of security and cooperation examined in this class are classical conceptions of human conflict, deterrence, 'game theory,' international regimes, feminist perspectives, and the 'constructivist' approach." ("International Security and Cooperation" syllabus 2002). Classroom discussions in this course involve focused examination of course readings and opportunities for students to evaluate the relative persuasiveness of competing theories of conflict and cooperation. Class sessions also provide opportunities for students to apply theories of security and cooperation to empirical case studies. Teaching strategies employed in the course include discussing historical case studies, analyzing competing theoretical perspectives, and utilizing simulations and role-playing exercises including a game theory unit involving a Prisoner's Dilemma exercise and an extended war game simulation.

By contrast, the mandate of the "War and Its Alternatives" course was to provoke students to debate war and peace as controversial topics. As mentioned, the course was a freshmen seminar required of all incoming students and was taught in multiple sections. As the course syllabus demonstrates, one of the overt and stated purposes of the course was to highlight the fact that because faculty were drawn from throughout the college, no member of the class (including the instructor) was any more an expert on the topic than anyone else: "Faculty who participate in the World Views program teach in a very different manner than if they were teaching in their discipline or area of expertise.... *In the World Views classroom, the teacher is more a facilitator than an authority*" ("World Views: War and Its Alternatives" course syllabus 2005, emphasis added). In keeping with the interdisciplinary nature of the course, among the stated objectives of "War and Its Alternatives" was to engage students in topical discussions, albeit ostensibly grounded in seminal texts on the subject. Students could be excused for not approaching the course with the same scholarly rigor as traditional classes that emphasized disciplinary methods. As the course syllabus stated, "The texts we will read and discuss this semester raise *provocative* questions about how nations decide to engage in warfare, what weapons to use, the effect war has on nations and individuals, and whether alternative to war exist. The texts also challenge us to review how we remember and reconstruct wars in *our personal and national history*" ("World Views" course syllabus 2005, emphasis added). In the "World Views: War and Its Alternatives" classroom instructors and students alike were encouraged by the faculty committee overseeing the course to treat war as a controversial topic and as a problem that had to be solved. Students and faculty members were prodded by the syllabus (which was not alterable by faculty teaching in the various sections of the course) to debate and to argue over the subject of war, not treat it as an outcome the causes of which are discernible through disciplinary methods. Faculty had discretion over the nature of the writing assignments they assigned to students, with many faculty opting for assignments that required students to take sides or to write a position paper. In addition, for two of the three years of "War and Its Alternatives" students had to complete a summer assignment in which they interviewed a personal acquaintance about his or her experience in war and then to write a personal reflection.

To sum up, the "International Security and Cooperation" course I teach in my political science department emphasizes the types of scholarly modes of inquiry I argue foster effective learning while the "War and Its Alternatives" course, by contrast, addressed many of the same topics of conflict and accord with the explicit aim of engaging students in a more open dialogue and debate that invited opinion alongside, if not instead of, academic inquiry. What, then, do student evaluations have to say about these courses? Although many of the student evaluations filled out for both courses did not include student feedback beyond the responses they gave to closed-ended statements that asked them to check off answers in the form of "agree" or "disagree" in varying degrees, those students who took the time to answer open-ended questions about the course responded with comments that are instructive. In the straightforward political science course "International Security and Cooperation" typical student comments included observations such as "It has been interesting to see the ways that these theories [of international security and cooperation] apply to other courses and current events;" "I really learned more about theories of international security. I think because I didn't know much before class I really learned a lot about how to analyze international interactions;" and "There were many intelligent discussions and relevant analyses of the material."

In the freshman seminar "War and Its Alternatives," by contrast, student comments highlighted the lack of academic rigor the course fostered through its encouragement of more open debate by faculty and students alike. Typical student comments included: "The World Views [committee] needs to de-emphasize their own viewpoints on war and allow students to draw their own conclusions;" "Unless [the course] presents a more balanced view, it is a huge waste of time;" "World Views should focus more on war and its alternatives. It was loosely organized and could have been more focused through the choice of text[s]. Perhaps reading more classics and more political books;" and "More emphasis needs to be placed on developing writing, speaking, and analytical skills." The most positive student comments were reserved for sections of the course that did emphasize analytical skills as opposed to what one student described as "opinion discussion."

What produced this negative reaction to this course? Student comments suggest that it was the design of the course that encouraged the sort of "opinion discussion" that students found to be counterproductive in promoting an understanding of the subject matter in question. As the excerpts from the course syllabus above show, students and faculty alike were encouraged to take the opportunity of the course to debate the question of war, not submit it to a rigorous scholarly analysis grounded in a clearly defined disciplinary perspective. This does not necessarily mean that it was the interdisciplinary aspect of the course that was problematic, but rather that the controversial nature of the topic of war took precedence over the disciplinary tools that might have been employed to subject war to a scholarly analysis. As students themselves reported, their learning was enhanced when "opinion discussion" was minimized and focused analysis was brought to bear.

Although the comparison of these two courses represents only a small sample, it is representative of similar findings from other social science disciplines in which studies have demonstrated the benefits of classroom strategies that encourage critical thinking and analytical skills over the airing of personal opinions. More research is necessary to confirm these results, but if the findings of other social science disciplines are a guide, many political science instructors likely will find that student evaluations of their own courses, in which a comparison of the type described above is possible, bear out these results.

Counterpoint

Of course there are those who would disagree with the premise and suggestions of this article on several counts. For example, there are some educators who would argue that permitting partisanship into political science courses is useful for promoting civic education. Groups such as the Center for Civic Education (http://www.civiced.org/), Justice Learning (http://www.justicelearning.org/home.asp), and the National Alliance for Civic Education advocate in favor of engaging students in learning about active participation in politics and governance. One strategy for doing this is to encourage students to think about issues that affect them personally in the context of course themes (see, for example, Shea and Harris 2006). Additionally, service-learning components can also put students directly in contact with individuals who are actively involved in the political process and thereby cultivate students' interest in politics (see, for example, Gorham 2005; Bennion 2006; Freyss 2006).[11] While there is merit to this argument, other strategies that offer fewer opportunities for students to make their own experiences the sole basis for civic education are possible. As discussed above, hypothetical situations can be just as stimulating for classroom discussion as real-life cases (see, for example, Brookfield 1990, 99). In fact, giving students hypothetical issues to discuss may broaden their ability to think about the range of issues that face civil society.

There are also those who point out that allowing students to draw on their personal political convictions is useful in sparking student interest in politics. There is no shortage of journal articles offering advice on how to bring more awareness of politics and current events into the classroom (see, for example, Ball 2005; Caruson 2005). These articles rest on the conviction that part of the purpose of political science courses is to bring politics into the classroom. In terms of the art of pedagogy, there are those who would argue that active learning is to be preferred over lecture-based classes and that appeals to students' political beliefs are useful in stimulating debate. There is no doubt that instructors in virtually every academic discipline look for ways to stimulate student interest in the subject matter at hand especially in an age of electronic communications and the potential for shortened attention spans that this can breed.

Still, there are ways of keeping students interested in politics without having to appeal to their personal opinions. More to the point, classroom discussions that draw on students' political preferences can alienate those members of the class who feel threatened by majority views. One would hope that the study of politics is interesting enough without having to appeal to students' personal beliefs. Moreover, as important political science classes can be for sparking student interest in politics, allowing students to indulge their personal convictions in class actually can be counterproductive because when students see the world from their own point of view they are less capable of understanding the bigger picture of society. As Kenneth Hoover (1992, 6) observes, "highly subjective accounts of life form a poor basis for the development of common understanding and common action." So, if the purpose of bringing personal experiences into the classroom is to cultivate more educated and informed students prepared to enter civic life, that goal may actually be frustrated by allowing students to indulge their previously held beliefs in classroom discussions.

Finally, one could argue that there is a virtue to draw on students' personal connection to politics to cultivate cultural sensitivity or empathy for political systems, cultures, or countries that are relatively alien to them (see, for example, Brooks 2005; Stover 2005). Obviously appeals to individuals' personal circumstances work in many contexts where the aim is to connect people to the larger world (see, for example, West 1998). The question then becomes if this is a legitimate goal in undergraduate political science courses. If that is the aim, then certainly discussion of personal beliefs can be invited in these classes. However, since most political science classes do not have this as an explicit aim, the need to make the connection between personal political convictions and the academic study of political science does not present itself as the norm.

Concluding Thoughts

The purpose of this article has not been to advocate a cleansing of the political science classroom so as to eliminate all opportunities for students to explore their personal political passions.[12] A political science classroom that fails to appeal to students' interest in politics is as ineffective as a biology classroom that fails to take into account students' fascination with the nature of life. However, just as students' personal beliefs about the *quality* of human life do not provide a sound basis for the scholarly investigation into the *nature* of life, students' personal political *preferences* are not an effective starting point for academic *explanations* for political outcomes. The political science classroom can be the site for lively debates over how best to theorize the nature of politics and governance. If students spend their time in political science courses preoccupied with what they personally believe, they will lose the opportunity to understand how political science helps explain the bases for those beliefs. Evidence from other social science disciplines supports this claim. Once students have a firm grasp of what forces shape the political world, they are then better equipped to pursue their political passions in the practical realm of politics.

Reprinted with permission from Michael P. Marks. 2008. "Fostering Scholarly Discussion and Critical Thinking in the Political Science Classroom." Journal of Political Science Education *4 (2). Taylor & Francis: 205-224. doi:10.1080/15512160801998080.*

Notes

1. I do not address in this article advocacy by instructors, although it is a related topic. Rightly or wrongly, a growing number of students perceive that faculty inject their personal political biases into the classroom. Organizations such as Campus Report Online (http://www. campusreportonline.net/), the Foundation for Individual Rights in Education (http://www.thefire. org/), NoIndoctrination.org (http://www.noindoctrination.org/), and Students for Academic Freedom (http://www.studentsforacademicfreedom.org/) regularly chronicle what they see as abuses of professors' position and inappropriate insertion of their personal political convictions into lectures, course readings, and classroom discussion. Among the most widely cited essays alleging liberal bias among college professors is Rothman, Lichter, and Nevitte (2005). Whether one agrees with these findings or not, there is a good case to be made that teachers should avoid injecting their personal opinions into the classroom. See Gardner (1998).

2. For an opposing point of view, see Omelicheva (2006).

3. On the intellectual purposes of college education see Bateman (1990), Brookfield (1990), Dressel and Marcus (1982), and Ignelzi (2000).

4. Hedley and Markowitz (2001) observe that in sociology classes students can be particularly prone to defending their personal beliefs in the face of sociological phenomena. On strategies for dealing with the emotions that are generated in the sociology classroom when controversial topics are raised, see also Roberts and Iyall Smith (2002).

5. On this point Kentish references Crookall and Sanders (1989), Sanders, Coote, and Crookall (1988), and Sanders and Gunn (1990).

6. A widget is defined generally as "a gadget" or "an unnamed or hypothetical manufactured article" (*The American Heritage Dictionary of the English Language*).

7. *The Simpsons* has also been found useful in the teaching of social psychology. See Eaton and Uskul (2004).

8. See, for example, the courses "Politics in Modern Science Fiction" taught by Sumana Harihareswara at the University of California at Berkeley (syllabus online at http://www.ocf.berkeley. edu/~sumanah/decalsyllabus.html) and "Science Fiction and Politics," taught by Courtney Brown at Emory University (syllabus online at http://www.courtneybrown.com/classes/scifi/ PrintableSciFiPoliticsSyl.html). In addition to science fiction, the world of fantasy can also be brought to near on international relations courses. See Nexon and Neumann's *Harry Potter and International Relations* (2006).

9. On critical thinking skills, see for example Piaget (1974), Fischer (1980), Meyers (1986), Sternberg (1990), and King and Kitchener (1994).

10. "War and Its Alternatives" was the then-current thematic focus of a freshman experience more broadly known as "World Views" that ran with a succession of themes over a series of four-year cycles. "War and Its Alternatives" was the last theme of the course before it was discontinued in favor of a freshman seminar in which each section's topic is chosen by the instructor.

11. Although as Susan Hunter and Richard Brisbin (2000, 626) point out: "Service learning, even with explicit classroom discussion,…is not a miracle cure for students' political apathy, civic disengagement, or lack of support for the values supporting pluralist participatory democracy."

12. In fact, passion about politics can be *increased* by encouraging a detached approach to course subject matter. Paul Gardner (1998, 802) astutely observes that "[d]etachment is a way to channel a passion to know into a means of knowing."

References

The American Heritage Dictionary of the English Language. 3rd ed. 1992. Boston: Houghton Mifflin.

Asal, Victor. 2005. "Playing Games with International Relations." *International Studies Perspectives* 6 (3): 359–373.

Asal, Victor and Elizabeth L. Blake. 2006. "Creating Simulations for Political Science Education." *Journal of Political Science Education* 2 (1): 1–18.

Bald, Suresht. 1996. "The Melian Dialogue." *Pew Trust Cases in International Affairs.* Washington, DC: Georgetown University.

Ball, William J. 2005. "From Community Engagement to Political Engagement." *PS: Political Science & Politics* 38 (2): 287 – 291.

Bateman, Walter L. 1990. *Open to Question: The Art of Teaching and Learning by Inquiry.* San Francisco: Jossey-Bass.

Bennion, Elizabeth A. 2006. "Civic Education and Citizen Engagement: Mobilizing Voters as a Required Field Experiment." *Journal of Political Science Education* 2 (2): 205–227.

Boehrer, John and Marty Linksy. 1990. "Teaching with Cases: Learning to Question." *New Directions for Teaching and Learning* 42: 41–57.

Boulding, Kenneth E. 1970. "The Task of the Teacher in the Social Sciences." In *Effective College Teaching: The Quest for Relevance.* Edited by William H. Morris. Washington, DC: American Association for Higher Education, 104–123.

Boyer, Mark A., Peter Trumbore, and David O. Fricke. 2006. "Teaching Theories of International Political Economy from the Pit: A Simple In-Class Simulation." *International Studies Perspectives* 7 (1): 67–76.

Brislen, William and Clayton D. Peoples. 2005. "Using a Hypothetical Distribution of Grades to Introduce Social Stratification." *Teaching Sociology* 33 (1): 74–80.

Brookfield, Stephen D. 1990. *The Skillful Teacher: On Technique, Trust, and Responsiveness in the Classroom.* San Francisco : Jossey-Bass.

Brooks, D. Christopher. 2005. "Learning Tolerance: The Impact of Comparative Politics Courses on Levels of Cultural Sensitivity." *Journal of Political Science Education* 1 (2): 221–232.

Cantor, Paul A. 1999. "The Simpsons: Atomistic Politics and the Nuclear Family." *Political Theory* 27 (6): 734–749.

Caruson, Kiki. 2005. "So, You Want to Run for Elected Office? How to Engage Students in the Campaign Process without Leaving the Classroom." *PS: Political Science & Politics* 38 (2): 305–310.

Chasek, Pamela S. 2005. "Power Politics, Diplomacy and Role Playing: Simulating the UN Security Council's Response to Terrorism." *International Studies Perspectives* 6 (1): 1–19.

Christopher et al.. 2004. "Using a 'New Classic' Film to Teach About Stereotyping and Prejudice." *Teaching of Psychology* 31 (3): 199–202.

Coghlan, Catherine L. and Denise W. Huggins. 2004. "'That's Not Fair!': A Simulation Exercise in Social Stratification and Structural Inequality." *Teaching Sociology* 32 (2): 177–187.

College of Liberal Arts Catalog. 2005–07. Salem, OR : Willamette University. Cook, Alan. 1998. "Using Hypotheticals for a Science, Technology and Society Curriculum Emphasis." *Australian Science Teachers Journal* 44 (3): 30–35.

Cowell-Meyers, Kimberly. 2006. "Teaching Politics Using Antigone." *PS: Political Science & Politics* 39 (2): 347–49.

Crookall, David and Danny Sanders, eds. 1989. *Communication and Simulation: From Two Fields to One Theme.* Clevedon, UK: Multilingual Matters.

Dressel, Paul L. and Dora Marcus. 1982. *On Teaching and Learning in College.* San Francisco: Jossey-Bass.

Eaton, Judy and Ayse K. Uskul. 2004. "Using the Simpsons to Teach Social Psychology." *Teaching of Psychology* 31 (4): 277–78.

Erskine, Toni. 2006. "Teaching the Ethics of War: Applying Theory to 'Hard Cases.'" *International Studies Perspectives* 7 (2): 187–203.

Ewing, Bradley T., Jamie B. Kruse, and Mark A. Thompson. 2004. "Money Demand and Risk: A Classroom Experiment." *Journal of Economic Education* 35 (3): 243–250.

Fischer, Kurt W. 1980. "A Theory of Cognitive Development: The Control and Construction of Hierarchies of Skills." *Psychological Review* 87 (6): 477–531.

Freyss, Siegrun Fox. 2006. "Learning Political Engagement from the Experts: Advocacy Groups, Neighborhood Councils, and Constituency Service." *PS: Political Science & Politics* 39 (1): 137–145.

Fryer, Roland G. Jr., Jacob K. Goeree, and Charles A. Holt. 2005. "Experience-Based Discrimination: Classroom Games." *Journal of Economic Education* 36 (2): 160–170.

Gardner, Paul. 1998. "Teaching at Its Best: A Passionate Detachment in the Classroom." *PS: Political Science & Politics* 31 (4): 802–804.

Goldsmith, Pat António. 2006. "Learning to Understand Inequality and Diversity: Getting Students Past Ideologies." *Teaching Sociology* 34 (3): 263–277.

Gorham, Eric. 2005. "Service-Learning and Political Knowledge." *Journal of Political Science Education* 1 (3): 345–365.

Haddad, Khristina. 2005. "What Do You Desire? What Do You Fear? Theorize It! Teaching Political Theory through Utopian Writing." *PS: Political Science & Politics* 38 (3): 399–405.

Harp, Shannon F. and Amy A. Maslich. 2005. "The Consequences of Including Seductive Details During Lecture." *Teaching of Psychology* 32 (2): 100–103.

Hassler, Donald M. and Clyde Wilcox, eds. 1997. *Political Science Fiction*. Columbia: University of South Caroline Press.

Hedley, Mark and Markowitz, Linda. 2001. "Avoiding Moral Dichotomies: Teaching Controversial Topics to Resistant Students." *Teaching Sociology* 29 (2): 195–208.

Holtzman, Mellisa. 2005. "Teaching Sociological Theory Through Active Learning: The Irrigation Exercise." *Teaching Sociology* 33 (2): 206–212.

Hoover, Kenneth R. 1992. *The Elements of Social Scientific Thinking*. 5th ed. New York: St. Martin's Press.

Hunter, Susan and Richard A. Brisbin, Jr. 2000. "The Impact of Service Learning on Democratic and Civic Values." *PS: Political Science & Politics* 33 (3): 623–626.

Ignelzi, Michael. 2000. "Meaning-Making in the Learning and Teaching Process." In *Teaching to Promote Intellectual and Personal Maturity: Incorporating Students' Worldviews into the Learning Process, No. 82 in the series, New Directions for Teaching and Learning*. Edited by Marcia B. Baxter Magolda. San Francisco: Jossey-Bass, 5–14.

"International Security and Cooperation." 2002. Course syllabus, Willamette University. http://www.willamette.edu/~mmarks/poli-373_syllabus.htm.

Josefson, Jim. 2005. "Don't Argue, Reflect! Reflections on Introducing Reflective Writing into Political Science Courses." *PS: Political Science & Politics* 38 (4): 763–767.

Kentish, Barry. 1995. "Hypotheticals: Deepening the Understanding of Environmental Issues Through Ownership of Learning." *Australian Science Teachers Journal* 41 (1): 21–26.

King, Patricia M. and Karen S. Kitchener. 1994. *Developing Reflective Judgement: Understanding and Promoting Intellectual Growth and Critical Thinking in Adolescents and Adults*. San Francisco: Jossey-Bass.

Knopf, Jeffrey W. 2006. "Doing a Literature Review." *PS: Political Science & Politics* 39 (1): 127–132.

Marks, Melanie, David Lehr, and Ray Brastow. 2006. "Cooperation versus Free Riding in a Threshold Public Goods Experiment." *Journal of Economic Education* 37 (2): 156–170.

Marks, Michael P. 1998. "Using the Game of Risk to Teach International Relations." *International Studies Notes* 23 (1): 11–18.

Marks, Michael P. 2002. "The 'We' Problem in Teaching International Studies." *International Studies Perspectives* 3 (1): 25–41.

McMenamin, Iain. 2006. "Process and Text: Teaching Students to Review the Literature." *PS: Political Science & Politics* 39 (1): 133–135.

McPeck, John E. 1990. *Teaching Critical Thinking: Dialogue and Dialectic*. New York: Routledge.

Meyers, Chet. 1986. *Teaching Students to Think Critically*. San Francisco: Jossey-Bass.

Murphy, James J. and Juan-Camilo Cardenas. 2004. "An Experiment on Enforcement Strategies for Managing a Local Environment Resource." *Journal of Economic Education* 35 (1): 47–61.

Nexon, Daniel H. and Iver B. Neumann, eds. 2006. *Harry Potter and International Relations*. Lanham, MD: Rowman & Littlefield.

Obach, Brian. 2003. "Barriers to Collective Action: A Classroom Simulation." *Teaching Sociology* 31 (3): 312–318.

Olsen, Jonathan and Anne Statham. 2005. "Critical Thinking in Political Science: Evidence from the Introductory Comparative Politics Course." *Journal of Political Science Education* 1 (3): 323–344.

Omelicheva, Mariya Y. 2006. "Global Politics on Trial: Using Educational Debate for Teaching Controversies of World Affairs." *International Studies Perspectives* 7 (2): 172–186.

Petrzelka, Peggy. 2005. "'They Make How Much?' Investigating Faculty Salaries to Examine Gender Inequalities." *Teaching Sociology* 33 (4): 380–388.

Piaget, Jean. 1974. *The Child and Reality*. Translated by Arnold Rosin. New York: Viking.

Pickhardt, Michael and Michael Watts. 2005. "Teaching Public Goods Theory With a Classroom Game." *Journal of Economic Education* 36 (2): 145–159.

Renzulli, Linda A., Howard E. Aldrich, and Jeremy Reynolds. 2003. "It's Up in the Air, or Is It?" *Teaching Sociology* 31 (1): 49–59.

Roberts, Alison and Keri Iyall Smith. 2002. "Managing Emotions in the College Classroom: The Cultural Diversity Course as an Example." *Teaching Sociology* 30 (3): 291–301.

Robertson, Geoffrey. 1986. *Geoffrey Robertson's Hypotheticals: Dramatisation of Moral Dilemmas of the 80s*. North Ryde, Australia: Angus and Robertson.

Robertson, Geoffrey. 1987. *Does Dracula Have AIDS? And Other Geoffrey Robertson Hypotheticals*. North Ryde, Australia: Angus and Robertson.

Robertson, Geoffrey. 1991. *Geoffrey Robertson's Hypotheticals: A New Collection from the Acclaimed ABC TV Series*. Crow's Nest, Australia: ABC Enterprises.

Rothman, Stanley, S. Robert Lichter, and Neil Nevitte. 2005. "Politics and Professional Advancement Among College Faculty." *The Forum* 3 (1): article 2. http://www.bepress.com/forum/vol3/iss1/art2.

Sanders, Danny, Alan Coote, and David Crookall, eds. 1988. *Learning from Experience Through Games and Simulations*. Loughborough, UK: SAGSET.

Sanders, Danny and R. Gunn. 1990. "The Assessment and Evaluation of Communication Skills Associated with Simulation/Gaming." *Simulation/Games for Learning* 20 (2): 215–234.

Santos, Joseph and Angeline M. Lavin. 2004. "Do as I Do, Not as I Say: Assessing Outcomes When Students Think Like Economists." *Journal of Economic Education* 35 (2): 148–161.

Shea, Daniel M. and Rebecca Harris. 2006. "Why Bother? Because Peer-to-Peer Programs Can Mobilize Young Voters." *PS: Political Science & Politics* 39 (2): 341–345.

Shellman, Stephen M. and Kürşad Turan. 2006. "Do Simulations Enhance Student Learning? An Empirical Evaluation of an IR Simulation." *Journal of Political Science Education* 2 (1): 19–32.

Sternberg, Robert J., ed. 1990. *Wisdom: It's Nature, Origins and Development*. Cambridge: Cambridge University Press.

Stover, William James. 2005. "Teaching and Learning Empathy: An Interactive, Online Diplomatic Simulation of Middle East Conflict." *Journal of Political Science Education* 1 (2): 207–219.

Weldes, Jutta. 2003. *To Seek Out New Worlds: Exploring Links Between Science Fiction and World Politics*. New York: Palgrave Macmillan.

Werth et al.. 2002. "Using Controversial Mock Trials in 'Psychology and Law' Courses: Suggestions from Participants." *Teaching of Psychology* 29 (1): 20–24.

West, Ellis M. 1998. "Some Proposed Guidelines for Advocacy in the Classroom." *PS: Political Science & Politics* 31 (4): 805–807.

Wilkinson, James and Heather Dubrow. 1991. "Encouraging Independent Thinking." In *Education for Judgment: The Artistry of Discussion Leadership*. Edited by C. Roland Christensen, David A. Garvin, and Ann Sweet. Boston: Harvard Business School Press, 249–261.

Winston, Fletcher. 2003. "What if Milgram Controlled Student Grades? A Simple Game for Teaching the Concept of Authority." *Teaching Sociology* 31 (2): 221–226.

"World Views: War and Its Alternatives." 2005. Course syllabus, Willamette University. http://www.willamette.edu/cla/wviews/syllabus.htm.

Wright, Wynne and Elizabeth Ranson. 2005. "Stratification on the Menu: Using Restaurant Menus to Examine Social Class." *Teaching Sociology* 33 (3): 310–316.

Young, Joseph H. 2006. "Simulating Two-Level Negotiations." *International Studies Perspectives* 7 (1): 77–82.

Turning the Classroom Upside Down: Experimenting with the Flipped Classroom in American Government

7

WENDY N. WHITMAN COBB

The classic picture of the college classroom is that of a stuffy, older professor standing in front of a blackboard lecturing to a large classroom of students, some falling asleep, some speaking with friends, and only a few paying attention. Undoubtedly, this is what many students dread, fear, and expect when walking in on the first day of class. Those of us who have been fortunate enough to have made it to the front of the classroom understand these challenges and fears as we often experienced them ourselves as undergraduates.

As teaching philosophies in higher education have evolved from a focus simply on research with teaching as a minor plot point to a sustained attention to the quality of teaching, professors have been forced to reevaluate their classrooms and to develop new methods through which to reach their students. One of those new methods is an approach known as "flipping the classroom" or the "flipped class." In general, a flipped classroom entails lectures being prerecorded so that students can listen to them at home on their own time, leaving classroom time for other activities such as discussion, debate, simulations, or group activities.

While the idea of a flipped classroom is attractive to many professors, there has been little research to date on its effectiveness as an educational method in higher learning. This article attempts to rectify that by utilizing a semester-long experiment of student success and perceptions across different learning environments. This article proceeds as follows: First, I summarize the concept of the flipped classroom, discuss some of the arguments proposed in favor of it and describe how I implemented this idea in my American Federal Government classes. Second, I describe the experimental design used to compare the flipped classroom to other instructional modalities: the traditional, lecture-based classroom and online classes. Finally, I analyze the results and discuss the conclusions drawn from this experiment. The results suggest that, while no distinct educational advantages were evident across these three classes, student perceptions of the classroom are nonetheless important in stimulating student interest and learning.

The Flipped Classroom

While there are as many definitions of a flipped classroom as there are teachers who do it, the basic idea behind the concept is that students take part in activities in the classroom instead of lectures. Lectures and lessons are instead available to students prior to class. The assignments that students are then asked to take part in can vary from discussions and debates to interactive simulations and group work (for further descriptions of the flipped approach, see Berrett

2012; Lage, Platt, and Treglia 2000). These activities give students a more hands on approach to learning, appealing to students with a wide array of learning styles.

The idea of the flipped classroom first developed at the K–12 level, particularly in high school. While the basic premise (active learning in the classroom) has been around for some time, in 2007, Jonathan Bergmann and Aaron Sams began to record their lectures for their classes at Woodland Park High School in Colorado. While out of the scope of this article, Bergmann and Sams have detailed their work in a series of blog posts for *The Daily Riff* (www. thedailyriff.com) and Knewton describes the origins and concepts of the flipped classroom in an infographic available at http://www.knewton.com/flipped-classroom/.

What is the methodological underpinning this approach? In fact, some argue that a flipped classroom is not a true flipped classroom unless some sort of active learning is going on (Brunsell and Horejsi 2013). The flipped classroom forces both instructors and students to focus on the active learning of students. Prince (2004, 223) defines active learning as "any instructional method that engages students in the learning process. In short, active learning requires students to do meaningful learning activities and think about what they are doing." What occurs in the flipped model, then, is the passive learning from lecture or other materials outside of the classroom, allowing for active-learning assignments within the classroom. Given the positive data surrounding active learning (for a good summary, see Prince 2004), the flipped model provides a framework through which instructors can include more of it in their classroom.

Similarly, Flip It Consulting, an organization focused on providing resources and ideas for professionals to flip not only the classroom but other professional activities, defines the flipped model as an acronym: Focus on your Learners by Involving them in the Process. As such, Flip It argues that compared to the lecture model, a flipped activity is focused on participants, is activity driven and places a larger emphasis on higher order thinking skills ("The Lecture vs. The Flip").

Partly because of how the flipped classroom can be applied, there is no ideal consensus on how much of the class needs to be flipped or the nature of the assignments that can be used. Some instructors utilize the flipped model to free up classroom time for engaging discussions that can be more fruitful with students being fully prepared ahead of time. Other instructors will utilize this model for only some portions of the class. Further, the flipped classroom can open up time for the utilization of simulations that can give students hands-on experience with the Congress, bureaucracy, or even the Supreme Court that they might not have grasped otherwise.

Given the relative newness surrounding the idea of the flipped classroom, research into its effectiveness has been rather limited. Robinson Meyer in *The Atlantic* (2013) reports on a three-year study examining the implementation of the flipped model in a graduate pharmaceutical course that found increased student learning gains and a growing student preference for the flipped model. Using the heading of "learning before lecture," Moravec et al. (2010) find that asking students to complete a short worksheet or lecture prior to an introductory-level biology course helped increase student learning. The flipped model is even making an appearance in law school classes (Rapoport 2013).

Other studies have examined specific teaching tools that are often used in support of the flipped model such as videos and podcasts. Fulton (2012) reports on results at the high school level that indicate that math proficiency increased anywhere from 5.1% in an algebra class to 9.8% in a calculus course. With respect to the use of videos in the classroom in general, Herreid and Schiller (2013) summarize the extensive literature concluding that videos alone have a positive influence on student attitudes, behavior, and performance. Examining videos in a flipped model specifically, a recent study on their use in a pharmaceutical class that aimed to educate students on renal pharmacotherapy led to increased student knowledge and improved student perception of the class (Pierce and Fox 2012).

Some researchers have been more critical of the flipped method. Ash (2012, 6) argues that some educators "believe that flipping is simply a high-tech version of an antiquated instructional method: the lecture." The root of this criticism comes from the fact that students are merely changing the location in which they listen to the lecture from the classroom to the home. Nielsen (2012) also discussed her own reasons for not flipping including the fact that not all students have the needed technology at home and that "flipped homework is still homework." Meanwhile, Mangan (2013) details student concerns over how they might perform in a classroom style that is unfamiliar to them.

One of the common complaints that professors have regarding their students is that they do not come to class having done the readings or being otherwise prepared for the day. In a flipped classroom, these concerns will not be alleviated because students may actually be asked to do more work (Meyer 2013). Further, this problem can be magnified in the college setting where there are fewer meeting days than high school or middle school environments where the flipped classroom has traditionally been implemented.

The literature and its focus to this point is problematic. First, studies such as Fulton (2012) and Herreid and Schiller (2013) looking at the effectiveness of the flipped classroom have focused on particular aspects of the teaching method such as the use of videos or podcasts. Other studies, such as Moravec et al. (2010), only flip a small part of the class. As such, few conclusions can be drawn about flipped classes as a whole class and not merely a part. Secondly, most studies of the flipped classes (including the ones noted above) have looked at science or math classes, not a social science class such as political science. This research builds on these gaps by applying the flipped model to an entire class in an introductory American government course.

Classroom Model Utilized

Because the flipped classroom is one of the independent variables of interest, it is necessary to explain the set-up of the class used, particularly since there is no generally accepted definition of flipping. The basic idea around which I organized the class was small groups of students who would work together throughout the semester on a series of engaging assignments. Before that could begin, however, I had to develop and record lectures that students could access outside of the classroom. Utilizing the Garage Band application for Mac, I recorded a series of MP3 s based on my actual classroom lectures. These lectures ranged in length from 15 minutes to 45 minutes depending on the topic. While some professors have chosen to video their lectures and to post the videos to the Web or YouTube or utilize other programs that allow them to sync their lectures with a series of slides, I chose MP3 s because they are the most portable. Students can download them onto their smart phones or burn CDs to play in their cars. They are not dependent on having to be near a computer in order to participate.

Once these lectures were recorded (a significant investment of time to begin with), they were posted to our learning management system, Blackboard. The key idea, however, is that, while some may initially believe the flipped classroom is technology dependent or, rather, high technology dependent, professors and students alike only require a basic minimum of technological experience to make the concept come alive.

I then developed a series of group projects, the descriptions for which are contained in appendix A. These assignments included the writing of their own group constitution, the creation of their own newspaper (which would then be "sold" in another class thereby simulating the conditions of real-world media problems), and the creation of their own interest group through the making of a Facebook (or "Fakebook" page). These assignments were topped off with a two-week-long simulation beginning with Senate Judiciary Committee hearings to confirm a slate of Supreme Court nominees and ending with those confirmed justices hearing and deciding a real-world Supreme Court case.

Overall, students were excited by these projects. In the constitution project, while some groups chose to focus on the American Constitution, other groups created constitutions for fictional worlds such as *The Hunger Games* or even "benevolent" dictatorships. In any case, all of the students were personally engaged in reading, examining, and understanding the US Constitution, an opportunity they do not usually get in a traditional classroom setting. In other projects, such as Newspaper Wars, groups put together quality newspapers that were quite competitive when it came to "selling" them in other classes. Finally, in the interest-group project, some students even created real Facebook sites to engage students across the university in movements centered around changing the available food options on campus. Overall, then, students found these assignments engaging and exciting while giving them hands-on experience with concepts of government.

To address a potential concern regarding group work, for many of the assignments, there were two components: a group assignment and an individual essay regarding the group portion. For the individual papers, students were usually asked to describe how their group came up with their ideas and how this connects back with the ideas discussed in the material. For example, following their group newspaper assignment, students are asked to discuss the decisions the group made about how they constructed their newspaper and what this says about the political economy of the media today.

The next major decision is how to schedule and organize the classroom. Because my classes met two days a week, I would break those days up as shown in the sample schedule in appendix B. The first day the class would meet, we would discuss the readings and the lecture so that I could ensure that the students fully grasped the material. On the second day, I would allow the students to work in their groups while I traveled from group to group addressing problems, answering questions, and ensuring that all students were fully participating.

Experimental Design

In order to examine the differences in learning across three different modalities—flipped, traditional (lecture-based), and online—I asked to be assigned three sections of American Federal Government in the Spring 2014 semester. At my university (a small, public, regional institution), American Federal Government is a general education course required of all students and so attracts those outside political science who might otherwise have a vested interest in taking the class. This is an important point for two reasons. First, political science majors may differ in some discernable way from nonmajors, which may affect the results here. To address this, future research may compare success in a majors-only introductory American government course and a nonmajors introductory American government course. Secondly, if we as political scientists hope to recruit new majors for our programs out of these introductory, required courses, it is all the more important that we design courses that are attractive and effective in order to energize and engage potential new majors.

In each of these, I randomly assigned a traditional teaching method, flipped method, and online class to each section. Students were aware of whether they were registering for an on-campus or online class, but they were not aware whether the on-campus class would be traditionally taught or flipped. While this design did not randomly assign participants to each model of teaching, it does control for most other extraneous factors including instructor, textbook, assignments, and exams. All readings, lectures, and notes were exactly the same across the three classes with the only minor difference in being how the group assignments were rephrased as individual assignments. This resulted in the traditional and online students oftentimes not only completing the work an entire group would be doing, but doing it on their own. To account for this, instead of asking for two parts as the flipped class was (described above), papers were shortened into one single paper.

I designed two surveys, one to be given at the beginning of the class and one at the end (appendices C and D, respectively). The preclass survey consists of three parts: The first asks for information regarding sex, age, academic status, and major as well as why students took the class. The second part contained a learning-style survey and the third contained a set of 10 questions drawn from the US Citizenship Test to measure student knowledge. The postclass survey asked students about their impressions of the class, how they would rate the instruction they received, and whether they would take a similar class again. Finally, the same 10 questions were given to measure any improved performance across the three sections.

For the on-campus classes, surveys were given anonymously in the first week of classes while the online class was asked to complete the survey within the first week via Survey Monkey. The response rates for the preclass survey were high: 93% for the flipped class (of 29 students), 97% for the traditional class (of 30 students), and 100% for the online class (of 11 students). The postclass survey was given the final week of class, again anonymously in the traditional and flipped classes and on Survey Monkey for the online class. For the post-class survey, response rates were 76% for the traditional class, 73% for the online class, and 72.4% for the flipped class. For both the preclass survey and postclass survey, students completed an Institutional Review Board-approved informed-consent form.

In reporting their majors, only one political science major was reported across the three classes (dual major with history) and the most common major was psychology (eight students) followed by nursing (seven students), and undecided or undeclared (six students). This further underscores that this class was directed mostly towards nonpolitical science majors. The most common reason given for registering for the class was because it is required (94%).

One major caveat that should be kept in mind with this design is that it is a one-semester snapshot of one set of students and does contain a small sample size, particularly with respect to the online section. It is entirely possible that the results may be different given a different set of students or a different mix of students. Ideally, this study could be continued over a series of semesters to confirm the findings; however, due to the teaching needs of my school and department, it was not possible to expand the study beyond one semester.

Results
Pre-Class Survey and Midterm Grades
The pre-class survey was designed to do two things: discern any differences between students demographically across the three sections that could affect student perceptions and performance and measure students' current knowledge regarding American government. Table 1 displays the modal responses across the entire study population and table 2 contains the modal responses in the traditional, flipped, and online courses.

According to table 1, the typical student was over 25, female, and an academic freshman with a grade point average (GPA) between 3.0 and 3.5. This matches well with the overall university's demographics (62% female, almost 30% freshmen, with an average full-time age of 25 as of Spring 2014).

The more important piece of information to come from these results is to know if any of the differences across the three sets of students are significant that could affect the eventual outcome of the study. Based on an initial examination of table 2, it would appear that there are differences in the classes as to age and GPA. To test this, I utilize an analysis of variance (ANOVA) with a Tukey posttest to determine significant differences. Table 3 displays the ANOVA results and table 4 displays the Tukey values for significant variables (Learning Style).[1]

While just slightly significant, learning style across the three classes appeared to differ. The Tukey test indicates that the differences are between the online and traditional classes; while the median for both classes was visual, the frequency with which they appeared in the two classes is slightly significant. Since the online class could be argued to be less visual in nature (since students are not personally watching the professor give a lecture but listening to it), it could affect the eventual success or failure of students in the online class.

At the midpoint of the class, following the midterm exam, I anonymously collected both the midterm exam score for each student as well as each student's overall class grade at the midterm. Table 5 displays the averages for each class and tables 6 and 7 provide ANOVA results for these two data points.

The first thing to notice is that on the midterm exam (which was the same for all three classes), the traditional class scored highest with a 77.93 average followed by the online class at 76.85 and the flipped class at 71.9. However, when looking at the overall class grade at the midterm, the flipped class has the highest average at 84.29. Interestingly, the only statistically significant difference in all of this was in the midterm exam grade between the traditional and flipped classes.

One possibility for the difference in average class grade at the midterm is the impact of group work. In the flipped class, students completed some assignments collectively whereas students in the traditional and online classes completed the same assignments on their own. This could lead to two outcomes that could be causing these differences: First, students who would not have otherwise completed the assignments were able to contribute minimally to the paper and still get the group grade. Second, with students working together, the assignment could simply be legitimately better than those completed by one student who would not have the opportunity to work with others. This could also lead to the problem of too many cooks in the kitchen, but this survey design is unable to discern that.

Post-class survey and Final Grades

While the pre-class survey looked at demographic differences, the post-class survey was designed to measure student impressions regarding the classes (the post-class survey appears in appendix D). Table 8 displays the average results both overall and within the classes for the impressions questions and tables 9 and 10 provide ANOVA Tukey results for the differences.

Taken together, these tables demonstrate that students in the three classes *perceived* their

Question	Modal response
What is your age range?	25+
What is your gender?	Female
What (academic) year are you?	Freshman
What is your approximate current GPA?	3.0–3.5
What grade do you expect to receive in this class?	A
Learning Style	Visual
Modality	Flipped

Table 1. Overall Pre-Class Survey Results

Question	Traditional	Flipped	Online
Age	25+	17–19; 25+	20–22
Gender	Female	Female	Female
Academic Year	Freshman	Freshman	Freshman
GPA	3.6–4.0	3.0–3.5	2.1–2.9
Grade Expected	A	A	A
Learning Style	Visual	Visual	Visual
Knowledge Pretest (Avg.)	7.5	7.1	7.2

Table 2. Pre-Class Survey Results by Modality

		Sum of Squares	df	Mean Square	F
Age	Between Groups	0.556	2	0.278	0.164
	Within Groups	110.209	65	1.696	
	Total	110.765	67		
Gender	Between Groups	0.018	2	0.009	0.044
	Within Groups	13.673	65	0.21	
	Total	13.691	67		
Year	Between Groups	4.912	2	2.456	2.991
	Within Groups	53.368	65	0.821	
	Total	58.279	67		
GPA	Between Groups	4.141	2	2.071	1.881
	Within Groups	71.55	65	1.101	
	Total	75.691	67		
Learning Style	Between Groups	15.184	2	7.592	3.402*
	Within Groups	145.051	65	2.232	
	Total	160.235	67		

Table 3. ANOVA results for preclass survey group differences

	(I) Modality	(J) Modality	Mean diff. (I-J)	Std. Error
Learning Style	Traditional	Flipped	−0.42656	0.3995
		Online	−1.35185	0.51828*
	Flipped	Traditional	0.42656	0.3995
		Online	−0.92529	0.51275
	Online	Traditional	1.35185	0.51828*
		Flipped	0.92529	0.51275

Table 4. Tukey Results for Learning Style
$*p < .05$

Modality	Average midterm exam (SD)	Average midterm class (SD)
Traditional	77.93 (11.262)	79.58 (11.046)
Flipped	71.9 (18.544)	84.29 (12.355)
Online	76.85 (12.765)	72.21 (11.344)

Table 5. Midterm Averages

classes very differently. In the case of the first three questions, which asked about student enjoyment in the class, rating of instruction in the class, and likelihood to take a class like it again, the traditional students had consistently higher ratings than the flipped and online students. Table 7 also bears out how large these differences are in the three questions by showing that the differences are statistically significant.

These perception differences are quite apparent when we turn to the comments offered by

		Sum of Squares	df	Mean Square	F
Midterm Exam	Between Groups	1898.277	2	949.138	4.155*
	Within Groups	14392.178	63	228.447	
	Total	16290.455	65		
Midterm Class Grade	Between Groups	268.492	2	134.246	1.045
	Within Groups	8095.699	63	128.503	
	Total	8364.191	65		

Table 6. ANOVA Results for Midterm Averages
*p < .05

	(I) Modality	(J) Modality	Mean diff. (I-J)	Std. Error
Midterm Exam	Traditional	Flipped	11.64049	4.04209*
		Online	6.68704	5.59515
	Flipped	Traditional	−11.64049	4.04209*
		Online	−4.95345	5.54276
	Online	Traditional	−6.68704	5.59515
		Flipped	4.95345	5.54276

Table 7. ANOVA Tukey Posttest for Midterm Exam
*p < .05

the students on the post-class survey. Table 11 summarizes the comments and includes the frequency of how many times a similar comment was made. In the traditional class, students most frequently enjoyed the teacher, followed by debate and discussion, and that it was a fun class. They did not like, however, that there were so many papers. In the flipped class, interestingly, group work was equally likely to be something that was liked and disliked by the students. Finally, online students were more critical of the class, with more comments about what was disliked (discussion boards, papers, lectures, textbook, teacher) than liked (lectures, teacher).

While there is a difference in student perceptions across the three classes, there does not seem to be much in the way of performance differences. While there was a slight difference statistically between the traditional and online classes in the knowledge portion, it was only at a p <.05 level. To further examine the actual performance differences, we can examine the final exam and final overall class scores. Table 12 has the averages for each class on the final exam and the final class score and tables 13 and 14 contain the ANOVA results.

With respect to the final exam grades, the traditional and online classes both outperformed the flipped class by approximately five points; however, as far as the final class grades go, the traditional and flipped classes are separated by only 0.07 points but are both 11 points higher than the online class average. These differences are borne out in table 13 with the ANOVA results demonstrating that the differences in final exam and final class grades were statistically significant. The Tukey results then show that with respect to the final exam, the traditional and online classes were statistically different and, with respect to the final class grade, grades in both the traditional and flipped classes and online classes significantly varied.

One final area of actual performance to examine is the pre- and posttest knowledge. Table 15 provides these data for the samples. Using a paired-samples t test, both the flipped class and online class showed a statistically significant increase in their knowledge of basic facts about

Question	Overall (SD)	Traditional (SD)	Flipped (SD)	Online (SD)
On a scale of 1–5, with 1 being the least and 5 being the most, how much did you enjoy this class overall?	M = 4.16	M = 4.73	M = 4.1	M = 2.75
	(1.027)	(0.550)	(0.625)	(1.488)
On a scale of 1–5, with 1 being the least and 5 being the most, how would you rate the delivery of instruction in this class?	M = 4.33	M = 4.68	M = 4.29	M = 3.5
	(0.792)	(0.646)	(0.644)	(0.926)
On a scale of 1–5 with 1 being the least and 5 being the most, how likely would you be to take a class like this again?	M = 3.53	M = 4.32	M = 3.33	M = 1.88
	(1.332)	(0.894)	(1.111)	(1.246)
What grade do you believe you earned in this class?	Mode = A, B	Mode = B	Mode = A	Mode = A
Are you enrolled for classes in the summer 2014 or fall 2014 semesters?	Mode = Yes	Mode = Yes	Mode = Yes	Mode = Yes
Knowledge Posttest	M = 8.2	M = 8.2	M = 7.9	M = 8.8
	(1.650)	(2.287)	(0.899)	(0.690)

Table 8. Overall PostClass Survey Results

		Sum of Squares	df	Mean Square	F
Enjoy Class Overall	Between Groups	23.072	2	11.536	18.661***
	Within Groups	29.673	48	0.618	
	Total	52.745	50		
Delivery of Instruction	Between Groups	8.275	2	4.137	8.613**
	Within Groups	23.058	48	0.48	
	Total	31.333	50		
Likely to Take Same Type of Class Again	Between Groups	36.391	2	18.196	0.000***
	Within Groups	52.314	48	1.09	
	Total	88.706	50		
Earned Grade	Between Groups	4.071	2	2.036	3.538*
	Within Groups	27.615	48	0.575	
	Total	31.686	50		
Enrolled for Summer or Fall	Between Groups	0.133	2	0.066	0.317
	Within Groups	10.024	48	0.209	
	Total	10.157	50		
Knowledge	Between Groups	4.895	2	2.448	0.895
	Within Groups	128.485	48	2.734	
	Total	133.38	50		

Table 9. ANOVA Results for the Postclass Survey
$*p < .05. **p < .001. ***p < .000$

American government, with the online class showing the largest increase. Taken together with the final exam and final class grades, however, success in the classroom seems to be mixed.

	(I) Modality	(J) Modality	Mean Diff. (I-J)	Std. Error
Enjoy Class Overall	Flipped	Traditional	−0.63203	0.23987*
		Online	1.34524	0.32667***
	Traditional	Flipped	0.63203	0.23987*
		Online	1.97727	0.32461***
	Online	Flipped	−1.34524	0.000***
		Traditional	−1.97727	0.000***
Delivery of Instruction	Flipped	Traditional	−0.39610	0.21145
		Online	0.78571	0.78751*
	Traditional	Flipped	0.39610	0.21145
		Online	1.18182	0.28615***
	Online	Flipped	−0.78571	0.28796*
		Traditional	−1.18182	0.28615***
Likely to Take Same Type of Class Again	Flipped	Traditional	−0.98485	0.31850**
		Online	1.45833	0.43374**
	Traditional	Flipped	0.98485	0.31850**
		Online	2.44318	0.43102***
	Online	Flipped	−1.45833	0.43374**
		Traditional	−2.44318	0.43102***
Earned Grade	Flipped	Traditional	0.16883	0.23140
		Online	0.66701	0.66071
	Traditional	Flipped	−0.16883	0.23140
		Online	−0.82955	0.31315*
	Online	Flipped	0.66701	0.31514
		Traditional	0.82955	0.31315*

Table 10. ANOVA Tukey Posttest Results
*p < .05. **p < .001. ***p < .000

Discussion

While the sample size is admittedly small, one of the most interesting findings from this experiment are the learning gains made in the online section compared to the other two sections. The online section had the lowest average final grade for the class, they had the highest class average on the final exam. Further, when comparing the pre- and posttest knowledge levels, the online class gained the most knowledge, with an increase in 2.72 points. Despite the seeming success of the students in the class, online students reported the lowest levels of satisfaction with the class. There could be any number of reasons for this discrepancy from a mismatch of work expectations on the part of students and the actual work load to differences in demographics as noted in table 2. Additionally, the sample may not be valid given the particularly small sample size and self-selection of students into the online section.

Examining table 11, which describes the types of comments students had about their respective classes on the post-class survey, the variety and frequency of student comments across the three sections should be noted. In the flipped section, students had six different types of positive comments compared to five different types in the traditional section and only four in

Modality	Like (Frequency of similar comments)	Did not like (Frequency of similar comments)
Traditional	How it was taught (3)	Notes not online (2)
	Videos used	Discussions (2)
	Teacher (9)	No extra credit
	Fun class (4)	Too many questions on midterm
	Debate and discussion (4)	papers (3)
Flipped	Lectures before class (2)	Too much reading (3)
	Group work (6)	Group work (6)
	Different teaching methods (3)	Online lectures
	Papers worth more than tests (2)	
	Wasn't boring (2)	
	Learning how government works (2)	
Online	Lectures (2)	Teacher
	Instructor (2)	Repetitive class
	Discussion boards	Discussion boards (2)
	Helped improve writing skills	Lecture
		Textbook
		Papers (2)

Table 11. Student Postclass Survey Comments

Modality	Average final exam (SD)	Average final class (SD)
Traditional	76.43 (13.658)	83.32 (9.502)
Flipped	71.21 (10.284)	83.25 (7.349)
Online	76.85 (27.004)	72.21 (11.979)

Table 12. Final Exam and Final Class Grade Comparisons

		Sum of Squares	df	Mean Square	F
Final Exam	Between Groups	1732.249	2	866.125	3.764*
	Within Groups	14268.466	62	230.137	
	Total	16000.715	64		
Final Class Grade	Between Groups	744.230	2	372.115	4.526*
	Within Groups	5097.259	62	82.214	
	Total	5841.489	64		

Table 13. ANOVA Results for Final Exam and Final Class Grades
*p < .05

the online section. This matches well with the lack of negative comments from students in the flipped class further demonstrating student attitudes towards the flipped class.

Embedded in these comments is also a split in student attitudes in the flipped class to group

	(I) Modality	(J) Modality	Mean difference (I-J)	Std. Error
Final Exam	Traditional	Flipped	5.21164	4.09179
		Online	15.32593	5.61580*
	Flipped	Traditional	−5.21164	4.091779
		Online	10.11429	5.58863
	Online	Traditional	−15.32593	5.61580*
		Flipped	−10.11429	5.58863
Final Class Grade	Traditional	Flipped	0.06853	2.44654
		Online	9.41289	3.35654*
	Flipped	Traditional	−0.06853	2.44564
		Online	9.34436	3.34030*
	Online	Traditional	−9.41289	3.35654*
		Flipped	−9.34436	3.34030*

Table 14. ANOVA Tukey Posttest Results
$*p < .05$

Traditional	Before: 7.27	−0.955
	After: 7.9	
Flipped	Before: 6.86	−4.422***
	After: 8.24	
Online	Before: 6.14	−4.80***
	After: 8.86	

Table 15. Knowledge Test Results Before and After Class (Out of 10)
$***p < .000$

work with six students noting the presence of it as a positive and six students noting it as a negative. For any instructor who has used group work and is familiar with student concerns about equity and fairness in the work, this split will be a familiar one. While it is out of the scope of this article to offer a solution to this problem, it does highlight a familiar drawback of the flipped approach.

The major results of this experiment, then, appear to be twofold: There does not seem to be any major difference in student performance across the three different modalities. Flipped classes do not appear to have any effect, positive or negative, on student performance. On the other hand, student perceptions of the class are very different between traditional, flipped, and online students with traditional students enjoying their class time more than the other groups of students.

Conclusions

While the data gathered here may not seem to lend much support to the flipped classroom, I believe the bigger conclusion is that there is no harm from it either. If anything is apparent from the results regarding student perceptions, it is that dynamic and engaging instruction is still of paramount importance to students. Regardless of the technology or model used, students still want a classroom experience that is fun as well as innovative and that can be given in any number of ways.

A major caveat to these findings, I believe, is required. Since there is no agreed upon definition of the flipped classroom, these findings are based on my idea of what the flipped classroom is and how to implement it. To the extent possible, I believe my flipped class keeps to the spirit of flipping and advances it at the college level in particular. The results, then, should not deter enterprising professors and teachers from developing their own ideas about the flipped class-room and testing them in their own environments. Another teacher in another school may indeed find more success with their students; at a minimum, the results show that the flipped classroom is not detrimental to our students and so should be encouraged in their pursuits of a more skilled teaching presentation.

Not central to the main question under study, it is also important to point out the poor performance of the online class in this study. While the student population was small (11 registered with only nine really completing the class), the overall performance of the students was poor compared to the other classes.

As a start to determining the comparative success of different teaching methods, this study makes headway in showing that, while performance may not vary much, student perceptions do. We must remember that as college professors and representatives of our fields of study, our goal should not only be to educate our students but to stimulate and encourage them and perhaps to collect a few converted majors along the way. When students enjoy a class, they are more likely to put more effort and interest towards it. The finding that students enjoyed a traditional-style class more than a flipped or online class should be taken seriously if we wish to not only please students but bring them along for future classes.

Reprinted with permission from Wendy N. Whitman Cobb. 2015. "Turning the Classroom Upside Down: Experimenting with the Flipped Classroom in American Government." Journal of Political Science Education *12 (1). Taylor & Francis: 1-14. doi:10.1080/15512169.2015.1063437.*

Acknowledgments
I would like to thank Edris Montalvo and the reviewers for their helpful comments.

Notes
1. I utilize the ANOVA test of significance throughout this article. When variables are shown to be significant, I then display the Tukey posttest values to determine which groups are statistically different for those significant variables only.

References
Ash, Katie. 2012. "Educators View 'Flipped' Model with a More Critical Eye." *Education Week* 32 (2): 6–7.

Berrett, Dan. 2012. "How 'Flipping' the Classroom Can Improve the Traditional Lecture." *The Chronicle of Higher Education*. http://chronicle.com/article/How-Flipping-the-Classroom/130857/.

Brunsell, Eric and Martin Horejsi. 2013. "Science 2.0: A Flipped Classroom in Action." *The Science Teacher* 80 (2): 8.

Fulton, Kathleen. 2012. "Upside Down and Inside Out: Flip Your Classroom to Improve Student Learning." *Learning and Leading with Technology* 39 (8): 12–17.

Herreid, Clyde Freeman and Nancy A. Schiller. 2013. "Case Studies and the Flipped Classroom." *Journal of College Science Teaching* 42 (5): 62–66.

Lage, Maureen J., Glenn J. Platt, and Michael Treglia. 2000. "Inverting the Classroom: A Gateway to Creating an Inclusive Learning Environment." *The Journal of Economic Education* 31 (1): 30–43.

Mangan, Katherine. 2013. "Inside the Flipped Classroom." *Chronicle of Higher Education* 60 (5): 18–21.

Meyer, Robinson. 2013. "The Post-Lecture Classroom: How Will Students Fare?" *The Atlantic*. http://www.theatlantic.com/technology/archive/2013/09/the-post-lecture-classroom-how-will-students-fare/279663/.

Moravec, Marin, Adrienne Williams, Nancy Aguilar-Roca, and Diane K. O'Dowd. 2010. "Learn Before Lecture: A Strategy That Improves Learning Outcomes in a Large Introductory Biology Class." *CBE-Life Sciences Education* 9: 473–481.

Nielsen, Lisa. 2012. "Five Reasons I'm Not Flipping over the Flipped Classroom." *Technology and Learning.* http://www.techlearning.com/default.aspx?tabid=100&entryid=3360.

Pierce, Richard and Jeremy Fox. 2012. "Vodcasts and Active Learning Exercises in a 'Flipped Classroom' Model of a Renal Pharmacotherapy Module." *American Journal of Pharmaceutical Education* 76 (10): 196.

Prince, Michael. 2004. "Does Active Learning Work?: A Review of the Research." *Journal of Engineering Education* 93 (3): 223–231.

Rapoport, Nancy B. 2013. "Rethinking US Legal Education: No More 'Same Old, Same Old.'" *Connecticut Law Review* 45.

Appendix A: Flipped Classroom Assignments

Assignment	Group Component	Individual Component
Create Your Own Constituion	Pretend you have been charged with rewriting the American constitution for today's day and age. Create a brief document outlining your constitution. Think about the status of states as well as how you would structure your new government. Your constitution should be at least three pages double-spaced.	In a two-page, double-spaced paper, explain how your group came to decide on your constitution. What do you like or not like about it? Why? How does it compare to the US Constitution?
Civil Liberties and Civil Rights	In a three-page write-up, identify the civil rights and civil liberties in your constitution. Why did you include what you did or why didn't you include them?	N/a
Public Opinion Polls	Each group will be assigned a different section of an opinion poll for which to write questions (demographics, political knowledge, political identification, etc.). Design three or four questions to be placed on a public opinion survey. The professor will combine these questions and provide results to the class as a whole.	In a two-page write up, interpret the results of the poll. Identify any problems or things that you liked in the poll.
Newspaper Wars	As a group, design and create a two-page (front and back) "newspaper." Decide on the layout, appearance, content, etc. The professor will run off copies of each group's newspaper to take to another class. In the separate class, each student will have the opportunity to pick one newspaper to "buy." The group who "sells" the most newspapers will receive extra credit.	In a two-page paper, discuss the role of the media in American government and what this assignment has to say about that. Why did the group choose to cover the stories it did? What went into the design decisions?
Interest-Group Facebook Page	As a group, create an interest group and design a Facebook page for your group. What policies would you like to see changed? How? At what level? Include a series of status updates (at least five) trying to convince browsers to join your group. As a group, you will present your page to the rest of the class.	N/a
Be the Bureaucrat: Interpreting the Clean Air Act	Pretend you are a regulator at the Environmental Protection Agency (EPA). As a group, you will be given a provision of the Clean Air Act and have to design and decide on how to implement a provision of the law. Each group should decide on a series of principles of how to implement the law. Each group will then present their proposed rules to the rest of the class.	N/a

Table A1. Flipped Classroom Assignments

Appendix B: Sample Flipped Classroom Schedule

	Monday	Wednesday
Week One	To be read/listened to: Chapters 1 and 2 in the textbook; Revolution and Constitution Lecture In class: Discuss readings and lecture	Work in groups on "Create Your Own Constitution"
Week Two	Due in class: Constitution assignments To be read/listened to: Chapters 3 and 4 in the textbook; Civil Liberties and Civil Rights Lecture In class: Discuss readings and lecture	Work in groups on "Civil Liberties and Civil Rights"
Week Three	Due in class: Civil liberties and civil rights assignment To be read/listened to: Chapter 10 in the textbook and Public Opinion Lecture In class: Discuss public opinion	Work in groups on "Public Opinion Poll"

Table B1. Sample Flipped Classroom Schedule

Supplementary Material

To view Appendix C: Preclass Survey and Appendix D: Postclass Survey, visit doi:10.1080/15512169.2015.1063437

Learning Through Discussions: Comparing the Benefits of Small-Group and Large-Class Settings

8

PHILIP H. POLLOCK III
KERSTIN HAMANN
BRUCE M. WILSON

D o the benefits of discussions in face-to-face classes vary depending on the type of discussion setting? Literature on active learning highlights the benefits of discussions for student learning; yet, we know relatively little about whether the setting in which a discussion takes place makes a difference for the benefits students derive from discussions. For example, do small-group discussions yield the same benefits to the learner as discussions involving the entire class? We also know little about whether different types of students participate equally in and reap similar benefits from different discussion contexts. Using student surveys, this study sets out to explore these questions for an upper-level political theory course and analyzes the participation and perceived benefits of different types of discussions taking into account student demographics. Questions concerning the effectiveness of discussions are important especially as college classes in many institutions of higher learning are growing in size and professors are faced with the task of developing strategies to involve students in discussions in large classes.

The next section presents a brief summary of the pedagogical value of discussions in different classroom settings. We then describe our study, data, and methodology and present our results. The conclusion reflects on implications for using discussions as an effective teaching tool.

The Benefits of Discussion

Lectures constitute a prevalent teaching strategy employed in many college classrooms and the literature has pointed to the benefits lectures can provide especially for transmitting information (e.g., Bligh 2000; Burgan 2006). At the same time, lectures have been found of limited effectiveness for satisfying other learner objectives, including stimulating interest and critical thinking (see, e.g., Bligh 2000; Buckley et al. 2004). Research highlights the advantages of other, more student-centered, active learning instruction, including discussions, for reaching these goals (see, e.g., Prince 2004). On the whole, studies assessing the usefulness of discussions conclude that they not only help develop students' oral communication skills (Dallimore, Hertenstein, and Platt 2008) but also improve learning (Bender 2003; Davis and Hillman Murrell 1993; Huerta 2007); they are considered an active learning technique and are credited with promoting critical thinking and higher-order, deep learning. Brookfield and Preskill (2005, 21–22) list 15 benefits of discussions, including the development of "intellectual agility" and "skills of synthesis and integration." Garside (1996, 215) argues that active learning is a key component for developing critical thinking skills, and discussion is one such strategy where students "elaborate, defend, and extend their positions, opinions, and beliefs." Discussions are one facet of cooperative learning, which also help students understand material better and develop new perspectives (see Garside 1996, 219). Comparing learner outcomes of material taught via lectures or discussion groups, the author finds that discussions yield "significantly more learning with regard to higher-level items" (Garside 1996, 212). Student-to-student interaction as a crucial component of critical thinking, problem solving, and deep learning is also emphasized by several other studies (e.g., Nicol and Boyle 2003; McCarthy and Anderson 2000; Philips 2005). Gall and Gall (1990, 25) cite research that credits discussions with improving students' mastery of the subject material and problem-solving ability, among others. Similarly, Ellis et al. (2004, 73) summarize some of the findings of research on discussions as a teaching and learning tool and point to literature that identifies discussions as a "quality approach to teaching." The authors conclude that discussions enhance student learning. Other authors, however, identify limitations to learning from discussion conducted among students. Laurillard (2002, 158–159), for example, finds that peer discussions do "not necessarily lead them to what they are supposed to know" since students might lack the knowledge to reach the desired learning outcome.

The assumption that discussions have beneficial effects on student learning is also implicit in scholarly work on how to structure discussions and discussion topics (e.g., Marks 2008). It is also present in studies that compare the effects of discussions in face-to-face classes compared to online learning contexts (see, e.g., Ellis et al. 2004; Meyer 2003; Tiene 2000) or in discussion analyses for courses taught entirely online (e.g., Clawson, Deen, and Oxley 2002; Hamann, Pollock, and Wilson 2009; Krentler and Willis-Flurry 2005; Pollock, Hamann, and Wilson 2005; Wilson, Pollock, and Hamann 2007).

Overall, then, a large body of research concludes that discussions are beneficial for learning, and especially for developing critical thinking skills. While many professors may thus be inclined to design some class time around discussions, some classroom environments make meaningful discussions difficult, and sometimes students are hesitant to participate in class. For example, studies have shown that up to two-thirds of students never or rarely participate in class discussions (cited in Caspi, Chajut, and Saporta 2008, 718). Nicol and Boyle (2003, 457) point to the difficulties professors face when they attempt to use "methods centered on dialogue and discussion" as class size increases. One way to overcome this limitation is to create small groups to generate cooperative team learning (see, e.g., Occhipinti 2003). This suggests that not all discussions are designed alike as some attempt to involve all students in the classroom, whereas others are structured around small discussion groups. Research has indicated that both peer instruction through small discussion groups as well as class-wide discussion "lead to improvements in students' conceptual understanding" (Nicol and Boyle 2003, 458). Similarly, Rabow et al. (1994, 1) argue that when students learn through discussion groups, they are required to become actively involved in the gaining of knowledge; discussion groups promote "a high level of analytical thinking" and help students master critical-thinking skills. These observations lead us to question whether all discussions have equal benefits, and if some students benefit more from some types of discussions than others.

Given that the literature establishes the benefits of discussions to result from active student engagement, we expect that small-group discussions are more likely to engage a higher number of students than discussions in large classes, which are often driven by just a few individual students (see Occhipinti 2003, 69). This assumption is also informed by research on communication patterns in small and large groups: In small groups (N = 5), more dialogues take place and group members are most influenced by those with whom they interact the most in dialogues; in large groups (N = 10), in contrast, less dialogue takes place and members are most influenced by the dominant speaker (Fay, Garrod, and Carletta 2000). Other research indicates that the quality of communication is higher in smaller face-to-face groups compared to larger ones (Lowry et al. 2006) and that students learn more from discussing physics material presented through videos in small groups (N = 3) compared to the whole class (N = 14) (Mayo, Sharma, and Muller 2009). Despite the relatively low number of participants in these studies' "large" groups, the findings concur that smaller groups are more effective in enhancing student learning than larger groups. While this research does not address larger class sizes, it nonetheless leads us to expect the benefits of discussions to be higher in smaller groups compared to the large class as the smaller group encourages more frequent participation, is less intimidating, offers fewer opportunities to disengage mentally from the discussion and thus furthers student engagement compared to the large-class setting.

The Study

Our study assesses different types of discussion in one upper-level political theory class. The course, offered in spring 2005 by one of the authors, enrolled 53 students and was conceptualized as a lecture class with substantial discussion components. The class met once a week in the evening for almost three hours.[1]

We were interested in finding out whether students perceive different benefits from different types of discussions.[2] We consider an upper-level theory course with over 50 students to be "large." This setting lends itself to varying the setting for discussions. We utilized two different types of discussion settings in the face-to-face environment. First, we planned discussions that invite the entire class to participate and students considered the assigned material in a plenary format. The discussions loosely followed the models of both "guided" and "reflective" discussions (Wilen 1990). Second, for some discussions the class was divided into groups of about five students; each group was assigned a discussion topic to deliberate for a specified amount of time, after which one of the group members had to summarize the discussion and report to the rest of the class. We evaluated two "large-class" discussions and two "small-group" discussions. The topics evaluated for the full-class discussions pertained to Mancur Olson's *Logic of Collective Action* and Tocqueville's *Democracy in America*; in both cases, the professor posed leading questions and guided the discussions. In one of the small-group discussions, each group was given a recent report on a case of a freedom of speech issue; the students were given questions to apply and evaluate John Stuart Mill's arguments from *On Liberty* for those cases. In the other small-group discussion, all students were given a brief article by Gabriel Almond (1991) on the relationship between democracy and capitalism; groups were then assigned one of the four main substantive sections of the article and provided with guiding questions for the discussion of their section. Attendance in class was not monitored or graded, and discussion participation was not graded.

We also wanted to find out whether all students participated equally in the different discussion settings, or whether there were systematic differences across the students enrolled in the class. In particular, we were interested in whether gender and race affected participation and perceived benefits. We also included GPA in the previous semester given previous findings on the differential effects of discussion participation on learner outcomes (although these findings relate to discussions in the online environment; see Hamann, Pollock, and Wilson 2009). Furthermore, research points to the significance of GPA in determining discussion behavior and group dynamics in that those students who are perceived by others to be of higher academic ability are more active and influential in cooperative groups than those of lower perceived ability; other studies show that students accept leadership from good students more readily than from poorer students (see Cohen 1994, 23).

Following each discussion, students completed a standard questionnaire[3] that was distributed at the end of the class period where the respective discussion occurred. The questions tapped the frequency of their participation (from "not at all" to "more than twice"), their impressions of the discussion environment, especially concerning the social function of discussions (for example, whether they got "to know other students better"), and their perceptions of the intellectual merits of the exercise, both in terms of substantive learner outcomes (the discussion helped promote the "understanding of the issue") and critical thinking (the discussion helped "apply the issue under consideration to a different context or a new situation"). The questionnaire also gauged overall satisfaction. Standard background demographics were included as well. (The questionnaire is reproduced in appendix A.) Our analysis is based on 67 questionnaires from the plenary discussions and 79 from the small-group format.

Results

Figure 1 contains side-by-side comparisons of the two types of discussions. The horizontal axis displays nine questionnaire items that measure various aspects of student behavior and perceptions. The vertical axis records the percentages of superlative responses to the questionnaire items ("to a large extent," "a lot," and so on). How do the different formats compare across the nine items? In line with our expectations, we find differences along the vertical axis. These differences suggest that small groups are superior vehicles of student engagement. Participation, the key behavioral attribute, is plainly more prevalent in small groups: one-third (32.9%) of small-group questionnaires reported high levels of participation, compared with less than

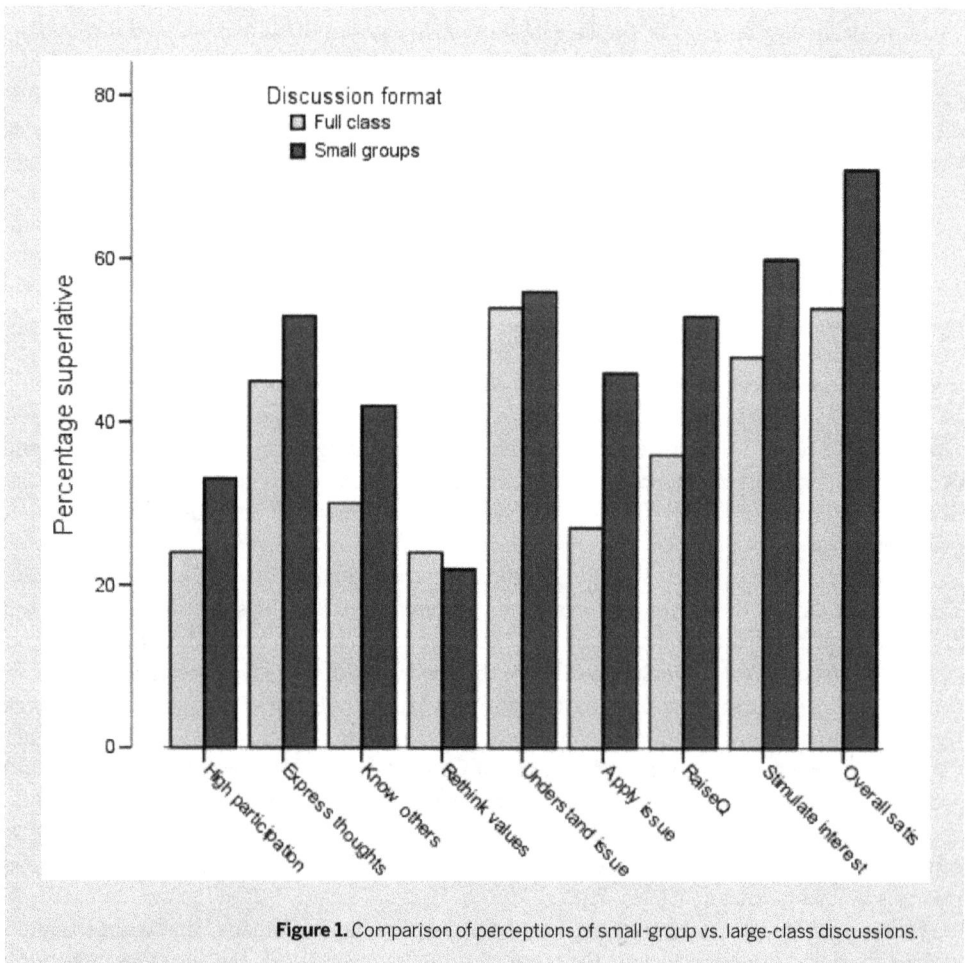

Figure 1. Comparison of perceptions of small-group vs. large-class discussions.

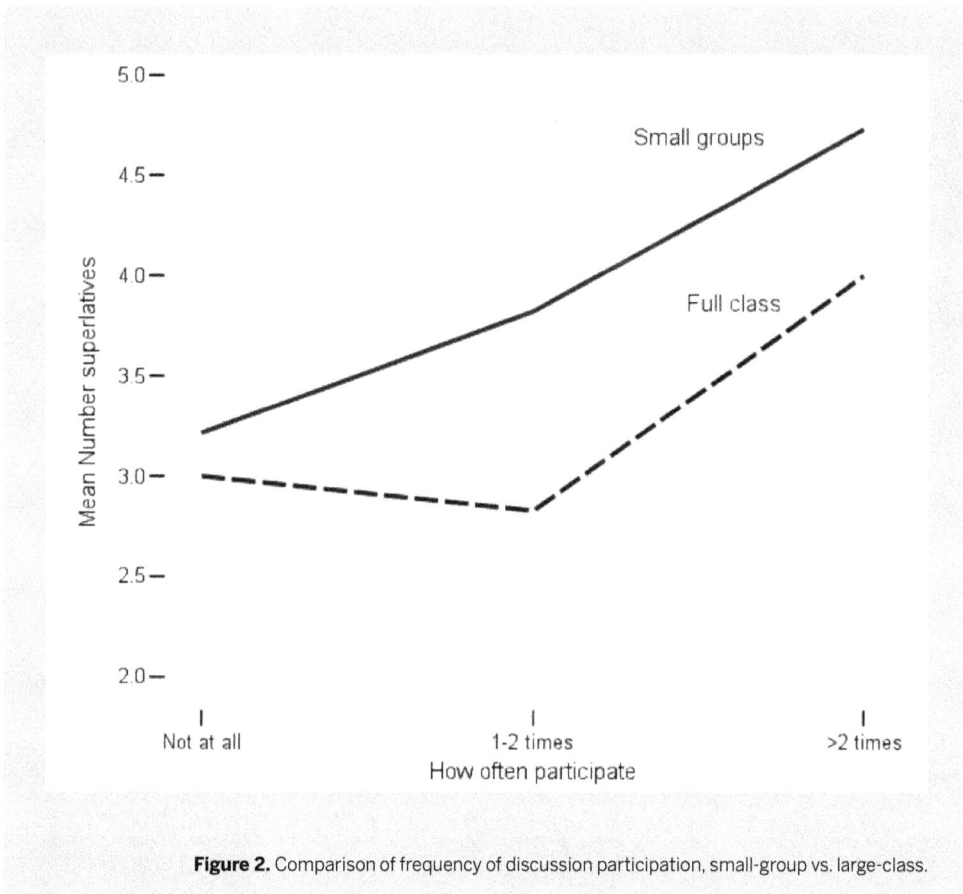

Figure 2. Comparison of frequency of discussion participation, small-group vs. large-class.

a quarter (23.9%) for the full-class venue. Predictably, too, students find that small groups are better places to express thoughts (53% versus 45%) and to get to know other students (42% versus 30%). The large-class setting performed slightly better in prompting students to rethink values (23.9% compared to 21.5% for small groups), perhaps because a larger range of opinions is present—and presented—in a larger group. In terms of promoting understanding of the issues, small groups were perceived to be just slightly more advantageous than discussion in the entire class. In contrast, small-group discussions yielded large relative returns on applying issues to new contexts compared to the large-class discussion (45.6% versus 26.9%); raising new questions (53.2% versus 35.8%); and stimulating interest (59.5% versus 47.8%). The percentages of questionnaires reporting the highest level of overall satisfaction, 70.9 for small groups and 53.7 for the full-class discussions, mirror the item-specific difference—overall, students perceive small groups to yield higher benefits than discussion in a large-class setting.

By what process does the small-group dynamic produce its salutary effects? Does the above-noted difference in participation between the two formats lead to more positive student evaluations of the small-group experience? To gain some leverage on this question, we first created, for each case in the dataset, a scale that sums the number of superlative responses to the eight student-perception items shown in figure 1. Scores on the nine-point scale range from 0 to 8. As the patterns of figure 1 would lead one to suspect, the small-group scale mean (4.01) was nearly a full point higher than the full-class mean (3.16), a statistically significant difference. Taking student participation into account produces more interesting differences.

Figure 2 displays mean differences between the formats, controlling for student participation.

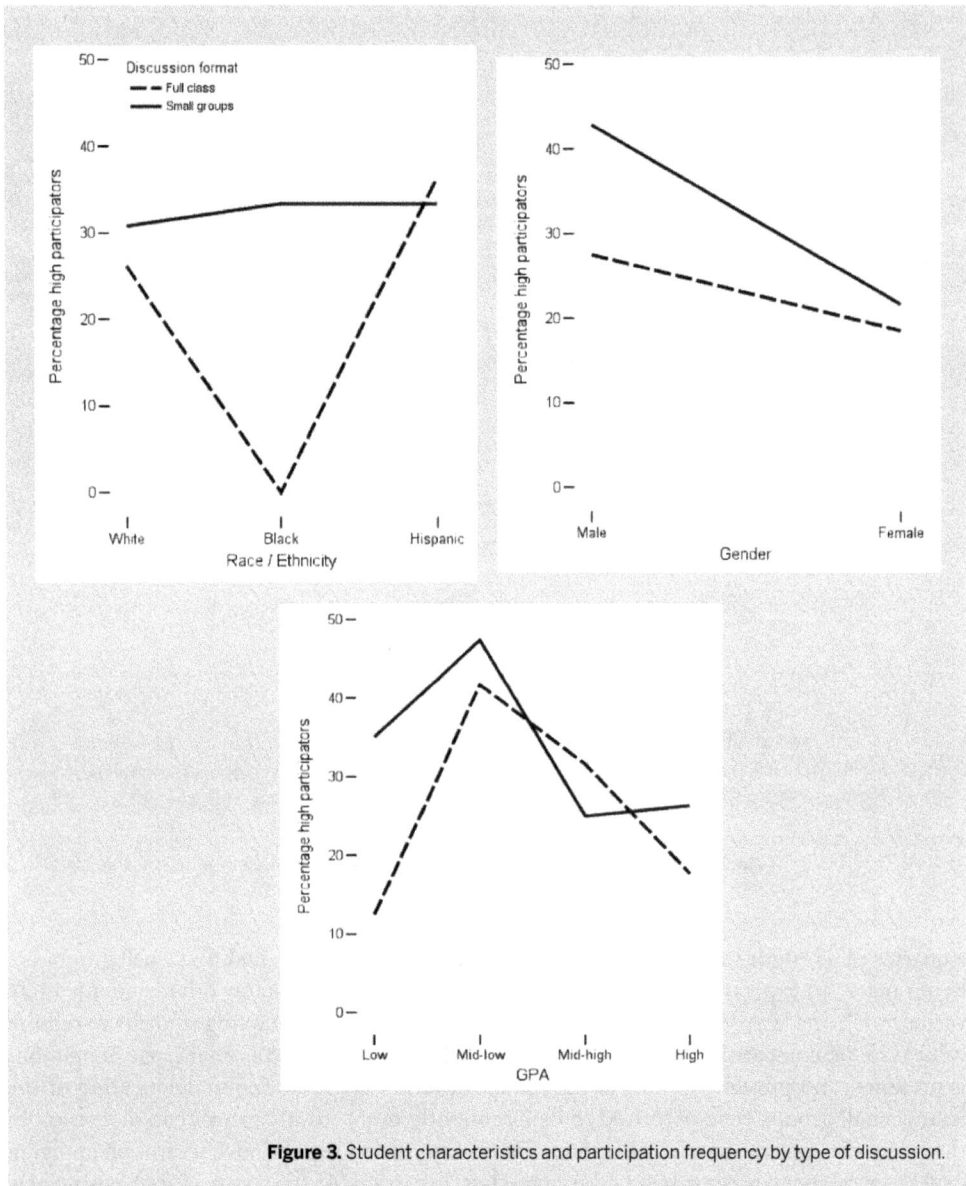

Figure 3. Student characteristics and participation frequency by type of discussion.

Clearly, and perhaps not surprisingly, non-participants reap few benefits from either setting: A mere 0.2-point mean difference separates the small-group and full-class numbers. But notice that the mean builds monotonically for small groups—from 3.2 for "not at all," to 3.6 for "1–2 times," to 4.7 for ">2 times." The more frequently individual students participated, the better their response to the discussion environment. For the full-class cases, by contrast, only the high participators had good things to report. Yet even here the ">2 times" mean (4.0) is virtually indistinguishable from the small-group "1–2 times" mean (3.8). The full-class numbers—a small, satisfied group of frequent participants—are consistent with the anecdotal profile of large-class participators.

Participation is more common in small-group discussions, and apparently more likely to produce positive perceptions. But who are those that participate? Are they the same types of students in small groups as in a large class? Is small-group participation also a "democratizing" experience, drawing in a more diverse pool of participants than one often finds in full-class settings? The panels of figure 3 provide some clues. The vertical axis of each panel displays the percentage of students reporting a high level of participation (">2 times"). The horizontal axis records student race/ethnicity (upper left), gender (upper right), and GPA (lower left). The relationships are shown for small-group (solid line) and full-class (dashed line) cases. A higher line means more frequent participation, and a flatter line means more equal participation.

The race/ethnicity panel conveys a hoped-for equalizing effect in the small-group setting. Whereas no African American reported frequent participation in the plenary discussions, one-third (33.3%) were frequent participants in small-group venues—a number equal to that for white (30.8%) and Hispanic (33.3%) students. The gender panel is less encouraging. Males claim substantially higher participation in small groups (42.9%) than in the full class (27.5%), but women do not—21.6% for small groups compared with 18.5% for full-class discussions. Thus the gender-participation relationship strengthens in the small-group setting. The finding that women contribute less than men in face-to-face learning environments is supported by much of the existing literature (see Caspi, Chajut, and Saporta 2008), and this inequity appears to remain unaffected by the size of the class or discussion group.

The relationship between student GPA and participation varies by discussion format. In the small-group setting, students with lower GPAs participated more frequently than did those with higher GPAs. Between one-third (35.0%) and half (47.4%) of students in the two lowest GPA quartiles were high participators, compared with about one-fourth of students in the two highest GPA quartiles (25.0% and 26.3%). Thus, in small groups the relationship is negative, at least in these zero-order findings. For the plenary discussions, we see a classic inverted-V: There is only a five percentage-point difference between the number of high participators in the lowest and highest quartiles (12.5% vs. 17.6%). By contrast, students in the two middle quartiles are much more likely to participate frequently than are students at either extreme. In terms of overall differences between formats, participation in the small-group setting appears to be more equal (the data range 22.4 points between the highest percentage and the lowest) than in the full-class setting (the data range 29.2 points).

A multivariate analysis supports and clarifies the zero-order relationships displayed in figure 3. Using logistic regression, we regressed a binary high-participator variable (0 = low participator, 1 = high participator) against a set of dummy demographics: African American, Hispanic, and female. Inasmuch as the relationship between GPA and participation is nonlinear, especially in the full-class modality, GPA is represented by three dummies: mid-low, mid-high, and high (low GPA is the base category). We also included a control for political science track. At the time, political science majors could either enroll in an American Politics track, an International Relations/Comparative Politics track, or a pre-law track. For the first two tracks, all students were required to take at least two political theory courses. Pre-law students, political science minors, and majors in other fields had no such requirement but were able to enroll in the class. Students in the International Relations/Comparative Politics track are coded 1; students in all other tracks are coded zero. We ran the model separately for the full-class data and the small-groups data. Table 1 displays the results.

Virtually all of the independent variables show sharper discriminating power in the full-class model than in the small-groups model. Hispanics are significantly more likely to participate than are whites (the excluded category) or African Americans. Moreover, the previously discussed GPA pattern is now shown in statistically precise relief: While students in the two middle quartiles are between 6 and 10 times more likely to participate than are students in the lowest quartile, the highest GPA group is no more likely to participate than their cohorts in the lowest GPA group. Surprisingly, the International Relations/Comparative Politics track students participated more often in either format—small groups or large class—than students in any other track or degree program. This is an interesting finding given that the discussion topics did not

Format

	Full class			Small groups		
Student characteristic	Coeff.	Sig.	Odds ratio	Coeff.	Sig.	Odds ratio
African American	−19.187 (14607.6) \§	.999	0.000	.121 (.997)	.904	1.128
Hispanic	2.416** (1.055)	.022	11.197	.048 (.723)	.947	1.049
Female	−.416 (.734)	.571	0.660	−.953* (.538)	.077	0.386
GPA mid-low	1.800* (1.096)	.101	6.051	.622 (.727)	.393	1.862
GPA mid-high	2.338** (1.191)	.050	10.359	−.350 (.774)	.651	0.705
GPA high	1.075 (1.142)	.347	2.931	−.121 (.760)	.873	0.886
IR/Comparative	1.796** (.880)	.041	6.024	.076 (.580)	.895	1.079
Constant	−3.881		.021	−.408		0.665
Cox-Snell R 2		.215			.076	
Nagelkerke R 2		.319			.105	

Table 1. Who participates? Student characteristics and discussion participation, full class and small groups compared

Note: Dependent variable is dummy coded 1 for students who participated more than twice, 0 otherwise. Standard errors are in parentheses. §There were no high-participation African Americans in the full-class discussions, resulting in a large standard error in the full-class regression. This variable remains in the model, however, in order to enable a direct comparison with the small-group regression.
*p < .10 **p < .05.

concentrate on comparative or international topics. While we do not quite know what drives students in the international/comparative track to participate more (perhaps they are used to more active learning in other classes, for example), the significance of this variable disappears in the small-groups model. What is more, the full-class model performs well, returning pseudo-R squares of.215 (Cox-Snell) and.319 (Nagelkerke). This contrasts with the weakly performing small-groups model, with pseudo-R squares of.076 and.105.

Of course, if equality of participation is the pedagogical goal, then one would prefer models that perform poorly—models in which "nothing makes a difference" in predicting the dependent variable. With one key exception, that is what we see in the small-groups equation. As expected, neither racial/ethnic dummy returns a significant coefficient. Similarly, the effect of GPA washes out under control. To be sure, in keeping with the figure 3 pattern, the mid-low dummy has a positive coefficient while mid-high and high are negative, but none of these coefficients achieves statistical significance. Gender effects remain the only factor at odds with the pattern of nothingness: After controlling for all other variables in the model, women remain significantly less likely to be frequent participants in small-group discussions.

Discussion and Conclusion

Much of the pedagogical literature has established that discussions can foster student learning as students become actively engaged. Our study, aimed at evaluating the effects of different types of discussions in an upper-level political theory course, shows that student perceptions, by and large, follow this positive assessment of discussions. Small-group discussions, in particular, seem to stimulate the interest of the students and engage them with the material, but discussions even in the large lecture classroom have positive effects and raise student satisfaction. These findings are encouraging despite the limitations of the study: We were not able to control for the topic of discussion (perhaps some students were more inspired by some of the discussion topics than by others) nor for the fact that students might have reacted differently to the discussions as the semester progressed. Nonetheless, students appear to find discussions stimulating and enriching, especially in the small-group format.

Our findings have practical implications for teaching. Professors have the option to infuse lecture-based classes with active learning components that benefit students. This holds true even as class sizes increase in many colleges and universities, including in upper-level classes, and instructors interested in active learning strategies may wonder how to keep students engaged through discussions when the class size prohibits a seminar-like atmosphere. Our research demonstrates that students can receive the salutary effects of discussions even in larger classes through discussions with the entire class, but more so when the class is split up into smaller groups. In fact, smaller discussion groups overall appear to be more conducive to critical thinking and higher-order learning than all-class discussions. Small groups also appear to stimulate more equal discussion participation for students from different ethnic backgrounds and with a wider range of previous academic achievements. Thus, even brief discussion periods during which class is broken up into small groups can enrich a large, lecture-based class by fostering greater student engagement from students with different ethnic and academic backgrounds, can usefully infuse critical thinking elements, and can increase overall student satisfaction with class discussions. Discussions, then, appear to be a valuable tool to enrich the lecture-class experience even in larger classes.

Reprinted with permission from Philip H. Pollock, Kerstin Hamann, & Bruce M. Wilson. 2011. "Learning Through Discussions: Comparing the Benefits of Small-Group and Large-Class Settings." Journal of Political Science Education *7 (1). Taylor & Francis: 48-64. doi:10.1080/15512169.2011.539913.*

Notes

1. In line with earlier research that points to the potential pedagogical benefits for students to be derived from online learning, confirmed by later studies (e.g., Botsch and Botsch 2001; Hamann, Pollock, and Wilson 2009; Wilson, Pollock, and Hamann 2006, 2007), one week was designated to replace the face-to-face meeting with a mandatory online component, including a small-group online discussion. Here, we focus on analyzing the face-to-face discussions only. For a preliminary analysis of the online discussion in comparison with the face-to-face discussions, see Hamann, Pollock, and Wilson (2010). The analysis showed that even though the students by and large were less satisfied with the online discussion than with the face-to-face interactions, they still thought that the online modality provided useful opportunities to express thoughts, to rethink values, and to apply issues.

2. For a similar approach to assessing the effects of different types of discussions, see Windschitl (1999) or Ellis et al. (2004), who utilize surveys and interviews to assess what students thought they learned from discussions.

3. Participation in the study was voluntary for a few extra-credit points; students who chose not to participate were able to complete a different extra-credit assignment. Some students evaluated only some of the discussions.

References

Almond, Gabriel. 1991. "Capitalism and Democracy." *PS: Political Science & Politics* 24 (3): 467–474.

Bender, Tisha. 2003. *Discussion-Based Online Teaching to Enhance Student-Learning.* Sterling, VA: Stylus.

Bligh, Donald A. 2000. *What's the Use of Lectures?* San Francisco: Jossey-Bass.

Botsch, Carol S. and Botsch, Robert E. 2001. "Audiences and Outcomes in Online and Traditional American Government Classes: A Comparative Two-Year Case Study." *PS: Political Science & Politics* 34 (1): 135–141.

Brookfield, Stephen D. and Stephen Preskill. 2005. *Discussion as a Way of Teaching: Tools and Techniques for Democratic Classrooms*, 2nd ed. San Francisco: Joessey-Bass.

Buckley, Geoffrey L., Nancy R. Bain, April M. Luginbuhl, and Mary L. Dyer. 2004. "Adding an 'Active Learning' Component to a Large Lecture Course." *Journal of Geography* 103 (6): 231–237.

Burgan, Mary. 2006. "In Defense of Lecturing." *Change* 38 (6): 30–34.

Caspi, Avner, Eran Chajut, and Kelly Saporta. 2008. "Participation in Class and in Online Discussions: Gender Differences." *Computers & Education* 50: 718–724.

Clawson, Rosalee A., Rebecca E. Deen, and Zoe M. Oxley. 2002. "Online Discussion Across Three Universities: Student Participation and Pedagogy." *PS: Political Science & Politics* 35 (4): 713–718.

Cohen, Elizabeth G. 1994. "Restructuring the Classroom: Conditions for Productive Small Groups." *Review of Educational Research* 64 (1): 1–35.

Dallimore, Elise J., Julie H. Hertenstein, and Marjorie B. Platt. 2008. "Using Discussion Pedagogy to Enhance Oral and Written Communication Skills." *College Teaching* 56 (3): 163–172.

Davis, Todd M. and Patricia Hillman Murrell. 1993. *Turning Teaching into Learning: The Role of Student Responsibility in the Collegiate Experience.* ASHE-ERIC Higher Education Report No. 8. Washington, DC: The George Washington University, School of Education and Human Development.

Ellis, Robert A., Rafael Calvo, David Levy, and Kelvin Tan. 2004. "Learning through Discussions." *Higher Education Research and Development* 23 (1): 73–93.

Fay, Nicolas, Simon Garrod, and Jean Carletta. 2000. "Group Discussion as Interactive Dialogue or as Serial Monologue: The Influence of Group Size." *Psychological Science* 11 (6): 481–486.

Gall, Joyce P. and Meredith D. Gall. 1990. "Outcomes of the Discussion Method." In *Teaching and Learning Through Discussion: The Theory, Research and Practice of the Discussion Method.* Edited by William M. Wilen. Springfield, IL: Charles C Thomas.

Garside, Colleen. 1996. "Look Who's Talking: A Comparison of Lecture and Group Discussion Teaching Strategies in Developing Critical Thinking Skills." *Communication Education* 45 (3): 212–227.

Hamann, Kerstin, Philip H. Pollock, and Bruce M. Wilson. 2009. "Learning from 'Listening' to Peers in Online Political Science Classes." *Journal of Political Science Education* 5 (1): 1–11.

Hamann, Kerstin, Philip H. Pollock, and Bruce M. Wilson. 2010. "Teaching Theory through Discussion: Evaluating the Benefits of Discussion in Small-Group, Large-Class, and Online Environments." Paper presented at the APSA Teaching and Learning Conference, Philadelphia, PA.

Huerta, Juan Carlos. 2007. "Getting Active in the Large Lecture." *Journal of Political Science Education* 3 (3): 237–249.

Krentler, Kathleen A. and Laura A. Willis-Flurry. 2005. "Does Technology Enhance Actual Student Learning? The Case of Online Discussion Boards." *Journal of Education for Business* (July/August): 316–321.

Laurillard, Diana. 2002. *Rethinking University Teaching: A Conversational Framework for the Effective Use of Learning Technologies,* 2nd ed. London: Routledge.

Lowry, Paul Benjamin, Tom L. Roberts, Nicholas C. Romano, Jr., Paul D. Cheney, and Ross T. Hightower. 2006. "The Impact of Group Size and Social Presence on Small-Group Communication: Does Computer-Mediated Communication Make a Difference?" *Small Group Research* 37 (6): 631–661.

Marks, Michael P. 2008. "Fostering Scholarly Discussion and Critical Thinking in the Political Science Classroom." *Journal of Political Science Education* 4 (2): 205–224.

Mayo, Ashleigh, Manjula D. Sharma, and Derek A. Muller. 2009. "Qualitative Differences Between Learning Environments Using Videos in Small Groups and Whole Class Discussions: A Preliminary Study in Physics." *Research in Science Education* 39 (4): 477–493.

McCarthy, J. Patrick and Liam Anderson. 2000. "Active Learning Techniques Versus Traditional Teaching Styles: Two Experiments from History and Political Science." *Innovative Higher Education* 24 (4): 279–294.

Meyer, Katrina A. 2003. "Face-To-Face Versus Threaded Discussions: The Role of Time and Higher Order Thinking." *Journal of Asynchronous Learning Networks* 7: 55–65.

Nicol, David J. and Boyle, James T. 2003. "Peer Instruction versus Class-Wide Discussion in Large Classes: A Comparison of Two Interaction Methods in the Wired Classroom." *Studies in Higher Education* 28: 457–473.

Occhipinti, John D. 2003. "Active and Accountable: Teaching Comparative Politics Using Cooperative Team Learning." *PS: Political Science & Politics* 36 (1): 69–74.

Phillips, Rob. 2005. "Challenging the Primacy of Lectures: The Dissonance Between Theory and Practice in University Teaching." *Journal of University Teaching and Learning Practice* 2 (1): 1–12.

Pollock, Philip H., Kerstin Hamann, and Bruce M. Wilson. 2005. "Teaching and Learning Online: Assessing the Effects of Gender Context on Active Learning." *Journal of Political Science Education* 1 (1): 1–16.

Prince, Michael. 2004. "Does Active Learning Work? A Review of the Research." *Journal of Engineering Education* 93 (3): 223–232.

Rabow, Jerome, Michelle A. Charness, Johanna Kipperman, and Susan Radcliffe-Vasile. 1994. *William Fawcett Hill's Learning Through Discussion.* 3rd ed. Thousand Oaks, CA: Sage.

Tiene, Drew. 2000. "Online Discussions: A Survey of Advantages and Disadvantages Compared to Face-to-Face Discussions." *Journal of Educational Multimedia and Hypermedia* 9 (4): 371–384.

Wilen, William M. 1990. "Forms and Phases of Discussion." In *Teaching and Learning Through Discussion: The Theory, Research and Practice of the Discussion Method.* Edited by William M. Wilen. Springfield, IL: Charles C Thomas.

Wilson, Bruce M., Philip H. Pollock, and Kerstin Hamann. 2007. "Does Active Learning Enhance Learner Outcomes? Evidence from Discussion Participation in Online Classes." *Journal of Political Science Education* 3 (2): 131–142.

Wilson, Bruce M., Philip H. Pollock, and Kerstin Hamann. 2006. "Partial Online Instruction and Gender-Based Differences in Learning: A Quasi-Experimental Study of American Government." *PS: Political Science & Politics* 39 (2): 335–339.

Windschitl, Mark. 1999. "Using Small-Group Discussions in Science Lectures." *College Teaching* 47 (1): 23–28.

Supplementary Material

To view Appendix A: Standard Survey Questionnaire for Discussion Analysis, visit doi:10.10 80/15512169.2011.539913.

Appendix B: Data for Figures 1, 2, and 3

	Full Class	Small Groups
Participation	23.9	32.9
Express Thoughts	45.0	53.0
Know Others	30.0	42.0
Rethink Values	23.9	21.5
Understand Issue	53.7	53.7
Apply Issue	26.9	45.6
Raise Q	35.8	53.2
Stimulate Interest	47.8	59.5
Overall Sats.	53.7	70.9

Table B1. Data (Percentages) for Figure 1
Note: Ns: Full class (67); Small groups (79)

Frequency of Participation	Full Class	Small Groups
Not at all	3.0 (22)	3.2 (14)
1–2 times	2.8 (29)	3.8 (39)
>2 times	4.0 (16)	4.7 (26)

Table B2. Data (Means) for Figure 2
Note: Ns on which means are based are in parentheses

Student Characteristics		Full Class	Small Groups
Race/Ethnicity	White	26.2 (42)	30.8 (52)
	African American	00.0 (7)	33.3 (6)
	Hispanic	36.4 (11)	33.3 (15)
Gener	Male	27.5 (40)	42.9 (42)
	Female	18.5 (27)	21.6 (37)
GPA*	Low	12.5 (16)	35.0 (20)
	Mid-low	41.7 (12)	47.4 (19)
	Mid-high	31.6 (19)	25.0 (20)
	High	17.6 (17)	26.3 (19)

Table B3. Data (Percentages) for Figure 3
Note: Ns on which percentages are based are in parentheses. *Mean GPA (range) for each category: Low: 2.33 (1.67–2.67); Mid-low: 2.97 (2.71–3.18); Mid-high: 3.35 (3.19–3.52); High: 3.74 (3.55–4.00).

Born Digital: Integrating Media Technology in the Political Science Classroom

9

LINDA K. MANCILLAS
PETER W. BRUSOE

American colleges and universities have increased their investment in technology over the past decade. Marketing data research showed that in 2010–2011 higher education spent approximately $10.3 billion on information technology (Center for Digital Education 2013). This commitment includes ventures into smart classrooms, collaboratories, online courses, increasing the number and strength of Wi-Fi connections, creating centers integrating both teaching and technology, and investing in training and technological capacity building for faculty. One of the driving factors for the emphasis on technology is effective student education and learning outcomes. The Millennial generation, also known as generation@, the Netgeneration, or the iGeneration, expects technology. A 2012 Pew Research Internet survey revealed that 95% of all teenagers were online in some manner (Brenner 2012). Today, educators face a student population that has never been without the Internet and some scholars refer to this generation as "mobile natives" or "digital natives" (Palfrey and Gasser 2008). Most prominent among current technologies are social networking sites such as Facebook and Instagram and user-uploaded multimedia sites such as YouTube (Jones and Shao 2011). Moreover, the Pew Internet Project reveals that college students are much more likely to engage in instant messaging, downloading and sharing music files, and browsing for fun than other Americans. Additionally, college students use Internet and email to interact with their professors, to organize online study groups, to plan assignments and projects, and even to see if college library materials are available (Duggan and Smith 2013). To meet the needs and expectations of these students, academia must acknowledge that modes of learning and teaching are rapidly changing and outdated pedagogical methods need transformation (Jones and Shao 2011).

Consequently, a debate around technology has emerged. Some scholars argue that technology has negative effects on learning outcomes and claim cautionary warnings concerning Internet technology in the classroom (Olson and Clough 2001). They argue that, while technology can assist teaching and learning, it may not encourage deep conceptual understanding. Therefore, dependence on technologies in learning may not tap into the student's prior knowledge and may hinder their ability to grapple with new experiences. Accordingly, students may not learn to struggle with understanding new experiences and may not have the opportunity for reflection or the time to deal with how new ideas connect with old ones. By increasing classroom technologies, students may actually fail to develop cognitive and emotional effort, to cultivate diligence, or to build perseverance. The end result could be only catching students' attention at the peril of less rigorous study (Olson and Cough 2001; Postman 1985).

Technology literacy is a necessity for today's college students. Technology competency includes the ability to utilize computer hardware and software, discernment of ethical issues when online, the ability to engage in productive electronic communication, and using technology to successfully produce learning materials (Langer and Knefelkamp 2008). Therefore, educators must integrate technology into teaching and learning activities with systemic purpose to maximize potential learning outcomes (Schrum, Skeele, and Grant 2003). One of the missions of the college classroom should be geared towards producing better informed information consumers (Chandler and Gregory 2010). Additionally, online-related activities and learning should produce greater self-expression and confidence (Guillot Pearson 2011).

Subsequently, the prevailing sentiment insists that failure to utilize developing forms of information technology will place students at a disadvantage in the ever-changing digital world. However, few studies have shown a connection between increasing use of technology and improved student performance. "Does academic performance improve with increased use of technology?" This is the question our study attempts to answer. Our experimental design tests this question by measuring academic performance on a pre-and posttest assessment. Our study contributes to the literature by utilizing an assessment of basic political science knowledge that was administered at the beginning and at the end of the semester in 100-level American Government classes.

In our study, many different technologies were employed, including Blackboard. In addition, individual and group emails were sent and online examinations were taken with instant feedback on performance and automatic entry to the student's online grade book. Short videos, documentary files, Power Point and Prezi presentations, and other technologies were also utilized, and, in one lecture, the students used TurningPoint response pads. In every class, students viewed online news articles with discussion. With each of these technologies, varying degrees of discussions took place relating the content to the lesson. Students were also encouraged to do online research to further generate questions and knowledge. The goal of using this technology was to increase student engagement and participation, therefore improving the educational experience. Our research shows that rather than technology improving academic performance, the experimental group scored lower on the posttest than the control group.

Hypotheses and Research Design

To assess the effect of technology in the undergraduate college classroom, we conducted a simple pretest–posttest experiment. A general American government pretest was administered at the beginning of the semester and a posttest of the same concepts was given at the end of the semester. For our survey population, we used three sections of Introduction to American Government at a university in Washington, DC, of the 2010 fall semester, where a coauthor was teaching. The coauthors had received special technology training from the Center for Teaching Excellence (CTE). The CTE had a "Green Technology" certification that encouraged instructors to use technology services to decrease their carbon footprint. One author was also awarded the Hybrid Teaching Certification from her present institution and the Problem Driven Learning: Innovative & Informed Curricular Design Certificate of Training from another university.

While students could not be randomly assigned into the different sections, we feel reasonably confident of the randomness of our sample and of its external validity for three reasons:

1. Students selected their classes without advanced knowledge of the experiment or the level of technology that would be used.

2. All classes were held two days a week during the late morning or afternoon for approximately 90 minutes.

3. Each class was a regular course with no honor sections or residential learning communities. Although we had no way of knowing at the start of the experiment, all three classes had a good mixture of higher and lower performing students based on midterm and final exam performance.

We assigned each class to Experimental Group 1 (EG1), Experimental Group 2 (EG2), or the Control Group. Experimental Group 1 had mandatory assignments on Blackboard and online participation was required. Experimental Group 2 was given the option to participate in extra Internet-based work. The Control Group had fewer Blackboard assignments with minor online participation. The Web-based participation consisted of different questions based on the readings and class lectures. To promote computer and technology literacy, each Experimental Group 1 student was required to post two comments on each question by making an original comment or responding to another student's post. This group was also exposed to supplementary videos and other multimedia, such as documentaries and YouTube, and were offered additional assignments every third week. Electronic submission of two assignments and two examinations was required.

Experimental Group 2 had the option of participating in online discussions, as well as to view material on Blackboard. No extra credit was awarded for this participation so there was no significant participation. Half the class participated in an online discussion at some point during the semester. However, participation was sporadic with about 10% of the class demonstrating active engagement on a weekly basis. Electronic submission of two assignments and two examinations was required. Since the students were "born digital," the experiment was designed to show the amount of interest students would voluntarily show without being required to participate.

The Control Group did not have access to the required online discussions. Only an LCD projector was used for lecture notes and displayed relevant information for class discussions. Assignments and notices were posted on Blackboard and email was used for communicating with students. The structure of this class followed the more traditional model with reading assignments and lectures and included only two online assignments and two online exams.

Our experiment focused on exam performance of basic political science concepts. We expected that academic performance would improve during the semester as students were exposed to more topics with multiple instructional practices to help them better comprehend the material. Since the type of knowledge students acquire matters, we designed questions to address a variety of skill sets including application of political science concepts and factual recollection. Some questions assessed simple facts; others required some application of political science concepts. The third type of question is a variation on the fact-based question but revolved around the Constitution and the US legal system. These concepts and issues are often most complicated for students to understand.

Examples of fact-based questions are defining "agenda setting" and understanding that it is a competitive process or being able to recall the number of African American Supreme Court Justices. An analytical question required the student to apply logical knowledge to the subject. For example, can the student identify gay marriage as a wedge issue? For the legal questions, students had to know what the antiestablishment clause was and where it could be found, or which constitutional amendment granted women the right to vote.

We postulate that if technology makes a major difference in academic performance, the greatest gains would be on test performance in the experimental group (EG1), followed by the quasi-experimental group (EG2), and the least gain among the control group regardless of the institution. Therefore, our hypotheses are the following:

H1: Average of test scores (experiment group is greater than the average of test scores from the control group).

H2: Average on analytical questions (experiment group) is greater than the average on analytical questions (control group).

To develop a baseline of political science knowledge, we administered a 24-question pretest the first week of class (see appendix A). The assessment was administered in paper form and consisted of 20 multiple-choice questions and five identification questions. Four questions pertained to current events questions and the remaining questions covered American political history, political science concepts, and the law. The identification section examined knowledge on congressional leadership, on members of the Supreme Court, and on a current event.

During the last week of the 2010 fall semester, each class was administered a follow-up posttest. The identification questions were the same as the pretest's identification questions. We were compelled to add current event questions covering the 2010 midterm elections and recent proposals by the debt-reduction panel. Additionally, we considered student interest in political science with the expectation that those who are more interested would presumably score higher than less interested students on current event questions.

We designed four questions to capture interest in political science including the following:

1. Is political science your Major/Minor/Neither my major nor minor?

2. How many years of political science/civics did you take in High School?

   a. 1

   b. 2

   c. 3

   d. 4

3. On a scale of 1 to 5, where 1 is very interested and 5 is very uninterested, how interested are you in politics?

4. Please circle any of the activities in which you have engaged:

   a. Volunteered on campaign

   b. Contacted your Member of Congress or Senator

   c. Voted in an election

   d. Wrote a letter to the editor

The level of political science experience varied and most students were political science majors. However, the experimental group included a fair number of nonpolitical science majors and minors. In the experimental and quasi-experimental groups, 70% had a year of political science or civics. Forty-nine percent of the control group had only one year, while 30% had two years of political science education. The majority of the students in all classes responded that they were interested or very interested in politics. This was expected as Introduction to American Government was not a required class for nonmajors. Therefore, students self-selected into this class and majors and minors were naturally interested in political science.

Political Science	Section as a Raw Number			
	EG1	EG2	CG	Total
Major	14 (47%)	25 (66%)	25 (68%)	64 (61%)
Minor	2 (7%)	1 (3%)	8 (22%)	11 (10%)
Elective	14 (47%)	12 (32%)	0 (0%)	26 (25%)
1 year	21 (70%)	27 (71%)	18 (49%)	66 (63%)
2 years	3 (10%)	7 (18%)	11 (30%)	21 (20%)
3 years	2 (7%)	2 (5%)	4 (11%)	8 (8%)
4 years	3 (10%)	2 (5%)	3 (8%)	8 (8%)
5 years or more	1 (3%)	0 (0%)	0 (0%)	1 (1%)
Very interested	11 (37%)	15 (39%)	13 (35%)	39 (37%)
Interested	11 (37%)	7 (18%)	8 (22%)	26 (25%)
Neither interested nor disinterested	1 (3%)	7 (18%)	2 (5%)	10 (10%)
Disinterested	4 (13%)	4 (11%)	7 (19%)	15 (14%)
Very disinterested	3 (10%)	5 (13%)	6 (16%)	14 (13%)
Volunteered for a campaign	12 (40%)	17 (45%)	12 (32%)	41 (39%)
Contacted their Representative or Senator	20 (67%)	14 (37%)	19 (51%)	53 (50%)
Voted in an election	17 (57%)	12 (32%)	15 (41%)	44 (42%)
Wrote a letter to the editor	0 (0%)	0 (0%)	0 (0%)	0 (0%)
Posttest				
Major	10 (38%)	20 (56%)	23 (66%)	53 (55%)
Minor	4 (15%)	1 (3%)	0 (0%)	5 (5%)
Elective	11 (42%)	14 (39%)	12 (34%)	37 (38%)
Very interested	9 (35%)	11 (31%)	7 (20%)	27 (28%)
Interested	11 (42%)	19 (53%)	20 (57%)	50 (52%)
Neither interested nor disinterested	3 (12%)	1 (3%)	7 (20%)	11 (11%)
Disinterested	1 (4%)	1 (3%)	1 (3%)	3 (3%)
Very disinterested	1 (4%)	2 (6%)	0 (0%)	3 (3%)
Contacted their Representative or Senator	20 (67%)	18 (47%)	28 (76%)	66 (63%)
Voted in an election	14 (47%)	22 (58%)	19 (51%)	55 (52%)

Table 1. Engagement in Political Activity

Finally, the political activities varied from class to class with 30% to 45% of the students having volunteered on a political campaign. In the experimental group, two thirds had contacted their US senator or representative. Meanwhile, only a third in the quasi-experimental group and just about half in the control group had contacted their senator or representative. The percentage of students voting was low, however. For many of the students, the November 2010 election was the first time that they were old enough to vote. To comply with university regulations, we did not inquire about citizenship status. Table 1 reports the raw numbers of activities and the respective percentages with the posttest answers reproduced in the table. We did see an increase in voting and contacting members of Congress; however, that behavior increased across the board and is not limited to one group. We suspect that part of this is the effect of living in the nation's capital, visiting Capitol Hill, and voting as a function of students turning 18 years of age.

Primary Source of Information	Section as a Raw Number			
	EG1	EG2	CG	Total
Internet	15 (50%)	23 (61%)	19 (51%)	57 (54%)
Printed Newspaper	6 (20%)	4 (11%)	5 (14%)	15 (14%)
Radio	0 (0%)	1 (3%)	1 (3%)	2 (2%)
TV News	12 (40%)	10 (26%)	11 (30%)	33 (31%)
Hours on Internet by Day				
0–1.9 hours	6 (20%)	4 (11%)	1 (3%)	11 (10%)
2–4.9 hours	22 (73%)	31 (82%)	32 (86%)	85 (81%)
5–10 hours	1 (3%)	3 (8%)	4 (11%)	8 (8%)
More than 10 hours	0 (0%)	1 (3%)	0 (0%)	1 (1%)
Do you own any piece of the technology?				
iPod	24 (80%)	20 (53%)	31 (84%)	75 (71%)
SmartPhone	14 (47%)	16 (42%)	17 (46%)	47 (45%)
Laptop	27 (90%)	36 (95%)	36 (97%)	99 (94%)
Desktop	3 (10%)	0 (0%)	1 (3%)	4 (4%)
Do you watch or visit any of the following sites?				
CNN	21 (70%)	27 (71%)	28 (76%)	76 (72%)
MSNBC	13 (43%)	7 (18%)	7 (19%)	27 (26%)
FoxNews	5 (17%)	8 (21%)	7 (19%)	20 (19%)
Drudge Report	2 (7%)	0 (0%)	1 (3%)	3 (3%)
Politico	7 (23%)	3 (8%)	6 (16%)	16 (15%)
Anderson Cooper	10 (33%)	2 (5%)	11 (30%)	23 (22%)
Rachel Maddow	8 (27%)	8 (21%)	4 (11%)	20 (19%)
O'Reilly Factor	5 (17%)	5 (13%)	5 (14%)	15 (14%)
Morning Joe	4 (13%)	3 (8%)	1 (3%)	8 (8%)
Colbert Report	14 (47%)	18 (47%)	23 (62%)	55 (52%)
Daily Show	18 (60%)	22 (58%)	22 (59%)	62 (59%)
News Hour	4 (13%)	0 (0%)	1 (3%)	5 (5%)
Wolf Blitzer	7 (23%)	5 (13%)	10 (27%)	22 (21%)
Internet	20 (77%)	2 (67%)	25 (71%)	69 (71%)
Printed Newspaper	1 (4%)	2 (6%)	1 (3%)	4 (4%)
Radio	0 (0%)	1 (3%)	0 (0%)	1 (1%)
TV News	5 (19%)	9 (25%)	9 (26%)	23 (24%)
Hours on Internet by Day				
0–1.9 hours	0 (0%)	2 (6%)	2 (6%)	4 (4%)
2–4.9 hours	14 (54%)	18 (50%)	20 (57%)	52 (54%)
5–10 hours	4 (15%)	9 (25%)	8 (23%)	21 (22%)
More than 10 hours	7	6 (17%)	5 (14%)	18 (19%)

Table 2. Internet and Information Sources

Our final questions focused on the students' source of news information and their use of technology. Overwhelmingly, most of the students received their news information from the Internet, followed by television and printed newspaper. While CNN remains the staple of a college student's media consumption, *The Colbert Report* with Stephen Colbert, and *The Daily Show* with Jon Stewart were watched by over half of the students—more than any other news outlet. The low percentage of students receiving information from printed newspapers is not surprising. The students spent between two to four hours on the Internet per day. Almost every student owned a laptop, most of them had an iPod, and about half had a Smartphone (iPhone, Droid, etc.). A full summary of Internet and information sources is listed in table 2.

During the study, there was no change in the sources of news used by students as they did not begin watching different television shows or become avid newspaper readers. This is important because it ensures that there was no intervening force impacting their consumption of political news. Use of the Internet as a new source increased across all groups. In the control group and in the experimental group, Internet usage increased by 20%, while the quasi-experimental group's Internet usage increased only by 6%. At the beginning of the semester, only 3% of the quasi-experimental group reported spending 10 hours or more on the Internet. At the end of the semester, there was a 14% increase of time spent on the Internet by the control group and a 17% increase by the quasi-experimental group. However, the experimental group showed a 23% increase, reporting 10 hours or more per day spent on the Internet.

The results of our pretest and posttest are illuminating and are displayed in table 3. On the multiple-choice section, the average pretest score was in the middle-to-high sixties. We analyzed the results by type of question asked: factual question, application question, and legal/constitutional question.[1] On the pretest, the students scored significantly better on the fact-based questions. When students were asked to apply political science concepts, their scores decreased. This is important for measuring the difference in the type of knowledge achieved. We suspect that this may be symptomatic of the nature of high school education that emphasizes factual based questioning. On average, the control group performed better than the other two sections. This is also consistent with their in-class examinations where the control group performed better. We think that the improved academic performance of the control group was related to more years of political science education and more use of news sources.

Finally, the third set of questions were related to the US Constitution and American law. Students scored higher on this part of the assessment than on the application questions, but scored lower than on the fact-based questions. Overall, the lowest performing question was on campaign contributions. Most students incorrectly answered that *Citizens United v. FEC* overturned the individual contribution limits established by McCain-Feingold. We suspect that this parallels the rhetoric being used in the 2010 midterm elections and the lack of familiarity with campaign finance law. The best performing question was, "What did abolitionists oppose?" with 93% in the experimental group, 97% in the quasi-experimental group, and 100% in the control group answering correctly.

Based on our discussion of the nature of analytical questions and being able to correctly apply a concept, we tested for that skill. To facilitate this, three questions were revised to better assess the analytical portion of the questions. For example, rather than asking the number of African American Supreme Court Justices, we asked about the number of female Supreme Court Justices. This tested if students were able to identify the members of the US Supreme Court. It was striking how many students incorrectly answered this question. Several students were able to recall Justices Sotomayor, Kagan, Ginsberg, or O'Connor but underreported the number of female justices. In another instance, we asked about the requirements for a US Senator in lieu of being president. Again, several students selected the incorrect answer to this question.

Additionally, changes were made to the "best" and the "worst" scoring questions from the pretest. We took the abolitionist question and asked students to identify which one of the four

Test Section	Pretest				Posttest			
	EG1	EG2	CG	All	EG1	EG2	CG	All
Multiple-Choice Section:								
Average Score All Questions	64%	68%	68%	66.40%	71%	65%	71%	69%
Difference Between Pretest/Posttest	7%	−3%	3%	3%				
Average Score Fact Based Questions	71%	80%	78%	76.22%	55%	56%	59%	57%
Difference Between Pretest/Posttest	−16%	−24%	−19%	−19%				
Average Score Application Questions	52%	61%	56%	56.05%	68%	59%	55%	61%
Difference Between Pretest/Posttest	16%	−2%	−1%	5%				
Average Score Legal/Constitutional Questions	66%	64%	68%	66.02%	63%	61%	73%	66%
Difference Between Pretest/Posttest	−3%	−3%	5%	0%				
Identify Political Leaders								
Identified Pelosi As Speaker	87%	84%	86%	86%	77%	81%	88%	82%
Difference Between Pretest/Posttest	−10%	−3%	2%	−4%				
Identified Reid as Majority Leader	50%	47%	57%	51%	50%	53%	51%	51%
Difference Between Pretest/Posttest	0%	6%	−6%	0%				
Identified Boehner as Minority Leader	20%	26%	32%	26%	50%	64%	62%	59%
Difference Between Pretest/Posttest	30%	38%	30%	33%				
Current Events								
Identified Arizona/DADT	47%	47%	59%	51%	46%	31%	26%	34%
Difference Between Pretest/Posttest	−1%	−16%	−33%	−17%				
Identified some other state and issue	7%	0%	3%	3%		5%		5%
Difference Between Pretest/Posttest	−7%	5%	−3%	2%				
Total Current Issue	53%	47%	62%	54%	46%	36%	26%	36%
Difference Between Pretest/Posttest	−7%	−11%	−36%	−18%				

Table 3. Test Performance

historical figures was an abolitionist. Students did poorly on this question with only 33% of the quasi-experimental group, 44% of the experiment group, and 40% of the control group correctly naming John Brown as an abolitionist. Moreover, 50% of the experimental group, 45% of the control group, and 63% of the quasi-experimental group identified Stephen A. Douglas as an abolitionist. We suspect that they confused Senator Douglas and ardent abolitionist Frederick Douglass.

The class average increased from 64% to 71% on scores. In the second experimental group, the scores decreased from 68% to 65%. The control group showed an increase in performance from 68% to 71% on the scores.

In addition, student performance on political leaders varied greatly in the pretest with 85% of all students correctly identifying Nancy Pelosi as Speaker of the House.[2] Nearly half of the students correctly named Harry Reid as Senate Majority Leader. Less than a third of the students could recall that John Boehner was the House Republican Minority Leader. The posttest saw a decline in the number of experimental group students able to name the House Speaker as Nancy Pelosi. This decline was not present in the control group. Across the board, however, students were able to correctly identify John Boehner as the minority leader. We suspect that the recent election may have generated some confusion.

For the current events question, students were asked to identify which state was being sued by the federal government and over what issue. About half of the students were able to answer Arizona and the immigration bill, SB1170. While not the answer we were looking for, students offered California and the legalization of marijuana, as well as Virginia and the lawsuit by Attorney General Ken Cuccinelli over the health care law, and the FBI investigation of former Illinois Governor Rod Blagojevich. We included these answers on a separate line because they were factually correct and salient when this test was administered. The posttest group was asked to recall that the Department of Defense released a new report on "Don't Ask, Don't Tell." The experimental group and the quasi-experimental group did better on this question than the control group did.

Consistent with the literature on political information, the results on identifying the Supreme Court Justices were dismal. On average, students could identify only two members of the US Supreme Court. We expected them to be able to name the two newest judges on the court, Justices Sotomayor and Kagan, due to the large amount of media coverage concerning their appointments. We also expected that Justice Kagan would be well known, given her confirmation happened over summer. In keeping with our expectations, Sotomayor was the most easily identifiable justice. However, in the experimental group, Justice Kagan was the sixth most identifiable justice with Justice Scalia. In the quasi-experimental group, she was tied for third with Justice Scalia and Justice Alito, and in the control group she was tied for fifth with Justice Scalia. The posttest did show an improvement on recalling Supreme Court Justices. On average students actually improved the number of justices they could name.

General Findings

This study failed to show improved performance from the group with the highest amount of technology exposure. Student groups that were exposed to a lower amount of technology, in a more traditional classroom setting, improved on the posttest assessment of basic political science knowledge. Moreover, we conducted a difference-of-means test across the different groups to determine the difference between pretest and the posttest scores. We are not necessarily concerned about the direction of the relationship at the outset of our test. Therefore, a simple one-tailed test was conducted. The p value for comparing the Experimental Group 1 to the control group was .972. The p values for comparing the Experimental Group 2 to the control group was .589 while the comparison across experimental groups was at .8533. We tested this at standard deviations of 1, 2, and 3 and none were statistically significant. This limited finding is most likely due to the small class size population. With the understanding that the results are not statistically significant, we want to discuss what the findings could suggest.

We expected a positive difference for the high-technology group but found a slight difference that was not significant in the wrong direction. This revealed no evidence that technology improved learning outcomes. This could be due to the relatively small sample size of the class populations. With a class size of 30 in the first experimental group, 38 in the second experimental group, and 33 in the control group, this gives us a very small sample size and could be the reason for the lack of statistical significance.

For the practical application of political science concepts, we found that the technology group had the greatest gain on the application questions. Given that the combined larger dataset was not statistically significant and that we have less degrees of freedom, we did not conduct a difference-of-means test. Perhaps the exposure to technology, while not having a positive impact on fact-based questions, had a positive impact on the students' ability to analyze and synthesize information.

Therefore, we are forced to reject our hypotheses that technology leads to improved academic results. However, although not statistically significant, this study suggests that students in the groups that had the mandatory level of technology did do better on the application questions.

Limitations

There are several limitations to this study, including the external validity of the students, the rapid change in technology, and the need to measure technology exposure. First, the students at this university are already predisposed to interest in American government and political science. Therefore, their academic results may be biased and their level of political awareness may be positively skewed. It is also possible that students were taking other political science courses and were exposed to concepts that are not captured in this study. Another limitation is the evolving nature of technology. The technology we used in our experiment may already be outdated. However, we must also consider that that not all students have exposure and competency in using technology. For the born-digital natives, we should have a constantly evolving understanding of how technology fits into our students' daily lives. Due to the small class sample size, our findings were not statistically significant. A marginal improvement difference between the three groups was in the opposite direction of what we expected. We would like to conduct a new version of our survey using a larger study population.

Further Research

Technology in the classroom is used to display information, to increase access to information, to improve information sharing, and to better organize the course material with the expectation of facilitating and enhancing the learning experience. However, we found that technology is not a magic bullet to improve academic performance. In this research, it seems that technology can hinder academic performance. Still, we need to explore why academic performance was hampered. Perhaps students spent more time learning how to use the technology and that took time away from learning the content material. One of the dangers of teaching a generation that was born digital is that we assume that students know how to use the tools and to make the best decisions on how to use technology.

Moreover, current research maintains that the college classroom should focus on hands-on, experiential, project-based learning that is aligned with students' interests. These learning strategies help students produce content, analyze material and develop a deeper understanding of complicated topics (Alliance for Excellent Education 2012). The relationship between technology use, teacher roles, and instructional strategies is vital (Bielefeldt 2012). The International Society for Technology in Education (ISTE) Classroom Observation tool (ICOT), created by ISTE, involves several learning attributes related to this integration, such as small student groupings, teachers as facilitators or moderators, and continued exploration of technologies by teachers and students (Bielefeldt 2012).

Others suggest that instructors should be cognizant of the unique context in the digital media environment and to offer the opportunity for a participatory-based digital media culture that fosters innovation in the classroom (Herro 2015). This setting consists of "technology-mediated, social and cultural communities to share, support, and refine expertise" (Herro 2015, 118). One way to achieve this is for teachers to realize that digital tools shift their role from "teachers modeling technology" to "teachers facilitating learning" (Herro 2015, 119).

Consequently, research specialists in education assessment should develop easy-to-administer evaluation tools that would enable education systems to conduct longitude studies on the efficacy of specific types of classroom technology. As a future project, we would like to introduce other technology components, such as student response pads into the classroom setting, and to explore the difference in the learning outcomes between a class that had response pads and a class that did not. Another area of interest is gender differences in the preferences of technology devices and amount of time spent online. It is a common perception that women are less interested in politics than their male counterparts. It would be interesting to see if the easy access to political information is attracting more female participation. Technology plays a major role in the life of college students and it is vital that we continue to explore models of pedagogy that will enhance the learning process.

Conclusion

In attending political science conferences over the past few years, we have learned that current research reveals no significant improvements in student-learning outcomes with increased utilization of technology. A new model is needed to capture what is really occurring in the digital higher education classroom. We know that there are several unique features required to effectively utilize online/Internet/Web knowledge such as mastering quick access to all types of available information, learning to grasp keyword knowledge, developing the ability to filter through the abundance of sources and to recognize reliable sources, cultivating skills to synthesize, summarizing and managing big data, promoting deep conceptual learning and understanding of important and relevant material, and being able to connect all this to prior knowledge. The challenge is to create learning and assessment tools that will express efficiency in information technology combined with what is found on these pre- and posttest models.

Reprinted with permission from Linda K. Mancillas and Peter W. Brusoe. 2016. "Born Digital: Integrating Media Technology in the Political Science Classroom." Journal of Political Science Education *12 (4). Taylor & Francis: 375-386. doi:10.1080/15512169.2015.1096792*

Supplementary Material

To view Appendix A: Pre-Test, Appendix B: Media Survey, and Appendix C: Post-Test, visit doi:10.1080/15512169.2015.1096792.

Notes

1. Fact-based questions are 1, 2, 4, 7, 8, 13, and 20; Application Questions are 3, 14, 16, 17, and 18; Legal questions are 5, 6, 9, 11, 12, 15, and 19.
2. The questions were structured as a free response. Some students wrote Pelozzi, Peloski, Pellosi Reed, Weed, Boner, or Banner. Credit was given for these responses.

References

Alliance for Excellent Education. 2012. "The Nation's Schools Are Stepping up to Higher Standards." http://www.huffingtonpost.com/2012/11/15/alliance-for-excellent-edn2140129.html.

Bielefeldt, Talbort. 2012. "Guidance for Technology Decisions from Classroom Observation." *Journal of Research on Technology in Education* 44 (3): 205–223.

Brenner, Joan. 2012. *PEW Internet: Teens.* The Pew Research Center's Internet & American Life Project. http://www.pewinternet.org/Commentary/2012/ April/Pew-Internet-Teens.aspx.

Center for Digital Education. 2013. *Key Market Data, Higher Education.* http://www.centerdigitaled. com/research/.

Chandler, Cullen, and Alison Gregory. 2013. "Sleeping with the Enemy: Wikipedia in the College Classroom." *The History Teacher* 43 (2): 247–256.

Duggan, Maeve, and Aaron Smith. 2013. *Cell Internet Use 2013.* The Pew Research Center's Internet & American Life Project, Washington, DC: Pew Research Center. http://www.pewinternet.org/ Reports/2013/Cell-Internet/Summary-of-Findings.aspx.

Guillot Pearson, Nancy. 2011. "Classrooms that Discourage Plagiarism and Welcome Technology." *The English Journal* 100 (6): 54–59.

Herro, D. 2015. "Sustainable Innovations: Bringing Digital Media, Games and Emerging Technologies to the Classroom." *Theory into Practice* 54 (2): 117–127.

Jones, Christopher, and Binhus Shao. 2011. *The Net Generation and Digital Natives: Implications for Higher Education.* York, UK: Higher Education Academy. http://www.heacademy.ac.uk/assets/documents/ learningandtech/next-generation-and-digital-natives.pdf.

Langer, Arthur, and L. Lee Knefelkamp. 2008. "College Students' Technology Arc: A Model for Under-standing Progress." *Theory into Practice* 47 (3): 86–196.

Olson, Joanne, and Michael Clough. 2001. "Technology's Tendency to Undermine Serious Study: A Cautionary Note." *The Clearing House* 75 (1): 8–13.

Palfrey, John, and Urs Gasser. 2008. *Born Digital: Understanding the First Generation of Digital Natives.* New York: Basic Books.

Postman, Neil. 1985. *Amusing Ourselves to Death: Public Discourse in the Age of Show Business.* New York: Penguin.

Schrum, Lynne, Rosemary Skeele, and Michael Grant. 2003. "One College of Education's Effort to Infuse Technology: A Systemic Approach to Revisioning Teaching and Learning." *Journal of Research on Technology in Education* 35 (2): 256–271.

Conflict in the Classroom: Considering the Effects of Partisan Difference on Political Education

10

APRIL KELLY-WOESSNER
MATTHEW WOESSNER

F ew people would deny the important role that higher education plays in the development of civic values. According to Nie and Hillygus (2001), "[the] Amount of formal education is almost without exception the strongest factor in explaining what citizens do in politics and how they think about politics" (30). Although there are several possible explanations for the relationship between education levels and political engagement (Emler and Frazer 1999; Hillygus 2005), there is some recent evidence that enrollment in specific courses or participation in other curricular experiences may prepare students to be better citizens (Beaumont, Colby, Ehrlich, and Torney-Purta 2006; Hillygus 2005; Nie and Hillygus 2001).

The task of creating thoughtful, informed citizens out of apathetic undergraduates falls most directly on those of us in the field of political science. Like all educators, we want students to respond positively to our instruction and to exert meaningful effort in our courses. We hope that, as a result of taking our courses, students acquire a basic understanding of the workings of government and take a greater interest in the political process. Yet, one should not assume that, upon entering the college classroom, students simply absorb the information required to make them responsible, informed citizens. The extent to which college instruction translates into civic knowledge and political interest is likely to vary across students, teachers, and courses, depending on a wide range of variables.

Despite public pronouncements about the importance of the subject (Bennett and Bennett 2001; Carter and Elshtain 1997; Snyder 2001), political scientists have yet to devote significant attention to the study of political education in the college classroom. In the analysis that follows, we examine the effect that students' perceptions of a professor's partisanship have on educational outcomes. Specifically, we hypothesize that students respond more favorably to professors whose partisan orientations are similar to their own and that perceptions of political disagreement have negative effects on effort in the course, interest in the subject, learning of the material, and students' overall satisfaction with their experience.

Communication Across Lines of Political Difference

Political disagreement has long been heralded as the hallmark of democratic governance, essential to the creation of an informed citizenry (Fishkin 1991; Mill 1848). Exposure to people with dissonant viewpoints leads to recognition of the legitimate rationales for disagreement and increased tolerance of others (Benhabib 1996; Gutmann and Thompson 1996; Mutz 2002b; Mutz and Mondak 2006; Price, Cappella, and Nir 2002). Exposure to dissimilar views may also lead to greater cognitive deliberation, deeper reflection on one's own views, and greater confidence in ones' ability to participate in the political process (McLeod et al. 1999; Sotirovic and McLeod 2001).

Research in the field of social psychology, however, suggests that exposure to new perspectives does not necessarily result in thoughtful analysis. Rather, people are often motivated to arrive at particular conclusions and direct their thinking accordingly (Kunda 1990). According to Lundgen and Prislin (1998), the motivation to protect prior beliefs leads people to "deeper and more favorable elaboration of arguments supporting those attitudes than arguments opposing them." Across a variety of situations, research subjects claim to find arguments more compelling when those arguments are consistent with prior beliefs (Lord, Ross, and Lepper 1979; Miller, McHoskey, Bane, and Dowd 1993). When faced with arguments that challenge previously held positions, people tend to expose these arguments to greater scrutiny (Ditto and Lopez 1992; Edwards and Smith 1996; Lord et al. 1979) and counter argumentation (Lapinski and Boster 2001; Zuwerink and Devine 1996). In scrutinizing the argument, research subjects also question the credibility of the message source (Lapinski and Boster 2001; Lodge, Taber, and Galonsky 1999).

Logically, many of these findings could apply to the classroom. In the educational setting, such resistance to new information would be especially problematic. Professors frequently expose students to new ideas and concepts, hoping that students will integrate these new ideas into existing cognitive frameworks in order to refine their reasoning and to clarify their own value positions. The research cited above generates some doubt as to whether educators can accomplish this goal. Yet college students are different from other groups of people.

As Sears (1986) aptly argues, when compared to other groups of people, college students have weakly developed social and political attitudes, easily damaged self-esteem, and great obedience to authority. Although their uniqueness may mean that we cannot generalize research findings from this population to other groups of people, the reverse is also true. Studies based on other samples may not apply to college students. As such, it is important that we devote specific study to this group when examining the development of political interest and knowledge, especially as related to the goals of higher education.

The unique attributes of college students are not the only causes for concern when applying research findings to educational settings. Even if we were able to select a random group of individuals and place them in the college classroom, the environment itself is unique in ways that may affect the reception and processing of information. First, the information flows may be more one-sided than in other settings, given the professor's authority and expertise. Even if the professor actively encourages discussion in the classroom, students may be unwilling to argue against the professor's perspective. This may mean that the benefits of political dialog and open disagreement (Mill 1848) may not materialize in a classroom environment. On the other hand, Mutz and Martin (2001) find that, in some settings, mere exposure to dissonant arguments can promote awareness of opposing viewpoints, tolerance for others, and more thoughtful consideration of one's own positions. It is possible that exposure to different viewpoints in a classroom environment would produce similar results, even if the flow of information is relatively one-sided.

Second, the classroom environment is also different from other communication settings in that participants are directly accountable for the material presented. Although some courses may require only memorization of facts and multiple-choice responses, others require students to articulate and to defend positions. In these cases, students should be motivated to consider the strengths and weaknesses of competing arguments. Tetlock (1983) demonstrates the importance of accountability on information processing and retention, in an experimental situation, where subjects only need to offer some justification for their position. The level of accountably is arguably much higher in the educational setting, where students must not only defend positions but also earn grades based on the quality of their arguments.

Finally, in a nonacademic setting, people may simply choose to avoid information that challenges existing viewpoints (Frey 1986). Yet, once enrolled in a course, students are a captive audience. In order to earn good grades, they must attend class. It is possible that students mentally tune out when professors present viewpoints that challenge their own. However, we believe that this is also unlikely given the high level of accountability described above. If resistance to counterattitudinal information does occur, it is likely that students adopt cognitive resistance strategies, such as denigrating the source (Zuwerink and Devine 1996) or counterarguing (Rucker and Petty 2004). This means that students may attempt to discredit the information by ascribing negative attributes to the professor or by searching for evidence that allows them to justify preexisting beliefs and to challenge the credibility of the message source.

Based on previous research findings, educators have good reason to be concerned about students' assessments of their credibility. Students are more motivated to perform (Frymier and Thompson 1992; Martin, Chesebro, and Mottet 1997; Myers and Martin 2006) and report learning more when they deem their instructors to be highly credible (Johnson and Miller 2002; Teven and McCroskey 1997). Not only is source credibility related to the acquisition of knowledge, referred to as cognitive learning (Mottet and Beebe 2006), but it also has an influence on affective learning. Affective learning occurs when students develop an interest in the subject matter, become self-motivated to learn more and apply material outside of the classroom (Mottet and Beebe 2006). Hence, in political education, affective learning may be especially important since interest in politics is a primary goal of instruction.

Although political discussions across lines of difference may produce some positive social outcomes, we do not yet know whether this occurs in educational settings, which are unique for the reasons cited above. Additionally, there is some evidence to suggest that exposure to disagreement may actually have negative consequences. Ulbig and Funk (1999) find that, in order to avoid conflict, some people simply choose not to engage in political discussion with people who hold dissimilar views. Although some might argue that even unwelcome or forced exposure to conflict is good for democracy, Mutz (2002a) concludes that exposure to frequent political disagreement may cause some individuals to avoid politics altogether in an effort to maintain amicable social relationships. Yet students are a captive, accountable audience and are unable to avoid professors' messages. Accordingly, students who tend to disagree with their professors' political views may find it more difficult to develop positive student-faculty relationships. Exposure to unavoidable conflict may also affect students' general attitudes toward the course.

As people encounter new perspectives, their confidence in their own political judgments may begin to erode. One theory is that "exposure to those with political views different from one's own also creates greater ambivalence about political options, and thus makes it more difficult to take decisive political action" (Mutz 2002a, 851). Although Mutz actually finds little evidence for the ambivalence effect, her results are based on populations known to hold more stable attitudes than those of college students. Additionally, Mutz examines casual conversations among peers. We might expect that the high credibility of the college professor as an information source and the students' compliance to authority may contribute to the creation of ambivalence in an educational setting. It is unclear as to whether students believe they learn more from politically opposed professors or from like-minded professors. On one hand, exposure to new ideas should generate greater learning and deeper reflection of the issues. On the other hand, students whose views are consistently challenged may have less confidence in their own political knowledge at the end of the day.

In sum, we are simply unable to apply previous research findings to college students and cannot predict how they will respond to political disagreement in the classroom. In the analysis that follows, we offer the first empirical study of the question. While we are unable to complete an exhaustive examination of the subject in the course of one article, we do believe that our findings shed some light on a previously unexplored topic and will serve as a starting point for future research.

Research Design

To test the effects of partisanship on education, we constructed a student survey, designed to be administered near the end of the college semester. The survey, modeled largely on the Individual Development and Education Assessment[1] (IDEA) format, provides the student assessments of the course on a number of potentially relevant dimensions including: effort in the course, interest in the subject, self-reported learning, assessments of the course, and rating of the instructor. Unlike typical course evaluation surveys, the instrument also included a battery of questions asking students about their own partisan/ideological views, as well as the views of their instructor and classmates.

The instrument was field tested in the spring and fall of 2004 with three professors from the researchers' institutions. The field test produced a sample of nine courses and 140 students. Failing to identify any problems with the instrument, we distributed identical surveys with cooperating faculty in undergraduate political science courses nationwide.

In order to obtain a large and diverse sample of students, we contacted 200 political science instructors, randomly selected from the faculty directory of the American Political Science Association. We asked these individuals to participate in a study by having students in their undergraduate classes fill out supplemental year-end evaluation forms. Of those who responded to our request, 27 individual professors agreed to participate in the study, 16 indicated they were not teaching undergraduate courses, and 22 declined to participate outright. The remainder of the sample did not respond to the initial request. The final dataset consists of the original field test and the later national study, producing 1385 student surveys from 69 individual courses, taught by 30 instructors at 29 different colleges and universities in 18 states. This sample, taken from both private and public institutions, contains respondents in both upper and lower division political science courses, with an average class size of about 20 students.

In order to demonstrate the importance of party affiliation on students' experiences in the classroom, we first examine how perceptions of partisan difference correlate with other assessments of the course and of the instructor, including measures of the instructor's credibility. We then run a series of models to demonstrate that perceptions of partisan difference affect student efforts, interest in the course material, learning, and overall course evaluations, even after controlling for these other assessment measures.

Dependent Variables
Interest in Politics

Clearly, one of the goals of civic education is to combat political apathy and to promote political interest. Students who are interested in a subject are more likely to learn the material and to apply it outside of the classroom. We measure these gains in affective learning by asking students to indicate, on a five-point scale, the extent to which they agree or disagree with the statement that "Taking this course increased my interest in this subject."

Learning about Politics

We operate under the assumption that learning in a political science class produces gains in political knowledge. While enrollment may or may not improve scores on traditional five-item knowledge scales (Delli-Carpini and Keeter 1996), students in political science courses should gain some understanding of how government works. In order to assess gains in political knowledge, we ask students to rate their learning in the course, as compared to other courses.

Some readers may question the accuracy of students' self-reported learning scores. Although it may be the case that student assessments of learning are vulnerable to various biases, they are still valid measures of achievement. Research by Chesebro and McCroskey (2000) shows that students' reports of learning are correlated with objective performance indicators, such as performance on a recall test. The authors conclude that "students can report accurately on their own learning" (301).

However, even if one does not accept the assumption that students can accurately report on their own learning, students' impressions of their learning are equally as important, as a measure of improved efficacy. One's confidence in one's knowledge of politics is important in predicting political participation (Pollock 1983). Students may, in fact, learn more about politics from a professor with whom they disagree. However, as explained previously, disagreement may also serve to create ambivalence and to erode confidence in one's own positions. In this sense, objective gains in factual knowledge may not be enough to promote political participation. Citizens must also *believe* that they are knowledgeable about politics and capable of making informed political decisions.

Effort in the Course
According to the social accountability theory (Mutz 2002a), people withdraw from political discussion in order to avoid conflict. We hypothesize that students respond in a similar fashion to disagreement and will be less engaged in a course when they perceive their views to be in conflict with those of the professor. We measure course engagement by asking students to rate the truthfulness of the statement that "I put more effort into this course than most others I have taken."

Overall Student Satisfaction
In addition to the learning outcomes above, we also include general measures of student satisfaction. These include an overall rating of the course, an overall rating of the professor, and a measure of the likelihood that students would recommend the course to others. If students are like others and prefer to avoid disagreement (Ulbig and Funk 1999; Mutz 2002a), we should expect to see higher satisfaction scores associated with greater partisan agreement between student and professor.

Independent Variables
Source Credibility Variables
Source credibility has been defined as the degree to which a source is thought to "portray the real world truthfully" (Austin and Dong 1994), to be "knowledgeable or trustworthy" (Rogers and Storey 1987), or to be "accurate, fair, unbiased and trustworthy" (Yoon 2005). Although attempts to define source credibility appear to be largely consistent and to describe a general "believability" (McCroskey 1998, 80; Yoon 2005), researchers have taken different approaches to measure the concept. Early studies measured source credibility in terms of "trustworthiness" and "expertise" (Hovland, Janis, and Kelley 1953). More recently, researchers include additional measures of credibility, including perceptions of "caring/goodwill" (McCroskey and Teven 1999; McCroskey, Valencic, and Richmond 2004; Teven and McCroskey 1997). Drawing from this body of literature, we use three measures of source credibility: focusing on perceptions of the instructors' knowledge or expertise, their fairness or objectivity, and their caring for students.

Learning Environment
We included a number of control variables for factors in the student's experience that would, theoretically, affect educational outcomes and that may be related to the partisanship of the professor and/or the class. For example, the political orientations of professors and/or classmates may have some impact on classroom discussions, with significant political differences leading

to heated debates. Students may be responding not merely to the partisanship of the professor but rather to the general tone of the classroom discussion. We control for this possibility by including a variable that asks students to indicate how often heated discussions occurred in class. Similarly, we ask students to assess whether or not the professor worked to provide a comfortable learning environment for students. Professors who make a directed effort to reduce political tensions and to welcome different viewpoints may be able to mitigate the effects of partisanship on the educational outcome variables.

We include a control variable for students' ratings of their professor's interest in the subject. Presumably, enthusiastic instructors will generate more interest in the subject. It is possible that students will find professors of one party to be more passionate or enthusiastic than professors of the other party and will rate them higher on the interest scale. This may be due to noted differences in personality traits between Democrats and Republicans (Carney et al. 2006).

Additionally, we include a variable that measures whether the students perceived grading standards to be fair and unbiased. It is likely that students' complaints of bias in grading are related to the partisanship of the professor, with students indicating less fairness when their own political orientations differ from those of the professor. It is possible that this reflects a real bias in grading, with professors finding arguments to be more compelling when they support their own beliefs. However, it is also possible that poor students attempt to justify low scores by reasoning that the professor must be biased against their arguments. Hence, the direction of the relationship between partisanship and fair grading are unclear. Whatever the case, we suspect that the two are related and that both serve to influence the educational outcome variables.

Students' Ideological Perceptions

It is possible that people's ideological orientations are related to other personality characteristics. Hence, students may honestly find that liberal instructors behave differently in the classroom. Students may also base their assessments of professors' political views on classroom behaviors and personality traits. For example, compassionate professors may be more likely to be labeled as liberal Democrats. It is also possible that students' political orientations reflect personality differences and that liberals make better or worse students than do conservatives. Finally, the ideological orientations of classmates may shape the learning environment. It is possible that students will find classes more interesting when surrounded by liberal/conservative students. We control for all of these factors: rating of the professor's ideology, student's ideological self-placement, and perception of classmates' collective ideology.

Partisan Distance

We use students' perceptions of the partisan difference between themselves and their professors as a measure of exposure to divergent viewpoints in the classroom. We believe that perception of partisanship is a more reliable measure of a professor's communication than is one's actual partisanship. Many professors attempt to be politically neutral in the classroom or may even play devil's advocate and adopt controversial positions. However, it is reasonable to assume that students' perceptions of professors are based largely on what the professors say in the classroom. Therefore, students may perceive a very partisan professor to be a moderate if the professor communicates a balanced view of the material. We argue, as do others (Mutz 2002a), that even if perceptions are not entirely accurate, it is this perception of disagreement that influences people's response to political information.

We measure perception of political difference by asking students to rate their own party affiliation as well as that of their professors, each on a five-point scale. We then calculate the difference between the two, such that a score of "0" indicates that a student identifies with the same party placement as the one assigned to the professor, while a score of "1" indicates that a student is one position away from the professor on the five-point scale.[2]

Results/Discussion

Among the 30 professors in our survey, student perceptions varied considerably, with average partisan ratings assigned to each professor ranging from strong Democrat ($M = 1.28$, $SD = 0.53$; $n = 77$) to fairly strong Republican ($M = 4.5$, $SD = 0.95$; $n = 92$). Twenty-three (77%) of the professors in our survey had average scores that placed them towards the Democrats (mean < 3), while only six (20%) of the professors were considered by their students to lean towards the Republicans (mean > 3). One professor had a mean party score of 3.0, directly in the center of the scale. Our findings are consistent with results from a national study conducted by The Brookings Institute (2001), which found that 78% of political science professors consider themselves either Democrats or Independents who lean Democrat. Overall, most students believed that their partisan preferences differed from those of their professor. Only 33% of students felt that they had the same partisan disposition as their instructor. Approximately 30% of students perceived a one-unit difference, 19% perceived a two-unit difference, and 18% observed a gap larger than two units.

In order to understand the relationship between partisanship and educational outcomes, we first ran a series of simple correlations between the partisan distance variable and the other variables in the model. As expected, *partisan distance* correlates with two of the three source credibility variables (see table 1). As partisan distance increases, assessments of the professors' *caring* and *objectivity* decrease. Surprisingly, partisan distance appears to bear no relationship to ratings of professor *expertise*. The fact that the students' ratings of instructor expertise are not related to the partisan difference variable is, in retrospect, not surprising. Although people may attempt to discredit counterattitudinal information by denigrating the source, they are limited in their ability to do so by what Kunda (1990) refers to as the "illusion of objectivity." In other words, people's judgments are constrained by their need to construct justifications for the judgments that would be credible to an objective observer. The vast majority of students (87%) rate their instructors as "excellent" in terms of expertise, regardless of the instructors' politics. Only three students in the sample rated their instructor's knowledge of the material as "poor." In this regard, the educational setting may be quite different from other communication contexts. In casual settings, people may dismiss dissonant viewpoints as uninformed. However, in the educational setting, respondents appear to recognize the superior knowledge of the highly educated instructor.

Students are less constrained in their ability to discredit the professor through other measures. Students rate politically similar professors as more caring and more objective than those believed to hold opposing party loyalties. Although it is possible that professors genuinely care more for students of their own party, we believe that this is not the most parsimonious explanation for the observed relationship between political agreement and perceptions of caring. Caring is a very subjective measure and one not as tightly bound by the "illusion of objectivity" discussed previously. Therefore, we suspect that students are engaging in source derogation. The objectivity measure is a bit more complex. It may be the case that students are dismissing sources as "biased," merely in an effort to discount different perspectives. However, it is also possible that students whose views are similar to the professors are less prone to generate counterarguments and, therefore, less aware if the professor is only presenting one side of a debate. Either way, assessments of objectivity are likely to influence classroom dynamics in a number of ways, only some of which we are able to explore here.

Among the variables measuring the learning environment, partisan distance correlates with the view that the professor worked to provide a *comfortable learning environment*. As one might expect, the greater the political difference between student and professor, the lower the rating of the professor's efforts. There appears to be no relationship between partisan distance and the three other environmental controls. Political difference between professor and student has no bearing on *heated debate* or *professor's interest*. Most notably, we find no relationship between

		Partisan Distance	Expertise	Caring	Objectivity	Heated Debate	Comf. Learning	Prof's Interest
Source Credibility Variables	Expertise	−0.050						
	Caring	−0.078**	0.183***					
	Objectivity	−0.094***	0.129***	0.320***				
Learning Envnt.	Heated Debate	0.003	−0.006	0.061*	−0.090***			
	Comfortable Learning	−0.066*	0.174***	0.654***	0.368***	0.055*		
	Prof's Interest	−0.049	0.302***	0.355***	0.224***	0.018	0.313***	
	Graded Fairly	−0.054	0.191***	0.514***	0.309***	−0.028	0.512***	0.339***
Student's Ideological Perceptions	Professor's Ideology	0.033	0.005	−0.116***	0.088**	−0.065*	−0.096***	−0.028
	Ideological Self-Placement	0.244***	−0.022	0.025	0.013	−0.040	−0.032	−0.003
	Class Ideology	−0.083**	0.001	−0.025	0.002	0.108***	−0.021	−0.025

Table 1. Correlation Matrix for Independent Variables
Significant correlations shown with * < .05, ** < .01, *** < .001 using a two-tailed test.

partisan difference and *graded fairly*. This appears to undermine recent claims from political activists that liberal professors use grading to penalize conservative students. At the very least, it appears that this does not occur on a large scale or that, if it does, students are not aware of a bias.

Partisan distance is also correlated, as predicted, with the educational outcome variables and with the student satisfaction measures.[3] However, we examine these relationships in much more detail in tables 2 and 3. We include the source credibility, learning environment, and ideological perception variables as controls in models predicting educational outcomes and student satisfaction. It is likely that partisan difference works through some of these other variables, bearing indirectly on the dependent variables. However, for the sake of parsimony, we focus on direct effects and attempt to demonstrate that partisan difference matters in education, even when controlling for other measures of student experiences.

The results shown in tables 2 and 3 are based on a linear-mixed model rather than a standard multiple regression model. Standard Ordinary Least Squares (OLS) regression assumes that the error term is distributed uniformly among the observations. Presumably, students in each classroom share a common experience that may collectively influence their assessments of that experience. The results of the mixed model provide a more accurate portrait of the relationship between the independent and dependent variables by accounting for correlated errors among students within the same class. Students in the class share a number of commonalities, including their instructor, class size, and college. While it may also have been possible to model these other variations (teacher, college, class size, etc.) as the basis for the random effects, we believe that classroom is the most appropriate unit. Each classroom has a unique dynamic in addition to these factors, based on the students in the class and the material covered. Accordingly, in

Dependent variables

Independent variables (Fixed effects)		Interest	Learning	Effort
(Constant)		0.7131 (0.3845)	0.3904 (0.3067)	1.5777*** (0.3714)
Source Credibility	Expertise	0.2003*** (0.0596)	0.1851*** (0.0471)	0.0411 (0.0564)
	Caring	0.2007*** (0.0438)	0.1862*** (0.0348)	0.0804 (0.0418)
	Objectivity	−0.0207 (0.0391)	0.0716* (0.0312)	0.0997** (0.0374)
Learning Environment	Heated Debate	0.1436*** (0.0260)	0.0800*** (0.0207)	0.1290*** (0.0251)
	Comfortable Learning Environment	0.2391*** (0.0490)	0.1660*** (0.0389)	0.0644 (0.0465)
	Professor's Interest	0.0914 (0.0661)	0.1508** (0.0527)	0.0192 (0.0631)
	Graded Fairly	0.1890*** (0.0425)	0.1465*** (0.0338)	0.0294 (0.0405)
Student's Ideological Perceptions	Professor's Ideology	0.0312 (0.0346)	0.0475 (0.0278)	0.0386 (0.0340)
	Ideological Self-Placement	0.0006 (0.0273)	0.0266 (0.0218)	0.0443 (0.0261)
	Class Ideology	−0.0256 (0.0334)	0.0387 (0.0268)	0.0508 (0.0326)
Partisan Distance		−0.1061*** (0.0269)	−0.0510* (0.0215)	−0.0617* (0.0257)
n		1223	1227	1226

Table 2. Linear Mixed Models of Educational Outcomes
Classroom variation set as the basis for the "random effects" in the linear mix models. Standard errors listed in (parenthesis) where * < .05, ** < .01, *** < .001 with a two tailed-test.

all of the results that follow, classroom variations are set as the basis for the random effects in a linear mixed model.

Table 2 outlines the three main statistical models predicting educational outcomes: *interest*, *learning*, and *effort*. In addition to the main partisan-distance variable, the models include the three measures of source credibility, the learning-environment measures and students' ideological perceptions, including perception of *professor's ideology*, *ideological self-placement*, and perceptions of the overall *class ideology*.

Overall, the source-credibility variables behave in predictable ways. Greater expertise is positively correlated with both increased interest in the subject and self-assessed learning. Instructors who rate high on the caring scale tend to elicit more interest and learning from their students. Somewhat surprisingly, professors' objectivity scores are unrelated to students' interest in the subject. Still, instructors' objectivity is positively associated with students' learning and effort.

Students seem to respond favorably to classes that evolve into heated debates. Frequent debates are associated with higher levels of interest, more learning, and greater reported effort in the course. Additionally, students report more learning when they believe the professor shows strong interest in the course. Both fair grading practices and a professor's efforts to provide a comfortable learning environment are positively associated with more student interest and learning.

Looking to the partisan/ideological estimates, there are two important findings. First, at least as it applies to the educational outcomes, none of the three measures of ideology are statistically significant. Interest, learning, and effort are unrelated to perceptions of the professor's ideological disposition, perceptions of classmates' ideological leanings, and student's ideological self-placement. This means that personal ideology does not predict student outcomes, nor does it predict faculty skill. Second, the partisan distance variable is related to interest, learning, and effort. Consistent with the theory, a smaller partisan divide is associated with a higher degree of interest, more learning and greater effort on the part of the students. Thus, while political views do not appear important to education in and of themselves, perceptions of political disagreement do matter.

It is worth noting that the statistical link between partisan distance and assessments of interest, learning, and effort is quite persistent. Even with substantial changes to the model's overall specification, the relationships remain. The inclusion of the source credibility variables, measures of professorial interest, assessments of fairness, etc., lend credence to the notion that perception of a partisan divide exert a real and independent influence upon educational outcomes.

Table 3 illustrates the impact that perceived partisanship differences can have on the classroom experience on the whole. Utilizing the same set of independent variables, the results mirror those provided in table 2. To an even larger extent than before, the source credibility variables consistently predict satisfaction with the *professor* and the *course* overall. Students are also more likely to *recommend* the course to others if the professor is politically compatible. Interestingly enough, students appear to prefer courses that involve heated discussion, yet show no preference for the instructors of these courses. Professors who show greater interest in the subject matter tend to generate higher scores, both for themselves and the course as a whole. The instructor's ability to provide a comfortable learning environment is highly correlated with every measure of overall satisfaction.

In an interesting departure from the results in table 2, perceptions of the professor's ideology are positively correlated with overall satisfaction in the course, but it remains unrelated to the assessments of the instructor. This result suggests that courses taught by the most liberal of instructors tend to score lower than courses taught by their relatively conservative[4] counterparts. It is difficult to know what to make of this finding. The statistically significant correlation with the course, rather than the professor, may suggest that the most liberal faculty in political science are either teaching inherently less desirable courses or are designing courses in a manner that makes them less appealing to students.

Once again, consistent with the findings in table 2, the partisan distance variable is independently correlated with overall assessments of the course, overall assessments of the instructor, and the students' propensity to recommend the course to others. Students who believe they share their professor's partisan affiliation report a better overall experience in the classroom. It is worth noting that prior research has identified simple bivariate correlations between student-faculty partisan differences and students' overall classroom experience (Kelly-Woessner and Woessner 2006). However, absent greater statistical controls, the meaning of this relationship remained somewhat unclear. One might argue that the partisan distance variable acted as a proxy for expertise, fairness, or liberalism. However, when estimated in a model of this scope and complexity, table 2 provides additional evidence that political difference is, in and of itself, a factor in students' assessments of their classroom experience.

Lest researchers conclude that perceptions of a professor's politics is the most important determinate in a student's classroom experience, table 4 provides a list of all of the statistically significant standardized coefficients for each of the six aforementioned models. Within each model, a small arrow identifies the independent variable that exerts the greatest influence on the dependent variable.

Perhaps not surprisingly, the belief that a professor cares about students is, in all but two of the models, the best predictor overall; Caring matters most for student assessments of learning and the three overall satisfaction measures. In terms of sparking student interest, the professor's level of caring is virtually tied with whether one is providing a comfortable learning environ-

Dependent variables				
Independent variables (Fixed effects)		Course	Professor	Recommend
(Constant)		−0.7094* (0.3200)	−0.0678 (0.2508)	−0.7524*(0.3527)
Source Credibility	Expertise	0.1796*** (0.0492)	0.1488*** (0.0390)	−0.1937*** (0.0538)
	Caring	0.2610*** (0.0364)	0.3151*** (0.0287)	0.3013*** (0.0398)
	Objectivity	0.1203*** (0.0326)	0.1386*** (0.0257)	0.0624 (0.0357)
Learning Environment	Heated Debate	0.0972*** (0.0216)	0.0322 (0.0169)	0.1085*** (0.0238)
	Comfortable Learning Environment	0.2462*** (0.0406)	0.2226*** (0.0321)	0.2658*** (0.0444)
	Professor's Interest	0.1304* (0.0550)	0.0966* (0.0435)	0.1650**(0.0602)
	Graded Fairly	0.2326*** (0.0353)	0.2145*** (0.0279)	0.2239*** (0.0386)
Student's Ideological Perceptions	Professor's Ideology	0.0836** (0.0290)	0.0250 (0.0224)	0.0117 (0.0321)
	Ideological Self-Placement	0.0207 (0.0227)	0.0101 (0.0179)	0.0496* (0.0249)
	Class Ideology	0.0004 (0.0279)	0.0256 (0.0217)	0.0197 (0.0309)
Partisan Distance		−0.0877*** (0.0224)	−0.0646*** (0.0177)	−0.0839*** (0.0246)
n		1227	1226	1227

Table 3. Linear Mixed Models of Student Satisfaction Classroom variation set as the basis for the "random effects" in the linear mix models. Standard errors listed in (parenthesis) where * < .05, ** < .01, *** < .001 with a two tailed-test.

ment for students. After levels of caring, educational outcomes and classroom assessments are most significantly correlated with the professor providing a comfortable learning environment, grading fairly, and encouraging or allowing heated debate to occur.

Perceptions of partisan distance, while consistently useful as a predictor of the classroom experience, falls consistently into the second tier of independent variables. Along with the professor's expertise and interest in the subject, the partisan distance variable lags behind assessments of ability to provide a comfortable learning environment, caring for students, and grading fairly in shaping educational outcomes and classroom assessments overall.

Theoretically, the perception of a vast partisan divide between the student and the instructor could affect more than student interest, learning, and assessments of the course. When confronted with countervailing arguments, people often become close-minded, subjecting the new information to unreasonable scrutiny (Lapinski and Boster 2001; Zuwerink and Devine 1996) or even denigrating the credibility of the source (Lapinski and Boster 2001; Lodge, Taber, and Galonsky 1999). As such, a sense of political alienation might color student opinion of the instructor's credibility, affecting assessments of the professor's expertise, caring, and objectivity. Having established a credible link between appraisals of source credibility and educational outcomes, it is worth restating that these measures of source credibility are correlated with partisan distance. In other words, it is likely that there are indirect effects as well, with partisan distance affecting source credibility. Additionally, we observed that partisan distance is also correlated with perceptions that the professor provided a comfortable learning environment, the most important variable in predicting educational outcomes and student satisfaction. Accordingly, the overall impact of partisan difference (as outlined in tables 2 and 3) might be somewhat understated.

Conclusion

One of the benefits of higher education is that it exposes people to new perspectives. There are benefits to political disagreement, including greater tolerance for others and deeper understanding of different perspectives. However, our research demonstrates that there are also drawbacks to political differences in the classroom. College students appear to gain the most from their educational experiences when they are paired with professors who appear to hold political dispositions similar to their own.

If people are uncomfortable with political disagreement, as Mutz (2002a) and others (Ulbig and Funk 1999) suggest, we would expect to see less effort from students who believe they are politically opposed to their professor. Indeed, this appears to be the case. Students report more effort when the professor is a political ally. An instructor's level of caring for students and objectivity are both characteristics that could make disagreement in the classroom tolerable. Yet, students' perceptions of these traits are also correlated with partisan difference. Still, it is no surprise to see that instructors rated lower in these measures also generate less student effort. Hence, our research demonstrates that political disagreement fails to excite students in the classroom and may actually cause them to disengage.

Students also report that they learn more from professors of their own party. This is a somewhat surprising finding. Presumably, students would learn more from hearing new per-

Independent variables (Fixed effects)		Dependent variables					
		Interest	Learning	Effort	Course	Professor	Recommend
(Constant)							
Source Credibility	Expertise	0.087	0.097	–	0.082	0.076	0.082
	Caring	0.165	0.186*	–	0.227*	0.307*	0.242*
	Objectivity	–	0.063	0.083	0.093	0.120	–
Learning Envnt.	Heated Debate	0.148	0.100	0.152*	0.106	–	0.109
	Comfortable Learning Envnt.	0.172*	0.145	–	0.187	0.189	0.186
	Professor's Interest	–	0.080	–	0.060	0.050	0.070
	Graded Fairly	0.140	0.132	–	0.182	0.188	0.161
Student's Ideological Perceptions	Professor's Ideology	–	–	–	0.074	–	–
	Ideological Self-Placement	–	–	–	–	–	0.047
	Class Ideology	–	–	–	–	–	–
Partisan Distance		–0.102	–0.060	–0.068	–0.089	–0.074	–0.079

Table 4. Statistically Significant Standardized Coefficient (Linear Mixed Models) Classroom variation set as the basis for the "random effects" in the linear mix models. * denotes the variable with the highest standardized coefficient.

spectives. One possible explanation for our finding is that students simply deem divergent sources to be less credible and discount the information presented. Indeed, there is a connection between the source credibility variables and learning. However, the relationship between partisan difference and reported learning is significant, even when controlling for the source credibility variables. Accordingly, we cannot be certain that information discounting is sufficient to explain the relationship between learning and partisan difference. It is quite possible that students do actually learn more from politically disagreeable sources but are less confident in their knowledge. Students whose views are confirmed by the professor may learn little, but become more confident in their previously held positions. However, this too is troubling, since recognition of one's learning is an important component to political engagement. Students who are confident in their political knowledge should be more inclined to participate in the political process. If gains in factual knowledge and exposure to new perspectives serve to create ambivalence and to erode political confidence, than they may be counterproductive to the goal of fostering political engagement.

In addition to improving political knowledge, political education may also serve to increase students' interest in politics. Yet, if students are conflict avoidant, exposure to dissonant viewpoints may have negative ramifications. Our study shows that this does occur in the classroom. Students appear to be turned off—or at least less turned on—by disagreement and rate the course and professor accordingly. Unfortunately, lack of enthusiasm for the course or professor may have broader implications; Political disagreement may interfere with the ability of political scientists to promote interest in politics more generally.

Finally, it is important to note that our findings do not measure levels of student effort, learning, and political interest over time. Thus, we are not arguing that students who are exposed to dissonant viewpoints in the political science classroom do not learn, or that they do not develop some interest in politics. Rather, we merely conclude that these students gain less from the experience than do students who share their professors' political orientations. This is still an important finding and one that should inform discussion of political education for the purpose of promoting engaged, informed citizens.

Reprinted with permission from April Kelly-Woessner and Matthew Woessner. 2008. "Conflict in the Classroom: Considering the Effects of Partisan Difference on Political Education." Journal of Political Science Education *4(3). Taylor & Francis: 265-285. doi:10.1080/15512160802202789.*

Notes

1. The IDEA (Individual Development and Education Assessment) center is located at the University of Kansas. Further information about IDEA evaluations is available online at www.idea.ksu.edu/.

2. Owing to the very few instances in which a student placed oneself on one end of the partisan spectrum, and the faculty member the other, we combined distances of three and four units into one collapsed measure, with a value of "3" indicating partisan distance of three or more points.

3. Pearson's R correlations between the *partisan distance* and the six dependent variables are as follows: *interest*, $R = - 0.128$; *learning*, $R = - 0.099$; *effort*, $R = - 0.066$; *course* evaluations, $R = - 0.136$; *professor* evaluations, $R = - 0.146$; *recommend* the course to others, $R = - 0.116$. Each of the correlations is statistically significant at the .05 level.

4. We use the term "relatively conservative," as the sample of perceptions is largely skewed toward the left. Only 20% of the students identified their professor as conservative. The bulk of the observable variation (72%) occurs between "moderates" and "fairly liberal."

References

Austin, Erica Weintraub, and Qingwen Dong 1994. "Source v. Content Effects of Judgments of News Believability." *Journalism Quarterly* 71 (4): 973–983.

Beaumont, Elizabeth, Anne Colby, Thomas Ehrlich, and Judith Torney-Purta. 2006. "Promoting Political Competence and Engagement in College Students: An Empirical Study." *Journal of Political Science Education* 2 (3): 249–270.

Benhabib, Seyla. 1996. *Democracy and Difference.* Princeton: Princeton University Press.

Bennett, Stephen and Linda Bennett. 2001. "What Political Scientists Should Know about the Survey of First-Year Students in 2000." *PS: Political Science & Politics* 34: 295–299.

Brookings Institution. 2001. "National Survey on Government Endeavors." Prepared by Princeton Survey Research Associates. http://www.brook.edu/comm/reformwatch/rw04_surveydata.pdf.

Carney, D. R, J. T. Jost, & S. D. Gosling. "The Secret Lives of Liberals and Conservatives: Personality Profiles, Interaction Styles, and the Things they Leave Behind." *Political Psychology* 29 (6): 807–840.

Carter, Lief H. and Jean B. Elshtain. 1997. "Task Force on Civic Education Statement of Purpose." *PS: Political Science & Politics* 30 (4): 745.

Chesebro, Joseph L. and James C. McCroskey. 2000. "The Relationship between Students' Reports of Learning and their Actual Recall of Lecture Material: A Validity Test." *Communication Education* 49: 297–301.

Delli-Carpini, Michael and Scott Keeter. 1996. *What Americans Know About Politics and Why It Matters.* New Haven: Yale University Press.

Ditto, Peter H. and David F. Lopez. 1992. "Motivated Skepticism: Use of Differential Decision Criteria for Preferred and Nonpreferred Conclusions." *Journal of Personality and Social Psychology* 44: 20–33.

Edwards, Kari and Edward E. Smith. 1996. "A Disconfirmation Bias in the Evaluation of Arguments." *Journal of Personality and Social Psychology* 71: 5–24.

Emler, Nicholas and Elizabeth Frazer. 1999. "Politics: The Education Effect." *Oxford Review of Education* 25 (1&2): 251–273.

Fishkin, James S. 1991. *Democracy and Deliberation: New Directions for Democratic Reform.* New Haven: Yale University Press.

Frey, Dieter. 1986. "Recent Research on Selective Exposure to Information." In *Advances in Experimental Social Psychology.* Vol. 19. Edited by L. Berkowitz. New York: Academic Press, 41–80.

Frymier, Ann B. and C. A. Thompson. 1992. "Perceived Teacher Affinity-Seeking in Relation to Perceived Teacher Credibility." *Communication Education* 41: 388–399.

Gutmann, Amy, and Dennis Thompson. 1996. *Democracy and Disagreement.* Cambridge, MA: Harvard University Press.

Hillygus, D. Sunshine. 2005. "The Missing Link: Exploring the Relationship Between Higher Education and Political Engagement." *Political Behavior* 27 (1): 25–47.

Hovland, Carl I., Iving L. Janis, and Harold H. Kelley. 1953. *Communication and Persuasion.* New Haven, CT: Yale University Press.

Johnson, Scott D. and Ann N. Miller. 2002. "A Cross-Cultural Study of Immediacy, Credibility, and Learning in the US and Kenya." *Communication Education* 51: 280–292.

Kelly-Woessner, April and Matthew Woessner. 2006. "My Professor is a Partisan Hack: How Perceptions of a Professor's Political Views Affect Student Course Evaluations." *PS: Political Science & Politics* 39 (3): 495–501.

Kunda, Ziva. 1990. "The Case for Motivated Reasoning." *Psychological Bulletin* 108: 636–647.

Lapinski, Maria Knight, and Franklin J. Boster. 2001. "Modeling the Ego-Defensive Function of Attitudes." *Communication Monographs* 68: 314–324.

Lodge, Milton, Charles S. Taber, and Aron Galonsky. 1999. "The Political Consequences of Motivated Reasoning: Partisan Bias in Information Processing." Paper presented at the APSA Annual Meeting. Atlanta, Georgia.

Lord, Charles G, Lee Ross, and Mark R. Lepper. 1979. "Biased Assimilation and Attitude Polarization: The Effects of Prior Theories on Subsequently Considered Evidence." *Journal of Personality and Social Psychology* 37: 2098–2109.

Lundgren, Sharon R. and Radmila Prislin. 1998. "Motivated Cognitive Processing and Attitude Change.". *Personality and Social Psychology Bulletin* 24: 715–726.

Martin, Mathew M., Joseph L. Chesebro, and Timothy P. Mottet. 1997. "Students' Perceptions of Instructors' Socio-Communicative Style and the Influence on Instructor Credibility and Situational Motivation." *Communication Research Reports* 14: 431–440.

McCroskey. James A.. 1998. *An Introduction to Communication in the Classroom.* 2nd ed. Acton, MA: Tapestry Press.

McCroskey, James C. and Jason J. Teven. 1999. "Goodwill: A Reexamination of the Construct and its Measurement." *Communication Monographs* 66: 90–103.

McCroskey, James C., Kristin M. Valencic, and Virginia P. Richmond. 2004. "Toward a General Model of Instructional Communication.". *Communication Quarterly* 52: 197–210.

McLeod, Jack M., Dietram A. Scheufele, Patricia Moy, Edward M. Horowitz R. Lance Holbert, Weiwu Zhang, Stephen Zubric, and Jessica Zubric. 1999. "Understanding Deliberation: The Effects of Discussion Networks on Participation in a Public Forum." *Communication Research* 26: 743–774.

Mill, John Stuart. 1848. *Principles of Political Economy.* Boston.

Miller, Arthur G., John W. McHoskey Cynthia M. Bane, and Timothy G. Dowd. 1993. "The Attitude Polarization Phenomenon: Role of Response Measure, Attitude Extremity, and Behavioral Consequences of Reported Attitude Change. *Journal of Personality and Social Psychology* 64: 561–574.

Mottet, Timothy P. and Steven A. Beebe. 2006. "Foundations of Instructional Communication." In *Handbook of Instructional Communication: Rhetorical and Relational Perspectives.* Edited by Timothy P. Mottet, Virginia P. Richmond, and James C. McCroskey. New York: Allyn and Bacon, 3–32.

Mutz, Diana. 2002a. "The Consequences of Cross-Cutting Networks for Political Participation." *American Journal of Political Science* 46: 838–855.

Mutz, Diana. 2002b. "Cross-Cutting Social Networks: Testing Democratic Theory in Practice." *American Political Science Review* 96 (2): 111–126.

Mutz, Diana and Jeffery Mondak. 2006. "The Workplace as a Context for Cross-Cutting Political Discourse." *The Journal of Politics* 68 (1): 140–155.

Mutz, Diana C. and Paul S. Martin. 2001. "Facilitating Communication across Lines of Political Difference: The Role of Mass Media." *American Political Science Review* 95 (10): 97–114.

Myers, Scott A. and Matthew M. Martin. 2006. "Understanding the Source: Teacher Credibility and Aggressive Communication Traits." In *Handbook of Instructional Communication: Rhetorical and Relational Perspectives.* Edited by Timothy P. Mottet, Virginia P. Richmond, and James C. McCroskey. New York: Allyn and Bacon, 67–88.

Nie, Norman H. and D. Sunshine Hillygus. 2001. *Education and Civil Society.* New Haven, CT: Yale University.

Pollock, Philip H. 1983. "The Participatory Consequences of Internal and External Political Efficacy: A Research Note." *Western Political Quarterly* 36 (3): 400–409.

Price, Vincent, Joseph N. Cappella, and Lilach Nir. 2002. "Does Disagreement Contribute to More Deliberative Opinion?" *Political Communication* 19: 95–112.

Rogers, Everett M. and J. Douglas Storey. 1987. "Communications Campaigns." In *Handbook of Communication Science.* Edited by C. R. Berger and S. H. Chaffee. Newbury Park, CA: Sage Publications, 817–846.

Rucker, Derek D. and Richard E. Petty. 2004. "When Resistance is Futile: Consequences of Failed Counterarguing for Attitude Certainty." *Journal of Personality and Social Psychology* 86: 219–235.

Sears, David O. 1986. "College Sophomores in the Laboratory: Influences of a Narrow Data Base on Social Psychology's View of Human Nature." *Journal of Personality and Social Psychology* 51 (3): 515–530.

Snyder, R. Claire. 2001. "Should Political Science Have a Civic Mission? An Overview of the Historical Evidence." *PS: Political Science & Politics* 34 (2): 301–305.

Sotirovic, Mira and Jack M. McLeod. 2001. "Values, Communication Behavior, and Political Participation." *Political Communication* 18: 273–300.

Tetlock, Philip E. 1983. "Accountability and the Perseverance of First Impressions." *Social Psychology Quarterly* 46 (4): 285–292.

Teven, Jason J. and James C. McCroskey. 1997. "The Relationship of Perceived Teacher Caring with Student Learning and Teacher Evaluation." *Communication Education* 46: 1–9.

Ulbig, Stacy G. and Carolyn L. Funk. 1999. "Conflict Avoidance and Political Participation." *Political Behavior* 21 (3): 265–282.

Yoon, Youngmin. 2005. "Examining Journalists' Perceptions and News Coverage of Stem Cell and Cloning Organizations." *Journalism & Mass Communication Quarterly* 82 (2): 281–300.

Zuwerink, J. R. and P. G. Devine, 1996. "Attitude Importance and Resistance to Persuasion: It's Not Just the Thought that Counts." *Journal of Personality and Social Psychology* 70 (5): 931–944.

Part Three

Field Research

Fieldwork in Political Science: Introduction

11

ROSELYN HSUEH
FRANCESCA REFSUM JENSENIUS
AKASEMI NEWSOME

Whether the aim is to build theory or test hypotheses, junior and senior political scientists alike face problems collecting data in the field. Most field researchers have expectations of the challenges they will face, and also some training and preparation for addressing these challenges. Yet, in hindsight many wish they had been better prepared—both psychologically and logistically—for the difficulties they encountered. The central theme of this section of the book is precisely these data collection problems political scientists face in the field and how to deal with them.

The articles in this section of the book are written by young scholars—PhD candidates and recent PhDs—who have spent considerable time in the field collecting qualitative and quantitative data for their dissertations and book manuscripts. The separate perspectives presented here contextualize particular challenges of data collection in different world regions within the trajectory of single research projects. The articles trace the challenges that analysts faced in field sites as varied as China, Germany, India, Kazakhstan, and Mexico. Describing the realities of fieldwork and resourceful strategies for dealing with them, these articles shed new light on several practical aspects of fieldwork in political science. They also bring together scholars who used multiple research methods, thereby illuminating the difficulties encountered in political science fieldwork from diverse angles. For this reason, these vignettes are relevant to researchers focusing on both qualitative and quantitative research methods.

There have been a few notable forays into the topic of fieldwork in political science, such as the symposia in the 2006 *APSA Qualitative and Multi-Methods Research Newsletter*, the April 2009 issue of *PS: Political Science & Politics*, as well as Kapiszewski et al.'s forthcoming book *Fieldwork in Political Science*. However, there is still a limited literature on fieldwork in political science that offers more than generalized advice and provides sufficient examples of ways to address problems that occur during the early, middle, and final stages of research projects. Most of the existing writing on fieldwork focuses on the planning stage and the transition from a research design to a data collection strategy. More discussion is needed of the problems that occur while in the field, whether they involve the complex dilemmas researchers face when negotiating the politics of identity, developing relationships with informants and respondents, or thoughts on how fieldwork findings can lead to a fundamental change in the focus of a project.

Researcher Identity

The first challenge addressed by the articles concerns how a researcher's identity shapes and constrains the quality of the data that can be collected. While researchers' identities are examined widely in both the anthropological and sociological literatures, it is seldom addressed in political science. The contributions to this section of the book by Suzanne Scoggins and Vasundhara Sirnate capture the ways in which gender, age, ethnicity, and race influenced their experiences of gathering interview and participant observation data. Scoggins spent years studying and working in China before embarking on fieldwork for her research project about policing practices; nevertheless, her ability to implement her research design at first seemed limited by her status as an outsider: a Caucasian woman with no professional experience in policing. Scoggins shares how she transformed her outsider status from a liability into an asset by using strategies that maximized opportunities. Social networking, diverse and dynamic interview settings, and nuanced language use enabled her to navigate informant expectations and collect data on politically sensitive topics.

Sirnate details how she managed her identity as a female researcher of a particular class, caste, and ethnicity during her fieldwork studying counterinsurgency strategies in India. Working in a patriarchal society, she found that informants were often put off by her presence as a woman traveling without male companions. People she encountered expressed a range of behaviors including aggression, hostility, incomprehension, and protectiveness on meeting her. To protect herself and access informants, Sirnate actively tried to give the male insurgents and soldiers roles as her "friends, protectors, and guides." By strategically shaping her relationships with those she encountered, she was able to obtain more honest answers to her questions and avoid dangerous situations.

Collecting Quantitative Data

Political scientists often associate fieldwork with qualitative methods. But many original data-sets, particularly those in developing countries, are the product of painstaking data gathering using strategies not unfamiliar to qualitative researchers. The second challenge addressed by the articles in this section of the book is the collection of quantitative data and how techniques associated with qualitative research can be used to get hard-to-access quantitative data. Although texts about political science methodology often talk about the importance of gathering reliable quantitative data, the actual process of collecting this data is, for the most part, neglected in the literature. Francesca Refsum Jensenius and Christopher Chambers-Ju discuss this challenge in their articles. Quantitative data that was supposed to be publicly available was often hard to locate, not available across all cases or time periods, or asymmetric in that different types of data were available at different levels of analysis.

For her study on the effects of electoral quotas in India, Jensenius spent more than a year collecting data for quantitative datasets that would allow her to study the actions of politicians and capture local level overtime variation in the delivery of various public goods. The challenge lay in the many logistical and bureaucratic difficulties of accessing the necessary data, as well as in the uneven data quality. To access data and assess their quality, Jensenius tracked multiple data sources, related to gatekeepers and data managers with respect, patience, and persistence, and partnered with local colleagues. She found that discussions of gaining entry and building rapport—familiar to us in the ethnographic literature—were also highly relevant for her field-work collecting quantitative data.

Over a fifteen-month period, Chambers-Ju visited Colombia, Argentina, and Mexico to conduct research on the electoral participation of teachers' unions. He outlines the problems he encountered collecting different types of data and describes the "workarounds" he took to overcome them. He emphasizes the importance of sequencing research activities to minimize costs in time and resources and developing extensive relationships with data brokers such as gatekeepers, organic intellectuals, local academics, and veteran field researchers to gain access to data.

Recrafting a Research Project

Fieldwork often leads scholars to reassess or fundamentally shift their core research questions. The third set of problems addressed in this section of the book is how to recraft a research project when prior expectations about the field do not pan out. Researchers may find that their original research questions are not appropriate for the cases they have selected, or that their proposed data collection strategy is not viable. The articles by Akasemi Newsome and Jody LaPorte highlight how data collection in multiple field sites forced them to rethink the core questions and outcomes of interest in their dissertations. They explain how they successfully reformulated the scope and design of their research during their fieldwork, while also generating new hypotheses for their adjusted projects.

Newsome's initial research question was why European trade unions varied in their responses to immigration flows after World War II. However, during her fieldwork, she faced the challenge of collecting equivalent and sufficient data to effectively answer the original research question in Denmark, Germany, and the United Kingdom. After realizing it was impossible to consistently collect data across the multiple indicators she would need in all three of her country cases, she decided to change her outcome of interest to one more modest in scope. Newsome's article details the analytical process by which she retooled her dissertation research design, including changing some of her cases, to accommodate her new, narrower dependent variable of cross-ethnic cooperation in union protests. Key to transitioning to a new research question was the use of substantive and temporal thresholds at regular intervals while in the field.

Also challenged by empirical realities, LaPorte modified her research by broadening her initial, narrow question of the causes of protests in the post-Soviet regimes in Kazakhstan, Azerbaijan, and Belarus. In preparation for fieldwork, she created a database of several hundred protests across her cases between 2002 and 2004. She planned to locate politicians and protesters who had been active in the incidents comprising her dataset in the field. Her interviews with informants, however, revealed that the time period her database covered was exceptional; there were broader political dynamics that were more interesting. Adjusting her research questions, recording new observations in regular structured memos, frequently consulting her advisers, and switching cases enabled LaPorte to expand her project's scope to explaining variation in the governing strategies pursued by wealth-seeking rulers in post-Soviet countries.

Through this collection of articles, we offer lessons for both researchers who are undertaking fieldwork and those who are training others preparing to go to the field. A common thread in this section of the book is that challenges in the field are unpredictable and not easily anticipated in advance. To address them researchers must be creative and flexible. It is also important to keep in mind the ways in which a researcher's identity can both create problems and serve as the key to solving them. Conducting fieldwork can be made easier by sharing experiences and providing ideas on how to maximize research resources and take advantage of opportunities. These articles explicitly connect problems encountered on the ground to solutions.

A common thread in this section of the book is that challenges in the field are unpredictable and not easily anticipated in advance. To address them researchers must be creative and flexible.

In these articles, we chose to err on the side of specificity rather than general applicability to show multiple examples of how problems may unfold and to provide examples of a range of different solutions. The highlighted complexities and practical solutions each researcher brought to bear showcase the iterative and often inductive process that enables political scientists to discover interesting puzzles. By highlighting the challenges of data collection and showing some of the paths that can be taken to address them, we hope to embolden others to pursue the rigors and joys of fieldwork, an experience we all found to be mentally and physically demanding, but also intellectually stimulating, exciting, and fun.

Reprinted from Roselyn Hsueh, Francesca Refsum Jensenius, and Akasemi Newsome. 2014. "Fieldwork in Political Science: Encountering Challenges and Crafting Solutions: Introduction." PS: Political Science & Politics *47 (2). Cambridge University Press: 391–93. doi:10.1017/S1049096514000262.*

Acknowledgements

Authors presented papers in this section of the book (previously a symposium) in February and April 2013 workshops generously supported by the Department of Political Science and Institute of International Studies at the University of California, Berkeley. We gratefully acknowledge comments provided by Pradeep Chhibber, David Collier, Diana Kapiszewski, and Steven K. Vogel during preparation of these manuscripts.

Navigating Fieldwork as an Outsider: Observations from Interviewing Police Officers in China

12

Suzanne E. Scoggins

U nderstanding how foreign governments operate is a cornerstone of political science fieldwork, but gaining access to representatives of the security state is difficult, particularly for foreign researchers. Scholars seeking to break into this world must identify points of entry, navigate cultural differences, and establish trust with their interviewees. Such tasks are challenging for any researcher, but they are particularly daunting for newly minted PhD candidates, many of whom set out for the field without prior experience conducting large, independent research projects. My own fieldwork on the police bureaucracy in China was filled with challenges, many of which related to my status as an outsider to China's policing world. Perceptions of my identity as a Caucasian woman with no professional experience in policing influenced my research by imposing limitations on where I could go, whom I could interview, and what kind of responses I received. Yet outsider status also opened up opportunities. Although some potential interviewees were reluctant to speak with me, other respondents were curious about foreigners and happy to tell their story to someone who was willing to listen. Cultural differences are thus a double-edged sword, wielding opportunities as well as obstacles. Researchers can capitalize on the former by learning as much as possible about their area of interest and by remaining flexible when implementing fieldwork plans.

Scholars have addressed outsider status as it pertains to subjects and interviewers by focusing on power dynamics (Merriam et al. 2001), the blurred distinction between insider and outsider (Dwyer and Buckle 2009; Naples 1996), and the ability of outsiders to gain valuable information from insiders (Herod 1999). Such discussions draw on debates in anthropology regarding insider-outsider status and the accumulation of knowledge (Merton 1972). Yet there remains a dearth of practical advice on the subject for young scholars facing a steep learning curve when implementing research projects. In the following pages, I discuss the obstacles I confronted in the field and detail the strategies I employed to make use of my identity and ultimately gather enough data for my dissertation. My goal is to pull back the curtain on my own fieldwork experience to expose the gritty details. When viewed together with the other articles in this book, these experiences provide insight into the type of struggles that accompany fieldwork-focused research projects and give real-world examples of how to overcome them.

Methodology and Recalculatons

My standard paragraph on methodology is clear cut: between 2010 and 2013, I spent 21 months in mainland China interviewing police officers as part of my research on the relationship between local state stability and China's public security bureau. I conducted 103 in-depth interviews with 51 police officers at the county, municipal, provincial, and central levels in five cities across four provinces. I also interviewed a handful of individuals with detailed knowledge of police activities. Finally, I spent two months at the Chinese University of Hong Kong conducting archival research. Nothing in this account reveals the difficulties I faced in the field, although readers might have an idea if they did the math and realized that 103 interviews over 21 months is slightly more than one interview per week. Indeed, one of the biggest challenges I faced in the field was finding people who would talk to me.

To build a pool of interviewees, I started with people in my social network. Before entering graduate school, I spent years working and studying in Beijing and Hong Kong. During that time, I taught English to a group of police officers and made friends with people whose fathers, uncles, and cousins were on the force. These contacts were my entry point because the prospect of a foreigner walking into a randomly selected police station and asking if they could interview officers was out of the question in China. Although I knew the drawbacks of snowball sampling (Hoyle, Harris, and Judd 2002, 188–89) there was no other way to access this group of hard-to-reach individuals. As it turned out, problems of representativeness would be the least of my concerns once I began the research.

I went into the field with the mistaken impression that rolling a few snowballs would trigger an avalanche of contacts, but after four months of lackluster interviews and few leads I returned to California feeling dejected. Fortunately, my advisors were skeptical when I floated the idea of relying solely on archival research. Interviews were the cornerstone of my dissertation plan. Other scholars had approached Chinese policing from the top down, but I was interested in the lived experience of frontline officers. Since this information was not available in the archives, I needed to interview street-level cops or go back to the drawing board.

Having learned that outsiders have a hard time when they are picky, I returned to China with a new goal—find any police officer who would talk to me.[1] Before, I was selective, looking for police officers of a certain rank who were engaged in specific activities. Now I was asking every friend and acquaintance I knew to help me locate officers of any type. If my point of contact requested more guidance, I asked them to introduce me to someone they knew fairly well and who would be willing to talk. I also let them know that location did not matter; I would travel anywhere. Such changes to one's research plan require hard choices. My new recruitment strategy of "any officer, anywhere" meant I had to throw away my case selection plan of six bureaus in six specific provinces chosen on the basis of economic development.

Rethinking Interviews

Managing one's outsider status also means learning the unwritten rules of how to communi-cate with subjects. During the summer of 2009, I conducted predissertation field research and quickly realized my mistake of thinking I could walk into a police station at a prescheduled time to ask questions with my notebook in hand. Instead, I did interviews at large banquet tables, small tea houses, Western coffee shops, and, occasionally, loud karaoke lounges. I never set foot in anyone's office. I also learned to leave the notebook at home. During the early days of my predissertation fieldwork, I conducted all interviews by dutifully writing down everything my interviewees said. Often these meetings were tense, and my efforts to put the interviewee at ease were unsuccessful. Only later after I heard a professor describe her experiences in the field did I learn that the best way to make an official in China uncomfortable was to visually remind them that every word out of their mouth was being recorded. Getting rid of the note-book meant relinquishing control of the interview.[2] This approach forced me to set aside my list of predetermined questions and let the conversation go where it would. Often this mean-dering led to far more interesting information than I would have obtained with my original questions.[3] This experience was fundamentally different from the journalistic-style interviews I once conducted as an undergraduate, but it was a necessary adaptation because it encouraged more open conversation.

Establishing Trust

Foreign researchers often struggle with getting interviewees to trust them. In China, my status as a foreigner was off-putting to certain subjects. On more than one occasion, a contact would set up an interview that would later fall through because the interviewee got cold feet over speaking to a foreigner about their work. My pool of interviewees was thus limited, which un-doubtedly affected the type of information I obtained. Many potential interviewees, however, saw the chance to talk to a foreigner as a novel opportunity. This opened doors that might have otherwise remained closed, but it also shaped the conversation in ways that were not conducive to research. For some of my respondents, this was their first conversation with a foreigner, and many of the others had previously experienced only limited contact. Dinners thus began with questions about whether or not I could use chopsticks and what my family ate for dinner. I was happy to answer questions, but I also needed to steer the conversation back to topics related to my dissertation. Sometimes I accomplished this by discussing policing in America, which in turn encouraged them to compare those stories with their own experiences.

Developing a rapport that goes beyond cultural exchange and comparison is not easy, and appropriate strategies are often location-specific. In my experience, many interviewees revealed little about their work at the first meeting, so the opportunity of a second, third, or nth meeting was critical for obtaining information. Having a mutual acquaintance set up additional meetings helped, but success also hinged on my ability to develop more meaningful connections. With female or younger officers this was relatively easy because we shared commonalities. It was far more difficult to relate to older, male officers. With these men, I found the best way to erase barriers to communication was to enter their world of banquet dining. This meant learning the local region's toasting traditions and drinking *baijiu*, a Chinese liquor. My adventurous eating habits also helped. The common assumption is that foreigners are unwilling to eat certain foods considered delicacies in China, so almost all of my interviewees were pleased when I tried and enjoyed their local cuisine. After a few glasses of *baijiu* and a good meal, the cultural and gender differences became less relevant and conversation flowed more freely.

Managing Political Sensitivities

Unfortunately, all the food and drink in the world cannot erase political sensitivities. Because China remains a semiauthoritarian state, research on the inner-workings of the government is sensitive for foreign and domestic researchers alike. Although the situation has improved—the type of research I did would have been far more difficult just 10 years ago—barriers remain, and knowing the political limits of a research project is crucial for conserving time and energy. I tried to identify these limitations before going into the field, but I inevitably ran into a few surprises along the way.

Learning to Use Proper Terminology

As Jensenius' article (this book) demonstrates, researchers must pay careful attention to nuances in language. Without proper care, seemingly small differences in terminology can quickly derail an interview, particularly when a topic is politically sensitive. At my first fieldwork interview with the supervisor of a friend's cousin, I was told no questions were out of bounds, so I jumped in and inquired about protests in the area. The supervisor soon cut me off to tell me that Amer-icans know nothing of what happens in China. His stern lecture stretched at least 20 minutes, making it obvious I had committed some dreadful, unknown faux pas. Weeks later, the puzzle was solved when I recounted the story to a friend. Within minutes, she stopped to ask why I was using a particular word for protest. I had relied on my dictionary to find the word *kangyi*. *Kangyi* is indeed a word for protest, but it denotes large-scale social unrest. *Shangfang*, the politically correct word for smaller scale incidents, was the word I should have used.

The *kangyi* kerfuffle taught me a lesson about politically charged words. Dictionaries were of limited use for identifying sensitive words, which can fall in or out of favor quickly. To prevent future mistakes, I began having more conversations with Chinese friends about my research topic because they would correct me without recrimination. I also paid careful attention to how interviewees used language. Whenever I heard a new term or phrase, I made a note that it was probably safe to use in future interviews.

Additional Research Design Limitations

Finally, political sensitivities place limits on the types of research methodologies outsiders can employ. Although other academics have conducted survey research in China with success,[4] I abandoned hopes of a survey early in my prospectus planning because my project was sensitive and I feared I would be unable to find enough respondents to give honest answers. I was also concerned that my attempts to collect information would attract unwanted attention to my project. By deciding against survey research, I may have unnecessarily engaged in self-censorship, but as a young researcher with few connections and limited experience, I decided it was not worth the risk.

Observational research was also out of the question. I initially hoped to spend time in local stations and observe police activity without having to ask questions and receive answers that were inevitably filtered. This type of organic observation would have added depth to my research, but every officer with whom I spoke agreed it was too conspicuous to allow a foreigner to spend long periods of time in their station. I instead had to settle for observing police action on the street in a somewhat haphazard way. Although this was not an ideal solution, there was no alternative.

Political sensitivities even put strains on my interview data. I found I could talk to officers about certain politically sensitive topics in one city but not in another, making the data I collected across cities incongruent. I agonized over these discrepancies for almost a year, hoping the inconsistencies would even out with time and more interviews, but the differences in the information I obtained only widened. Eventually, I decided to reorganize my data around actors instead of field sites. This allowed me to make full use of the information I had obtained while simultaneously sidestepping comparability issues within cases.

Conclusions

The problems and strategies discussed herein are highly context specific and bound by both time and space, but some themes remain constant. Interview research requires time, patience, self-awareness, and a willingness to adapt. Foreign researchers do well to keep this in mind at all stages but especially when designing their project, applying for funding, and beginning their fieldwork. Adaptation is particularly important, because plans can go awry quickly. In these situations, paying attention to cultural cues such as language and local customs is just as important as recognizing the limits of your methodologies. Often this means making hard, project-altering decisions when you are thousands of miles away from your advisors, colleagues, and family.

Researchers should also keep in mind that personal identity cannot be divorced from their research project. The specific examples I give from my fieldwork in China illustrate how outsider status shaped my research design and interviews, but the influence of identity also crops up in more subtle ways. Importantly, our identities can affect what types of projects we pursue, how we frame our research, and what kinds of larger questions we ask. Consciously reflecting on where one stands in relation to one's interviewees, what some have called the insider-outsider continuum (Hellawell 2006), is the first step toward recognizing these influences. Good research depends on identifying limitations, planning projects accordingly, and acknowledging the influence of personal identity in our work.

Reprinted from Suzanne E. Scoggins. 2014. "Navigating Fieldwork as an Outsider: Observations from Interviewing Police Officers in China." PS: Political Science & Politics *47 (2). Cambridge University Press: 394–97. doi:10.1017/S1049096514000274.*

Notes
1. Solinger (2006) provides a detailed account of the how conversations with a wide variety of respondents can be used as an effective strategy when conducting fieldwork in China.
2. Converse and Schuman (1974) is a good resource for those who want to learn more about how to engage respondents when conducting in-depth interviews.
3. For a detailed discussion of how open-ended interviews improve research by enabling theory building, see O'Brien (2006).
4. Manion (2010) provides a comprehensive overview of survey research in China. See Tsai (2010) for a discussion on managing political sensitivities surrounding surveys.

References

Converse, Jean M., and Howard Schuman. 1974. *Conversations at Random: Survey Research as Interviewers See It.* New York: John Wiley.

Dwyer, Sonya C. and Jennifer L. Buckle. 2009. "The Space Between: On being an Insider-Outsider in Qualitative Research." *International Journal of Qualitative Methods* 8 (1): 54–63.

Hellawell, David. 2006. "Inside-Out: Analysis of the Insider-Outsider Concept as a Heuristic Device to Develop Reflexivity in Students doing Qualitative Research." *Teaching in Higher Education* 11 (4): 483–94.

Herod, Andrew. 1999. "Reflections on Interviewing Foreign Elites: Praxis, Positionality, Validity, and the Cult of the Insider." *Geoforum* 30: 313–27.

Hoyle, Rick H., Monica J. Harris, and Charles M. Judd. 2002. *Research Methods in Social Science.* 7th ed. Fort Worth, TX: Wadsworth.

Manion, Melanie. 2010. "A Survey of Research on Chinese Politics: What Have We Learned?" In *Chinese Politics: New Sources, Methods, and Field Strategies.* Edited by Allen Carlson, Mary Gallagher, Kenneth Lieberthal, and Melanie Manion. Cambridge: Cambridge University Press, 235–45.

Merriam, Sharan B., Juanita Johnson-Bailey, Ming-Yeh Lee, Youngwha Kee, Gabo Ntseane, and Mazanah Muhamad. 2001. "Power and Positionality: Negotiating Insider/Outsider Status Within and Across Cultures." *International Journal of Lifelong Education* 20 (5): 405–16.

Merton, Robert K. 1972. "Insiders and Outsiders: A Chapter in the Sociology of Knowledge." *American Journal of Sociology* 78 (1): 9–47.

Naples, Nancy A. 1996. "A Feminist Revisiting of the Insider/Outsider Debate: The 'Outsider Phenomenon' in Rural Iowa." *Quantitative Sociology* 19 (1): 83–106.

O'Brien, Kevin J. 2006. "Discovery, Research (Re)design, and Theory Building." In *Doing Fieldwork in China.* Edited by Maria Heimer and Stig Thøgersen. Honolulu: University of Hawaii Press, 27–41.

Solinger, Dorothy J. 2006. "Interviewing Chinese People: From High-Level Officials to the Unemployed." In *Doing Fieldwork in China.* Edited by Maria Heimer and Stig Thøgersen. Honolulu: University of Hawaii Press, 153–67.

Tsai, Lily L. 2010 "Quantitative Research and Issues of Political Sensitivity in Rural China." In *Chinese Politics: New Sources, Methods, and Field Strategies.* Edited by Allen Carlson, Mary Gallagher, Kenneth Lieberthal, and Melanie Manion. Cambridge: Cambridge University Press, 246–65.

Positionality, Personal Insecurity, and Female Empathy in Security Studies Research

13

VASUNDHARA SIRNATE

"He is a very nice man. There is no need to be scared or worried," said Mr. Saikia,[1] the driver of the car that was carrying me to a high-profile interviewee. He had correctly guessed that I was worried about an impending meeting with a known Assamese ex-insurgent. A woman traveling alone in India can confront a high level of personal risk, and, I was seeking interviews with people whom the state had routinely described as "terrorists," "insurgents," "militants," and "murderers."

I had been asked to be present at a predetermined pick-up location with instructions to bring no one else and not to mention this meeting to anyone. It was only 5 pm. We came to a halt before a white gate that was guarded by large men carrying assault rifles and holstered handguns. Three SUVs were parked outside in the dirt track that led to this dwelling.

I spent the next three hours interviewing a former militant of the United Liberation Front of Assam, who was one of its highest-ranking officials during the 1990s. He surrendered for personal and ideological reasons and was granted freedom from prosecution under the Government of India's surrender policy for insurgents. This pattern repeated itself a few more times over the next three years, and almost always involved all male environments with heavily armed men.

My research is on differential counterinsurgency strategies of the Indian state. Northeast India, the "field" for my project, is a region that has seen up to 56 tribal insurgent groups operating during the last 60 years with varying degrees of success and longevity. My task was to study perceptions of the Indian state about its insurgent adversaries. For this, I began by gaining access to local police and paramilitary organizations that were heavily engaged in counterinsurgency. I documented their interviews and the small bits of information they provided about how insurgencies are conducted.

I conducted fieldwork in northeast India[2] and in central India between 2008 and 2011. In northeast India levels of state violence and insurgent violence have been consistently high for six decades. Civilian and security forces casualties have been high as well, and despite transparent electoral processes, people remain suspicious of the Indian state. Socially, the landscape consists of hundreds of tribal and subtribal groups, and racially, most of these tribes look more East Asian and Southeast Asian than the typical South Asian, and practice different religions.

To broaden the scope of my study, I also began studying the Indian state's counterinsurgency response to the tribal Maoists that operate in Chhattisgarh state. These responses included the raising of a private armed tribal militia called the *Salwa Judum*, which was later declared unconstitutional by the Indian Supreme Court.[3] I was in Chhattisgarh to study subcontracted counterinsurgency campaigns. I conducted 120 interviews with counterinsurgency personnel, surrendered and current militants, journalists, academics, local bureaucrats, local economic and political elites, students, and other people sympathetic to insurgencies in their areas.

Some of the articles in this book highlight the difficulty in gaining access to communities, such as in China (Scoggins), or in collecting quantitative data (Jensenius). I relied more on my training as a journalist, than on my methods training, to gain access to communities. In every location, I contacted the bureau chiefs and stringers of news channels and local papers and presented them with my credentials. This way, I also obtained some very sensitive interviews, which were given confidentially. When people heard that I had written for some Indian newspapers and magazines, they were more likely to help and more willing to talk. I presented them with the plan of my research and the main questions I was trying to answer. Some even made suggestions on my project proposal.

Although I was conducting fieldwork technically in my own country, I was unprepared for the linguistic, religious, and racial diversity I saw. The tight-knit tribal communities meant that if I showed up in one place, most people knew what I was doing by the end of the week. This made it easier to get interviews.

Political Science and the "Field"

Political science teaches us to see a particular geographical region as the "field," construed as a cluster of measurable independent and dependent variables. The people I was studying were political actors; their strategies and political decisions and competing rationales would become the bulwark of a massive dissertation on Indian counterinsurgency. These individuals ceased to be actors, data points or sound-bytes to me. They become friends, protectors, and guides.

The field is a constantly evolving, dynamic, and unpredictable universe. Qualitative investigations into the field are movements through social spaces that are designed and redesigned as they are moved through by a researcher (Tewksbury and Gagné 1997). The field offers several challenges to the best research designs, and often research projects are altered beyond recognition.

Anthropologists and sociologists have written at length about positionality (Chacko 2004; Sultana 2007), insider/outsider status (Sherif 2001), buy-ins into different communities (especially stigmatized ones), and status similarity between the researcher and the researched (Tewksbury and Gagné 1997). Such writing that focuses on the trials and triumphs of fieldwork also rests on the intensely personal experiences that fieldwork offers researchers.

No two researchers have the exact same fieldwork experiences because no two researchers are the same. The researcher's identity leads to the calibration of fieldwork experiences that can be fraught with tension if, for instance, the researcher studies a stigmatized community and cannot show empathy (Tewksbury and Gagné 1997) or it can smooth the course of fieldwork if the researcher shares some status similarity with the researched.

Positionality is the relative position of an individual vis-à-vis others, or, how an individual is situated in society in terms of class, caste, gender, ethnic identity, sexual orientation, and so forth (Chacko 2004; Katz 1994; Mohanty 1988). A researcher's positionality has some effect on the answers she gets.[4]

Identity and Positionality

Positionality is often a proxy for relations of power. Some people are more equal than others, and most societies work on this premise. In this context, when researchers proceed into a different geolocation to study political outcomes and processes, they bring a set of competing identities, which interact with the identities of people in the field creating several social and ethical dynamics that often inform research projects. Positionality also has an effect on the personality of the researcher because it often means moving from a position of relative power to one of disempowerment or one where there is less mobility. For female researchers, it could involve moving from a relatively permissive social environment to one where women's clothing, movement, and behavior is closely monitored (Sherif 2001). The opposite is also possible. White male researchers are reported to have an easier time studying closed societies than, for instance, a female researcher of any race (Tewksbury and Gagné 1997).

These situational permutations of the self/other, insider/outsider, gender, caste and/or race dynamics of the researcher while doing fieldwork inform the researcher's project and the access, acceptability, and answers she gets. This situation has led some scholars to argue for the "management of the fieldwork" identity, by revealing less or more information to make the researcher more socially acceptable (Tewksbury and Gagné 1997).

The management of fieldwork identity becomes important because the basis of any relationship between the researcher and the researched in qualitative research projects rests on the perceptions that each has about the other. These perceptions are amplified by interpretations of others' behavior. For instance, a researcher's ability/inability to speak the local language can facilitate access or impede it. Many researchers can often manipulate self-presentation to get a more credible buy-in into a community, often a stigmatized one.

"Don't You Get Scared While Doing All This?" Managing Being Female in Security Studies Research in India

Little discussion exists about the experience of female researchers who conduct research in conflict zones and work directly with actual conflict actors. Women who study security are aware that this field of research is still shaped by male researchers and often abide by high degrees of professional standards. They often do not articulate gender issues they face in the field for fear of being seen as weak-kneed by their colleagues.

During three years of fieldwork, I was exposed to personal insecurity, sometimes had my ideas put down by men or "mansplained" some very obvious issues. I recount here a few instances of how I managed fieldwork identity to enhance my personal security by reducing the risk of predatory behavior and gain the trust of people who were uncomfortable with talking to female outsiders.

Chhattisgarh, India: Negotiating the Limits of Personal Independence

Two armed men of the Border Security Force (BSF) were driving me to the Counterinsurgency and Jungle Warfare College in a Maoist dominated district called Kanker, in Chhattisgarh state in January 2011. Our vehicle was a white SUV with fake license plates. It was a four-hour drive between my base in Raipur city and Kanker. There were no stops on the way and we drove as fast as possible for security reasons. The fake license plates and civilian make of the SUV were to ensure that no Maoists attacked the vehicle. Misdirection was the key to survival for the BSF officers.

As an Indian woman, from an upper-caste background, operating under the protection of the BSF, I was supposed to play by the rules that govern Indian women: no skin showing, no unnecessary chatter and familiarity (often called fraternizing by the Indian military men). I was dressed traditionally and spoke little although I knew I could get come candid commentary on this four-hour nonstop ride. Finally one of the escorts, whose assault rifle rattled at his feet, broke the silence and said, "Madam, don't you get scared while doing all this?"

I thought about this for a moment. Through the three years I had traveled alone in conflict zones, many men had chosen bemusement or predation as a form of response to a single woman in her late 20s trying to, in their mind, meddle in the affairs of men. I wondered if this was an earnest question born out of curiosity, or if this was some sort of entry into a session where I would be warned about "girls like me" traveling alone. Given the South Asian context, where working women are routinely seen as lacking in "character" by different groups of men, I heard these warnings several times from various men *and* women.

I said quietly, "If people like you are along, I have no reason to be afraid." In this response I had put the onus of protection and responsibility on the men who accompanied me. I was managing my identity through careful sartorial decisions and minimum speech. My response to their question broke the ice. They felt more powerful. I had talked to them in Hindi, assumed the role of someone who needed protection (a very feminine role in India), and the BSF men were suddenly talking about the Maoists with a strange amount of sympathy, albeit, reducing the Maoists to primitive tribals with no sense of politics.

I offered honest details when quizzed and showed interest in their families. This allowed me to carry the tag of being a "homely girl." After half an hour, I shifted the discussion to the operations of the Maoists and what I should expect from the counterinsurgency school. Another hour later, I was being referred to as *didi*, which means "elder sister."

I had, in my mind, successfully managed being seen as "respectable." Assuming a traditional Indian woman's role was a tough matter personally because it involved giving up an independent identity and assuming the mantle of tradition under which the rules that govern Indian women can be quite severe and disempowering. I had made a simple calculation: I would gain no cooperation from the men if I defied their perception of how Indian women should behave. I was already defying it by being a single woman, traveling alone, without a brother, father, uncle, husband. I didn't need to push that image any further.

Other female researchers working in middle-eastern countries have faced similar dilemmas. However, the crucial thing female researchers report is that choice of dress and capacity to manage and manipulate personal identity sends signals that are interpreted by people in the field (Sherif 2001). As researchers, this can raise ethical dilemmas. If we want honest answers from interviewees to very personal questions that we pose and if we are recording very personal insights of the people we study, are we unethical in manipulating our fieldwork identities?

I think about this in terms of access and security. For me, my personal security was paramount. I needed the men to feel responsible for my security, and I had to earn my own safety from them. Translating the researcher-researched dynamic into one that was a more familial one, where I was a "sister" and they my *bhaisaabs* or brothers, achieved both.

Meghalaya, India: On Being Given an Identity

In November 2008, I arrived in the northeastern state of Meghalaya, home to four active insurgent groups. I was aware of the extent of disaffection many groups in the region felt toward the Indian state and how they had a natural tendency to distrust anyone from what they called "mainland" India. For the previous two months, however, I had lived in Guwahati, in Assam, where many Assamese still thought of themselves as Indian. So I was surprised when I found that in Meghalaya I had a new identity: a "mainlander."[5]

A mainlander was an Indian who did not possess northeastern racial characteristics, spoke Hindi or some affiliated language, watched Bollywood movies, and did not tolerate separatism of any kind. Mainlander was code for "unsympathetic outsider." I was marked for exclusion. I decided that to accept the label but present myself as an empathetic outsider would be the best strategy to overcome hurdles placed by lack of access. As far as I could tell, the problem with my position was that I was seen as someone who could not understand tribal society, was of the wrong race and religion, and *must* be sympathetic to the Indian state project.

My first brush with the antagonism against mainlanders came during an interview I did with a local student leader of an exclusivist group. My interviewee, Mr. L., started the interview in English saying, "Our entire movement was directed against people like you. We wanted to drive you guys away". In Meghalaya the local Khasi tribe held a long-standing economic grievance against Hindu merchants from the mainland. In the 1980s the Khasi launched a massive political agitation to drive away Marwari Hindu traders. This movement was initially led by students of the Khasi Students Union, but soon there were other similar groups that mushroomed (Sirnate

2009). Mr. L. belonged to one such associated group.

The line was delivered with much vehemence. Mr. L had also provided an audience of two other people from his group. I made the decision to not be kowtowed by his offensive. Instead, I ignored it and proceeded with the interview as if nothing had happened. I made sure to pepper my questions with lines that I believed Mr. L needed to hear: "Perhaps this is hard for you to talk about," "that sounds like a very tough situation that you had to deal with," "I am so sorry to hear that they arrested your friend," "I hope the government listens to your group."

During the next two hours, the interview proceeded with some measure of language difficulty but I was able to get good behavioral responses and turned what could have been an even harder or shorter conversation into something more useful. Mr. L, who had become much easier to talk to as the interview progressed, left that afternoon promising that he would show me around rural Meghalaya, shook my hand, and thanked me for coming.

I had used empathy to deal with what I thought was a bad situation. To Mr. L, I symbolized New Delhi, which he saw as an agent of domination over his people. I had been completely honest about my research project, and he knew I had "connections" with the military. His distrust and initial aggression was understandable, if not justified.

It was important to the objectivity of the research project that I not be seen as someone who endorsed the problematic manner in which the Indian state operated in northeast India. I used female empathy to gain the confidence of Mr. L. In an odd way, I fell into yet another gender trap where women are seen as nonaggressive and placating. Perhaps, because I did not respond to his comment, he may have later seen my empathetic statements as the performance of a gender role he was comfortable with and could understand.

Conclusions: Managing Identity In Challenging Contexts

In the initial months of fieldwork, I was clear that I was an inquirer. What mattered was my professional identity and I hoped that because I did not assert a personal cultural identity, no one else would either. In both instances that I have described, strong political points had been made.

Now, I discuss an issue that is subsumed in much writing on fieldwork and methods: the possibility of sexual predation during fieldwork. India is a country where sexual harassment and violence against women occurs on a fairly regular basis. As an outsider, who was unable to speak local languages, I took extreme precautions to safeguard my personal security. This meant setting clear rules for fieldwork— what time to venture out and when to return (never after dark because of the lack of public transport), what to wear, and how to present myself (clothes that provided full coverage and an acceptance of temporary disempowerment), how long to stay during an interview in someone's office, planning an exit strategy for each interview, especially those conducted in strange locations.

During the course of fieldwork, I drifted in and out of various roles. I was sometimes a knowledgeable outsider and at other times an empathetic one. I was also diffident when required and learned how to set boundaries quickly during interviews. I was careful not to demonstrate any one political preference and also cautious about my interviews with military actors. When talking with the coercive arm of the state, I was cautious about not revealing anything about my sources from the underground. Also, I was careful to emphasize that empathy with an interviewee did not imply sameness. It may sound as if I had a well-devised strategy and had thought through these issues before stepping into the field. However, the rules and norms and strategies evolved on a case-by-case basis.

Reprinted from Vasundhara Sirnate. 2014. "Positionality, Personal Insecurity, and Female Empathy in Security Studies Research." PS: Political Science & Politics *47 (2). Cambridge University Press: 398–401. doi:10.1017/S1049096514000286.*

Notes

1. Name changed to protect identity.
2. I worked in the states of Assam, Meghalaya, Tripura, Mizoram, Arunachal Pradesh, Manipur.
3. See "Supreme Court Judgment in Salwa Judum Case", in The Hindu, July 6, 2011. Can be accessed online at http://www.thehindu.com/news/resources/supreme-court-judgment-in-salwa-judum-case/article2185766.ece
4. These answers are not always the product of a methodological individualistic encounter between the researcher and the researched. In India, for instance, a question posed to one person often involves a response generated by a surrounding collective and such socially produced responses may defy the survey method. See Rudolph (2005).
5. Because I had mostly used a snowball sample to gain interviews, I was often referred to as a mainlander on phone conversations where I heard only one side of the conversation. The person recommending me for a meeting would often say, "she is a mainlander."

References

Chacko, Elizabeth. 2004. "Positionality and Praxis: Fieldwork Experiences in Rural India." *Singapore Journal of Tropical Geography* 25 (1): 51–63.

Katz, Cindi. 1994. "Playing the Field: Questions of Fieldwork in Geography." *The Professional Geographer* 46 (1): 67–72.

Mohanty, Chandra T. 1988. "Under Western Eyes: Feminist Scholarship and Colonial Discourses." *Feminist Review* (30): 61–88.

Rudolph, Susanne H. 2005. "The Imperialism of Categories: Situating Knowledge in a Globalizing World." *Perspectives on Politics* 3 (1): 5–14.

Sherif, Bahira. 2001. "The Ambiguity of Boundaries in the Fieldwork Experience: Establishing Rapport and Negotiating Insider/Outsider Status." *Qualitative Inquiry* 7 (4): 436–47.

Sirnate, Vasundhara. 2009. "Students versus the State: The Politics of Uranium Mining in Meghalaya." *Economic and Political Weekly* 44 (47): 18–23.

Sultana, Farhana. 2007. "Reflexivity, Positionality and Participatory Ethics: Negotiating Fieldwork Dilemmas in International Research." *ACME: An International E-Journal for Critical Geographies* 6 (3): 374–85.

Tewksbury, Richard and Patricia Gagné. 1997. "Assumed and Presumed Identities: Problems of Self-Presentation in Field Research." *Sociological Spectrum* 17 (2): 127–55.

The Fieldwork of Quantitative Data Collection

14

FRANCESCA REFSUM JENSENIUS

For many political scientists, fieldwork means conducting focus groups in villages, attending campaign rallies, or interviewing political elites in government offices. When I present the mainly quantitative findings from my PhD work on electoral quotas for the Scheduled Castes (the former "untouchables") in India, colleagues are sometimes surprised to hear that I spent more than a year conducting fieldwork for the project. To study the effects of quotas in India I wanted to combine statistical work with interview-based case studies. I collected some of the quantitative data needed for the project during two initial field trips, and then returned to India for another nine months of fieldwork, intending to conduct interviews and collect more data. The main surprise was how easy it proved to get interviews, whereas considerable time and effort were needed to get access to "publicly available data." This article is about some of the failures and successes of my fieldwork, focusing particularly on the social relational aspects of collecting quantitative data.

Fieldwork-based work is often contrasted with quantitative data work, but while some quantitative datasets can be downloaded from the Internet or bought from data-collection agencies, other datasets are the result of months and months of pestering officials, searching through archives, or accompanying data-entry people in the field. To gather this type of data, one spends considerable time on both gaining access and building rapport with gatekeepers, topics familiar from discussions of qualitative data collection (Berg 2003; Harrington 2003; Scoggins, this book). Local knowledge also gives insights into how large datasets are collected, where their weaknesses lie, and how to spot irregularities in the data. This insight can be key to ensuring data reliability, an issue frequently discussed in methodological texts for political science (e.g., Kellstedt and Whitten 2013, chapter 5). By sharing some examples from my own field trips, I hope to show the importance of fieldwork for quantitative data collection and ways of dealing with the frustrations resulting from trying to collect data in the field.

Getting into the Building

The first hurdle in trying to access quantitative data is how to gain access to the building where the data are stored. This is a very physical and concrete version of ethnographers' challenge of "entry" (e.g., Johnson 1975, 52). My fieldwork was full of frustrations related to getting into buildings, compounds, and archives. In India's largest state, Uttar Pradesh (UP), the legislative assembly and its archives are surrounded by a tall fence with intimidating gates and guards. When I first came there to consult the archives, I was pointed to a small office by the entrance gate that issued entry passes. There was a long line of people waiting, and since I did not want to use my "foreigner-card" to skip the line, I waited there for a long time. When I finally came to the head of the line, I was told that I could not get an entry pass unless I had an appointment with someone working inside the compound. The legislative archives in India are supposed to be open to researchers, but although I showed my research visa and letters confirming my academic affiliation I was told I could not get access without such an appointment. Because I had previously visited archives in other states of India, I insisted that I was entitled to access the archives. The officer on duty then told me that I would need permission from the head librarian, but when I called the head librarian to ask to see her she told me I could not meet with her unless I had an entry pass to enter the compound! I finally accepted defeat. Fortunately, a colleague with whom I was traveling had some local political connections who arranged an appointment for me with one of the head civil servants working inside the compound. Once inside, it was easy to get the additional permissions.

A similar situation occurred in the state assembly of Haryana, also in northern India. In this case my colleague and I passed through the main gate of the legislative assembly compound by showing letters proving our research affiliation and explaining that we wanted to access the archives. Here the challenge was to get into the actual archives because the staff at the reception desk claimed that only politicians were allowed to enter. Here too we insisted, and in this case I believe it was the fact that I as a foreign woman pleaded to them in Hindi that made them soften up and allow us access. The staff were not following any procedure: they made an arbitrary choice of granting us access.

What these stories show is that to get through the doors where data are stored you often need to be persistent, use contacts, and plead nicely to gatekeepers for access. This can be frustrating, humiliating, and time-consuming. For me it has proved to be a huge advantage to travel with a friend or colleague, and I now try to do that as often as I can.

Convincing Gatekeepers to Give You Data

When inside the right building, the next step is to convince the people who have access to the data that they should give it to you. This too can be time-consuming, and is often about building trust and "rapport" in much the same way as researchers who collect qualitative data (see Glesne and Peshkin 1992; Marcus 1997; Scoggins, this book).

In one case I was trying to obtain some publicly available education data in UP. During my fieldwork in the northern state Himachal Pradesh (HP) I had discovered a fascinating survey of infrastructure, teachers, and students covering all public schools in India. The civil servant in charge of the data collection had given me the entire raw dataset for that state, so I was excited about collecting it for the state of UP, too.

The office responsible for collecting the education data in UP was about half an hour's travel from where I was staying, and I went there in an auto-rickshaw with an Indian colleague. When we got to the correct office we asked for the data-entry people. From previous experience, I had learned that it is vital to know exactly what is available on file before making requests to the officials in charge. Having ascertained that they had all the data I wanted, we then asked whom we should ask for permission to get the data. We were sent to one civil servant, but because he was away for the day we were told to come back the next day. Not too disappointed, we traveled the half-hour back to our lodgings and came back again the next morning. When I met with the civil servant and explained what data I was looking for he told me that nobody had ever asked for this data before and that he was not sure whether he could authorize giving it to me, so he sent me to a higher-level official. However, that person was not in the office, and I was told to come back another day.

The following day I was sent to yet another person, the head of the department. He told me that I needed to submit a written application for him to consider my request. I left his office, wrote up an application on my laptop, printed it in a shop down the street, and returned to his office with the completed application. By that time he had gone out for lunch. So we waited for him for two hours, but he did not return. By now a bit tired of the situation, we traveled back to the city center again and returned the next day to give him my application. He told me to leave the application with him and that he would get in touch with me. However, wise from earlier experience, I insisted on waiting. He then told me to wait outside his office, but then left through another door and did not return for many hours.

Realizing at this point that the officials simply did not want to give me the data, I asked my Indian colleague to make some enquiries. From the civil servant we had first approached, we learned that there had been a lot of internal discussion about my visits, and that the leadership had decided not to give me the data because they were worried that I would discover the poor quality of the data. Apparently, there had been major problems with how the data had been collected and coded, and if we studied it we might discover some of these weaknesses. Nobody wanted to take the blame for having given me the data in case I should publish something that resulted in a public scandal. In this case I did not get the data I needed because I failed to create the feeling of trust necessary for them to believe that my intentions were really to do long-term research and not to create a media scandal.

In the end I accessed this data through the central office in New Delhi. However, having learned about the poor quality of the data from the UP office, I was far less enthusiastic about it than I had been initially. This story shows the importance of building rapport and trust, as well as the importance of trying several avenues for getting the same data. It also shows the value of traveling with a colleague, in this case a local scholar. Being a foreigner I can usually gain access to high-level officials, but when it comes to hearing about office gossip, being local is a huge advantage. When traveling back and forth to the office, and then waiting for hours, it is also nice to have company.

As the previous example shows, trust is central to getting access to data. In two other cases I was initially refused access to data sources because other scholars had broken the trust of people working with the data. In one case I was refused access to an archive because another scholar had taken pictures of data sources although this was explicitly not allowed. The librarian was upset about this disrespectful behavior and took out his anger on me. I was consequently refused access to the documents I needed, although the person in charge of the archive had granted me access. It took several hours of drinking tea with the librarian to calm him down and convince him that I would indeed follow the rules.

In another archive I was refused access because another foreign scholar had tried to get some data from an archive, and, finding the process too slow, had gotten a powerful political friend to put pressure on the librarian. The librarian was deeply offended by this behavior, and because I was the next foreign scholar to come along, she gave me a long speech about how disrespectful all foreigners are and how it gave her a "bitter taste in the mouth" to help us out with our work and then get this kind of behavior in return. She consequently refused to help me, and again I had to spend considerable time talking with her about my work to gain her trust and be allowed access to the resources in the archive.

These experiences were frustrating, but also taught me the important lesson of always being respectful and polite to all the officials I encounter in my work. The importance of being respectful is often discussed in connection with qualitative fieldwork, but not in the context of quantitative data collection. The people in charge of entering, storing, and administering data are often hard-working individuals who do not receive much gratitude for the work they do. They must take time out of their already busy schedules to help researchers who come to request data. Naturally, they feel upset when they find that their work, time, and operating procedures are not respected. Being respectful, as well as patient and persistent, has therefore become a major rule for how I approach data collection.

Data Lost, Damaged in a Fire, Never Existed

Another challenge arises when those who are supposed to have data claim that the data never existed or cannot be found. This is often not out of ill will, which means that neither good access nor good rapport is helpful. A clear example of this occurred during an early field trip, when I was trying to obtain lists of villages that fell under each political district in India to merge political data with development data. Expecting this information to be fairly readily available, I went to the Election Commission of India to ask for it. And here I believe the official I talked to was willing to provide the data—but when he asked one of the men working in his office to give me the CDs with lists of villages for each state, they could not find them. They were sent out to search, and came back with several CDs that I was allowed to view on my computer and copy. Some of them contained information I had been looking for, but data for several large states were missing. After many rounds of phone calls we heard that the remaining CDs had been lost in a flood in one of the basement offices during the last monsoon. I do not know whether these files were actually lost in a flood, or had simply been misplaced. What I do know is that a few years later, when I returned to the same office to ask for some other information, the officer in charge asked me timidly whether I would be willing to share with them the data for the states I had copied, because they had misplaced more of the CDs and no longer had access to this information themselves.

In another case I was trying to get access to the district-wise census booklets that the Census of India had prepared for the Election Commission of India for use in delimiting new political districts in the 1970s. After a few visits to the Census office and the Election Commission offices, where I was varyingly told that these documents had never existed or had never been archived, I was finally sent to an obscure archive on the outskirts of the city, where copies of these documents were supposed to be kept. There I was told that the collection had been lost in a fire 10 years earlier. Later, I discovered these booklets in the Election Commission archives. Because these were historical documents that the Election Commission no longer needed, no one knew that they were there. This experience taught me to always look for myself, rather than simply accepting that something does not exist.

Data Reliability and Usefulness

Here is a final challenge: although some data may be easy to obtain, they may prove unreliable or useless. Previously I discussed poor quality of the education data from UP. My visit to the HP archives to gather information about the bills introduced and passed in the Assembly over the years is another example. This information is available in the minutes of the debates for each legislative session that are stored in the archives and in booklets summarizing each of the debates. When I told the librarian what I was looking for, she enthusiastically explained that my work would be easy because one of the staff in the library had already gathered all of the information. And indeed, my colleague and I were soon handed a complete list of all the information we were looking for. Somewhat surprised at achieving our goal so easily, we asked whether we could still see the archives and the books. We soon discovered that many of the collated figures were incorrect. I do not know whether the person working on this had been sloppy or whether the information was gathered only from certain publications, for example only those issued in Hindi, but we ended up spending several days assembling a new version of the dataset, with quite different figures.

I will end with the story of one of my major disappointments in the field. After I established contacts in the secretariat in one Indian state, a high-level civil servant promised to use his power to help me get data on how state-level politicians spend their development funds—a discretionary cash fund that politicians can allocate to development projects of their choosing within their political districts. He told me that the secretariat kept records of the spending of the funds and usually did not share this information, but that he would do me the favor of having it entered for me in Excel format. Having high hopes for the usefulness of this data, I returned to that office many days in a row to follow the progress of the data entry. After several days of waiting, the civil servant proudly handed me a printout of the new Excel spreadsheet. However, I was in for a disappointment: the data sheet had one column with the name of each politician in the state assembly and then a column for spending—with 100% listed in each row. All politicians had spent all of their development funds. There was no variation in the spending patterns and there were no records of how they had spent it. The only information kept in the secretariat was what percentage—100%—of the allocated funds had been spent. I thanked the civil servant for his help, and left the secretariat feeling miserable.

Conclusions

As the above examples show, data gathering often requires much of the same use of persistence, patience, local language skills, and relationship building as other forms of fieldwork. A main lesson from my work has been that it can be a huge advantage to work together with others in the field. Traveling with others can make the work safer, easier, and more enjoyable. I also learned never to rely on getting data from one source, but to try various avenues. This is important for ensuring the reliability of data and for getting anything. Finally, I learned that it is essential to be polite, respectful, and to take the time to talk properly with people working with the data you are collecting.

In the previous text I have focused on some of my failures in data collection, to show that data collection could be hard work, requiring many of the same skills as other types of fieldwork. But there have also been many success stories. In many cases I obtained access to large data sources very easily. While conducting qualitative interviews, or simply spending time in the field, I also got to hear about datasets or sources of data of which I had been unaware. Overall I hope these examples, both negative and positive, serve as reminders of the importance of fieldwork for quantitative data collection.

Reprinted from Francesca Refsum Jensenius. 2014. "The Fieldwork of Quantitative Data Collection." PS: Political Science & Politics 47 (2). Cambridge University Press: 402–4. doi:10.1017/S1049096514000298.

References

Berg, Bruce Lawrence. 2003. *Qualitative Research Methods for the Social Sciences.* 5th ed. Boston: Pearson.

Harrington, Brooke. 2003. "The Social Psychology of Access in Ethnographic Research." *Journal of Contemporary Ethnography* 32 (5): 592–25.

Glesne, Corrine, and Alan Peshkin. 1992. *Becoming Qualitative Researchers: An Introduction.* White Plains, NY: Longman.

Johnson, John M. 1975. *Doing Field Research.* New York: Free Press.

Kellstedt, Paul and Guy Whitten. 2013. *The Fundamentals of Political Science Research.* New York: Cambridge University Press.

Marcus, George E. 1997. "The Uses of Complicity in the Changing Mise-en-Scène of Anthropological Fieldwork." *Representations* 59: 85–108.

Data Collection, Opportunity Costs, and Problem Solving: Lessons from Field Research on Teachers' Unions in Latin America

15

CHRISTOPHER CHAMBERS-JU

As I prepared to leave Mexico, my efforts to access an important dataset for my dissertation became increasingly desperate. A newspaper article mentioned that the Mexican teachers' union endorsed nearly 2,000 political candidates in the 2012 election.[1] I wanted to solicit this list. For three weeks I made daily treks to the Mexican teachers' union's headquarters in downtown Mexico City. The union was in a dark, cavernous building. I wandered through smoked-filled offices with impressionistic portraits of the union's president, Elba Esther Gordillo. I sought "Geraldo," a leader of the union's political action committee, who could tell me whether the data I sought was obtainable, or give me closure with a simple "no."[2]

One day I received news that Geraldo could meet. After hurrying to his office, the receptionist told me that her boss had just stepped out to take an urgent call. Confused, I sat and waited. When it became clear that Geraldo would not appear, I left. Later I was told what had happened. Apparently, after agreeing to the interview, Geraldo informed the union's top brass that I wanted to know about the union's political endorsements. Because of a recent damaging leak to the press, Geraldo was ordered not to speak to me, and I was warned to stop contacting union leaders. A gatekeeper had slammed the door on my research.

This article examines the challenges related to getting data in the field. Researchers can be confused about what to do when data exists but, because of bureaucratic barriers, cannot be accessed; researchers may face challenges just "getting into the building" (Jensenius, this book). Rich data may be found, but putting it together may require significant work—the amount of effort may outweigh the data's added value. Comparative researchers may encounter data that is asymmetric and only available for some cases, and they must decide whether to present incomplete data in their final analysis. This article lays out these challenges and then suggests paths forward.

The approach to field research outlined in this article is informed by my experience in Argentina, Colombia, and Mexico studying the electoral participation of teachers' unions. I wanted to analyze how teachers came together as an organized voting bloc, whether teachers influenced the vote choice of low information voters, why union leaders became political candidates, and what conditions enabled teacher-based parties to form. I collected electoral data from official government sources, teacher surveys, newspaper archives, and databases of legislator CVs. I draw from my experience throughout this article to illustrate general points with specific examples.

The Cost Structure of Data Collection

Field research promises high rewards because original data can make valuable contributions to the field.[3] Graduate students may postpone graduation because of these payoffs. By conducting interviews and communicating directly with the actors involved in generating data, analysis is sharpened and made more credible. There is broad agreement that more data is better than less and that more types of data—qualitative and quantitative—are better than fewer. However, data collection involves labor, capital, and time. Empirically minded social scientists almost always encounter problems related to data collection. Analysts tend to specialize in collecting and analyzing only a few types of data—be they interview transcripts, survey data, or others—because of the costliness of working with various data structures. Many activities in the field have a high marginal cost because of the costs associated with conducting searches, which ex ante are unknowable.[4] For instance, the per-unit cost of conducting an additional face-to-face interview involves contacting, scheduling, preparing questions, transportation, carrying out the interview, and then transcription, coding, and analysis. The marginal cost of one more interview is quite high.

Field research is one of the most costly forms of data collection, especially at the beginning of a project and early in an academic career. Graduate students face opportunity costs; they could instead learn new quantitative methods or graduate early. Data collected for theory building is open ended. Few guidelines are available about what is needed and what is not. Usually, a significant chunk of the data that is collected is not used in the final analysis.[5] Graduate students are expected to soak and poke, and then quickly move to a research question and an empirical strategy. They must commit to a project before knowing exactly what it is or whether it will work.

Gathering data in a foreign country also adds a dimension of complexity. There may be different levels of access depending on country context; developing countries present considerable hurdles. Not all countries have freedom of information acts and laws requiring transparency and disclosure. Working with data in a foreign language is also more challenging. Gathering data in multiple foreign countries compounds these problems. As the complexity of a project increases, something is likely to go wrong.

Data Collection Problems

The costliness of data collection gives rise to various problems. Projects motivated by important questions often run into a gap between the research design and the available data. Ideally, analysts will find data that is structured. Yet, analysts often encounter data that is nonexistent, unstructured, hidden, or asymmetric. Table 1 presents a typology of data that analysts may encounter in the field, with a brief description of the challenges that each poses.

Type of Data	Description
Structured	Data exists, is clean, and is ready to be analyzed.
Nonexistant	Data does not exist. Alternative indicators must be found or new data must be generated.
Hidden	Data exists, but it is diffi cult to access.
Unstructured	Data exists, but it is costly to collect and clean.
Asymmetric	Data exists, but it is partial or incomplete for key cases; it is difficult to analyze.

Table 1. Types of Data Problems

Structured Data

Structured data serves as a standard against which more complicated types of data can be compared. Structured data is complete, clean, and ready to be analyzed. Interuniversity Consortium for Political and Social Research has complete datasets that are publicly available. Similarly, government agencies also can be transparent and have easily downloadable data. For my research, I found that electoral data was easily accessible through the websites of government agencies. Getting data on the territorial distribution of the vote share of candidates and parties linked to the teachers' union proved relatively straightforward.

Nonexistent Data

Important research questions can call for data that does not exist. Nonexistent data is a problem commonly encountered when conducting historical research. It is more problematic if the analyst has reason to believe that data, in fact, exists, and significant time must be spent to verify that it does not. When there is evidence to suggest that data is nonexistent, the analyst must make decisions; whether to search for alternative indicators, or proxies, that can indirectly get at the research question, or whether to generate new data, for instance, through a survey. Generating original data can be orders of magnitude more costly than collecting data.

For my research, I sought the results of elections for the Colombian teachers' union's executive committee—for 1994 and 1998—to understand how union electoral results influenced the decisions of union leaders to pursue public office. Several helpful union leaders told me that the union lacked "institutional memory;" union leaders had not archived this data and it did not exist. I chose to move on and seek out other data that would be more useful.

Unstructured Data

Data—in some form—exists for most significant social and political phenomena that have occurred over the past 20 years; most leave an electronic footprint. The problem, however, is that data is scattered among various sources and is quite messy. The more disorganized data is, the higher the costs of putting it together. For example, when data is found in newspaper articles, it must be collected from various sources, coded, and then aggregated. Data for different years or for different regions may be housed in various locations. For my research, putting together a census of union leaders who went into public office required me to organize unstructured data. First, I searched databases with legislator CVs to find former union leaders who entered the national legislature. This data, however, was incomplete. I then printed tables with the names of union leaders who had gone into public office and circulated these tables in interviews. I asked current union leaders to verify that the legislators I had found did, in fact, have ties to the union and to identity other union leaders who had gone into government as well as friends of the union. I would then check these names online. This iterative approach yielded interesting data but constructing this dataset required me to invest a significant amount of time consulting multiple sources.

Hidden Data

Data known to exist may be hidden. Finding and accessing it can be difficult, and a lot of time can be wasted in fruitless searches. Some of this data may be accessible through networking, creativity, and luck; others may be nearly impossible to access, short of paying large sums of money. The candidate endorsement data I sought from the Mexican teachers' union is a good example of hidden data. After being told to stop contacting union leaders, I decided to move on and search for low-hanging fruit.

Asymmetric Data

Analysts conducting comparative research frequently encounter asymmetric or incomplete data. Data may be available and complete for one or more cases, but nonexistent for others. Data can also be coded or operationalized in different ways, rendering it non-comparable. Asymmetric data raises difficult questions that must be addressed in the final analysis. In some cases, asymmetric data is sufficiently interesting that it can be presented in an incomplete form.[6] Yet, data with too many holes must be thrown out. Comparative researchers must make decisions about how much asymmetry their analysis can tolerate.

Teacher surveys were an important point of asymmetry in my research. I wanted to analyze teachers' attitudes toward elected representatives linked to their union and whether the union contacted them during political campaigns. I obtained data from a 2009 teacher survey in Bogota, Colombia by Rocio Londoño and Javier Saenz (Londoño et al. 2011). Although this data shed light on the variables associated with teachers' political support for union leaders who entered public office in Bogota, I was unable to get comparable data for Argentina or Mexico. In my final analysis, I need to decide how prominently to feature this data because my research question concerns teachers in all three cases.

Problem Solving

What should analysts do when they encounter roadblocks in the field? Data problems do not have easy, one-size-fits-all solutions. However, while frustrating, data problems are rarely insurmountable. Many workarounds require improvisation; they must be figured out on the ground, using limited information and gut feeling. This section considers strategies for coping with the aforementioned problems, and it considers guidelines on how to invest scarce resources.

Networks

Fieldwork is a messy, social process that involves building trust and establishing long-term relationships. It involves constructing networks that are multinodal; they should include a variety of different types of data brokers. This section sketches out some of the data brokers who can help access hidden data, confirm concerns that a database does not exist, and suggest strategies for efficiently pursuing unstructured data.

Gatekeepers can unlock hidden data. They can also allay concerns about whether data exists. Gatekeepers can be low-level functionaries, such as receptionists and assistants, who may make discretionary decisions about whether to help a researcher. I encountered gatekeepers who opened doors, and helped me obtain hidden data. These included sympathetic union leaders, government officials, and workers at nongovernmental organizations. I convinced these brokers to help me by cultivating relations of trust and conveying the important implications of my research for their organization. I also encountered gatekeepers who closed doors and prevented me from accessing data. Developing good working relationships with gatekeepers can yield unexpected positive consequences.

Organic intellectuals are nonacademic observers who know a lot about a given substantive topic. They may be analysts at think tanks, journalists, or public intellectuals. Organic intellectuals have tremendous substantive knowledge and can provide another perspective on a given research topic; they often interact with local academics. These brokers can help to correctly interpret data and understand how it was generated. In my research, organic intellectuals from the Colombian think tank the Center for Investigation and Popular Education, most notably Alvaro Delgado, gave me invaluable feedback as I advanced my project. Aside from having extensive networks and knowledge of how to get data, they also helped guide me when I had to make decisions about how to pursue unstructured data.

Local academics are trained and work at local universities. They offer important insights regarding the substantive topic and usually have established professional networks. In Mexico, several distinguished local academics helped me connect to leaders in the teachers' union and gain access to hidden data. Karla Fernández, Aurora Loyo, Aldo Muñoz, and Carlos Ornelas all had established networks and access to valuable data sources that are not public. Local academics had a different perspective on my research question than professors at my home university. Theses Mexican professors knew substantially more about the Mexican teachers' union than my dissertation committee and their input kept the project on track during periods of confusion.

Veteran field researchers are usually trained in American universities and work on the same substantive topic. They have established networks and can also provide useful advice regarding data sources that can be accessed. Unfortunately, over time these academics may switch topics and lose touch with the data brokers they once knew well. For me, Maria Lorena Cook of Cornell University and Maria Victoria Murillo of Columbia University both generously shared their experiences studying teachers' unions and put me in touch with contacts, who offered to share data.

The importance of networks that include multiple types of data brokers reinforces arguments for an area studies approach to comparative research. Because it is costly to assemble these networks, the best way to organize research is to have analysts commit to studying a few countries. They can then develop relationships of trust and reciprocity, as well as deep case knowledge.

Sequencing

Research often involves collecting a lot of data and then only using a small subset. The more a project is properly sequenced, the more time can be spent chasing critical data. Unfortunately, knowing what is most important for a given research question often can only emerge from the fieldwork experience itself. Properly sequencing a project can help to minimize wasted resources when putting together unstructured data or seeking out hidden data. Analysts must build theory before testing theory. Too often, because of skewed incentives, theory building is not given enough time. Grants are awarded for concrete data collection proposals—even if these proposals lack well-developed research questions. Pressure to publish induces a rush to collect data and test hypotheses. By moving forward too quickly, many well-funded projects end up wasting grant money. Theory building should involve iteratively moving between data and theory, and reflexively considering new directions for the project, based on what data is found to be available.

Researchers should invest in costly data collection activities at the end of a project. They should identify multiple data sources before deciding which to use. When the project is quite advanced, specific and costly tasks can begin: launching a survey, conducting content analysis of newspaper archives, or coding archival materials. It can be useful to perform triage, and differentiate between essential and nonessential (albeit quite interesting) data. It can also be helpful to decide whether data can be gathered in small pieces or whether it must be collected in one big chunk.

Sequencing can also be thought of in terms of an academic career. Graduate students have relatively few resources—in terms of research funds, research assistants, networks, and coauthors—in comparison to professors. Graduate students should be realistic about their constraints. They can plan to pursue bigger projects with more costly data collection activities later in their careers.

I carried out several short trips to the field before spending a full year conducting field research on teachers' unions. I dedicated a substantial amount of time to soaking and poking, experimenting with ideas, and trying to understand how teachers' unions actually operated. When my project finally developed a strong foundation, I began to carry out repetitive tasks—constructing a candidate recruitment database, searching for teacher survey data, and structured queries of newspaper archives.

One question that should constantly be asked is, "is this data essential for this project?" Flexibility is important. Theory can be tested using nondata intensive methods. For example, the concept of observable implications does not require "smoking gun" evidence in support of a theory (Collier 2011, 825–26). Instead, it requires limited, albeit significant, observations to bolster a theory's plausibility. A well-specified theory can be built around a thoughtful set of observable implications. It is not always necessary to laboriously compile a complete, rectangular dataset. Case studies are regularly used to test key assumptions and predictions of formal models. Some—although by no means all—projects can be defended with limited data.

Flexibility also involves thinking creatively about the substitutability of indicators and clever proxy variables. The concept of triangulation, now a cornerstone of multimethod research, can provide a path forward (Brady and Collier 2010).[7] This method enables analysts to make inferences based on multiple data sources—if none individually provide "smoking gun" evidence.

Conclusions

Data collection has important downstream consequences for data management and analysis. Too often, data collection is approached as an informal and idiosyncratic part of the research process and graduate students are expected to figure this out alone. This article aims to flesh out some common challenges that are encountered in the field and guidelines for thinking about how to confront them.

Fieldwork involves shoe leather. The epidemiologist John Snow, in dogged pursuit of data that would help him understand the spread of cholera, wore out the soles of his shoes walking around London (Freedman 2009). For political scientists, data collection involves going out into the street, talking to people, and trying to understand what is actually happening on the ground. Full immersion in the field is the best way to figure out the most interesting part of a research project and to find the data necessary to successfully complete it.

Reprinted from Christopher Chambers-Ju. 2014. "Data Collection, Opportunity Costs, and Problem Solving: Lessons from Field Research on Teachers' Unions in Latin America." PS: Political Science & Politics *47 (2). Cambridge University Press: 405–9. doi:10.1017/S1049096514000304.*

Notes

1. Nurit Martínez. "Impulsa el SNTE a casi 2 mil candidatos." El Universal June 27, 2012.
2. Geraldo is a pseudonym.
3. For example, Eggers and Hainmueller (2009, 517-19) used a very costly data collection strategy in their analysis of the economic returns to office holding. They identified British MP candidates who barely won and barely lost elections by coding parliamentary candidate biographies from an archive of The Times of London. They then identified the date of death of these candidates, using a genealogy database, and collected data on their probate values (which is a legal record of the size of an individual's estate). This is a good example of a costly and complex data collection process that yielded substantial professional and analytic payoffs.
4. Some activities involve a significant fixed cost, in the form of specialized training, but have a low marginal cost. For example, web scraping involves learning how to write code in a programming language. However, when an analyst can write code, the marginal cost of assembling data drops significantly. Amazon's Mechanical Turk and online surveys also have low marginal costs. Because these tools make data collection less costly, analysts can experiment with various datasets before committing to the one that yields the most interesting analysis.
5. By contrast, gathering data for theory testing or replicating the results of an existing study is focused and highly structured.
6. Chhibber and Kollman (1998, 338) acknowledge a problem of asymmetric data but are able to proceed in their comparison of the United States and India. In table 1 they run a regression on the effect of government fiscal centralization on the effective number of parties in the United States. However, they are unable to find corresponding data in India to run the same regression. "Because there are too few cases for meaningful regression analyses, we do not replicate table 1 for India."
7. Brady and Collier (2004, 310) describe triangulation as a "research procedure that employs empirical evidence derived from more than one method or from more than one type of data. Triangulation strengthens the validity of both descriptive and casual inference."

References

Brady, Henry and David Collier, eds. 2004. *Rethinking Social Inquiry: Diverse Tools, Shared Standards*. Oxford: Rowman and Littlefield.

Chhibber, Pradeep and Ken Kollman. 1998. "Party Aggregation and the Number of Parties in India and the United States." *American Political Science Review* 92 (2): 329–42.

Collier, David. 2011. "Understanding Process Tracing." *PS: Political Science & Politics* 44 (4): 823–30.

Eggers, Andrew and Jens Hainmueller. 2009. "MPs for Sale? Returns to Office in Postwar British Politics." *American Political Science Review* 103 (4): 513.

Freedman, David A. 2008. "On Types of Scientific Enquiry: The Role of Qualitative Reasoning." Edited by Janet Box-Steffensmeier, Henry E. Brady, and David Collier. *The Oxford Handbook of Political Methodology*. Oxford: Oxford University Press: 309–18.

Londoño, Rocio, Javier Saenz. Carlos Lanziano, Bibana Castro, Vladimir Ariza, and Mario Aguirre. 2011. *Perfil de los docentes del sector público de Bogotá*. IDEP, Secretaria de Educación Distrital.

Knowing When to Scale Back: Addressing Questions of Research Scope in the Field

16

AKASEMI NEWSOME

espite extensive preparation and familiarity with field sites, researchers can face questions of scope during the implementation of their research design. It may be difficult or impractical to visit all the country cases or collect different types of data at equal levels of detail across geographic space (Lieberman 2004). Informants who expressed interest in participating may later be nonresponsive. Researchers may then need to adjust their research question midway through data collection. Whereas I arrived at my field site to begin a project that would explain different trade union responses to immigration in Europe, I returned to my home institution with a new outcome of cross-ethnic cooperation in protest.

I adjusted my outcome of interest because the scope of my original outcome was too broad, rendering the collection of comparable data across multiple dimensions difficult. With a new, narrower outcome I could locate more equivalent types of data via interviews with informants and observational and archival research. This article details the issues of scope and the different stages of my research when I faced these issues while in the field in Western Europe. It addresses potential pitfalls that can lead to questions of scope and offers strategies to deal with those challenges. Establishing *substantive* and *temporal thresholds* and confirming these with local academics and knowledgeable colleagues stateside as a way of "assessing progress periodically," aided in transitioning to a new, narrower research question (Lynch 2004, 11).

The Challenge of Logistics

The unit of analysis of my original research question was the union, and I planned to explore the question of differing responses by labor unions to immigration through data collection across three countries (Denmark, Germany, and the United Kingdom (UK)) and two sectors (elder care homes in the public sector and food manufacturing firms in the private sector). I conceptualized unions as having two categories of responses, internal and external. Internal responses included organizational discourse within unions referring to immigrants and representation of immigrants as a fraction of the membership and elected positions. External responses covered lobbying by the union in society on behalf of immigrant concerns. For my initial data collection plans, I completed a pilot research trip in 2009 and planned to spend 13 additional months abroad from 2010 to 2011 conducting in-depth interviews with trade unionists, activists, employers, politicians, and journalists across these three country cases and two sectors. I also planned to do surveys of elected union representatives in each country, compile observational data by visiting six workplaces, one in each sector per country, as well as visit archives.

Logistical challenges presented themselves with an early set of interviews in November 2010. I had received introductions to five officials responsible for immigration issues, each affiliated with a different sectoral union in Germany. My informants' locations ranged from two- to five-hour train rides from my research base in Berlin, Germany. I faced the logistic challenge of scheduling all the interviews within a two-week period, physically getting to the places and staying long enough to follow up with any referrals to additional informants or worksites. After scheduling these interviews, I realized that it had taken me two weeks with those five informants to coordinate and cluster the interview appointments, while the interviews would take place over the following three-week period. Scheduling a handful of interviews within one of my country cases took more than twice as long as I expected, therefore I discovered it would probably be quite challenging to maintain the scope of the project across multiple countries, sectors, and types of data.

To move forward, I had to decide whether to scale back my ambitions or to press ahead. Because I thought that it was too early to change course and drop a country case, sector, or type of data, and I was unsure if a windfall of data was just around the corner, I settled on a strategy involving regular evaluations of the data-gathering process. I committed myself to sticking with my research project as long as I met reasonable *substantive* and *temporal thresholds*. For example, the substantive goal I set for those five interviews with informants was to secure leads to worksites where I could collect observational data and gain permission for and aid with the distribution of a survey of union representatives. For temporal parameters, I allowed myself a month after each interview to set up worksite visits and the surveys, assuming my informants were willing and able to help me. I also shared these thresholds with local academics and members of my dissertation committee to get advice about the feasibility of my expectations and to create accountability.

Recognizing the Impracticability of the Survey

During early trips to field sites in the UK and Denmark in 2010 and 2011, I talked to informants and local academics about possible worksite locations where I could collect survey data. Some informants quickly expressed their inability to help me field surveys in a straightforward fashion. One British informant at the executive level of an industrial union said that the union could not afford to let me loose to do my own survey because of what I might find. Union officials would only allow outside researchers to add questions if the union had already committed to conducting their own survey. Another British informant at a public sector union told me she did not have the authority to give me permission to do the survey and that she could not direct me to anyone with that authority. I faced similar obstacles in Denmark, however, union officials stated that I would also need the permission of employers to field a survey, and their permission would be difficult to obtain without an affiliation with a Danish university and Danish academic partners.

A more difficult situation arose when informants conveyed enthusiasm about aiding me with my research, but weeks and months later did not respond to emails or phone calls about the specifics. For example, in March 2011, I had a particularly informative and congenial interview with a midlevel union official in a public sector union in Denmark. At the end of the interview, I broached the topic of locating a worksite for observation and fielding a survey. He reeled off several potential places that he thought could be feasible based on his professional connections to union representatives and managers and told me to follow up with him by email and phone so that we could arrange my visit during the next two months. Although I sent several emails and left a number of voicemail messages, I was never able to contact him.

Setting substantive and temporal thresholds proved useful in my decision to abandon the survey. As an initial visit to the UK in November 2010 involved contact with local academics only, I allowed myself a month to follow up with referrals directly connected to potential worksites as union representatives or employers and an additional month to set up interviews and worksite visits. When none of the British informants I met in January 2011 could commit to helping me field a survey, I decided to abandon the survey in the UK. By January 2011 I was sure the worksite surveys would no longer be part of my dissertation, but decided to try in Denmark. If I succeeded in fielding a survey in even a single country case, I could still use the data for an article or book project later. However, as described earlier, although some Danish informants expressed interest in helping me in March 2011, they were nonresponsive during April and May, which led me to abandon the survey portion of my data collection by the end of May.

Changing Sectors to Access Comparable Data

In addition to managing geographic distances when accessing data across country cases and deciding to drop one type of data—surveys— questions of scope can also crop up for scholars when attempting to acquire the remaining data types in equivalence across cases. Setting the parameters of this project to include multiple cases, sectors, and types of data seemed feasible owing largely to the success of a pilot foray into the field. I spent two months in the summer of 2009 locating and contacting 40 potential interviewees in Denmark and was able to interview nearly 30 of them during that short visit. Yet, extrapolating from the relative ease with which I located contacts in my 2009 pilot trip proved to be a mistake. In the process of getting feedback from local academics on substantive and temporal thresholds for setting up interviews, I realized that I had to change my sectors of focus a few months after arriving in the field in 2010.

In Denmark, I found contacts from 2009 willing to facilitate workplace visits to a food manufacturing plant and elder care home. Yet, before I had organized parallel workplace visits in Germany and the UK, local academics urged me to change my sectoral focus because of the difficulty I would have obtaining comparable data. Although these sectors had union presences in Germany and the UK, unions had a more visible presence in major manufacturing firms and public services such as metal manufacturing/autos and public hospitals, respectively. Most important, immigrants in Germany and the UK were more likely to come in contact with unions in these sectors. The chance that immigrants might have little contact with unions in my two original sectors made them potentially poor sites to gather evidence on my outcome of differences in union responses to immigration across country cases.

Turning to a New Outcome

Researchers may at times exit from fieldwork abroad with a new dependent variable. Factors such as difficulties obtaining comparable data across cases, locating informants, or the discovery of local knowledge contradicting the existing literature (LaPorte, this book), can force scholars to change their outcome. At the end of several months of fieldwork, rather than seek to explain differences in union responses to immigration, my project shifted to instead explain when native and immigrant union members were able to cooperate to take part in workplace protests such as strikes.[1] My arrival at a new outcome unfolded as I conducted fieldwork for my original question and highlights the iterative and often unpredictable nature of research in comparative politics. Just as scholars cannot extrapolate from past experiences in the field and need to prepare for developments that may be hard to foresee, scholars can also stumble on important caches of data or "opportunities for observation" and insights into innovative analysis (Bissaillon and Rankin 2013).

The first inkling of this impending change came after a conversation in July 2010 with a prominent German scholar of immigration with whom I had coffee at the beginning of fieldwork. I told him about my interest in understanding why trade unions had such different responses to immigration, and he said that one reason might be because German unions, more than their British and Danish counterparts, have a greater reliance on the strike capacity of members.

After this scholar's suggestion, including questions about strikes or any other workplace protests became part of my interview scripts. Yet, until I changed my sectors of focus from food manufacturing and elder care to metal manufacturing/autos and public hospitals by the end of 2010, the strike/protest questions did not result in particularly useful responses from informants. At my first worksite visit to a public hospital in March 2011, I was able to interview several union members, some of them union reps and works councilors, many of them with immigrant backgrounds. One of the things I asked them was how they decided to join the union, and whether they thought the union was doing anything for immigrant integration. I received a variety of responses on the integration question, however some of the platitudes about how great the hospital and union were at integration contrasted with other complaints my interviewees had about obstacles to promotion they faced at work.[2] One interviewee got involved in the union because he wanted higher wages and thought that approaching the union as an individual would be the best way to do it. Yet what he discovered when talking to the union rep was that it was not something he could do alone. The condition of union help was getting his colleagues on board with the demand for higher wages. Certainly, in those interviews, I realized that union representatives encouraged collective action as a problem solving strategy, yet I still did not think about collective action as an outcome for my research. Not until the very last interview I conducted a few weeks before returning to the United States, for a different hospital work site, did I suddenly grasp the potential of protests as a new outcome.

Talking to bystanders and participants in May Day protests in Berlin, I learned about a hospital strike nearby. Halfway through an interview with one of the strike organizers, he shared a surprising piece of information. Work in the hospital was bifurcated not only by skill but also, largely by ethnicity. Most immigrants worked in low paid, insecure jobs for a private contractor in cleaning and catering while Germans held highly skilled, secure public sector jobs in medical care at the hospital. German trade unionists directly employed by the public hospital decided to combine their protest for higher wages, with that of the immigrants in the hospital working for the private contractor. What surprised me was that German trade unionists would not gain materially from this alliance, yet they had gone out of their way to set it up. I asked my informant why they were doing this. He gave me several reasons: solidarity, ideological opposition to privatization, poor work conditions, and a sense that immigrants as a group lacked a lobby. I wondered if their immigrant partners would give the same reasons for cooperation. When I asked my informant if the alliance had succeeded, he said that it had been very difficult to maintain. When the German skilled workers had won concessions, most of them returned to work, although the immigrant workers had not yet achieved their goals. A small hard core of German trade union activists remained committed to helping the immigrants.[3] Immediately, I wanted to know why, and I wanted to know more about the immigrant partners. What would they have to say about the partnership? Why did these groups cooperate at all?

The following spring of 2012, I returned for follow-up interviews with other activists at the hospital and researched newspaper coverage of the protests to put together a fuller picture of partnership between immigrant and German workers. The fact that I uncovered this fascinating case after changing my sectoral focus, caused me to actively rethink what I had assumed and what I had learned during fieldwork. I considered the likelihood that parallel dynamics in the export-oriented manufacturing sectors and sheltered public sectors probably influenced the way natives and immigrants cooperated in protest at work. When I switched sectors from food manufacturing and elder care to metal manufacturing/autos and public hospitals, I had only thought of manufacturing as the sector where globalization influenced relations between native and immigrant workers. Employers regularly threatened manufacturing unions with offshoring jobs in Eastern Europe and further afield (Harrison 1997; Jacoby 1995), and sometimes, native workers saw immigrant fellow workers as symbolic scapegoats of foreign competition. In public hospitals, local authorities face limited budgets partly because of globalization and the reduced ability of the state to collect tax revenue from corporations. One of the ways public hospitals can continue to provide services and balance budgets is by contracting out nonclinical services, often to global or European firms (Bach and Givan 2010; Boehlke and Schulten 2008; Broadbent, Gil, and Laughlin 2003; Mosebach 2007). Although immigrants bear the brunt of new low-wage employment created by contracting, this type of privatization is unpopular and may also lead to scapegoating of immigrants.

Conclusion and Lessons for Others

The central lesson of this article is that scholars have to be aware of the likely possibility that one's research question may change. Even with extensive preparation before fieldwork, it can be hard to know in advance what part of the project will actually be doable and most importantly, what aspect will be the most stimulating. Being open to inspiration and stimulation in the field is valuable because it can propel one through the hard work of writing and rewriting after returning from the field. For scholars of interest groups and organizations in particular, fieldwork showed how even heavily bureaucratized organizations such as unions can be fairly dynamic on the inside. It was fascinating to get a sense of splinter groups and fragmentation in specifically corporatist unions, which had been characterized by the literature as organizations where change happened very slowly. Along this vein, another lesson is to be aware that sometimes the way that the literature describes the phenomena under study can be outdated (Chambers-Ju, this book). Although this article discusses questions of scope and setting substantive and temporal thresholds as strategies allowing one to decide when to pare back the parameters of a project, this should not be confused with an admonition to embark only on narrowly defined projects.

Reprinted from Akasemi Newsome. 2014. "Knowing When to Scale Back: Addressing Questions of Research Scope in the Field." PS: Political Science & Politics 47 (2). Cambridge University Press: 410–13. doi:10.1017/S1049096514000316.

Notes

1. Currently, the outcome of cross-ethnic cooperation over protests has expanded to protests and day-to-day workplace activity.
2. See the way Lee Ann Fujii (2010, 232) addresses the importance of understanding "contradictions" and "silences" as "meta-data" that can provide information about the phenomenon under study while conducting interviews.
3. Author Interview with Arnim Thomass, Berlin, Germany, July 2011.

References

Bach, Stephen, and Rebecca Kolms Givan. 2010. "Regulating Employment Conditions in a Hospital Network: The Case of the Private Finance Initiative." *Human Resources Management Journal* 20 (4): 424–39.

Bisaillon, Laura and Janet M. Rankin. 2013. "Navigating the Politics of Fieldwork Using Institutional Ethnography: Strategies for Practice." *Forum: Qualitative Social Research* (Sozialforschung) 14 (1): 1–27.

Boehlke, Nils and Thorsten Schulten. 2008. "Unter Privatisierungsdruck (Under Pressure to Privatize)." *Mitbestimmung* 6: 24–28.

Broadbent, Jane, Jas Gil, and Richard Laughlin. 2003. "The Development of Contracting in the Context of Infrastructure Investment in the UK: The Case of the Private Finance Initiative in the National Health Service." *International Public Management Journal* 6 (2): 173–97.

Fujii, Lee Ann. 2010. "Shades of Truth and Lies: Interpreting Testimonies of War and Violence." *Journal of Peace Research* 47 (2): 231–41.

Harrison, Bennett. 1997. *Lean and Mean: The Changing Landscape of Corporate Power in the Age of Flexibility*. New York: Guilford Press.

Jacoby, Sanford M. 1995. *The Workers of Nations: Industrial Relations in a Global Economy*. New York: Oxford University Press.

Lieberman, Evan. 2004. "Preparing for Field Research." *Qualitative Methods: Newsletter of the APSA Organized Section on Qualitative Methods* 2 (1): 3–7.

Lynch, Julia. 2004. "Tracking Progress While in the Field." *Qualitative Methods: Newsletter of the APSA Organized Section on Qualitative Methods* 2 (1): 10–15.

Mosebach, Kai. 2007. "Institutional Change or Political Stalemate: Healthcare Financing Reform in Germany." *Eurohealth* 12 (4): 11–14.

Confronting a Crisis of Research Design

17

JODY LAPORTE

Like many eager PhD candidates, I set off for the field with a compelling research question, a set of carefully adjudicated hypotheses, and a long "to get" list of data to obtain (Lieberman 2004). My dissertation was to examine why some authoritarian regimes allow protests to occur, focusing on three country cases from post-Soviet Eurasia: Kazakhstan, Azerbaijan, and Belarus. The Azerbaijani government regularly permitted demonstrations; in contrast, protests in Belarus and Kazakhstan were rarely permitted. This variation would allow me to say something important about the different cross-national strategies of authoritarian rule. However, as I pursued my field research, I realized that the empirics of these cases were much different than I expected. Not only was my original hypothesis wrong; the data challenged the premise of my entire research design.

Many field researchers confront evidence that contradicts their initial hypotheses. In some cases, the alternative explanations turn out to be true. In other cases, data collected in the field reveals a causal process that is unexpected and far more interesting than the researcher imagined. Such discoveries can be unsettling, but often lead to major theoretical insights (Kapiszewski, MacLean, and Read 2014; Lynch 2004).

What I faced was a different—and more fundamental—problem. A "crisis of research design" occurs when fieldwork questions the appropriateness of the research question, dependent variable, or case selection mechanism. Under these circumstances, researchers may have no choice but to redesign the project while in the field.

This article examines options for researchers who encounter substantive challenges to their research design while conducting fieldwork. The article's premise is that these crises can be productively resolved by maintaining the original intent of the project, even as the research design evolves. Drawing on my experience conducting research on nondemocratic regimes in Central Asia, I illustrate the iterative and highly inductive process of reformulating a research project while still in the field. In some cases, a crisis of research design can be solved by *narrowing* one's focus (Newsome, this book). In my case, the empirical realities that I confronted during fieldwork challenged me to *broaden* the scope of my analysis. In the following text, I discuss how and when to broaden one's analysis, as well as how to avoid this in the first place.

Causes of a Crisis

A common misconception is that crises of research design result from insufficient preparatory work. In practice, however, graduate students spend years developing their projects. By the time they have developed a coherent research project, survived the prospectus defense, and secured travel funding, their projects have passed several rounds of rigorous review.

In reality, all empirical research projects run some chance of running into crisis. Two fundamental and unavoidable aspects of positivist social science create this risk. First, social scientists routinely import theories, concepts, and methods developed in one context and apply them to another. We identify empirical or theoretical puzzles and generate likely answers using information gleaned from other people, places, and times. Generating and testing hypotheses is at the heart of our work. However, caution is necessary. To avoid a crisis of research design, the concepts, tools, or theory must resonate with your specific cases and reflect empirics at your specific field site. Importing a dependent variable is particularly risky. Hypotheses can be tested, modified, and retested in the field. Retooling a dependent variable, however, is likely to have major implications for other aspects of the research design.

Second, political scientists tend to study contemporary phenomena; we study moving targets. Major empirical events can upend carefully constructed research plans. Unexpected, cataclysmic political developments—such as revolutions, economic crises, and major policy changes—can happen just as a researcher is about to embark for the field. As the recent Arab Spring illustrates, a case of regime stability quickly can become one of regime breakdown.

Some projects entail higher risk. Scholars who study lesser-known topics or cases are more likely to rely on imported concepts and theories when developing their projects. Studying understudied cases is an important enterprise, and one to which many scholars are committed. However, the practice also generates higher levels of uncertainty when developing a research design. No established body of literature exists that lays out the main theoretical debates for these cases. Nor is there scholarly agreement on what constitutes an empirically meaningful development. Preliminary data may be more difficult to obtain. In addition, dissertation advisors may be general experts on the topic or region, but likely are not an expert on your specific countries. Under these circumstances, a researcher is more likely to "import" theories and concepts originally developed in other contexts.

These risks are exacerbated when a long lag exists between defending the prospectus and leaving for the field. The problem is particularly acute for graduate students who rely on external grants to fund their fieldwork. Polished, well-specified grant applications are due in the fall; awards are announced in the spring; and travel may commence in the late summer or early fall. Thus, graduate students may wait an additional year before heading into the field. This lag increases the likelihood that preliminary work can become outdated.

My project scored high on these risk factors. My dissertation focused on understudied cases. More than a year lapsed between defending the prospectus and leaving for the field. Crucially, I imported the outcome to be explained: state response to protest. I wanted to study the interaction between government, opposition, and average citizens within nondemocratic regimes. These interactions usually occur behind the scenes. Mass protests and their consequences seemed to be an observable way to study these dynamics. I knew that protests had been an important phenomenon across the post-Soviet region since perestroika (e.g., Beissinger 2002; Ekiert and Kubik 1999). When I defended my prospectus in 2006, the "color revolutions" had recently toppled governments in Georgia, Ukraine, and Kyrgyzstan. In Uzbekistan, by contrast, government troops had used force to quell an uprising in Andijon, massacring hundreds of protesters. These events exposed important aspects of government-opposition dynamics in seemingly similar post-Soviet countries. I inferred that studying state response to protest would expose the underlying dynamics in my case studies as well.

Warning Signs in the Field

What does a crisis of research design look like? Four warning signs follow.

First, researchers should take heed if data collected in the field contradicts their preliminary coding of the dependent variable. As previously discussed, these discrepancies could occur if a major political event has transformed the situation on the ground or if your preliminary research is outdated when you arrive at your field site. Scholars also can be misled by biased sources used during preliminary research. For scholars who do international research, the sources available in the United States rarely reflect the full range of viewpoints as those on the ground. Most user-generated online content—such as Facebook updates, YouTube videos, or blog posts—reflect the opinions of younger, urban, upper-class citizens. Official policy analyses conducted by international aid agencies or the local government frequently advance a political agenda. Easily accessible research contacts often include friends-of-friends, official spokesmen, or members of a diaspora community. These groups are unlikely to be representative of the larger population. My preliminary work was based on a protest event dataset that I constructed using news articles from Azerbaijan, Kazakhstan, and Belarus. These articles were available through the US Department of State's FBIS reports. However, most of these articles were from opposition-affiliated newspapers, which overestimated the importance of their activities.

A second red flag involves conceptualization. Fieldwork may reveal important dimensions of the dependent variable. A project may need reworking if interview data, personal observation, or quantitative evidence suggests that the outcome does not capture the full story. One interview subject in Kazakhstan, for example, told of a major protest that was allowed to proceed. Police stood by as thousands marched through the city, but undercover security agents hid inside streets and back alleys, arresting participants on their way home. Thus, the protest appeared to be tolerated, although the participants incurred harsh administrative and coercive penalties.[1] My conceptualization had not accounted for this more complex state response.

Third, field research may expose unforeseen anomalies in your case selection. I faced this problem with the longitudinal aspect of my case selection. I had focused my dataset on the years 2002 to 2004, which allowed for a tidy research design. During this time, the governments in Azerbaijan, Belarus, and Kazakhstan responded quite differently to protests, although they were ruled by regimes with nearly equal levels of political openness (Marshall and Jaggers 2006) and maintained similar levels of security personnel (Institute for Strategic Studies 2004). However, my interviews in the field revealed that these years were highly unusual, especially in Azerbaijan. In the early 2000s in Azerbaijan, the state did sanction hundreds of antigovernment protests, as the news reports had suggested. However, those years corresponded to a time of political transition in Azerbaijan, as power was passed from President Heydar Aliyev to his son, Ilham. This contentious issue existed both inside and outside of government, so protests were more frequent and more tolerated. Today, Ilham Aliyev has a solid hold on power. Azerbaijan's government has tightened legal and administrative measures against expressions of public dissent. Few political protests have occurred since 2005.

The fourth, and most serious, signal that a project needs to be reworked occurs when respondents attribute different meaning to the events under study. In both Kazakhstan and Azerbaijan, I heard during interviews that protests were not significant. When asked whether protests were important to understanding the political process, one expert responded, "In practice and concretely, in Kazakhstan they are not important. They don't play a role in politics because no one goes to protests."[2] Another person summarized that "much of politics in Kazakhstan is a performance (*spektakl'*)" designed to impress outsiders.[3] In Azerbaijan, many protests in the early 2000s were described as "small" and "not significant," despite their heavy coverage in the media.[4] These comments implied that protests were not the most accurate lens to study government-opposition relations in these countries.

Redesign in the Field and Beyond

Researchers need to make a choice when confronted with these warning signs. They may proceed with the original research plan or choose to shift the design of the research project. Retooling in the field is imperative when your original project is premised on data or assumptions that were factually incorrect. But the decision is rarely so straightforward. Sometimes other mitigating factors must be considered. For example, retooling is advised if these warning signs are accompanied by a quest for data that turns out to be hidden or nonexistent (Chambers-Ju, this book).

Navigating this decision requires close attention to your own motivations. What drives your interest in this project? Some projects find purpose in making a theoretical contribution——by resolving a theoretical debate, or elucidating an overlooked concept. Other projects are motivated by the potential to make an empirical contribution—shedding light on an understudied set of cases, or highlighting an underappreciated development. Indeed, successful research projects accomplish both. Nonetheless, identify the unique contribution of your research and your motivation for pursuing it.

I considered sticking with the original research design. After all, my preliminary research was not wrong; it just did not capture the whole story of politics in these countries. Doing so, however, would have left two key problems unsolved. First, given the closure of political regimes in these countries since 2004, it was difficult to collect high-quality data from my interviews. Furthermore, I could not shake the feeling that, across my cases, these individual protest events were embedded within larger patterns of government-opposition interaction. It seemed less accurate to consider a narrow time period or to focus on the micro-level analysis of protest events. With great trepidation, I abandoned my neatly controlled research design. I broadened the scope of the project in ways that I hoped would capture some important aspect of politics in these countries. Doing this required reworking the design in the field as well as continued revisions after I arrived home.

Retooling in the Field

Here are four steps I took while in the field.

(1) Adjusted the Interview Questions

I broadened the scope of my interview questions by asking my respondents to place these events into context for me. What did these protests mean? In Azerbaijan, why had protest activity died down after the mid-2000s? I asked about the steps that each government took to preempt contentious political activity. I also posed less-structured background questions to give my interview subjects a chance to teach me about politics in their country. What is the most important thing to know about how politics works here? How do people express dissent here? Who is the opposition, and what do you think about them?

(2) Wrote Memos

Advisors commonly suggest keeping a fieldwork journal to record your progress and to process your ongoing reactions. In the early months of fieldwork, I recorded my surprising findings and panicked reactions. The journal created a paper trail for how and why I modified the project and proved crucial for later discussions with advisors and funding agencies. As I was rebuilding the project, however, I wrote directed memos. Every two weeks in the field, I wrote a three- to five-page document summarizing what I knew about a single topic in that country. I focused these memos on events, processes, or potential causal factors that had come up repeatedly in my interviews. These memos helped to organize my thoughts, and they ultimately provided the analytical framework for my dissertation.

(3) Revised the Case Selection

After conducting fieldwork in Kazakhstan and Azerbaijan, I decided that it was not feasible to pursue fieldwork in Belarus. Belarus no longer provided adequate variation within the larger research project. Therefore, I developed an alternative plan to conduct research in Georgia and Ukraine. Both Georgia and Ukraine had experienced electoral revolutions in the mid-2000s, when mass protests about fraudulent elections culminated in the defection of the security apparatus and the ruler's resignation. The protests provided broader perspective on the interaction between government and opposition, including the different ways that the state might respond to opposition mobilization. By expanding the range of outcomes and cases, I increased variation in the outcome of interest and created the opportunity for a richer, deeper analysis.

(4) Consulted with Advisors and Funding Agencies

Discussing these problems with advisors and funding agencies was daunting. It is difficult to admit that things are not going well in the field. In addition, advisors may be hard to reach, and funding agencies are generally unwilling to approve major changes. Regular written communication was key. Documents to my dissertation committee detailed what I had learned, problems that had arisen, and new directions that had opened. My funding organization required me to submit periodic written reports, which helped me organize my thoughts and communicate how the project was evolving. In addition, as I neared the end of my stay in Azerbaijan, I prepared a detailed memo for the funding organization requesting approval to change field sites. The memo outlined why conducting fieldwork in Belarus was not feasible and why Ukraine was an appropriate substitute. I explained to whom I had consulted in obtaining this information, the specific problems that I anticipated, and an alternative plan that preserved the character of the project.

Further Reworking at Home

The process of reconstructing my project continued after I returned to the States. I continued to write memos as I processed and analyzed the data. For months, I reworked the argument and revised the analytical framework before writing the first draft chapter. In the end, the overall point of inquiry remained similar from my prospectus to the dissertation, and ultimately to the book manuscript. The project continues to ask why some nondemocratic regimes give political opponents significant leeway to organize, while others enforce strict limits on these activities. However, the manuscript uses political opposition groups as the unit of analysis, rather than certain activities. I conceptualize political opposition quite broadly—as any organization that criticizes the government—a definition that reflects the situation on the ground. The causal argument is something that I would not have predicted before fieldwork. Based on data collected in the field, I argue that these policies can be traced to divergent patterns of state corruption. *The Logic of Kleptocracy* thus contributes to the growing literatures explaining variation among non-democratic regimes and the sustainability of non-democratic rule.

Conclusion

Conducting original research is an iterative process of deductive and inductive reasoning. Within this process, fieldwork can serve several purposes: revealing exciting new data sources, suggesting new hypotheses for exploration, or offering a fresh perspective on your topic. Fieldwork also may lead to more distressing developments, even raising doubts that your original research plans are appropriate for the context.

In conclusion, here is a short list to confronting and resolving a crisis of research design.

1. In the field, keep sight of your original motivations. There is a distinction between modifying your research design versus abandoning a project altogether.

2. Consult with advisors as soon as problems arise, and apprise funding organizations.

3. Write memos summarizing what you have learned. Yet, many of these problems can be mitigated by careful attention in the preliminary research stage.

4. Plan a preliminary trip to your field site. Even a short trip can establish feasibility, expose the broader context, and field-test the methods of data collection.

5. Stay up to date on developments in your case studies. Factors that seem external to your project may take on relevance later.

6. Develop a backup plan. Entertain the possibility that your question, method, or case selection will prove not feasible. Discuss this possibility with your advisor before leaving for the field, and build flexibility into your research plans.

Reprinted from Jody LaPorte. 2014. "Confronting a Crisis of Research Design." PS: Political Science & Politics *47 (2). Cambridge University Press: 414–17. doi:10.1017/S1049096514000328.*

Notes

1. Author Interview, Respondent 4116, Almaty Kazakhstan, May 2008.
2. Author Interview, Respondent 9387, Almaty Kazakhstan, March 2008.
3. Author Interview, Respondent 4815, Almaty Kazakhstan, March 2008.
4. Author Interview, Respondent 8480, Baku Azerbaijan, November 2008.

References

Beissinger, Mark. 2002. *Nationalist Mobilization and the Collapse of the Soviet State.* Cambridge: Cambridge University Press.

Ekiert, Grzegorz and Jan Kubik. 1999. *Rebellious Civil Society: Popular Protest and Democratic Consolidation in Poland, 1989–1993.* Ann Arbor: University of Michigan Press.

Institute for Strategic Studies. 2004. *The Military Balance.* London: Institute for Strategic Studies.

Kapiszewski, Diane, Lauren Morris MacLean , and Benjamin Read. 2014. *Field Research in Political Science.* Cambridge: Cambridge University Press.

Lieberman, Evan. 2004. "Preparing for Field Research." *Qualitative Methods: Newsletter of the APSA Organized Section on Qualitative Methods* 2 (1): 3–7.

Lynch, Julia. 2004. "Tracking Progress While in the Field." *Qualitative Methods: Newsletter of the APSA Organized Section on Qualitative Methods* 2 (1): 10–15.

Marshall, Monty and Keith Jaggers. 2006. Polity IV Dataset. College Park, MD: Center for International Development and Conflict Management, Univ. of Maryland. www.cidcm.umd.edu/polity.

Part Four

The Profession and the Public

Political Science and the Public Sphere Today

18

ROGERS M. SMITH

L ike many other political scientists I have over the years worried, sometimes in print, about our discipline and its broader contributions to public life. In the mid-1990s, I participated an interdisciplinary conference organized by the American Academy of Arts and Sciences to analyze transformations in four disciplines over the last fifty years. That experience prompted me to become more of a student of the history of American political science, its problems, and its contributions to knowledge and to public life (Bender and Schorske 1997; Smith 1997, 271–305). Then in fall 2000, I was one of the initial recipients of a manifesto from a "Mr. Perestroika" decrying the state of political science and I participated in the listserv discussions the manifesto quickly generated (Monroe 2005, 9–11). Though I did not agree with every particular, I shared many of the basic concerns Mr. Perestroika and others expressed. I drafted an open letter summarizing them that many leading political scientists signed and sent it to the editor of *PS: Political Science & Politics*, and I then went on to write several pieces elaborating "Perestroikan" views (Smith 2002a; 2002b; 2005). Later I participated in discussions organized by the Social Science Research Council addressing the relationship of various academic disciplines to the public sphere in the twenty-first century.[1] Most recently I served on the American Political Science Association's Task Force on Public Engagement in 2013–2014.[2] These experiences have reinforced some of my longstanding concerns about political science but have added new ones that seem important to raise today.

To preview the main points: the analysis of the intellectual challenges facing the discipline that I offered in the past, focused on the tensions between trying to achieve rigorous science and trying to serve American democracy, seems to have held up well. All that means, however, is that despite real progress on some fronts, those tensions remain and have in some ways become still more debilitating, particularly for the capacities of political science to enrich the public sphere. But the discipline is now also challenged, probably more severely challenged, by changes in modern American higher education, including declining public support and the increased segregation of higher education faculty members into a small cadre of high-paid researchers who do limited teaching, and a large number of economically insecure teachers who lack time and resources for research.

These transformations in higher education affect all disciplines. But I believe they especially compound the difficulties facing good political science research and teaching, in ways that diminish the discipline's capacities to enhance broader public understandings of politics. I do not despair for the future of political science or higher education due to these difficulties. But they do define intellectual and institutional challenges that all contemporary academics must confront.

My focus here is on American political science and American higher education. But America is not *so* exceptional; I will also draw on the broader analyses provided in a *European Political Science* journal symposium that featured the Canadian John Trent's analysis of various efforts by the International Political Science Association to assess the state of political science around the globe (Trent 2011, 191–209). I will first discuss how tensions between goals of intellectual rigor and public relevance, and efforts to minimize or deny the often deleterious consequences of these tensions for political science scholarship and teaching, continue and in some ways have worsened today. Then I will turn to trends transforming and, frankly, threatening higher education to clarify why these longstanding tensions in political science and related disciplines pose heightened dangers now. I conclude with some observations on how political scientists might better respond to the challenges we face in the twenty-first century.

The Tensions in American Political Science, Past and Present

From its inception, the discipline of political science in the United States has been shaped by a desire to be as rigorous a science as possible, on the one hand, and to serve American democracy, on the other (Smith 1997, 271, 273–275). From the profession's formation in the early twentieth century, most of its leaders have conceived of science as involving extensive, accurate data collection used for systematic testing of hypotheses derived from theories that generally have taken one or more of the natural sciences, and sometimes economics or psychology, as their models. The object of this work has always been in part, as Charles Beard argued in 1908, "to seek the truth" about politics "simply in the spirit of science" (Beard 1993, 127). But like most political scientists, Beard also contended that such research would enable the "teacher" of political science to convey "necessary" knowledge that would prepare each pupil "as a citizen of this great nation" to engage in wiser "thought and action" (Beard 1993, 127).

In the past I argued that historically, these disciplinary goals have often proven to be in conflict. In fact there have been three conflicts: first, scientific "truth" about politics has often appeared to discredit instead of affirming the feasibility and desirability of democracy; second, scientific truth has also appeared to challenge many of the claims Americans advance to celebrate their country; and third, some political scientists have concluded that serving democracy and serving America are in many ways two very different, sometimes opposed projects. Most US political scientists, however, have still presented themselves as simultaneously seeking to advance science and to serve democratic citizens and American institutions.

For example, after leading a very successful APSA Presidential Task Force, Theda Skocpol and Lawrence Jacobs argued that "political scientists have responsibilities and obligations in return for our privileges. One of our responsibilities is to maintain rigorous standards for research... For more than a century, though, political scientists have also appreciated that... (we also) have broader responsibilities to use our research capacities and teaching opportunities to scrutinize the health of our democracy." They contended it was part of "our duty as citizens in a democracy...to pursue rigor in the service of the public good" (Jacobs and Skocpol 2006). Like these scholars, many political scientists have not expressed concern that there might be deep incompatibilities in these goals, that the pursuit of rigor might not serve democracy, America, or the public good. I believe they have not focused on such possible conflicts in part out of sincere conviction, in part because they have wished the discipline to appear valuable in the eyes of the American government agencies, private donors, and mass publics that have provided its material bases.

Today, despite its name, the American Political Science Association rarely expresses its aims in overtly American-centered terms, but its basic goals remain the same. Its official "core objectives" begin with "promoting scholarly research and communication, domestically and internationally," followed by "promoting high quality teaching and education about politics and government." The objectives conclude with "serving the public, including disseminating research and preparing citizens to be effective citizens and political participants."[3] The assumption remains that by discovering and disseminating truth about politics and government, political science research and teaching will in fact serve "the public," however defined, and equip "citizens" to participate effectively in "politics," presumably democratic politics allowing for civic participation—rather than discrediting the feasibility and desirability of democratic citizenship. These objectives also express the assumption that political science research and teaching go hand in hand, a long-fragile belief that has further eroded in the last two decades, as I will discuss.

There are two notable patterns in the discipline's history related to the tensions between discovering scientific truths about politics and aiding American democracy. On the individual level, many leading American political scientists, including Charles Beard (who was president of the American Political Science Association before becoming president of the American Historical Association), Arthur Bentley, Charles Merriam, Harold Lasswell, David Easton, Gabriel Almond, and Robert Dahl, stressed making political science more scientific early in their careers; but all came to place greater stress on serving democracy later in their lives (Smith 1997, 275). Yet on the collective level, the discipline has over time given greater priority to becoming more truly scientific, rather than to contributing to democracy or America—while continuing to seek to minimize the tensions among those goals (Smith 1997, 276). That trend has persisted despite periodic outbursts of resistance, such as the protests of the Caucus for a New Political Science in the late 1960s. The predominance of the quest to become a true science contributed to the ascendancy of rational choice theory and more sophisticated quantitative analyses through the 1980s and into the early 1990s (Smith 1997, 277–278). I judged in 1996, however, that rational choice theory was coming to be seen as an important source of "tools and hypotheses" for the discipline, but not as a credible "grand unifying theory" of politics. The profession seemed headed instead into an era of intellectual pluralism in which the strongest emphasis would be on more empirically rigorous testing of hypotheses that were parts of "middle-level" theories of particular political phenomena (Smith 1997, 288, 291).

What has happened since then? At the turn of the century, political science experienced another uprising, this time termed the "Perestroika" movement, protesting what its participants, including me, saw as the discipline's undue privileging of quantitative methods and rational choice theory over other forms of analysis, and its neglect of important political questions not readily amenable to such methods (Monroe 2005; Tarrow 2008). By then I saw a further specification of the tension between the discipline's scientific and its public service aspirations. Often the only questions that could be answered at what was taken to be the highest level of scholarly rigor were relatively narrow, technical aspects of larger issues—so the discipline ended up saying very little of substance about those issues (Smith 2002b, 199–201).

Robert Putnam's 2002 American Political Science presidential address, "The Public Role of Political Science," exemplifies the predominant response of the profession to these concerns. Putnam insisted that various scholars, including me, had overstated the tensions between "rigor and relevance," and that "scientific rigor and public relevance" were in fact "mutually supportive," just as "the founders of the APSA" had believed (Putnam 2003a, 251). But he agreed that "in recent years" the "salience" of the goal of contributing to "public understanding and the vitality of democracy" had "dimmed" in the profession, though he also believed that political science was "nearing the end of a period in which activism has been de-emphasized and even de-legitimated by our professional norms" (2003a, 249, 251). He advised his "more scientific" colleagues, "Better an approximate answer to an important question than an exact answer to a trivial question," and his "less scientific" colleagues, "More precise is better" (2003a, 252).[4] He called for a political science that used many methods, engaged many disciplines, and that ecumenically included both "problem-driven" and "method-driven" work while returning to "a phase of more active engagement in the world" (2003a, 252–253).

Putnam's positions—that early twenty-first century political science did need to seek more active engagement with real-world problems and needed to do so in methodologically pluralistic fashion, but that all scholars should see the quest for scientific rigor, defined chiefly in terms of "counting and modeling," as overwhelmingly "supportive" of these goals—capture well what I see as the prevailing sensibilities in American political science today. The discipline's leaders endorse intellectual pluralism and the need to address substantively important questions more strongly than many did prior to the perestroika "revolt," while largely adhering to the view that formal modeling and quantitative methods, now more often including randomized field experiments, generally if not always represent the most rigorous forms of political science. David Laitin, for example, responded to what he understood to be perestroikan concerns by arguing that narratives had useful roles to play in social science in conjunction with formal models and quantitative analyses, but he cautioned against "a pluralism that sees formal and statistical research as only two of a thousand flowers that should be permitted to bloom" (Laitin 2003, 179). They were instead essential to modern social science endeavors. Though many disciplinary leaders agree, a number are more skeptical than Laitin and some influential rational choice scholars have often been about rational choice theory as a candidate for a grand, unifying theory of all politics.

Notable in this regard is Jon R. Bond's presidential address to the Southern Political Science Association, published in 2007. Bond professed his wholehearted commitment to the scientific method as conventionally understood. But just for that reason, he was "not persuaded that rational choice theory will provide the Newtonian breakthrough for political science" because he saw it as "nonfalsifiable" (Bond 2007, 95). Bond maintained that though we can test whether actors pursue particular goals rationally, we can always imagine an alternate rational choice model in which the actors' goals are defined as doing whatever they are in fact found to have done. So we cannot falsify the theoretical claim that all behavior can be deemed rationally instrumental to the achievement of some goals. At most we can find that some behavior was not rational for the goals we thought, perhaps incorrectly, that the actors held. While that finding may lead us to reconsider our characterizations of their goals, it leaves the question of whether we should regard their conduct as rational unanswered. Bond concluded that rational choice provides particular models that are falsifiable, but no testable general theory of politics.

Because many of the most scientifically committed political scientists like Bond have now reached this conclusion, and no alternative grand theory of politics has subsequently emerged, the discipline now displays considerable intellectual pluralism, though as much by default as by conviction. Scholars seeking to achieve a more scientific political science have felt compelled to identify that quest simply with the use of scientific methods, not with any particular substantive or theoretical focus. At the same time, those commitments have continued to arouse anxieties that too much modern political science research is purely "method-driven" and so does not illuminate important political problems in ways that can inform and advance debates and deliberation in the public sphere (Soss et al. 2006).

Yet despite Robert Putnam's hope for an upsurge in publicly-relevant research, and despite general disillusionment with the most sweeping ambitions of rational choice theorists, the different camps are still by no means equal in size or status. Political science has continued to trend toward the predominance of research that is most focused on achieving rigorously specified and tested findings, with only secondary concern for how far those findings are relevant to major aspects of contemporary public issues. That focus may explain why there is a tiny number of contemporary American political scientists whose professional research results have made them prominent contributors to public debates. The best-known political scientists, such as former Secretary of State Condoleeza Rice and the now-notorious David Patraeus, are famous for what they have done in public service and private life, not for their political science scholarship.

In recent years, the two closest candidates for "public intellectual" standing due to their scholarly contributions were probably Nobel Prize Winner Elinor Ostrom and Putnam himself. As a crude measure of their public impact, Putnam's most cited work, *Bowling Alone: The Collapse and Revival of American Community*, has close to 35,000 citations on, while Ostrom's *Governing the Commons: The Evolution of Institutions for Collective Action* has over 20,000. Yet *Bowling Alone* primarily addresses the forms of social life that are and are not conducive to the formation of "social capital" (Putnam 2000). It rarely directly addresses politics or most public issues, though social capital is found to be conducive to political engagement. The same is true of Putnam's more prescriptive book, *Better Together: Restoring the American Community*. Its emphasis is on initiatives by community groups and businesses in civil society, not on government action—not even on why government action would be inappropriate—though it cannot avoid discussing government as a sector pertinent to these initiatives (Putnam 2003b). In comparison, though Ostrom's seminal book has a wide audience among scholars and policymakers, and though it does assess government responses to public resource issues among other alternatives, it has not put a signature idea into public circulation in the manner of Putnam's "bowling alone" and "social capital" concepts. Insofar as it has had a broader impact, the book has conveyed a similar "civil society" message suggesting that local voluntary associations are often better than national governments or markets for resolving resource development and allocation problems (Ostrom 1990).

There are, to be sure, a few other political scientists whose ideas published in their scholarly works have affected important public debates. Most notable, perhaps, are the late Samuel P. Huntington, whose *Clash of Civilizations* book and preceding article together have more than 23,000 citations, and his student Francis Fukuyama, whose *End of History* book and article have more than 18,000 (Fukuyama and Huntington 1996). But unlike the Putnam and Ostrom books, few regard those works primarily as examples of modern, "professional" political science. And while the *New York Times* once called Princeton's Robert P. George "this country's most influential conservative Christian thinker," and George's ideas are laid out in his books, those works, too, are not seen as exemplars of modern political science, and in comparison with the writings of Putnam, Ostrom, Huntington, and Fukuyama, they are not read nearly so widely in the profession (Kirkpatrick 2009; George 1995).[5] George is most influential due to his advisory roles with Catholic leaders, government agencies, and the Federalist Society.

Apart from Putnam and Ostrom, the work of "professional" political science that may have had the greatest public impact in the United States since 2000 is Donald Green and Alan Gerber's *Get Out the Vote: How to Increase Your Vote Turnout*, which has become the Bible for contemporary campaign organizations (Green and Gerber 2008; Nielsen 2012). But this book, with roughly 420 citations (though their related scholarly articles add close to 1500 more) has influenced the tactical conduct of political professionals far more than it has public understanding of politics. Even so, by getting campaigners to knock on doors and talk to people instead of running more television ads, it may have done more than most academic works to inspire active participation in democratic self-governance.

Not only is the list of American political scientists whose professional scholarship has had a substantial public impact very short; it also has a political tilt that is understandable but disturbing. Even though the authors of these works are by no means all conservatives or neoconservatives—only George and at times Fukuyama have been politically active in those circles—their messages have nonetheless been broadly consonant with the conservative tide in American politics over the past generation. These works tend to celebrate many traditional American values and institutions, to express concern about loss of older civic virtues, and most importantly, to favor decentralized, civil society solutions to common problems—not big government, certainly not any radical egalitarian reform agendas. It is not surprising that political science scholarship that is more in keeping with the dominant political mood of an era should attract more attention than work that is out of step. But if one believes that there are at least aspects of that mood that warrant criticism, then it is questionable whether these patterns show that modern professional political science is doing all it ideally should to improve public life.

To be sure, the still-recent creation of this journal, *Perspectives on Politics*, has provided a venue in which political scientists often draw on their professional research to highlight its pertinence to major public issues in accessible fashion; and political scientists are also contributing to the ever-burgeoning blogosphere, sometimes influencing discussion in the mainstream media and broader public debates.[6] But these impacts still appear limited. They have not visibly altered the predominant tendencies in most published political science research.

The patterns I discern in recent American political science fit broadly with the global trends portrayed by John E. Trent in his 2009 presentation to the World Congress of the International

Political Science Association held in Santiago, Chile. Trent, a former Secretary General of the IPSA, based his remarks on his work as coeditor of a book series on the state of political science around the world and on papers presented at a 2008 IPSA conference in Montreal devoted to the condition of international political science.

Trent argued that, globally, twenty-first century political science benefits from much better databases and improved quantitative methods than in the past. But rather than being entirely devoted to such quantitative work, the discipline still displays "an eclectic, pluralistic set of approaches to political analysis" (Trent 2011, 193–194). There is neither methodological nor theoretical consensus. Trent perceived that in particular "rational choice theory was generally condemned" as a candidate to be an overarching theory of all politics, and he also saw "appreciation of historical sociology and normative theory" on the rise (Trent 2011, 194–195). Nonetheless, Trent reported that more generally, "almost all the political science research paradigms are severely questioned," and tensions "run deep between 'scientific' and 'political' orientations," with a "mainstream/non-mainstream division and deprecation between quantitative (e.g., empirical/scientific) versus qualitative (e.g., philosophical/institutional) practitioners" (Trent 2011, 194–195).

Overall, Trent portrayed a fragmented, overspecialized "discipline in search of its soul and out of touch with the real world of politics." He called for political scientists to have a greater sense of their responsibilities to be relevant to the concerns of "the public and the political class, society and democracy" (Trent 2011, 196–197, 199) He also thought, however, that these difficulties were mainly with "the theory and research side of the discipline, rather than our teaching" (Trent 2011, 204).

His presentation drew a sharp response from former IPSA president and leading German political scientist Max Kaase, who noted that "many important scientific inventions were initially made without any concern for any broader social relevance" and that "differentiation and specialization lead to both academic and human progress" (Kaase 2011). He thought any undue emphasis on quantification was primarily a North American, not a global problem, and he did not see it as a great problem anywhere, because he saw "research specialization" as "a *conditio sine qua non* for progress in political science knowledge creation" (Kaase 2011, 231) Yet Kaase also stressed, contrary to Trent, that the growing numbers of university students in many places, combined with the need for specialized research, was "probably increasing the distance between teaching and research." Specialization, while good for "the development of the field," was "clearly a challenge to teaching" (Kaase 2011, 230–231).

The Trent-Kaase exchange suggests that the trends discernible in American political science are more than simply a US phenomenon. It also raises the vital issue of whether teaching is endangered by these trends; and though I am in many ways sympathetic with Trent, here I think Kaase's perception is correct. More than I recognized twenty years ago, developments in higher education are producing new challenges in all disciplines to older models of professors as both researchers and teachers. These developments appear particularly threatening for the research and teaching contributions of the discipline of political science, in ways that may well be damaging for the profession's contributions to the public sphere. To understand why, it is useful to review some of the recent transformations in higher education that are becoming all too familiar.

The Transformations in Higher Education and Implications for Political Science

The most important transformations are, first, the expansion of modern higher education that has fostered increased teaching needs at precisely the same time that more and more colleges and universities have sought to become research centers, not just teaching institutions (Geiger 2004, 2). Second is the potentially lethal combination of higher university costs and declining public funding. The resulting revenue challenges have produced cutbacks in non-income-producing programs and much higher tuition rates—accompanied by increased reliance on potentially lucrative university-corporate partnerships and an embrace of bottom-line focused corporate managerial styles within universities (Ginsberg 2011, ch. 6; Geiger 2004, 3, 24–25, 29–33, 41, 44, 47, 180–231). Third, and most notorious, is the increased reliance on adjuncts, graduate students, and other sorts of lesser paid, non-tenure track faculty members to do the bulk of the instruction in American research universities and even many American teaching-oriented institutions.

At the same time, within the ranks of tenured and tenure track faculty, fissures are deepening. Often because cutbacks in faculty size have accompanied rising number of students, many state universities and community colleges are requiring their standing faculty to teach more, even as they also increase adjunct and graduate student teaching. But scholars in more affluent research universities (including me) are being asked to do less teaching than in the past (Geiger 2004, 170–172). Such research scholars are, however, often expected to do more to win grants from foundation, corporate, and government research funding programs, even as most of these are shrinking. So many scholars devote their time chiefly to income-generating centers rather than to classrooms or to forms of research that do not attract large grants (Geiger 2004, 172–179).

As Joanna Scott and I have stressed, these transformations are massive in scale: in 1960, three-quarters of college instructors in the United States were full-time tenured or tenure-track faculty. By 2009, only 27 percent were, with adjuncts and graduate students providing most of the rest of the teaching (Stainburn 2010; Scott and Smith 2010). And in the last 30 years, the full costs of four-year public universities in the United States has risen almost 500 percent, while the main source of student financial aid for these institutions, Pell grants, rose much more slowly—so that these grants only cover 33 percent of public university costs, versus almost 70 percent in 1980 (Scott and Smith 2010; Carey 2010) As students and their families have paid more and more for less and less teaching by senior tenured faculty members, sharp criticisms of the costly scholarship and teaching being provided by modern American colleges and universities and calls for substantial restructuring including elimination of tenure have mounted. Strikingly, the authors of many of these critiques are themselves leading university administrators and academics (Bok 2007; Hacker and Dreifus 2010; Arum 2011).[7]

These transformations pose major challenges to all disciplines and all institutions of higher education, even though there are important variations: top private universities and a few elite public research universities are less burdened than most public institutions. Scholars in the STEM—science, technology, engineering, and math—disciplines, along with health researchers, are faring better than most in the humanities and social sciences. But throughout higher education, trends are working against maintaining the "symbiosis of multiple purposes" long achieved by having scholars who were both researchers and teachers, with great academic freedom to do both, as the typical faculty members in post-secondary institutions (Geiger 2004, 13–14).

There are good reasons to think that increasing the distance between research and teaching has real costs. Even in the STEM fields, one recent study found that graduate students who taught displayed greater improvement in their research skills than graduate students who did not teach, as evaluated by how their research proposals improved over time. A qualitative survey of economists produced a similar finding (Berrett 2011). But many education reformers, including the Texas Public Policy Foundation, a think tank associated with former Texas governor and recurrent presidential candidate Rick Perry, have argued that "transparency and accountability" can be improved by instead "emphasizing teaching and research as separate efforts in higher education" (Berrett 2011). They are thereby adding political reinforcement to the modern patterns in which more academics are becoming either researchers or teachers but not truly both.

Even so, it is chiefly market competition for top research scholars—competition that education scholar Roger Geiger terms "the arms race"—that has generated the trends toward providing the most prestigious researchers with reduced teaching. Of course this means that often demands for college-level instruction are met by assigning to other scholars teaching loads so great that doing serious research becomes difficult if not impossible (Geiger 2004, 13, 59–60, 237–238).

And the comparatively light teaching duties at top American research universities are being achieved and preserved through more visible embrace of ties to wealthy donors, corporate and individuals on which universities feel they must rely. For example, the leading public university political science department in the United States at the University of California–Berkeley is now officially the "Charles and Louise Travers Department of Political Science," named for an alumnus donor who made a fortune in mineral development. A top private university, New York University, houses "The Wilf Family Department of Politics," named for a family of real estate developers and businessmen that includes several NYU alumni. Undeniably, both public and private universities in America have always partly depended on gifts from wealthy alumni, often recognized in the naming of buildings and endowed chairs. But the recent overt identification of prominent departments with particular private donors symbolizes how this reliance is becoming a yet more significant part of modern American university life.

Although these developments affect virtually every facet of academia today, they interact with the traditional and still-present tensions in political science in ways that are distinctively consequential. However its goals may be conceived, political science is the one discipline above all that cannot avoid being "political." Politics is our profession's subject matter. Whatever methods its practitioners employ, whatever the particular substantive foci of their research and teaching are, political scientists are always likely to produce results that are controversial from some political point of view—either because the results question aspects of the political status quo, or because they affirm aspects of the political status quo, or simply because they emphasize some aspects of politics and neglect others. Even attempting to do "apolitical, pure science" research on politics involves making a sharply contested political choice. There is no safe option.

These realities have been dramatized for political scientists in recent years by the repeated and partly successful efforts of conservative members of Congress to reduce or eliminate National Science Foundation funding for our discipline (Basken 2013). Journalists have perceived these initiatives as hostility to studies "tainted by left-wing biases" (Glenn 2009). That may well be true; but their largest target has been the University of Michigan's American National Election Studies, the survey research many regard as the bedrock of "professional" quantitative political science. Oklahoma Senator Tom Coburn claims that even such work has "little, if anything, to do with science," and he has urged that NSF funds go to "finding solutions for people with severe disabilities, or the next generation of biofuels, or engineering breakthroughs," leaving "political science" to "pundits and voters" (Glenn 2009).

The American Political Science Association has responded in various ways, including its Task Force on Public Engagement appointed by President John Aldrich and chaired by Arthur Lupia, on which I had the pleasure to serve (Lupia and Aldrich 2014). Its report includes many salutary recommendations, including creation of an Outreach Director and Outreach Committee, new public education ventures utilizing modern media, and strengthening writing in the discipline. But change will be difficult. And this recent history confirms that whenever scholars discuss politics in any way, there is always the inescapable risk of upsetting persons in power. Again, that is a risk that political science, more than any other discipline, cannot avoid without ceasing to exist.

I have also long contended that precisely because governments, major media firms, private corporations and nonprofit think tanks of various stripes can and do hire skilled researchers to document and analyze politics, the profession of academic political science should see itself as having special responsibilities that only heighten these risks (Smith 1997, 276–278). The intellectual agendas of all researchers employed outside academia inevitably reflect the interests of the government agencies, media outlets, corporations and think tanks that finance their studies. If academic political science is to make a distinctive contribution, its agenda should therefore be different from the work that such non-academic researchers are doing. That often means asking questions powerful interests do *not* wish to see pursued.

For even if academic political scientists simply strive to provide value that others cannot, they will often feel compelled to question the empirical and normative assumptions and the adequacy of the data and analyses offered by these other, often more "public" researchers, along with those of scholarship generated within the discipline. And when academics seek to explore significant political topics that non-academic researchers neglect, much of their research will turn out to focus on the circumstances of those who are not wealthy, not powerful, and not socially influential—because those groups are not able to commission research in non-academic venues. But if political scientists pay special attention to the poor and to marginalized communities, they are likely to be accused of, at best, not addressing what better-off Americans sees as the nation's most pressing concerns, and of, at worse, doing nothing beyond spouting liberal biases.

Yet even though political scientists should nonetheless address such neglected subjects, let me emphasize that academic political scientists should also feel a special responsibility to pursue many topics that are already standard fare in mainstream "professional" political science. Some political research questions are neglected by non-academic researchers because they present rarefied technical challenges that can be overlooked when the push is to get quickly to "useful" results. Other political science projects address historical issues or require extensive data collection that government agencies, corporations, and think tanks may not see as sufficiently connected to their immediate agendas to warrant support. I have long believed that political scientists should see themselves as "gadflies" in the tradition of Socrates, asking uncomfortable fundamental questions. But it would be wrong to deny that much irreplaceable work is done and must be done by academic political scientists who seek instead to be professional "worker bees," industriously contributing to the collective project of building up a body of reliable scientific findings about politics. The lesson of the NSF controversy, again, is that current trends endanger *both* political science worker bees and gadflies. To many politicians, all the buzzing of all the different types of academic insects sounds the same—and they just start swatting.

Nevertheless, the fact that even "mainstream" quantitative political science is coming under criticism only shows further how the longstanding internal tensions in American political science, and the trends in the discipline's responses to those tensions, are now interacting with external developments in American higher education in ways that justify concern for the profession's vitality. The contested but predominant internal trend to give priority to the goal of becoming more scientific has been bolstered by the external trends separating research from teaching, and by the increasing need to rely on nongovernmental research funding, which goes primarily to what is seen as more "scientific" work. But the profession's research contributions may well prove to be narrowed and skewed by these developments. As top research scholars are increasingly relieved of many of their teaching responsibilities, it becomes easier to pursue highly technical, often esoteric dimensions of the discipline's internal theoretical debates, since those topics are generally not suitable for undergraduate courses. At the same time, however, pressures to focus on dimensions of their research agenda that have value in the eyes of private individual and corporate donors may mount. These conditions increase the risk that research will be excessively tied to donor agendas, or unduly remote from any major substantive political debates, or perhaps even both.

And though political science courses remain popular at most American universities, fewer and fewer political science instructors are now having their teaching fueled by the insights gained from designing and executing significant research projects on a continuing basis—even as the work of research scholars in political science is becoming less informed by experiences of learning student concerns, of seeking to have something to say to them, and of finding how to communicate that content effectively. Widely publicized recent controversies such as the uproar over the University of Illinois' revocation of a tenure offer to Steven Salaita also suggest that non-tenured teachers of political topics, and indeed many of the tenured faculty members who work at financially-stressed public institutions, may be endangered if they teach about politics in unpopular ways.[8] Those anxieties matter, because as is true of political science research, any political science teaching worthy of the name must examine controversial political matters and must present unpopular views concerning those subjects. The more teaching about politics is done by teachers who feel themselves to be in highly vulnerable positions, wary of offending taxpayers, governmental officials, or corporate donors, the more likely it is that political science teaching will be done in ways that simply canvass conventional perspectives, rather than promoting wide-ranging critical reflection and deeper public understanding of important political concerns.

I do not wish to exaggerate these dangers. My perception is that most political scientists in America today still feel very free to pursue the research that they regard as important, while most teachers of political science in modern American higher education classrooms, regardless of rank, still feel they can challenge students with a range of critical perspectives. But it is entirely possible that for many of us, these beliefs are already partly a form of denial, because at some level we know that we run risks if our research or teaching goes very far in unpopular directions. It also seems likely that if current trends continue, these pressures on political science research and teaching will loom larger. It is notable that one of America's leading beneficiaries of higher education, President Barack Obama, is now among those most vociferously championing new rules to make institutions of higher education more accountable for their performance (Shear 2014). The chorus of criticism is broad and growing.

The Road Ahead for Political Science?

In many ways, to be sure this is healthy. These heightened criticisms of higher education are being accompanied by initiatives to improve the accessibility and resources for higher education in important regards, such as President Obama's proposals to fund enrollments in community colleges (Associated Press 2015). And I wish to stress that it is not only politically unrealistic, it is not defensible for political scientists or other academics to seek to be wholly immune from accountability to the governments, private donors, and citizens who supply the resources that enable us to do the research and teaching that we do. Being a professor of political science or anything else is not a matter of divine right. But it also remains true that to study and teach about politics well, political scientists must be conscious of the dangers of having their agendas or their messages dictated closely by any powers that be, including government officials, wealthy corporations, foundations, or individuals, or even democratic public opinion. Political science's contribution to the public sphere must not become only the provision of an echo chamber for the voices of the powerful, rather than the supplying of valuable new political facts or freshly conceived ideas.

Yet if political science is to fare better in fulfilling its core missions, the road forward cannot simply be a road back. The trends I have sketched are largely not reversible, nor would many types of reversal be desirable. Although I do not agree with David Laitin's suggestion that *all* political science research should include formal models and statistical analyses, he is right that it is silly to disdain statistical empirical work and formal modeling. Over the years I have come to believe that political scientists can better serve themselves and others by reflecting more than we often do on how we can combine and build on different sorts of work, instead of arguing about which sorts are better. In recent writings I have suggested that political scientists of all methodological stripes should bear in mind the larger "spirals of politics" in which their studies fit—the paths of political development in which contexts first generate ideas for change; then movements and coalitions form to achieve those changes by gaining control of governing institutions (or tearing down some and creating new ones); and then the policies and institutions of governing coalitions reshape contexts, often generating new political conflicts and developments (Smith 2014, 2015). Perhaps too optimistically, I think that by attending to how the subject matters of our particular studies fit into broader patterns of political development, we can see more clearly how research projects that utilize different methods and that focus on different phases of politics can nonetheless inform each other and collectively contribute to cumulative advances in understanding politics. At a minimum, I suggest that both the discipline's intellectual quests for rigor and significant findings, and its mundane quests for material support, counsel in favor of exploring vigorously how different types of work in political science can be combined to amplify the discipline's overall contributions.

If that message makes me sound like a recent convert to a (very hard to achieve) kind of disciplinary ecumenicalism, I also still insist that such amplification requires us to recognize that scientific rigor is *not* defined by systematic data collection and hypothesis testing alone. Just as fundamentally, rigor requires intellectual honesty about the presumptions that drive our research, about how certain our findings really are, and about what bearing the substance of our research really has on the important substantive political concerns that it is the discipline's mission to address. The intellectual honesty that is the heart of true science also involves communicating the aims and results of our work, in our scholarship and in our teaching, in terms sufficiently comprehensible to our various audiences so that they can judge whether we are doing work that matters in their eyes. Our research must be presented in ways that at least have the potential to be understood, assessed, and utilized productively in the public sphere. For if the reality is that what we are doing, accurately understood, simply does not matter for the public sphere in the eyes of virtually all its participants, it is likely that we are deceiving ourselves about whether the political knowledge we are providing is really worth our efforts, or anyone's support. Self-deception is not good science.

Yet seeking to insure that our work is communicated effectively may well only intensify the pressures arising from external trends. Many in the public may be even more dissatisfied with us when they really comprehend the sorts of questions we are pursuing and the sorts of findings we are producing—particularly when our questions and findings are highly relevant to them, well-conceived and executed, and deeply disturbing. The main response of contemporary American academics to these risks, apart from ignoble choices to write on obscure topics in impenetrable fashion, is to seek to protect academic freedom by maintaining the institution of tenure. It appears increasingly likely, however, that we American academics will not be able for too much longer to continue to justify having jobs for life, without even mandatory retirement, when no other sector of the American economy enjoys such privileges. If so, our battle will have to be not for tenure but for long-term contracts that can protect academic freedom without seeming to evade accountability.

But more fundamentally, we have to use our professional protections and privileges well. This means doing our research in ways that do more to unite the contributions of different flavors of political science and that also address more effectively topics that matter to participants in modern public spheres. It also means something else. In America today, perhaps much more than in other nations, political scientists particularly need to resist the pressures and temptations to move further away from the researcher/teacher model of academic life and toward disciplinary segregation into those who are almost exclusively researchers and those who almost exclusively teach. Despite the volley of recent critical studies, the evidence from enrollments is that many parents and teachers still greatly value political science teaching in institutions of higher education, probably more than they value the great bulk of our research. Many seem unconcerned if our teaching raises serious questions about American institutions, values, and practices, so long as we teach in ways that are informative and thought provoking, not heavily polemical and one-sided. Most value the development of capacities for critical, independent thought, and most recognize that this goal requires challenging inquiries into conventional ways of conducting politics. At the moment, most in the American public are not too happy with the state of contemporary American politics—so many are receptive to hearing at least some critical perspectives. And in an era of declining resources, political science sorely needs the public support that teaching helps to generate.

Indeed, given the limited public impact of most late twentieth-century and twenty-first century American political science scholarship, it is possible, even likely, that today we American political scientists contribute to the public sphere more extensively and distinctively through our teaching than we do in any other way, just as many in the public appear to believe. As I have suggested, there is also good reason to believe that combining teaching and research, difficult as it can be to do, ultimately strengthens both—meaning that if we in American political science strive harder than we have been doing to resist recent trends and maintain, or indeed strengthen, our commitment to being active researchers *and* active teachers, then *both* our research and our teaching may become more valuable to more people. If for much of the twentieth century, leading U. S. political scientists decided late in their careers that the quest to be more scientificshouldnot in theend take priority over the quest to strengthen democracy in America, then early in the twenty-first century, it may be time for political scientists to decide humbly that the best path to strengthening our contributions involves not only doing more rigorous, more interconnected and cumulative, more substantively significant, and more accessible scientific research. We must equally strive to maintain and strengthen our teaching, seeking to combine and do both teaching and research as well as we possibly can.

Reprinted from Rogers M. Smith. 2015. "Political Science and the Public Sphere Today." Perspectives on Politics *13 (2). Cambridge University Press: 366–76. doi:10.1017/S1537592715000225.*

Notes

1. http://publicsphere.ssrc.org/smith-political-science-and-the-public-sphere/. This current paper is a mildly updated version of that discussion. I am grateful to Roy White for excellent research on the earlier version and to Anne Norton for helpful discussion of its themes.
2. http://www.apsanet.org/files/Task%20Force%20Reports/APSA%202014_Task%20Force%20 Report.pdf.
3. American Political Science Association, "Core Objectives"; http://www.apsanet.org/content. asp?contentid51.
4. As a target of Putnam's thoughtful and courteous criticism, let me note that I agree entirely with both these admonitions, though not entirely with the designation of the groups as "more" and "less" scientific.
5. This work, George's most influential, has roughly 500 citations on.
6. *New York Times* columnists David Brooks and Thomas Edsall, for example, regularly cite writings by political scientists as well as other social scientists in writing about public issues.
7. Bok is a former president of Harvard University. Hacker is professor emeritus in political science at Queens College, City University of New York, and Dreifus is an adjunct associate professor at Columbia University. Arum is a sociologist at New York University and director of education research for the Social Science Research Council, and Roksum is a sociologist at the University of Virginia.
8. In response to the apparent influence of specific donors in the revocation of his tenure offer, Salaita has sued both the university and those donors; see Flaherty (2015).

References

Arum, Richard, and Josipa Roksum. 2011. *Academically Adrift: Limited Learning on College Campuses.* Chicago, IL: University of Chicago Press.

Associated Press. 2015. "Obama Proposes Publicly Funded Community Colleges for All." http://www. nytimes.com/aponline/2015/01/09/us/politics/ap-us-obama.html.

Basken, Paul. 2013. "Senate Moves to Limit NSF Spending on Political Science." *Chronicle of Higher Education.* http://chronicle.com/article/Senate-Moves-to-Limit-NSF/138027/.

Beard, Charles A. 1993. "Politics." In *Discipline and History: Political Science in the United States.* Edited by James Farr and Raymond Seidelman. Ann Arbor: University of Michigan Press.

Bender, Thomas, and Carl E. Schorske, eds. 1997. *American Academic Culture in Transformation: Fifty Years, Four Disciplines.* Princeton, NJ: Princeton University Press.

Berrett, Dan. 2011. "Want to Be a Good Researcher? Try Teaching." *Chronicle of Higher Education.*

Bok, Derek. 2007. *Our Underachieving Colleges: A Candid Look at How Much Students Learn and Why They Should Be Learning More.* Princeton, NJ: Princeton University Press.

Bond, Jon R. 2007. "The Scientification of the Study of Politics: Some Observations on the Behavioral Evolution in Political Science." *Journal of Politics* 69: 95.

Carey, Kevin. 2010. "That Old College Lie." *Democracy* 15 (Winter). https://democracyjournal.org/magazine/15/that-old-college-lie/.

Flaherty Colleen. 2015. "Going After the Donors." *Inside Higher Ed.* https://www.insidehighered.com/news/2015/01/30/steven-salaitas-long-anticipated-lawsuit-against-u-illinois-includes-twist.

Fukuyama, Francis. 1992. *The End of History and the Last Man.* New York: Simon & Schuster.

Geiger, Roger L. 2004. *Knowledge and Money: Research Universities and the Paradox of the Marketplace.* Stanford, CA: Stanford University Press.

George, Robert P. 1995. *Making Men Moral: Civil Liberties and Public Morality.* New York: Oxford University Press.

Ginsberg, Benjamin. 2011. *The Fall of the Faculty: The Rise of the All-Administrative University and Why It Matters.* New York: Oxford University Press.

Glenn, David. 2009. "Senator Proposes an End to Federal Support for Political Science." *Chronicle of Higher Education.*

Green, Donald P., and Alan S. Gerber. 2008. *Get Out the Vote: How to Increase Voter Turnout.* Washington, DC: Brookings Institution Press.

Hacker, Andrew, and Claudia Dreifus. 2010. *Higher Education? How Colleges Are Wasting Our Money and Failing Our Kids—and What We Can Do about It.* New York: St. Martin's Press.

Huntington, Samuel P. 1996. *The Clash of Civilizations and the Remaking of the World Order.* New York: Simon & Schuster.

Jacobs, Lawrence R., and Theda Skocpol. 2006. "Restoring the Tradition of Rigor and Relevance to Political Science." *PS: Political Science & Politics* 39 (1):27–31.

Kaase, Max. 2011. "Should Political Science Be More Relevant? A Comment on the Paper by John E. Trent." *European Political Science* 10: 228–231.

Kirkpatrick, David D. 2009. "The Conservative-Christian Big Thinker." *New York Times.* December 20, MM24.

Laitin, David D. 2005. "The Perestroikan Challenge to Social Science." *Politics & Society* 31: 179.

Lupia, Arthur, and John H Aldrich. 2014. "Improving Public Perceptions of Political Science's Value." Report of the Task Force on Improving Public Perceptions of Political Science's Value. Washington, DC: American Political Science Association.

Monroe, Kristen Renwick, ed. 2005. *Perestroika: The Raucous Rebellion in Political Science.* New Haven, CT: Yale University Press.

Nielsen, Rasmus Kleis. 2012. *Ground Wars: Personalized Communication in Political Campaigns.* Princeton, NJ: Princeton University Press.

Ostrom, Elinor. 1990. *Governing the Commons: The Evolution of Institutions for Collective Action.* New York: Cambridge University Press.

Putnam, Robert D. 2000. *Bowling Alone: The Collapse and Revival of American Community.* New York: Simon & Schuster.

Putnam, Robert D. 2003a. "The Public Role of Political Science." Presidential Address. *Perspectives on Politics* 1 (2): 249–255.

Putnam, Robert D. 2003b. *Better Together: Restoring the American Community.* New York: Simon & Schuster.

Scott, Joanna Vecchiarelli, and Rogers M Smith. 2010. "Teaching: The Issues Perestroika Neglected." *PS: Political Science & Politics* 43 (4): 751.

Shear, Michael D. 2014. "Colleges Rattled as Obama Seeks Rating System." *New York Times.* May 25, A1.

Smith, Rogers M. 1997. "Still Blowing in the Wind: The American Quest for a Democratic, Scientific Political Science." In *American Academic Culture in Transformation: Fifty Years, Four Disciplines*. Edited by Thomas Bender, and Carl E. Schorske. Princeton, NJ: Princeton University Press.

Smith, Rogers M. 2002a. "Putting the Substance Back in Political Science." *Chronicle of Higher Education* April 5, sec. 2: Chronicle Review 47: B10–11.

Smith, Rogers M. 2002b. "Should We Make Political Science More of a Science or More about Politics?" *PS: Political Science & Politics* 35 (2): 199–201.

Smith, Rogers M. 2005. "Of Means and Meaning: The Challenges of Doing Good Political Science." In *Perestroika: The Raucous Rebellion in Political Science*. Edited by Kristen Renwick Monroe. New Haven, CT: Yale University Press.

Smith, Rogers M. 2014. "Ideas and the Spiral of Politics: The Place of American Political Thought in American Political Development." *American Political Thought* 3 (1): 126–136.

Smith, Rogers M. 2015. Political Peoplehood. Chicago, IL: University of Chicago Press.

Soss, Joe, Condon Meghan, Holleque Matthew, Wichowsky Amber. 2006. "The Illusion of Technique: How Method-Driven Research Leads Welfare Scholarship Astray." *Social Science Quarterly* 87: 798–807.

Stainburn, Samantha. 2010. "The Case of the Vanishing Full-Time Professor." *New York Times* January 3, ED6.

Tarrow, Sidney G. 2008. "Polarization and Convergence in Academic Controversies." *Theory and Society* 37: 513–36.

Trent, John E. 2011. "Should Political Science Be More Relevant? An Empirical and Critical Analysis of the Discipline." *European Political Science* 10: 191–209.

Disenchanted Professionals: The Politics of Faculty Governance in the Neoliberal Academy

19

Timothy Kaufman-Osborn

On Wisconsin! (A Drama in Three Acts)

Act I: On October 8, 1971, Governor Patrick Lucy signed into law a bill that merged the University of Wisconsin at Madison with the several branches of the Wisconsin State University system. Two years later, the governance structure of the reorganized system was codified in state statute, and the specific role of the faculty was defined as follows:

> The faculty of each institution, subject to the responsibilities and powers of the board, the president, and the chancellor of such institution, shall be vested with responsibility for the immediate governance of such institution and shall actively participate in institutional policy development. As such, the faculty shall have the primary responsibility for academic and educational activities and faculty personnel matters. (Wis. Stat. § 36.09(4) 1973)

With this last sentence, the legislature ascribed to the faculty principal jurisdiction over affairs pertaining to its domains of professional competence, but left unclear what it intended by rendering the exercise of that capacity "subject to the responsibilities and powers" assigned to the governing board and its executive appointees.

Act II: In 1992, a suit concerning the respective roles of the governing board, administrators, and faculty in fashioning a plan to allocate salary increases required the Dane County Circuit Court to clear up the ambiguity left unresolved by the legislature two decades prior. Ruling in favor of faculty and union plaintiffs, in *Spoto v. Board of Regents of the University of Wisconsin System*, the court concluded:

> It is clear that, in order to give the shared governance concept full effect, the term "subject to" may not be defined as an equivalent as "subordinate to." Although the board and its administration are responsible for shared governance and policy, the defendants may not treat shared governance as a matter of administrative convenience... If the faculty's right to participate is to be given any effect, the administration may not exercise unbridled power where it reaches an impasse with faculty over the salary distribution decision. (*Spoto v. Board of Regents...* 1994–95, 15)

On this basis, the court held that the board and its agents had overstepped the limits prescribed by law when they unilaterally imposed a salary plan on faculty, but, at the same time, that any proposal advanced by the faculty was subject to veto by the board or administrators. Doing so, this ruling effectively concluded that adherence to the principle of shared governance implies that no affirmative course of action can be undertaken on matters for which the faculty has "primary responsibility" absent the negotiated concurrence of all three participants.

Act III: Two decades later, in 2013, the Republican Speaker of the Wisconsin State Assembly charged a working group with recommending reforms aimed at re-structuring the "balance of power" among the several parties to university governance in order to enhance its "operational efficiency" (*UW System Shared Governance Reform* 2013).Left unmodified, the report's authors contended, faculty members will continue to affirm their statutorily-guaranteed "primary responsibility for academic and educational activities," as ratified in Spoto, and, in doing so, render the system unable to shift "from an emphasis in a liberal arts education towards an educational background that better prepares them [students] for the job marketplace and utilizes vocational training" (Potts et al. 2013).[1]

Acting on the working group's recommendations, the legislature approved a bill that was signed into law by Governor Scott Walker on July 12, 2015. Aside from replacing gender-specific language, this statute retains a section of the 1973 law that reads as follows:

> Subject to board policy, the chancellors of the institutions in consultation with their faculties shall be responsible for designing curricula and setting degree requirements; determining academic standards and establishing grading systems; defining and administering institutional standards for faculty peer evaluation and screening candidates for appointment, promotion and tenure; recommending individual merit increases; administering associated auxiliary services; and administering all funds, from whatever source allocated, generated or intended for use of their institutions. (Wis. Stat. § 36.09(3) 2015)

The new law, however, eliminated the structure of overlapping jurisdiction inherent in its 1973 predecessor by inserting the phrase "for advising the chancellor regarding" into the passage that had previously ascribed to the faculty "primary responsibility for academic and educational activities and faculty personnel matters." And, in order to lay the specter of *Spoto* forever to rest, the statute provides that the phrase "subject to the responsibilities and powers" of the governing board, the president, and the chancellor shall henceforth be construed as "subordinate to" (Wis. Stat. § 36.09(3m) 2015). What was once the practice of shared governance at Wisconsin is thereby supplanted by an order that reduces the faculty to the status of an advisor whose counsel in all matters, including those for which it is most expert, bears only as much force as its superiors will countenance.

That recent events in Wisconsin are emblematic of a phenomenon extending well beyond its borders is implicit in the title of Larry Gerber's 2014 book, The Rise and Decline of Faculty Governance: Professionalization and the Modern American University. This work offers the best history of faculty participation in the governance of higher education within the United States now available, and the story Gerber relates is one we should all come to know. My concern here is not with that story's particulars, but, rather, with the account Gerber offers for the faculty's shifting fortunes, which, were he to address it, would no doubt include the dissolution of shared governance in Wisconsin. As its title intimates, for Gerber the professionalization of the professoriate accounts for the rise of faculty governance and de-professionalization accounts for its decline; and the phenomenon of de-professionalization he explains in turn by invoking the category of corporatization. In sum: "In recent years the greatest threat to the practice of shared governance has come from those administrators, governing board members, and public officials who seek to corporatize American higher education," and essential to that enterprise is the move to "deprofessionalize the professoriate" (Gerber 2014, 8).

While I do not consider this explanation entirely misguided, I do want to perplex it. To foreshadow this complication, consider Gerber's contention that professionalism is an "ideal premised on the possibility of individuals using their expertise in a disinterested way to achieve the common good" (Gerber 2014, 166). The contrary argument I develop in this essay was anticipated by Sheldon Wolin more than thirty-five years ago:

> Perhaps no single factor has done more to conceal the political nature of the current developments in higher education than the reluctance of academics to admit that there are political stakes and determinants in matters of knowledge. At a time when colleges and universities are desperately seeking to make themselves attractive to government, corporations, and "consumers," and to find ways of patenting research in genetic engineering, of developing real estate, and of diversifying stock portfolios, the academic clings to the rhetoric that portrays the academy as a "community of scholars" devoted to "disinterested truth" (Wolin 1981, 50).

Whereas Gerber contends that the professoriate qua profession has been corrupted in recent decades by the forces of "corporatization," I argue that the project of modern professionalism since its inception has been deeply political not merely in the sense that it is affected by, but also in the sense that it is thoroughly implicated in the generation and legitimation of specific configurations of power. To say this is not to deny that the faculty's capacity to exercise some measure of collective self-governance as well as to determine the trajectory of the colleges and universities that employ them is today under sustained assault. But it is to say that we will not understand what has happened at Wisconsin so long as we remain captivated by an ideal that deflects attention from the key role played by the professional professoriate in assimilating the modern American research university within the regime of liberal and, more recently, neoliberal capitalism.[2]

The Modern Professional Ideal

In the United States, the ideal of modern professionalism is a creature of the late nineteenth and early twentieth centuries, and more specifically, of the Progressive movement (see Abbott 1988; Freidson 2001; and Larson 2013). To furnish an adequate historical context for this movement and so this ideal would require an account of the displacement of an agricultural by an industrializing economy, the replacement of competitive by corporate capitalism geared to mass production, the proliferation of bureaucratic administrative agencies at all levels of government, etc. For present purposes, suffice it to say that each of these developments played a part in opening up new occupational opportunities for those, especially in the urban centers of the Northeast, who aspired to an economic standing between wealthy elites and poor workers. The emerging professions afforded a path to middle-class status, and the Progressive movement gave voice to their ambitions.

Articulation of the modern professional ideal turns on two central principles, both of which are presupposed by Gerber's characterization of it through reference to the deployment of "expertise in a disinterested way to achieve the common good." First, modern professionalism affirms that its claim to expertise is grounded in the form of reason that is modern science; and, second, modern professionalism affirms that its practice constitutes a vocation. Woven together, the authority of modern professionalism turns on its construction as an occupational sphere that rises above the fray of politics because its conduct is rooted in knowledge that is not implicated in power and directed toward goals that are not partisan.

Prior to the twentieth century, the term "expert" was employed in vernacular reference to someone whose skill was rooted in extensive experience within any given domain. (This is the sense that informs the question of a soldier who, in Shakespeare's All's Well That Ends Well, inquires about a captain's reputation for "valour, honesty, and expertness in wars" [Shakespeare 1602, VI, iii, 2264–65]). What distinguishes the specifically modern expert is the grounding of skilled practice in the reason of modern science. Granted, during the half-century following the Civil War, what counted as modern science in the United States was defined more by what it was not than by what it was. For example, the inquiry claiming this mantle, whether taking shape as the disciplines that gradually emancipated themselves from the once-comprehensive category of "natural philosophy" or those that emerged from "history" and "political economy" as the several social sciences, was distinguished from the deductive moral and metaphysical systems that were quickly losing their cultural cachet. Moreover, incessant invocation of the "experimental method" made clear that modern science was something other than a mere extension of antebellum empiricism, which was chiefly characterized by Baconian induction that generated taxonomic classifications of observed phenomena. Rhetorically speaking, the affirmative sense of the appeal to modern science at the turn of the twentieth century is well-understood as a distinctively American articulation of the Enlightenment conviction that the progress of civilization is inseparable from the advance of a form of reason whose aspirations are indicated by a cluster of proto-positivist terms including "objective," "neutral," "disinterested," "facts," and the like.

Appropriation of the ascending authority of scientific reason by the emerging professions was key to affirming their work's superiority over that performed by other occupations. At its most elemental, this was a matter of securing an invidious distinction between professional work and inexpert manual labor. But it was also a matter of distinguishing such work from semi-skilled and subdivided industrial labor (think of the eighteen distinct operations involved in making Adam Smith's pins) as well as the specialized but un-subdivided labor of skilled artisans (think of early modern mechanical watch-makers). More generally, mastery of bodies of knowledge that cannot be acquired via empirical experience, no matter how extensive, became key to differentiating professionals from amateurs, whether they be licensed physicians as opposed to snake oil salesmen, certified lawyers as opposed to unscrupulous pettifoggers, or examined civil servants as opposed to corrupt party bosses.

The second defining ingredient of the modern professional ideal is its enactment as a vocation. To provide an adequate account of this element would require a careful tracing of the slow secularization of the Christian representation of clerical work. For present purposes, suffice it to say that Max Weber essentially got matters right when he explained how the Puritans, extrapolating the Calvinist idea of a "calling," came to conclude that one's earthly career constitutes the fulfillment of one's spiritual occupation (see Kimball 1992).

This construction sustains the characterization of modern professional work as the performance of a service on behalf of others. However, an orientation to useful service in and of itself is insufficient to differentiate modern professionals from others who also serve, whether they be merchants who supply goods to customers or politicians who furnish favors to constituents. What renders professional work of elevated status is its conduct on behalf of ends, like those conferred by its ministerial precursors, that transcend those regarded as base. These are the inherently valuable ends—e.g., justice, truth, goodness, well-being—that are essential to human flourishing. To affirm that these ends are universal or "common," to employ Gerber's term, is to insist that they promote the true interests of all, and that is so even though they may not always be embraced as such by their beneficiaries.

The foundation of the distinctively modern professions in the reason of modern science grounds their claim to cognitive superiority over other occupations, and their standing as vocations devoted to transcendent ends establishes their complementary claim to moral superiority. Because their practice is regulated by the highest form of worldly knowledge and subordinated to humanity's most noble goods, the temptations that might otherwise incline the professional toward the partial interests of the self are effectively checked. It is the self-disciplined asceticism of modern professionalism in turn that grounds its claim to special stature when invidiously compared to conduct that pursues mere pecuniary gain or that is immersed in the unsavory machinations of political power.

The Professional Professoriate

The birth of the modern professoriate in the United States is appropriately situated within the late nineteenth/early twentieth-century context adumbrated above. Specifically, it is but one of several occupations that seek to take advantage of newly-materializing opportunities for middle-class employment and so to achieve a class position that is distinguished from wealthy elites as well as manual laborers. Key to this effort is the struggle to secure recognition of its status as a modern profession.

As Gerber reminds us, for two and a half centuries following the founding of Harvard in 1636, the power of rule in American colleges was "largely in the hands of presidents, who more often than not came from the ministry, and of lay governing boards" (Gerber 2014, 3; see also Veysey 1965; Thelin 2011; and Geiger 2015). Leaving aside a few elite institutions, most instructors prior to the late nineteenth century were poorly compensated, of indifferent status, and but modestly prepared for their work as agents of moral uplift and mental discipline. Retained as what the law would eventually come to categorize as "at-will" employees, they had little basis for challenging the presidents who hired and fired them with or without cause and still less claim to participate in institutional governance.

Some of the features that unevenly materialize in the late nineteenth century and that in time come to define the professional professoriate include the expectation that employment in higher education will assume the form of a full-time salaried career characterized by upward mobility through academic ranks on the basis of merit; the expectation that research, in addition to teaching, will be part of that career; the presumption that graduate training and receipt of a doctoral degree are generally anticipated qualifications for faculty appointment; and the emergence of trans-institutional disciplines as well as the associations that represent them.

These articulations of the modern professorial ideal cannot be understood apart from invention of the modern research university whose origins are conventionally identified with the founding of Johns Hopkins in 1876, whose numbers increased dramatically between 1890 and 1920, and whose collective identity was cemented via formation of the American Association of Universities in 1900. For present purposes, what is most significant about the modern American university is its critical role in consolidating the professoriate's standing as what, given the German institutions from which it drew its primary inspiration, we might call the "uber-profession." In his history of US higher education, Roger Geiger notes that "professional education, with the partial exception of theology, grew progressively estranged from the college during most of the nineteenth century and similarly distanced from the frontiers of knowledge" (Geiger 2015, 315). One of the principal victories of the modern American university was its reversal of this trajectory by securing effective jurisdiction over professional education. It did so principally by creating graduate programs that successfully claimed a monopoly over the specialized training that defined the practice of other professions and, more specifically, by securing exclusive authority to grant the degrees that attest to mastery of all other forms of vocational expertise. Doing so, the emerging modern professoriate joined forces with, for example, the elite cohort of attorneys who in the late nineteenth century sought to disqualify the law offices that provided apprenticeships in civil law to those with no post-secondary education. So, too, did many proprietary teaching hospitals affiliate with research universities in an effort to discredit nineteenth-century spiritualists, railway surgeons, and others who competed for business in ministering to the woes of the body (see Geiger 2015, 380–94).

In sum, the general ideal of modern professionalism provides the foundation for the specific ideal of the professional professoriate. What both share is a claim to cognitively-based expertise that cannot be acquired via ordinary experience, no matter how extensive, and whose work in the world assumes the form of a secular vocation. What renders the professoriate the most special profession is its institutionally-secured and state-sanctioned status as the sole authorized provider and certifier of the education necessary to practice not just the academic calling, but all other distinctively modern expert vocations as well.

Professorial Prerogatives

The unique nature of the academic calling provides the ground for justifying the workplace prerogatives that distinguish the professoriate from non-professional occupations and, in certain instances, other professions as well. The lead agent in promoting these prerogatives was another Progressive era invention, the American Association of University Professors (AAUP). Mimicking a strategy employed by the nascent legal and medical professions via formation of the American Bar Association in 1878 and the American Medical Association in 1897, the AAUP's establishment in 1915 encouraged faculty members to envisage a form of collective identity and hence the sharing of interests that transcended their status as employees of specific colleges and universities.

However inchoate, this identity enhanced the professional professoriate's struggle to affirm its status vis à vis occupations that could claim neither the mantle of modern science nor a vocational character. Staking his position in a controversy that would vex the Association for the next half century, in his 1919 presidential address, Arthur Lovejoy insisted that the relationship of faculty to their employers was essentially different "from that of the wage-earner bargaining with the private capitalist over the division of the profits of industry," (Lovejoy 1919, 26; see also Benjamin 2015) and hence that the AAUP should not be confused with trade unions since the latter are focused exclusively on their members' economic well-being. Arguably, this same pejorative construction informed the AAUP's seminal "1915 Declaration of Principles on Academic Freedom and Tenure," which insisted on a categorical distinction between the purpose of a university and that of "an ordinary business venture." The unique purpose of "the academic calling," stated the Declaration, is to secure the "progress in scientific knowledge" that is "essential to civilization." An essential purpose of the AAUP, accordingly, is to "enhance the dignity of the scholar's profession" and, more particularly, to ensure that faculty possess the freedom that enable them "to perform honestly and according to their own consciences the distinctive and important function which the nature of the profession lays upon them" (American Association of University Professors 2015, 6). In other words, and recapitulating the general logic of modern professionalism, the professoriate masters bodies of knowledge that are distinguishable in kind from that possessed by even the most skilled non-professional workers because they can only be acquired through "prolonged and specialized technical training;" and, furthermore, it employs that knowledge, "exempt from any pecuniary motive," in the service of ends that transcend those rooted in self-interest even when, as in the case of unions, that interest is common to many.

It is only because the essential purpose of the academy transcends the parochialism of class interest that the professional professoriate can lay claim to workplace prerogatives unavailable to those employed in non-professional occupations. One such prerogative concerns the faculty's title to take part in governing the institutions by which it is employed. This claim derives principally but not exclusively from its specialized expertise in matters educational. To illustrate, however halting and partial, if an early faculty accomplishment in securing control over its work consisted of exerting authority over course offerings, later accomplishments are well-understood as efforts to extend that governance role to domains that bear on the curriculum. (For the culmination of this process, recall the broad language of the 1973 Wisconsin statute, which vested in the faculty "primary responsibility for academic and educational activities.") It is on these grounds that faculties during the twentieth century justified their right to determine, for example, graduation requirements, to participate in formulating annual budgets, to have a voice in the selection of presidents, chief academic officers, and department chairs, and so forth.

A second workplace prerogative also turns on the faculty's claim to expertise, but is more especially reliant for its rhetorical force on the vocational dimension of the professorial ideal.

This privilege consists of the claim to immunity from disciplinary interventions that would compromise the faculty's duty to fulfill its unique mission, whether that take the form of advancing knowledge via research or disseminating knowledge via teaching. This threat arises because the practice of the professoriate, as is true of all vocational professions, must ultimately be governed by the true needs of those whom it serves and from whom it anticipates deference in virtue of its specialized expertise. And yet such deference can never be taken for granted because the goods advanced by the professions may sometimes be unrecognized, unvalued, or even rejected by their beneficiaries. Should that occur, to quote the 1915 AAUP declaration, "society at large" will fail "to get from its scholars, in an unadulterated form, the peculiar and necessary service which it is the office of the professional scholar to furnish" (American Association of University Professors 2015, 6). Accordingly, some measure of occupational autonomy is the sine qua non of the faculty's capacity to pursue knowledge for its own sake, independent of all class interest, including its own, and so discharge the duty that only it can accomplish.

As the AAUP effectively acknowledged when it worried about the "tyranny of public opinion," (American Association of University Professors 2015, 8) and as recent events in Wisconsin confirm, professorial autonomy is jeopardized in a distinctive way within a capitalist democracy. No matter how great the gap between theory and practice, modern political democracies are predicated on the ideal of popular sovereignty; and the doctrine of popular sovereignty presupposes that individual citizens and their elected representatives are the best judges of their own interests. By the same token, in principle, a capitalist economy is predicated on the ideal of consumer sovereignty, which is premised on a similarly egalitarian conviction about individual rationality expressed not in the polling place but in the marketplace. Accordingly, inherited forms of privilege are suspect in a capitalist democracy, whether based in birth, wealth, or any other ascriptive foundation. And so too are all other affirmations of elite status including those based in claims to cognitive superiority, that contravene a culture wedded to a myth of the self-governing individual.

The AAUP's earliest response to this danger relies on the logic of apolitical professionalism, but, intriguingly, draws on an analogy taken from the sphere of politics. Quoting again from its 1915 declaration, the AAUP affirms that professional academics, unlike other workers, "are the appointees, but not in any proper sense the employees" of the institutions that hire them. Likening them to judges who are selected and confirmed by politicians but who are neither required nor expected to do their bidding in the act of adjudicating, professional academics are obligated to perform duties that may sometimes bring them into conflict with the lay governing boards to whom they are ultimately subject as well as the administrators who rule in their name:

> For, once appointed, the scholar has professional functions to perform in which the appointing authorities have neither competency nor moral right to intervene. The responsibility of the university teacher is primarily to the public itself, and to the judgment of his own profession; and while, with respect to certain external conditions of his vocation, he accepts a responsibility to the authorities of the institution in which he serves, in the essentials of his professional activity his duty is to the wider public to which the institution itself is morally amenable. (American Association of University Professors 2015, 6)[3]

To say this is not to deny that the professional academic is required to perform the tasks outlined in a contract specifying the terms of employment and the compensation to be paid for services rendered. Nor is it to say that the professional academic is immune from discipline for incompetence, refusal, or failure to satisfy these terms. But it is to insist that the terms of employment are not exhaustive of the academic's obligations as a professional, for these are owed to ends that transcend the walls of any specific college or university. And it is to insist that the professional academic should be immune from regulation and sanction when engaged in work conducted in accordance with professional norms even should that constraint be imposed by or at the behest of the public.

To safeguard this autonomy, the AAUP campaigned for specific practices aimed at securing some measure of protection from the harsh logic of capitalist employment to which the vast majority of workers are subject. Certain of these practices are generally consistent with those affirmed by other modern professions. For example, the principle of collective self-regulation manifest in the practice of academic peer review is embraced by the medical and legal professions insofar as they affirm their authority, subject ultimately to state jurisdiction, to define the standards by which their members are to be evaluated and to ensure that judgments of competence are entrusted to those qualified to make them. The practices of academic freedom and tenure, however, are specific to the modern professoriate, and that renders them simultaneously remarkable and vulnerable. They are remarkable insofar as they testify to the unique prestige of education within American democratic culture. There, the fulfillment of individual talent is rendered possible for everyone, at least in principle, via equal access to schooling; and such talent is the only unproblematic foundation for inequalities of status. But these practices are also vulnerable because tenure and academic freedom afford exclusive workplace privileges to those whose vocational expertise entitles them, at least in principle, to acquiescence on the part of all who lack professional stature. In short, if higher education is taken to be a key to meritocracy's fulfillment in the United States, we should not be surprised to find the professional professoriate held in high esteem. But no amount of esteem is sufficient to quell entirely the resentment engendered by workplace perquisites that shelter the professoriate from the indignities to which ordinary workers are so often subject.

In sum, what the AAUP championed in its early years were the terms of a fragile compromise delineating the situation of the professional professoriate within a liberal capitalist regime. As Clyde Barrow taught us a quarter century ago, that settlement did nothing to challenge the formal legal control over, and indeed ownership of, the academy by governing boards whose members at the turn of the twentieth century were ever more drawn from corporate boardrooms rather than the pulpit or state and local governing bodies. But, by representing the academy not as a "private propriertorship" but as a "public trust" invested with a unique cultural mission, and the professional faculty as the privileged guardians of that mission, the AAUP was able to inaugurate modest but not insignificant impediments—most notably the adequate cause and due process provisions that define tenure—to the otherwise unchecked operation of at-will employment. While this "accommodationist strategy," (Barrow 1990, 174) to quote Barrow, did help to secure for faculty the esteem it considered its due, it remained vulnerable to populist revolts from below as well as assaults initiated by political and economic elites who had little patience for academic conceits regarding, for example, the best form of college or university governance.

The Politics of the Professional Professoriate

Were Gerber to draw a graph in order to depict the overall arc of the argument advanced in The Rise and Decline of Faculty Governance, I suspect he would place on the horizontal axis a timeline that begins in the last quarter of the nineteenth century and extends through the early decades of the twenty-first. On the vertical axis, in order to explain why by the 1960s "the general principle of shared governance had become a widely accepted norm in higher education," (Gerber 2014, 6) Gerber would draw a line whose upward slope represents the uneven but more or less steady trajectory of professorial professionalization. Sometime in the early 1970s, that line would begin to tail downward depicting the faculty's de-professionalization, which in turn explains the decline of shared governance that culminates in Wisconsin. Finally, at the apex of this parabola, Gerber would inscribe the explanatory epithet "corporatization."

There is no denying that the character of academic labor has undergone a major transformation since the 1970s; nor is there any doubt that this transformation has undercut faculty participation in the governance of higher education. Manifestations of the de-vitalization cited by Gerber include the characterization of departments as revenue production units and cost centers, which renders them subject to reduction or discontinuation based on non-academic considerations; the creation of distance learning programs and especially online courses that bypass conventional curricular approval processes; the proliferation of for-profit institutions whose "faculty," as at-will employees only minimally protected against arbitrary dismissal, are ill-positioned to exercise any substantive control over academic programs; the "unbundling" of instruction as its once more or less unified elements are sub-contracted to discrete providers, including "course development specialists," "web managers," "student learning assistants," and the employees honorifically dubbed "professors" but whose educational role is restricted to on-camera lectures; the use of market-based metrics for assessing the "performance" of faculty members, which undermines peer review by shifting authority from colleagues to managerial personnel; and, to return to the scene of our opening tragedy, the calls issued by officials in Wisconsin and elsewhere for removal of all impediments, including faculty participation in governance as well as tenure, that hinder the transformation of higher education into a more efficient locus of worker training.

The question I raise in this section is not whether these changes have occurred, but, instead, whether they are adequately understood through appeal to a category of "de-professionalization" that is itself parasitic on an ideal of professionalism "premised on the possibility of individuals using their expertise in a disinterested way to achieve the common good." From this depoliti-cized perspective, should the professoriate become implicated in political power, that can only be explained through reference to its illegitimate subordination to partisan purposes. On this construction, that possibility will remain foreclosed so long as professional expertise remains true to the universal ends that sustain its vocational character. Should these ends be violated, however, that must be explained either through reference to individual neglect of occupational obligations, i.e., the professorial equivalent of malpractice, or alternatively, through reference to corruption of these ends by what Gerber labels, the pervasive influence of a market-based culture in which "all incentives are defined solely by the pursuit of self-interest and the laws of supply and demand" (Gerber 2014, 165).

Better, I argue, to acknowledge that the project of the professional professoriate in US higher education is and always has been a political enterprise whose claim to authority depends in large measure on disguising that character. The distinctive part played by the professoriate in repro-ducing the larger order within which it is situated is principally a function of its monopolistic authority over the issuance of degrees certifying formal educational accomplishment. This is a role that neither state nor corporation can meet (although the proliferation of corporate "uni-versities" as well as competence-based certification programs signals erosion of that monopoly). Engaged in this task, the work of the professoriate is political insofar as it reinforces the status hierarchies that define the professional ideal, whether they turn on the disparagement of inex-pert work or conduct oriented to self-interested gain. This work is political insofar as it installs higher education faculty as the gate-keepers who determine who will and who will not gain admission to and, once inside, be certified as masters of the esoteric forms of knowledge that yield the privileges of professional occupation outside the academy. And this work is political insofar as its most esteemed occupational residence, the modern research university, is deeply enmeshed in the constitution of a regime that yokes state power to a capitalist economy. The question, then, is not when the professional professoriate was deflected from its true end, but, rather, how the form of its entanglement has changed over time.

I cannot provide that history here. But, to intimate what it should include, let me suggest that the "Wisconsin Idea" in its early years exemplifies one of its key moments. Although its intellectual antecedents can be located in the writings of John Bascom, Richard T. Ely, and John R. Commons, invention of the Wisconsin Idea is typically ascribed to University of

Wisconsin president Charles Van Hise and Governor Robert La Follette. The cornerstone of this quintessentially Progressive endeavor is this:

> The Wisconsin Idea pledged the University of Wisconsin to serve the state by applying its research to the solution of public problems, by training experts in the physical and social sciences and joining their academic efforts to the public, administrative functions of the state, and by extending the work of the University, through its personnel and facilities, to the boundaries of the state. (Hoeveler 1976, 282)

As David Hoeveler explains, this appeal to "serve the state" is well-read as a secularized rendition of the Social Gospel's call to realize the will of God on earth via the university's performance of a mission in the guise of a vocation. Anticipating Gerber's representation of professionalism, the Wisconsin Idea promised to replace the competitive, partisan, and ineffectual intrigues of politics with the principles of "scientific management." Whether applied to government or any other domain of collective life, reform based in these principles augured the dispassionate triumph of instrumental efficiency, enlightened transparency, and democratic accountability.

The specific character of the professional professoriate's simultaneous autonomy from and yet implication in this regime can be metaphorically illustrated by considering the mile-long stretch of road that is State Street in Madison, which separates but also joins the capitol at one end and the university at the other. The purpose of the Wisconsin Idea, as first advanced, was not to collapse the distance between capitol and university, but, to quote from an official history, to facilitate their "partnership" in diverse exchanges:

> The services carried out in its name yielded mutually beneficial exchanges between the university and the people of the state. From the establishment of a lecture service for teachers in 1860, farmers institutes in 1885, a mechanics institute in 1888 and continuing with the development of summer classes, applied research, public lectures and many other extension activities, the university has viewed individuals as the direct beneficiaries of its outreach... In parallel efforts, Van Hise and La Follette promoted university service to state government, which took various forms, such as drafting proposed legislation and serving as members of state boards, commissions, and administrative departments. (Knox and Curry 1995, 181)

If the first form of exchange referenced here consisted of programs whereby faculty offered technical expertise to laborers outside the academy, the second consisted of expert counsel provided to legislators involved in crafting remedies to problems stemming, in large part, from the advance of capitalist industrialization—e.g., urban poverty, corporate monopolies, hazardous consumer products, unsafe labor practices, etc. This mutation of the university's "public trust" into work performed at the behest of state elites acting in the name of the people was anticipated by the AAUP when, in its 1915 declaration, it insisted that the "training" of experts equipped to address the "complexities" of modern life has "become an important part of the work of the universities; and in almost every one of our institutions of learning the professors of the economic, social, and political sciences have been drafted to an increasing extent into more or less unofficial participation in the public service" (American Association of University Professors 2015, 7).

We are thus invited to imagine State Street as the materialization of a hyphenated relationship whose participants require one another, but who remain sufficiently independent to render the professional ideal not entirely fanciful. It would be a mistake, however, to construe this "partnership" between state and university as one of egalitarian reciprocity. Indeed, as early as 1858, prefiguring the report submitted by the Wisconsin Assembly's shared governance working group in 2013, a legislative committee declared that its citizens have "a right to ask that the bequest of the government [to the university] shall aide them in securing to themselves and their posterity, such educational advantages as shall fit them for their pursuits in life, and which, by an infusion of intelligence and power, shall elevate those pursuits to a dignity commensurate with their value" (Carstensen 1956, 182).

On the face of it, the state's demand that the university be harnessed to the improvement of ordinary occupations and, in doing so, render their work worthy of respect it cannot otherwise command makes this a profoundly political enterprise. The professional professorial ideal, however, requires that this representation be denied so that it can sustain the characterization of its work as the apolitical provision of specialized vocational expertise. But, as we have seen, a constitutive feature of such expertise is the ethical orientation as well as the cognitive foundation that renders it superior to unskilled, semi-skilled or even skilled labor. That labor remains inferior so long as it is merely a matter of earning a wage and so long as its conduct is ungrounded in forms of knowledge that are "theoretical" in the sense that they are abstracted from empirical practice. This affirmation of professional authority over ordinary work becomes self-reinforcing when insistence on the apolitical character of academic expertise serves as an essential prop for the faculty's justification of the practices, including tenure, academic freedom, and shared governance, that demonstrate the elite nature of its work relative to those who remain subject to the routine degradations of non-academic employment.

"We should seek to withdraw as many questions of statesmanship and social science as we can from the sphere of party politics, and hand them over to the investigation and experiments of our scholars" (Francis March, a faculty member at Lafayette College, in Veysey 1965, 72). The excision of scientifically-informed administration from the political domain was institutionally consolidated via creation of the US Civil Service in 1871, and that agency was defined by its commitment to the meritocratic appointment of public servants on the basis of technical competence acquired through university education and demonstrated by competitive examination. And yet the anti-political ideal symbolized by the Civil Service is itself deeply political insofar as it gestures toward a rationalized utopia ruled by experts in which, to quote once more from the AAUP's 1915 declaration, the "hasty and unconsidered impulses of popular feeling" are rendered "more self-critical and more circumspect" by the discipline of "scientific method" (American Association of University Professors 2015, 9). As the major universities during this period quickly pivot toward meeting the burgeoning demand for technically-trained labor power, exemplified by their rapid incorporation of agricultural and mechanical institutes within doctoral programs in engineering, the leading edge of the professional professoriate helps to ensure that the contradictions and excesses of capitalism will be managed rather than overcome, and that the reality of bureaucratic domination will be hidden beneath a veneer of non-partisan administration.

Were I to recount adequately the changing character of the research university's political implication over the course of the twentieth century, I would discuss with some care the reconstitution of the professionalized professoriate as the United States shifted from the competitive capitalism that defined the Progressive era to the state-managed capitalism that defined the Cold War. Although anticipated as early as 1916 via creation of the National Research Council, for present purposes, suffice it to say that this era was defined by a more complete integration of the research university within the nation state, as the power exercised by economic and political elites was jointly directed toward the achievement of post-war global supremacy. This integration was accomplished in large part through massive infusions of federal funding supporting scientific research, much of which was not immediately subordinated to the imperatives of technological pay-off or commercial value. Although the growing financial dependence of the research university on state funding certainly eroded the professional professorial ideal, that work's characterization as "basic" rendered not entirely incredible the representation of faculty inquiry as disinterested expertise governed by vocational norms.

The state-managed capitalism of the Cold War era required extensive public expenditures not just in defense, but also in health care, education, and other social welfare plans necessary to secure a productive workforce. With these investments came rapid expansion of the professions in general, as scientific knowledge was declared essential to the conduct of virtually all spheres of collective life. More comprehensively realizing the utopia imagined by Progressive era reformers, the authority of expertise insinuated itself within, for example, the managerial and accounting practices of corporate capitalism, the demographic initiatives undertaken by governmental agencies, and even the nuclear family as child-rearing came to be seen as a practice whose success turns on its conformity to medical and, later, psychological prescription. The enhanced prestige afforded to the reason of modern science redounded to the benefit of a professionalized professoriate not merely in virtue of its standing as privileged generator of the knowledge that grounds expert practice, but also because, as the uber-profession, it monopolized the right to confer the post-secondary degrees that certify competence exercised in all other domains. In addition, given that the general project of modern professionalism is inseparable from the economic aspirations of its participants, and given that the professionalization of the professoriate has always been a class project as well, it is not surprising to learn that the Cold War era saw considerable augmentation of the material benefits that follow from this inflation of academic status.

Under these circumstances, it is also not surprising to learn that the three decades following the end of World War II represent the heyday of faculty participation in college and university governance as well as consolidation of the workplace prerogatives that distinguish the academic career from other occupations, non-professional as well as professional. Gerber depicts the relationship between the faculty's more extensive participation in institutional rule and its Cold War context as co-constitutive:

> The rise of American higher education to a position of global preeminence after 1945 was certainly a result in good part of the nation's postwar prosperity, which allowed the United States to invest immense resources in its college and universities. However, the preeminence achieved by American colleges and universities was also tied to the substantial professional autonomy, significant role in institutional governance, and academic freedom enjoyed by faculty members. The widespread recognition of these faculty rights and responsibilities helped create an environment that fostered the pursuit of new knowledge and helped keep academic priorities at the forefront in the operation of American colleges and universities. (Gerber 2014, 6)

A skeptical interpretation of this relationship might ask whether the professoriate's empowerment during this era was chiefly enabled by considerable excess demand for academic expertise and hence vigorous competition among colleges and universities for its labor. This reading might also ask whether the "substantial professional autonomy" cited by Gerber was tolerated not so much because the ideal of the professional professoriate was universally endorsed, but because the secular work ethic of the self-disciplined vocational subject required only modest supplementation by external controls or, more probably, because the exercise of workplace prerogatives within the academy posed no real challenge to the advance of American hegemony.

The Oxymoron of Neoliberal Professionalism

For Gerber, the sorry fate of shared governance in the post-Cold War era is a function of higher education's hostile takeover by the agencies of "corporatization." This story takes on a different complexion when told from the vantage point of "neoliberalization." No matter how one tells the history of neoliberalism, as it has unfolded over the course of the past four decades or so, it seems clear that it has involved a more thoroughgoing incorporation of the modern research university within the political economy of the United States. That in turn has entailed a radical reconfiguration of the academic workforce, one whose specifically political import cannot be adequately conceptualized via a category that effectively reduces to professionalization thrown into reverse.

One element of the university's structural transformation is captured by what Sheila Slaughter and Gary Rhoades label the "shift from a public good knowledge/learning regime to an academic capitalist knowledge/learning regime" (Slaughter and Rhoades 2004, 8). Their analysis of this regime's consolidation since the 1970s calls attention to the active engagement of many faculty in fostering revenue-generating collaborations between corporations and the academy as well as the state's participation in legally structuring these affiliations via, for example, the 1980 Bayh-Dole Act as well as later copyright and patent legislation. Within this university, in contrast to that of the Progressive era, we can no longer speak uncritically of neutral experts traversing the length of State Street in order to offer dispassionate counsel to the occupants of political office. Nor, in contrast to the university of the Cold War era, can we speak artlessly of disinterested researchers whose objective discoveries are fashioned by governmental agencies into instrumentalities of state power. In a neoliberal regime, the distinction between neutrality and partisanship as well as that between basic and applied mischaracterize the work performed by that sizeable segment of the contemporary professoriate whose entrepreneurial endeavors generate forms of cognitive capital that are smoothly integrated into the global circuits of production, accumulation, and exchange as these are hard wired by the state.

To illustrate, consider a contemporary incarnation of the Wisconsin Idea. According to its website, University Research Park (URP) in Madison "is an internationally recognized research and technology park that supports early-stage, and growth-oriented businesses in a range of sectors, including engineering, computational and life sciences."[4] Situated at neither end of State Street, this complex does not entirely dissolve the distinction between government, economy, and university, but it commingles their energies and resources in ways that render it practically impossible to tell where one begins and the others leave off. The irrelevance of the AAUP's 1915 account of the university's unique vocation, let alone the affirmations of academic freedom and shared governance that turn on that account, is revealed by URP's strategic plan, which offers this statement of its "mission:" "To encourage technology development and commercialization that advances the economy and benefits research and related educational programs at the University of Wisconsin-Madison, and serve as UW-Madison's primary real estate development arm, providing facilities and entrepreneurial real estate development service."[5] On this account, the public good served by the university is conflated with increase in the value of its real estate holdings, construed as investments that enhance its constitution as something not unlike a private equity firm.

No understanding of the professoriate's neoliberalization will prove adequate, however, if its focuses only on its esteemed commercial and technology vanguards and so disregards its neglected remainder. That these are flip sides of the same neoliberal coin is indicated by erosion of the middle class status to which early modern professionals aspired, as the academic labor force ever more recapitulates the yawning inequalities that now stratify American labor more generally. This is most strikingly disclosed by modification of the contractual terms of academic employment during the several decades defined by aggressive adoption of neoliberal strategies aimed at reducing labor costs. In 1969, to be specific, over three-quarters of instructional appointments in American higher education were to full-time tenure-track positions whereas, today, 70 percent of faculty members are employed in contingent positions, and over half of those appointments are part-time (see Kezar and Maxey 2013; Kezar 2014).

As a result, the instructional workforce is now bifurcated into a privileged minority and what we might euphemistically call an "under-privileged" majority, but which is perhaps better characterized as a reservoir of surplus and hence disposable labor. A 2014 report issued by Democratic staff members of the US House Committee on Education and the Workforce described this segmentation as follows:

The post-secondary academic workforce has undergone a remarkable change over the last several decades. The tenure-track college professor with a stable salary, firmly grounded in the middle or upper-middle class, is becoming rare. Taking her place is the contingent faculty: nontenure-track teachers, such as part-time adjuncts or graduate instructors, with no job security from one semester to the next, working at a piece rate with few or no benefits across multiple workplaces, and far too often struggling to make ends meet. (US House Committee on Education and the Workforce 2014, 1; see also Curtis and Thorton 2014; Finkelstein, Conley, and Schuster 2016)

In this universe, what may once have qualified as a more or less cohesive profession is now divided between, on the one hand, the few who are compensated well, who are covered by institutional health care and pension policies, who enjoy the relative security of tenure and academic freedom, who experience some measure of autonomy and control over their work, and who are afforded significant prestige as well as the obeisance that accompanies it, and, on the other hand, everyone else. Here I acknowledge that this undifferentiated category occludes multiple sources of stratification internal to it, including but not limited to that between part-time workers paid on a piecework basis and those who are full-time and who are sometimes fortunate enough to be granted multi-year contracts. Even so, under these circumstances, especially when neither teaching nor research is a necessary condition of membership, it is not clear what it means to place all postsecondary "instructional" employees in the same occupational category.

Students of contemporary work have invented terms like "casualization" and "precarity" to name the neoliberal strategies deployed in order to exercise greater control over labor by exposing it to the vagaries of capitalist unemployment and, when working, by subjecting it to intrusive (although often invisible) technologies of discipline. True, the exact form assumed by these strategies may differ in the specifically academic workplace, but what, we should ask, is the difference in kind between the modes of surveillance to which most "non-professional" labor is now subject and their kinder and gentler appearance in the assessment metrics that monitor faculty work in the name of greater efficiency? And what is the difference in kind between poorly-compensated on-demand work performed by "independent contractors" in a "gig economy" and instructional work paid on a per course basis by part-time instructors on short-term contracts subject to renewal or non-renewal with little if any notice? And what is the difference in kind between the out-sourcing of those elements of production that can be accomplished by unskilled manual labor and the unbundling of faculty work that enables those tasks that require little or no skill to be delegated to wage-earners who receive none of the perquisites of professionalism? And, finally, what is the difference in kind between the lived experience of at-will service workers employed by vertically-organized capitalist corporations and that of contingent instructors subject to the authority of administrative personnel schooled in managerial techniques that are anathema to the norms of a self-governing community of scholars?

The relative ease with which elite as well as non-elite segments of the academic workforce in the United States have been reconstituted in accordance with neoliberal imperatives testifies at least in part to the failure of the historical project of academic professionalization. "Professionalism may be said to exist," writes Eliot Freidson, "when an organized occupation gains the power to determine who is qualified to perform a defined set of tasks, to prevent all others from performing that work, and to control the criteria by which to evaluate performance" (Freidson 2001, 12). If an indispensable marker of a profession's reality is creation of an effective labor market shelter, as Freidson suggests, then the project of the modern professoriate succeeded insofar as the universities founded during the late nineteenth and early twentieth centuries did secure a reasonably firm monopoly over the authority to certify professional competence in multiple occupations, including its own, via the granting of post-secondary degrees.

In most other ways, however, this project has proven weak and thus vulnerable. Its relative impotence is apparent in the academic profession's inability to summon governmental muscle to discipline unqualified practitioners (unlike the legal and medical professions, which can still call on state power to sanction those who practice absent appropriate credentials and to revoke the licenses of those deemed incompetent). It is apparent in the inability of the supra-professional association that is the AAUP to do more than chastise institutions that violate key markers of professional status, including academic freedom, peer review, and shared governance, as well as its inability to enforce a code of ethics whose very existence appears unknown to most. It is apparent in the professoriate's inability, if not to restrict the production of doctorates and so ensure the scarcity that is a key condition of labor market power, then at least to thwart the indiscriminate replacement of tenure-track with contingent positions. And, finally, it is apparent in the professoriate's incapacity to curb the proliferation of competitors, most notably for-profit enterprises, to provide the good that defined the public trust it alone was once deemed qualified to fulfill.

This final example is telling because it indicates how neoliberal colonization of the university undoes the professoriate's organizational integrity as a profession, but also, and perhaps equally important, compromises the very ideal that once sustained it. It does so by rendering the fruits of academic labor a utilitarian good, which, like all other commodities in a service economy, is sold by profit-minded merchants of skill and purchased by buyers well-advised to heed the motto "caveat emptor." On one construction, the neoliberal imaginary seeks to disembed and so free market rationality from associational forms, including the traditional academy, that constrain its unfettered operation. On a more ambitious construction, the neoliberal imaginary seeks to extend market rationality into all forms of collective association predicated on non-capitalist logics, whether that be family, church, or academy. On its most radical construction, however, the neoliberal imaginary seeks to rid the world of all contrary rationalities whose persistence might provide the basis for contesting its hegemony. This, I take it, is what Wendy Brown is getting at when she writes:

> To speak of the relentless and ubiquitous economization of all features of life by neo-liberalism is thus not to claim that neoliberalism literally marketizes all spheres, even as such marketization is certainly one important effect of neoliberalism. Rather, the point is that neoliberal rationality disseminates the model of the market to all domains and activities—even where money is not at issue—and configures human beings exhaustively as market actors, always, only, and everywhere as homo economicus. (Brown 2015, 31)[6]

As neoliberal rationality vanquishes older imaginaries, the university and hence the professoriate are ever more pressed to justify their existence not via recourse to the tattered ideals of self-cultivation, citizenship, or the progress of civilization, but via an appeal to their efficient contribution to goods framed exclusively in economistic terms. Just how pervasive this logic has already become is indicated by the desperate effort to affirm the relevance of a liberal arts education by representing it as an investment that will pay off in the long run by equipping students with the skills they require in order to succeed in the multiple jobs they will hold within an economic order whose ceaseless disruptions demand continuous occupational retraining and so a talent for "lifelong learning." For much the same reason, in time, we should anticipate that the lexicon of professionalism, with its melancholy appeals to "self-sacrifice," "the public good," and "impartial expertise," will be evacuated of substantive sense. No doubt, these terms will still be pressed into service to rally the troops when, for example, the next legislature seeks to gut faculty participation in institutional governance. But, in the long run, these relics are likely to collapse under the weight of neoliberal cynicism regarding all verbiage that pretends to mask the omnipresent promptings of unvarnished self-interest.

On Wisconsin? (A Tragedy in One Act)

However lamentable if not deplorable, the fate of the American professoriate should not surprise us all that much when we consider its status within a neoliberal regime that yokes the research university to a political economy geared to capital accumulation within interdependent globalized markets that show little respect for national borders. Nor should we be overly surprised by the fate of the anachronistic traditions of shared governance when we recall that this regime's bottom line turns in large measure on marginalization or elimination of unrationalized practices that restrain the rapid circulation of capital as well as the mobile reallocation of labor. Stripped of the patina of professionalism, much like occupational safety regulations, faculty participation in university and college governance, like tenure, is at best an expensive luxury and at worst an impediment that compromises the academy's capacity to inculcate the flexible skills required of malleable human capital.

Given this bleak conclusion, as academic norms prescribe, perhaps I should end by asking what is to be done. But, aside from urging that analyses of the plight of the professoriate appreciate its political dimensions, I have no answer to that question. Rather than pretending to know what I do not, I want to close by asking what we stand to lose if we relinquish the ideal of the professional professoriate inherited from the Progressive era; and then I want to ask what costs we may incur if, instead, we cling to an ideal that compromises our ability to grasp the faculty's present situation.

If we concede that the vision of professionalism informing Gerber's narrative is a relic whose day has come and gone, there is indeed much we must surrender. The presuppositions inherent in the ideal of disinterested expertise exercised on behalf of the common good enable and invite certain kinds of criticisms that we will no longer be able to advance in good faith. No longer, for example, can we claim that academic work is "corrupted" when bought and sold like any other commodity in a capitalist economy. Nor can we claim that our labor is "deformed" when subordinated to bureaucratic managerial norms, including that of efficiency or, when inflected by market rationality, cost-effectiveness. Nor can we claim that the fruits of scholarly endeavor are "degraded" when twisted to the ends of state power. Each of these expressions of outrage is tacitly informed by representation of the professional professoriate as an agent of vocational expertise whose service is subject to compromise or conquest by that which is fundamentally alien. True, we may still choose to affirm the faculty's "autonomy" as well as the institutional conditions that render it real. But, if we do so, we must acknowledge that the sense of this term is necessarily constituted by what it is not, just as the terms "day" and "night" each derive sense from their implicit reference to the other, and so we must regard the achievement of autonomy as a heteronomous and fragile accomplishment whose political character we deny at our peril.

And yet if we jettison the conception of autonomy that depends for its coherence on the professional ideal, arguably, we lose the familiar conceptual underpinnings, which, since the founding of the AAUP, have informed and justified much that we hold dear, including tenure, academic freedom, and the faculty's title to participate in institutional governance. Today, after Foucault, that ideal's representation of knowledge as apolitical appears naïve in its failure to acknowledge the necessary inter-implication of truth and power. And today, after Weber, that ideal's representation of work as a calling appears implausible given rationalization's relentless disenchantment of once-sacred values. If these are the essential normative ingredients of modern professionalism, but we no longer find them credible, either we must abandon the practices justified in the name of professionalism or find some other way to defend them.

Given these very real perils, it is tempting to do what we can to prop up the ideal of the professional professoriate even at the risk of hypocrisy. To see why this strategy is so seductive, recall that this ideal is deeply implicated in status differentials, and, in particular, with the self-identity of academics as something other than mere employees in a capitalist economy. Precisely that point was made by the AAUP in 1915 when, to extend a quotation cited earlier, it declared that any representation of the university "as an ordinary business venture, and of academic teaching as a purely private employment, manifests... a radical failure to apprehend the nature of the social function discharged by the professional scholar" (American Association of University Professors 2015, 6). Here, the term "professional" references a specific occupation whose members, like lawyers and doctors, do or at least should enjoy considerable autonomy and authority in the workplace in virtue of their recognized vocational expertise.

How, though, might the sense as well as the work accomplished by this term mutate when the material conditions of that autonomy and authority are shredded and this occupation's members are ever more regarded as and treated like mere job-holders? Under those circumstances, might it seem all the more urgent to affirm professional status, but now as a compensatory category whose avowal cloaks the fact that, for most, the lived reality of academic work no longer secures its relative prestige? Indeed, is it possible that it was Marco Rubio's failure to demonstrate the respect due to professionals that explains, at least in part, the indignation expressed in Inside Higher Ed and elsewhere when, not long ago, he insisted that what the world needs now are fewer philosophers and more welders (e.g., see Weisbuch 2016)?

Affirmation of a status common to all faculty will merely obfuscate, however, if it occludes the stratifications internal to the contemporary academic workforce. As illustrated, for example, by the AAUP's "one faculty" campaign, announcement of interests shared by all academics, however unintended, may mask the structural conflicts that render those at opposite ends of the socioeconomic spectrum within higher education more foe than friend.[7]

The import of these conflicts can be suggested by returning one last time to Wisconsin. In addition to rendering faculty members mere consultants in matters of institutional governance, the 2015 statute significantly eroded the tenure provisions previously embedded in state law by authorizing the Board of Regents to "lay off or terminate any faculty member when such an action is deemed necessary due to a budget or program decision requiring a program change" (Wis. Stat. § 36.22(2)(a) 2015). Like Act 10, which four years earlier hobbled the collective bargaining rights of public sector unions in Wisconsin (see Beck 2016), this provision is but one more tactic within a comprehensive neoliberal campaign designed to remove constraints on the unfettered exercise of employer prerogative. Not surprisingly, the amended tenure provisions provoked a vigorous campaign to persuade the board to adopt policies aimed at reinstating the due process protections now stripped from state law. Yet even were this campaign to succeed, this victory would only advantage a privileged minority whose members already derive significant benefit from the offloading of undesirable tasks, such as grading undergraduate work, to those least able to object. I am not quite ready to conclude that this is a battle to be forsaken, but I do worry that a fixation on tenure may discourage us from imagining alternative strategies aimed at securing for all faculty members freedom from the exploitation inherent in at-will employment as well as that measure of workplace autonomy that is essential to good teaching and research (see Bérubé and Ruth 2015).

Whether we are likely to prove able to think our way beyond the invidious distinctions that divide us within a neoliberal age is a question posed by Wendy Brown when she writes:

> Faculty interpellated by neoliberal rationality are generally unable to grasp, let alone resist, what is happening to postsecondary education. Distinguished faculty who enjoy the privileges of the top end of privatized publics tend to be focused on their own research, publications, invitations, prizes, fellowships, rankings, offers, and counter-offers. Younger faculty relentlessly socialized by neo-liberal careerism are frequently unaware that there were or could be alternative academic purposes and practices to those organized by a neo-liberal table of values. (Brown 2011; see also Kaufman-Osborn 2016)

This is no doubt so, but, as presented here, this claim fails to acknowledge the meritocratic presuppositions, which, especially when afforded a neoliberal spin, explain why the contemporary drama of faculty within US higher education is perhaps best framed as a tragedy.

Max Weber taught us that the project of modern professionalism is a key element within the more comprehensive dynamic of rationalization. As such, modern professionalism is committed to filling occupational positions not on the basis of charisma, tradition, or wealth, but on the basis of demonstrated cognitive accomplishment. There are no good reasons for thinking that the uber-profession that is the modern professoriate should or will remain immune to this meritocratic ideal, especially since this ideal draws much of its force from vocationalism's assurance that hard work performed as an ascetic duty will be rewarded in this world. Indeed, given the indispensable role played by formal education in perpetuating the conviction that rewards are rationally distributed to those most deserving, we should be surprised if we were to learn that faculty members in the United States are not deeply invested in this individualizing fiction.

The neoliberal intensification of the myth of meritocracy, sometimes dubbed "responsibilization" (see Brown 2015, 131–34), is manifest in the self-congratulatory confidence on the part of tenure-track and tenured faculty that they earned their positions and, although seldom uttered aloud, that those who fail in the so-called "job market" deserve their fate as well. Internalization of this central pillar of professional self-identity is yet another reason to suspect that Wolin was right to note the "reluctance of academics to admit that there are political stakes and determinants in matters of knowledge." And that reluctance in turn is one more reason to dread the denouement foreshadowed by Gerber's lament: "The ideal and practices of shared governance are not yet altogether dead" (Gerber 2014, 164).[8]

Reprinted from Timothy Kaufman-Osborn. 2017. "Disenchanted Professionals: The Politics of Faculty Governance in the Neoliberal Academy." Perspectives on Politics *15 (1). Cambridge University Press: 100–115. doi:10.1017/S1537592716004163.*

Notes

1. To illustrate what might qualify as such a shift, the report cited the UW Flexible Option plan, which is an online program that enables adults to acquire workplace skills and demonstrate their successful acquisition by earning certificates of competence.

2. The argument I advance here, while not inapplicable to other institutional types, is most germane to faculty within what the Carnegie Commission identifies as R1 doctoral universities. (For the Commission's classification system, see http://carnegieclassifications.iu.edu/classification_descriptions/basic.php) I focus on faculty in R1s, first, because they most fully embody the conception of professionalism that provides the foundation for the professoriate's claims to governance prerogatives as well as employment immunities; and, second, because it is the modern research university that is most fully integrated within and of concern to the regime within which higher education is situated more generally.

3. It is seldom recalled that the characterization of faculty employment advanced by the AAUP in 1915 finds earlier expression in a 1914 report adopted by the Joint Committee on Academic Freedom and Tenure and prepared on behalf of the American Economic Association, the American Sociological Association, and the American Political Science Association. That report, written by Edwin Seligman, rejected the representation of "academic teaching" as a "purely private employment, resting on a contract between the employing authority and the teacher." Instead, Seligman wrote, the work of the academic professional "must be regarded as a quasi-public official employment in which the original appointment is made by the authorities who are bound to act not as private employers or from private motives but as public trustees" (380).

4. See http://universityresearchpark.org/about/.

5. See http://urp2014.mhwebstaging.com/wp-content/uploads/2014/03/URP-Strategic-Plan-for-2013-2014-.pdf.

6. The website for Wisconsin's University Research Park intimates the comprehensive utopia projected by the neoliberal imaginary when it states that, in addition to providing a locus of research and a place to work, the park encompasses "a commercial and residential 'New Urbanist' development that aims for environmentally friendly, walkable neighborhoods where people can live and work." Available at (http://universityresearchpark.org/about/).

7. See https://www.aaup.org/get-involved/issue-campaigns/one-faculty.

8. Arguably, those who best understand what Wolin called the "political stakes and determinants" of higher education are those who are least prone to be taken in by meritocratic ideology; and, arguably, we see the most adequate expression of that realization on the part of contingent faculty engaged in struggles to unionize. As Schmidt 2014 explans, it is unseemly but true that often the loudest voices raised in opposition to faculty unionization are those of tenured and tenure-track faculty.

References

Abbott, Andrew. 1988. *The System of Professions: An Essay on the Division of Expert Labor*. Chicago, IL: University of Chicago Press.

American Association of University Professors. 2015. "Declaration of Principles on Academic Freedom and Academic Tenure." *Policy Documents and Reports*. 11th ed. Baltimore, MD: Johns Hopkins University Press.

Background Materials. 2013. UW-System Governance Reform Summer Workgroup. Wisconsin State Assembly.

Barrow, Clyde. 1990. *Universities and the Capitalist State: Corporate Liberalism and the Reconstruction of Higher Education, 1894–1928*. Madison, WI: University of Wisconsin Press.

Beck, Molly. 2016. "Assessing the impact of Act 10 on Wisconsin, 5 years later." *Wisconsin State Journal* February 11. http://host.madison.com/wsj/news/local/govt-and-politics/assessing-the-impact-of-act-on-wisconsin-years-later/collection_66ea3487-a88a-5c0a-aa13-87ceae934104.html.

Benjamin, Ernst. 2015. "How Did We Get Here?" *Academe* 101 (1). https://www.aaup.org/article/how-did-we-get-here#.V1m7EigrKUk.

Bérubé, Michael and Jennifer Ruth. 2015. *The Humanities, Higher Education, & Academic Freedom*. New York: Palgrave Macmillan.

Brown, Wendy. 2011. "The End of Educated Democracy." *Representations* 116: 1–19.

Brown, Wendy. 2015. *Undoing the Demos: Neoliberalism's Stealth Revolution*. Brooklyn, NY: Zone Books.

Carstensen, Vernon. 1956. "The Origin and Development of the Wisconsin Idea." *Wisconsin Magazine of History* 39 (3): 181–88.

Curtis, John W. and Saranna Thorton. 2014. "Losing Focus: The Annual Report of the Economic Status of the Profession, 2013–14." *Academe* 100 (2): 4–17. https://www.aaup.org/sites/default/files/files/2014%20salary%20report/zreport_0.pdf.

Finkelstein, Martin J., Valerie M. Conley, and Jack Schuster. 2016. "Taking the Measure of Faculty Diversity." New York: TIAA-CREF Institute. https://www.tiaainstitute.org/public/pdf/taking_the_measure_of_faculty_diversity.pdf.

Freidson, Eliot. 2001. *Professionalism: The Third Logic*. Chicago, IL: University of Chicago Press.

Geiger, Roger. 2015. *The History of American Higher Education*. Princeton, NJ: Princeton University Press.

Gerber, Larry. 2014. *The Rise and Decline of Faculty Governance: Professionalization and the Modern American University*. Baltimore, MD: Johns Hopkins University Press.

Hoeveler, David J. 1976. "The University and the Social Gospel: The Intellectual Origins of the 'Wisconsin Idea.'" *Wisconsin Magazine of History* 59 (4): 282–98.

Kaufman-Osborn, Timothy. 2016. "Faculty Members Play a Role in the Erosion of Shared Governance." *Inside Higher Ed*. https://www.insidehighered.com/views/2016/05/26/faculty-members-play-role-erosion-shared-governance-essay.

Kezar, Adrianna. 2014. "Changing Faculty Workforce Models." New York: TIAA-CREF Institute. https://www.tiaainstitute.org/public/pdf/changing-faculty-workforce-models.pdf.

Kezar, Adrianna and Daniel Maxey. 2013. "The Changing Academic Workforce." *Trusteeship Magazine* 21 (3). http://agb.org/trusteeship/2013/5/changing-academic-workforce.

Kimball, Bruce. 1992. *The "True Professional Ideal" in America*. Cambridge, MA: Blackwell Publishers.

Knox, Alan and Joe Curry. 1995. "The Wisconsin Idea for the 21st Century." *Wisconsin Blue Book, 1995–1996*. Madison, WI: Wisconsin Legislative Reference Bureau.

Larson, Magali Sarfatti. 2013. *The Rise of Professionalism: Monopolies of Competence and Sheltered Markets*. New Brunswick, NJ: Transaction Press.

Lovejoy, Arthur. 1919. "Annual Message of the President." *Bulletin of the American Association of University Professors* 5 (Nov./Dec.): 10–40.

Potts, Crystal, Lauren Clark, Scott Coenen, Heather Moore, Justin Phillips, and Dan Posca. 2013. "UW Shared Governance Reform." Presented at the Wisconsin State Assembly Republican Caucus Meeting.

Schmidt, Peter. 2014. "Union Efforts on Behalf of Adjuncts Meet Resistance within Faculties' Ranks." *Chronicle of Higher Education*. http://chronicle.com/article/Union-Efforts-on-Behalf-of/145833/.

Seligman, Edwin. 1915. "Preliminary Report of the Joint Committee on Academic Freedom and Tenure." *American Political Science Review* 9 (1): 374–381.

Shakespeare, William. 1602. *All's Well that Ends Well*. http://www.opensourceshakespeare.org/views/plays/play_view.php?WorkID=allswell&Act=4&Scene=3&Scope=scene.

Slaughter, Sheila and Gary Rhoades. 2004. *Academic Capitalism and the New Economy*. Baltimore, MD: The Johns Hopkins University.

Spoto v. Board of Regents of the University of Wisconsin System. 1994–95. Dane County Circuit Branch 14, Case No. 92 CV 5046. Unpublished.

Thelin, John. 2011. *A History of American Higher Education*. 2d ed. Baltimore, MD: Johns Hopkins University Press.

US House Committee on Education and the Workforce. 2014. *The Just-in-Time Professor: A Staff Report Summarizing eForum Responses on the Working Conditions of Contingent Faculty in Higher Education*. http://democrats-edworkforce.house.gov/imo/media/doc/1.24.14-AdjunctEforumReport.pdf.

UW System Shared Governance Reform. 2013. UW—System Governance Summer Reform Workgroup.

Veysey, Laurence. 1965. *The Emergence of the American University*. Chicago, IL: University of Chicago Press.

Weisbuch, Robert. 2016. "The Liberal Arts at War." *Inside Higher Ed*, May 15. https://www.insidehighered.com/views/2016/05/05/values-liberal-arts-and-enlightenment-are-under-attack-essay.

Wolin, Sheldon. 1981. "Higher Education and the Politics of Knowledge." *Democracy* 1 (2): 38–52.

The Most Important Topic Political Scientists Are Not Studying: Adapting to Climate Change

20

Debra Javeline

The world is being transformed by climate change.[1] Without human intervention, hundreds of thousands of species are threatened with extinction; infectious diseases are emerging in new areas; ecosystems on which humans depend for food, water, and clean air are increasingly dysfunctional; and urban environments are at risk from rising seas, storm surge, heat waves, and the resulting harmful effects on public health and critical infrastructure (IPCC 2007b). Even if today all countries could somehow immediately reduce greenhouse gas emissions, existing emissions guarantee considerable climate change, and that climate change has considerable impact (e.g., see Anderegg et al. 2010).

Although we need to continue mitigation efforts (steps to reduce emissions) to minimize the damage, the unfortunate reality is that we also must learn to live in a world transformed by climate change. Countries, states, cities, communities, businesses, and individuals are now compelled to develop strategies that allow societal "adaptation" to inevitable climate change. Adaptation, according to the Intergovernmental Panel on Climate Change (IPCC), is the reduction of vulnerability to climate change.[2] Adaptation involves protecting our coasts, cities, water supply, food supply, public health, ecosystems, and infrastructure. While not an alternative to mitigation, adaptation has become a crucially necessary accompaniment and a growing interdisciplinary field of study.

This new critical field, climate change adaptation, is currently populated by climate scientists, ecologists, NGOs, environmental lawyers, urban planners, engineers, computer scientists, development experts, resource managers, and policymakers. Political scientists have been largely absent from the conversation, despite the importance of the topic and the need for their contributions. Many of the most pressing questions about adaptation are less about science and more about political, social, and economic behavior and the institutions that facilitate or obstruct that behavior—questions that political scientists are uniquely trained to answer. Such questions include why some people, land, infrastructure, and ecosystems get protected but not others, why some protective mechanisms are chosen over others, and how we can account for variation in the sources and quantities of funding for protection.

Environmental research, broadly conceived, is an increasing presence in political science. The subfields of international relations and political theory are probably the biggest contributors to the general environmental literature. Scholars of international relations have focused on institutions, negotiations, and policies between nations that affect global environmental outcomes (e.g., see Selin 2010), including our current lack of progress in mitigating climate change (Roberts and Parks 2007; Young, King, and Schroeder 2008; Aldy and Stavins 2009; Keohane and Victor 2011). Scholars of political theory have focused on questions of social justice and the relative responsibilities of different nations, social groups, and generations for mitigating climate change and the rights of victims of climate change to compensation (e.g., see Vanderheiden 2008; Hiskes 2009; Gardiner et al. 2010; Baer 2011; Dietz 2011; Gardiner 2011; Howarth 2011; Brooks 2013). In comparative politics, scholars in and outside the field have contributed cross-national studies of domestic environmental politics, such as disaster management and recovery (e.g., see Perrow 2007; Boin, McConnell, and Hart 2008; Kunreuther and Useem 2010), domestic mitigation efforts (Bättig and Bernauer 2009; Harrison and Sundstrom 2010; Christoff and Eckersley 2011), and the domestic impacts of climate change (e.g., see Dalby 2009; Matthew et al. 2011). Scholars of American politics have contributed a large literature on American environmental politics and decision making (e.g., see Mullin 2009), including our largely-failed climate policy efforts (e.g., see Keller 2009) and public opinion about those efforts (Dunlap and McCright 2008; Krosnick 2010).

Yet even with the expansion of research relevant to climate change mitigation, there is little acknowledgement of the separate and increasingly important field of climate change adaptation. Adaptation, as I will describe, is not and should not be a small subfield of environmental politics; if anything, it is a large and growing super-field that connects almost all existing fields of political science. When we talk about adapting to climate change, we are talking about everything from urban politics to international development, public opinion to national security, interest groups to federalism to a variety of other seemingly disparate fields. The need to adapt to climate change will affect nearly every political decision in the coming decades, making adaptation relevant to political parties, elections, civil society, business and politics, and most other political phenomena as citizens and political officials grapple with changing conditions.

Some political scientists are beginning to recognize these connections. On occasion, the distinct topic of adaptation has been mentioned by international relations scholars discussing the new international institutions designed to help fund adaptation in the least developed countries (Keohane and Victor 2011,12), by scholars of the European Union interested in adaptation strategies within and across member states (Jordan 2010), and by political theorists who appreciate the numerous justice questions that surround adaptation funding and implementation (Adger et al. 2006; Duus-Otterstrom and Jagers 2012).

Beyond these cases, we are hard pressed to find even passing reference to adaptation. A search of the 152 political science titles in JSTOR using the phrases "climate change adaptation," "adapting to climate change," and "adapt to a changing climate" as of May 2013 reveals a single article that has such a phrase in the title, a 2010 Policy Sciences article on alleviating flood impacts in Australia (Tryhorn and Lynch 2010). A full-text search on the same key phrases reveals 41 articles, most published in non-mainstream journals and including little more than the phrase "adaptation" with no meaningful discussion or analysis and sometimes having only a tangential connection to the topic.[3] Indeed, to call any of the articles "adaptation research by political scientists" would be misleading. Only a single article—Robert Keohane and David Victor's "The Regime Complex for Climate Change," published in Perspectives on Politics— goes beyond mentioning the phrase "climate change adaptation" and includes some discussion.

With the level of heat-trapping carbon dioxide in the atmosphere having just surpassed an average daily level of 400 parts per million in May 2013 (Gillis 2013), and with adaptation occupying more and more of the political discourse in important forums such as the forthcoming IPCC Fifth Assessment Report and the forthcoming US National Climate Assessment Report,[4] discussion of adaptation by political scientists must become more frequent and central to our discipline. We must continue discussing greenhouse gases and policies, but we must also seek to understand the urgent and directly political questions surrounding where people live, whether they are safe from disease and disaster, whether the land, water, and air can provide for them in their current locations, and what, if anything, is being done when the answer is "no."

Here I make the case for political scientists from all subfields to contribute to climate change adaptation research and advance the adaptation conversation in mainstream political science. Recognizing that political scientists are more likely to engage in needed research if the startup costs are lowered, I first summarize the most essential scientific points about climate change, climate change impacts, and adaptations. I then describe how scholars with different specialties could apply their knowledge to help the world adapt to climate change while using adaptation to illuminate research questions and test hypotheses. Political scientists who seek theory-driven research questions with practical and even urgent implications will find a wealth of opportunity in the study of adaptation. The goal is to define a research agenda on the politics of adapting to climate change.

Adaptation 101 for Political Scientists

Political scientists could participate actively in adaptation research without undertaking a lengthy course of study in climate science or ecology, in much the same way that political scientists study political economy without becoming economists. There are many short volumes that provide sufficient introduction to climate change, its impacts, and potential adaptations, with the most authoritative and useful being the IPCC's Summary for Policymakers (IPCC 2007a, 2007b). Here I briefly review the most essential scientific findings that political scientists might need to know in order to assess where their own contributions could be most meaningful.

Climate Change Basics

Most major impacts of climate change follow from a few basic scientific and historical facts (IPCC 2007a). First, human emissions of carbon dioxide, nitrous oxide, methane, and other greenhouse gases have increased dramatically since the beginning of the industrial age when humans became dependent on burning fossil fuels for comfort and economic gain and on large-scale changes in land use such as deforestation, urbanization, waste management, and industrial agriculture. Second, these excess greenhouse gases trap thermal infrared radiation (heat) in quantities that exceed the historical equilibrium and enhance the greenhouse effect, causing the atmosphere and the earth's surface to warm. The earth has *already* warmed almost 1°C in the last 100 years—this is a fact well established by empirical evidence (IPCC 2007a, 5)—and projections for future warming range from 1–6°C, based on different "emissions scenarios," with previously unthinkable projections becoming more and more likely as new data accumulate (Brysse et al. 2013).

Third, and very relevant for understanding climate impacts, warmer air holds more water. Fourth and similarly relevant, warmer air warms the oceans, and warmer ocean water expands. Fifth, excess carbon dioxide in the atmosphere gets absorbed by ocean water and turns the oceans more acidic, potentially more acidic in the coming centuries than in the past 300 million years (Caldeira and Wicket 2003). Climate science is certainly more complicated than my summary of these five facts can convey, but these facts are sufficient for political scientists to understand the impacts that follow, their urgency, and their relevance to politics.

Climate-change Impacts

Why should we care about higher temperatures? Higher temperatures increase evaporation and the amount of moisture held in the now-warmer atmosphere. The evaporation and higher atmospheric water content culminate in increased rainfall, but the rainfall is not uniform. Some areas experience drought and losses in soil moisture, which in turn leads to reduced crop yield, reservoir depletion, hydroelectric interruptions, other power shortages, land degradation, economic loss, diminished livelihood opportunities, hunger, and even desertification, famine, and human dislocation (Adger et al. 2007, 734; Roberts 2010; Webber 2012). Other areas experience heavy rainfall and major floods, which in turn can lead to increased soil erosion, turbidity, water pollution, toxic mold, water-borne gastrointestinal illness and other disease, and death. Heavy precipitation also increases power outages and puts at risk commercial and residential real estate, transportation infrastructure, oil and gas infrastructure, and other assets. Some areas experience both droughts and floods. For example, they alternate between dry and rainy seasons, or they are downstream of rapidly melting glaciers that threaten to flood and then cause freshwater dams and reservoirs to run dry.

Higher temperatures also cause the sea level to rise. A warmer atmosphere warms the ocean, which in turn increases in volume in a process known as thermal expansion. Melting glaciers, ice caps, and ice sheets also contribute to the increased ocean volume, and once huge amounts of ice melt and dark water replaces shiny white ice, surface reflectivity is reduced, which only serves to accelerate warming and sea level rise. During the twentieth century, the global average sea level rose about 15–20 centimeters, and the IPCC estimates a continued global average rise of between.2 and.6 meters in the next century, threatening many populous metropolitan areas (IPCC 2007a, 13). A rising sea contributes to coastal erosion, wetland and coastal plain flooding, salinization of aquifers and soils, and loss of habitats for fish, birds, plants, and other wildlife, not to mention humans who will lose fresh water supplies. Sea level rise, like rainfall, is not uniform around the globe, meaning that some species, ecosystems, and coastal communities are affected more severely than others. In the case of future potentially uninhabitable island-states, climate-induced sea level rise threatens not simply lifestyles but state sovereignty and citizenship.

Higher temperatures increase the severity of extreme weather events and natural disasters. Given that the warmer air holds more moisture and the warmer sea rises, when hurricanes, cyclones, and other natural disasters hit, there is more water in the atmosphere to pour down, and the sea has less distance to travel before wreaking havoc. While scientists debate whether climate change has increased the number of extreme weather events, most agree that climate change has contributed to the greater scope, intensity, and destructive power of recent hurricanes, tropical cyclones, fires, and other otherwise "natural" events.

Higher temperatures by themselves and in combination with low moisture, sea level rise, flooding, or extreme weather events have impacts on human health and infrastructure. When higher temperatures are relentless ("heat waves"), they increase the likelihood of dehydration, kidney failure, respiratory disease, and death, and they can overtax hospitals, emergency services, and health care budgets. Higher temperatures increase the range and reproductive frequency of insect-borne diseases such as malaria, dengue, West Nile, and Lyme, as well as the incidence of air and water pollution and associated diseases such as asthma and cholera. By drying crops, reducing agricultural productivity, and thus driving up food prices worldwide, higher temperatures can exacerbate malnutrition and poverty (Jones 2011; Reardon 2011). By increasing evaporation and drying soil and plant life, higher temperatures increase the likelihood of wildfires and their accompanying human and economic costs in evacuations, property loss, fire-fighting resources, and death, in addition to the tremendous natural value of lost forest and its carbon-capturing abilities. Tropical cyclones expose about 120 million people each year to hazards and kill more than 12,000 people a year (UNFCCC 2009, 421). As human settlements continue to expand into already vulnerable coastal areas, destruction is expected to increase. All of these impacts increase climate-induced human migration and displacement, which again increases disease risk as more people clump together in urban slums.

Higher temperatures cause things to melt or expand—important things, like railroad tracks, roads, and other infrastructure that are now stressed beyond their design limits (Wald and Schwartz 2012). Metals suitable in the historical climate can expand and kink in higher temperatures and cause trains to derail; previously suitable but now softened asphalt can cause aircraft to stick; and hot, dry soil can shrink and lead highways to buckle or crack, creating road hazards and costing thousands or even millions of dollars to repair. In some areas, higher temperatures cause the ground itself to melt. Permafrost, permanently frozen subsoil, remains intact at 32°F (0°C) or lower, but just a few degrees of warming turns the soil mushy and unstable, causing ground collapse, landslides, and "drunken forests." The resulting "thermokarst" no longer provides solid support for houses, buildings, pipelines, highways, railroads, and other infrastructure (Dean 2012).

Higher temperatures lead to species extinction and ecosystem dysfunction (Hansen, Biringer, and Hoffmann 2003; Fischlin et al. 2007, 242-4). The relationship is both direct and indirect, since climate change impacts like desertification reduce habitat for endangered plants and animals and threaten their survival, and many species, such as those with restricted diets ("specialized predators") or those living on mountaintops or islands or near cities, farmland, or other human-made barriers, are unable to adjust on their own by evolving or moving to new locations. This is the plight of the climate change poster species, the polar bear. Higher temperatures affect lifecycles and the availability of nutrients, especially for species at the bottom of food chains, such as plankton and coral, which then triggers reactions up the food chain and threatens entire ecosystems (Richardson and Schoeman 2004). It does not take much warming to induce this effect. A mere 1–2°C increase over the usual summer maximum temperature causes coral bleaching and the losses of potentially thousands of fish and marine creatures that feed off the coral, as well as the use of corals and reef animals and plants for medicinal purposes and tourism (Fischlin et al. 2007, 235).

As with most climate change impacts, these losses are not distributed evenly, and crucial ecosystems such as coral and mangroves—and the communities that depend upon them—suffer sooner and more extensively than others. Even where extinction is not the main risk, species may decrease in abundance, threatening fish stocks, timber supply, pollination, and other ecosystem provisions for humans. Subsistence farmers and communities directly dependent on fisheries and agriculture are most affected by these ecosystem changes (Adger et al. 2007, 734).

For marine life, the effects of higher temperatures are compounded by the effects of increased ocean acidity. Acidification reduces the water's content of calcium carbonate and hampers the shell-building, growth, and reproductive capacity of shellfish, crustaceans, mollusks, and species of plankton and coral that are critical to food chains. At even low projections of acidification, coral skeletons begin to dissolve, and reefs fall apart (Fischlin et al. 2007, 235). The inability of plankton to maintain their shells could threaten their survival in some areas and lead to the collapse of entire ecosystems (Orr et al. 2005).

Adapting to These Impacts

People often respond to climate change impacts by coping, or employing short-term remedies to immediate problems. For example, victims of food shortage may receive humanitarian assistance, or victims of flooding might seek shelter at higher elevation, wait for the flood to recede, and then begin the process of cleanup and rebuilding. Adapting to climate change differs from coping. Adaptation is a more permanent change—a change in "business as usual"—that results in a community's reduced vulnerability to future climate change impacts. Perhaps a community begins to acquire its food differently, regardless of whether an acute crisis is predicted, or perhaps the community elevates infrastructure, builds new infrastructure such as seawalls, or relocates.

Just a few years ago, policymakers, environmentalists, and even scientists avoided talking about adaptation and focused exclusively on mitigation. The concern was that such discussions seemed defeatist or accepting of climate change. If human and natural systems are adaptable, then perhaps the climate change deniers would have further ammunition to stymie mitigation efforts. Perhaps, too, adaptation discussions might give the false impression that adaptation is easily attainable. At the level of the United Nations, policymakers feared endorsing a course of action without the financial assistance such action would require (Schipper 2009, 362).

Increasingly, the call for adaptation research and policy has grown. While mitigation continues to be the primary concern, adaptation is now seen as a crucial accompaniment. Chief among the many reasons is that temperature change is a reality that even the most intense mitigation efforts now cannot stop. The greenhouse gases already emitted into the atmosphere "commit" the planet to further warming and the oceans to centuries of thermal expansion. Even in a best-case scenario, the world must adapt (IPCC 2007b, 19; Pittock and Jones 2009).

However, most if not all adaptation strategies are controversial. Because we are living in a "no analog future," tremendous uncertainty surrounds the costs, benefits, and potential effectiveness of most adaptation decisions. In best-case scenarios, adaptation strategies still often involve high costs such as the expense of building and maintaining seawalls and irrigation systems or relocating entire human populations of soon-to-be-engulfed island nations, communities in vulnerable coastal cities such as Mumbai or Dhaka, or even small villages in Alaska (Bicknell, Dodman, and Satterthwaite 2009; Western Governors' Association 2010, 6). In worst-case scenarios, measures ostensibly designed to reduce vulnerability may end up increasing vulnerability and become "maladaptations." For example, irrigation may encourage the continuation of agriculture in arid locations with unreliable water sources that cannot sustain agriculture in the long term. Levee construction or insurance practices may encourage more people to underestimate their risk, move to flood-prone areas, and even build new homes and infrastructure directly in harm's way—the so-called "levee effect."

The controversies—and the politics accompanying the controversies—present obstacles to action. Despite the heightened awareness and increased conversation about the critical need to adapt, very little adaptation has actually been implemented anywhere in the world.[5] It is especially telling that the city known for having one of the best climate-preparedness plans in the world, New York City and its PlaNYC,[6] is not prepared and recently suffered billions of dollars of losses from Hurricane Sandy.

One potential route to minimize the controversies and facilitate action would be in the provision of knowledge about adaptation. However, little is known so far about the potential effectiveness or harm of various adaptations and the causes of variability in effectiveness (IPCC 2007b, 19; National Research Council 2010, 60). Even less is known about how adaptations come to be—how governments or publics come to accept the need to adapt to climate change and move from acceptance to action (National Research Council 2010, 77, 213–4).

A New Interdisciplinary Field, Minus Political Science

Scholars in a variety of fields are trying to address this knowledge deficit. There is tremendous dialogue among climate scientists, ecologists, legal scholars, urban planners, engineers, architects, public health experts, geologists, hydrologists, agronomists, economists, computer scientists, development experts, and more. Climate change adaptation is thoroughly interdisciplinary.

However, to date, the field of political science has contributed virtually nothing. Our absence is noteworthy and problematic because most adaptation questions are fundamentally political (Moser 2009a), and political scientists possess tools of analysis that make them uniquely equipped to contribute vital insights. For example, an engineer can decide where to build a seawall to best protect a city from sea level rise, and an engineer combined with a climate scientist might determine how high to build the seawall, how thick, and with what material and what procedure. The engineer, however, does not decide *whether* to build the seawall—a question that involves political officials and the people who vote for them, as well as political institutions, the economy, and other factors that potentially constrain or facilitate action (Karl, Melillo, and Peterson 2009, 156).

We know this even about mitigation. Climate scientists can employ the most sophisticated analyses of General Circulation Models (GCMs) to project future global mean temperatures, but those models are really a function of politics. If today, the US Congress and other legislatures around the world issued currently unthinkable laws rationing gasoline or restricting driving, greenhouse gas emissions would be reduced, and the margin of error in the GCMs would decrease because of new information guiding the "emissions scenario." The 2008 Olympics in

Beijing hinted at this possibility: The Chinese restricted diesel truck traffic, limited automobile traffic, shut down heavily polluting factories, raised auto fuel emission standards, and halted construction, and as a result, carbon dioxide emissions in Beijing were 47 percent lower than the year prior (Schreurs 2011, 457). Politics explains much of what the GCMs can't.

Consider even something as seemingly apolitical as nature. To some extent, species extinction is a political decision. Do we allow species to go extinct, or do we implement wildlife adaptations to try to save them? If we try to save them, how do we decide which ones? Given estimates of Earth's biodiversity of 5 to 80 million species (Mace, Masundire, and Baillie 2005), and given projected extinctions between 9 and 40 percent, or one-half to eight million of those species (MacLean and Wilson 2012; Javeline et al. 2013), such decisions will involve only a few winners and many losers, making the decisions highly controversial. Assuming we succeed at selecting species, how do we decide on adaptation strategies? These decisions too are highly controversial, given the spatial and financial demands of most forms of conservation and the competition of conservation goals with the other societal goals for a human population predicted to reach 9 billion by the year 2050. Whatever decisions are made will require bargaining and trade-offs and most likely laws, public financing, and leadership—that is, politics.

Changing crops or diversifying crops as an agricultural adaptation is also extraordinarily political. In the US and elsewhere, farmers choose their crops based largely on subsidies and other political incentives, which in the US leads them to emphasize corn and to a lesser extent cotton, wheat, rice, and soy. Climate change adaptation is not as simple as saying "change which crops you grow" and having this outcome materialize. Lawmakers must agree which crops to subsidize in the new climate, and they must negotiate with lobbyists and each other and "sell" any new farm bill to constituents.

Politics also play a decisive role in coastal adaptations, especially those involving the possibility of coastal retreat. Research in geology, oceanography, economics, and other fields may show that moving away from the coastline is the only available long-term option for some coastal communities, but such research is unlikely to encourage relocation. Residents are often invested in their communities, financially, socially, culturally, and emotionally, and they may resist the science-based advice to move. Opposition to a perfectly scientific and sensible solution to climate change impacts is not a salient research topic for most geologists, but it can be for many political scientists.

Even the most severe climate change impacts that may have advanced beyond our capacity to adapt can still be the subject of important political science research. For example, if coral reefs are truly beyond conservation (Bradbury 2012), we may then allocate funds not to saving ecosystems but to economic structural adjustment for communities and industries that depend on coral reefs and to studying how these new ecosystems could provide food and other ecosystem goods and services. If higher temperatures and accompanying water shortages make nuclear reactors too risky in certain locations (Wald and Schwartz 2012), we might consider alternative sources of energy. Political scientists could contribute to our understanding of how these political decisions get made, how the decisions vary across countries and other geopolitical units, and the implications of these decisions for the environment, electoral outcomes, and other ecological and political variables.

Bringing Political Scientists to the Table

Almost every subfield of political science has potential relevance for climate change adaptation. Table 1 presents a dozen or so such subfields, as well as examples of research questions that specialists in these subfields could address. Together, these represent a huge untapped opportunity for political scientists to contribute to the adaptation literature. The table is by no means exhaustive, and there are undoubtedly other important applications of political science to climate change adaptation research. Also, while the table suggests ideas for research within conventionally-defined subfields, the multifaceted nature of climate change and its impacts often demands research that bridges subfield and methodological divides. To expand on a few of these ideas, we now turn to examples from four subfields and their currently unaddressed research questions.

Comparative Politics

Specialists in comparative politics could address the question, "Why do some countries adapt to climate change better than others?" Country-level adaptation questions are important because climate change impacts such as a flooding river or a drying water supply often cross local or regional jurisdictions, and political decisions to adapt must therefore often happen at higher administrative levels or not happen at all (Giddens 2009, 167). The national government often plays a role in policy formation, policy enactment, stimulating innovation, and research funding. If any government level is going to identify vulnerabilities throughout the country and coordinate a plan of action, it will probably be the national level (Berrang-Ford, Ford, and Paterson 2011, 32).

The relative adaptation performance of countries is acknowledged in the so-called "grey literature" (literature that may originate from government agencies, think tanks, or non-governmental organizations but is not commercially published), but the subject is not systematically studied. Adaptation specialists often describe the United States as a laggard among developed nations, due to our lack of a comprehensive national adaptation strategy that assesses our nation's vulnerabilities and offers strategies for reducing them (e.g., see Moser 2009b; Ebi 2010). There is a fair amount of adaptation planning in the United States at the state and city levels but no national-level adaptation mandate, grand master plan, or funding, let alone national-level action. Conversely, adaptation specialists usually describe the United Kingdom and the Netherlands as adaptation leaders, partly because they—along with Germany, Portugal, Spain, France, Belgium, Denmark, Switzerland, Hungary, Sweden, and Finland—have adaptation plans at the national level, often referred to as National Adaptation Strategies.[7]

Because these National Adaptation Strategies are reasonably accessible, adaptation planning receives more attention than actual adaptations. At times, the (non-political science) literature seems to conflate the plans with actual adaptations, despite the absence of empirical evidence that adaptation plans translate more quickly and efficiently into adaptation implementation and can serve as reasonable proxies for adaptation (Farber 2011, 366–8). A rare recent study moves in the right direction by focusing on activities rather than potentially unfilled plans (Berrang-Ford, Ford, and Paterson 2011; Ford, Berrang-Ford, and Paterson 2011), but to my knowledge, no study as yet has attempted the more labor-intensive work of determining which countries have reduced their vulnerability to specific climate impacts such as heat waves, drought, coastal erosion, or disease outbreak, and no study systematically analyzes the causes of variability in adaptation and thus allows us to understand and learn from success.

Within the developing world, a potential source of information for cross-national comparative analysis is the National Adaptation Programmes of Action (NAPAs) from 47 Least Developed Countries as of January 2012.[8] Like the NAS of the developed world, many of the NAPAs represent plans more than actual adaptations, but there is the possibility to compare projects in specific economic sectors and country priorities across sectors. Outside these clusters of countries—the European Union and Least Developed Countries—few if any one-stop-shopping sources of information exist that would allow comparison of adaptation efforts and results across countries. The need for such a database is strong, especially one that is regularly updated to monitor adaptation progress in every country of the world, including national-level legislation, commitment or disbursement of funds, implementations, specific dates, specific amounts of money, and which agencies do the organization and implementation. Political scientists could use their skills to fulfill this need.

Subfield	Sample Research Questions
Comparative Politics	Why do some countries adapt to climate change better than others?
Regimes & Regime Change	Do democracies adapt better than authoriatrian governments or vice versa?
Foreign Assistance	Is climate change adaptation in developing nations facilitated by international actors? If so, which circumstances are conductive to effective aid?
Urban Politics	Why do some cities adapt to climate change better than others?
State Politics/ Subnational Governments	Why do some states take greater initiatives than others? Why do some states work together on adaptation issues? Why do some state adaptation plans get implemented while others do not? Of the implementations, what accounts for variation in success?
Federalism	How do center-periphery relationships or the presence of multiple layers of governance affect adaptation? Is there is an optimal allocation of adaptation tasks between different government levels?
Bureaucracy	How can the problems of regulatory fragmentation be minimized for adaptation? How can institutions be structured to help governments and publics best adapt to climate change? Is mainstreaming or centralizing adaptation efforts the most effective institutional approach?
International Development	What is the effect of development on adaptation and adaptation on development? Can poverty reduction and the reduction of vulnerability to climate change be jointly pursued, and if so, how?
Business & Politics	Why do some businesses adapt to climate change better than others? What is the role of government in encouraging or discouraging the private sector to take adaptation action? What is the most effective mixture of market and government responses to climate change?
Political Economy	How can the value of nature or natural capital be incorporated into adaptation decision making?
Political Theory	How do we justly allocate the burdens and benefits of climate change adaptation between the developed and developing world, the wealthy and poor (especially indigenous peoples), current and future generations, men and women, and humans and non-humans?
Public Knowledge, Opinion, & Behavior	What accounts for public awareness of adaptation options, opinions on those options, and public willingness to support adaptation policy and to implement individual adaptations?
Media	What is the content and message of adaptation reporting? Does adaptation reporting vary cross-nationally (or even between states and cities in the same nation), and if so, what are the effects of this variation?
Social Capital	When does social capital have positive versus negative implications for adaptation?
Civil Society	What are the causes and implications of limited civil society involvement in adaptation?
Interest Groups	What is the role of the carbon-intensive industry lobby, environmental organizations, and other interest groups in adaptation policymaking and implementation?
Elections	What, if any, are the incentives for office-seeking politicians to promote adaptation over time? Under which circumstances might voters reward an incumbent for planning and implementing adaptation or vote a candidate into office specifically on the promise to adapt? Under which circumstances might politicians lead voters by raising awareness of climate change impacts and "selling" adaptation policies?

Table 1. Political Science Research Questions on Climate Change Adaptation

Subfield	Sample Research Questions
Political Parties	Does partisanship drive adaptation decision making? What is the influence on adaptation of a viable green party, other minority parties, a strong or weak left wing party, rules of the electoral system, a two-party versus multi-party system, and a presidential versus parliamentary system?
Political Conflict & National Security	Can climate change adaptation diminish the likelihood of conflict and increase national security, and if so, under which circumstances? Which adaptations hold the greatest promise of reducing or resolving conflict versus causing or enhancing conflict?
Human Migration & Displacement	How can climate change migration be governed and managed effectively so that humanitarian crises are minimized and conflicts are avoided? How will relocations be funded, and if they are not funded, what becomes of climate refugees and the health and financial systems where they migrate?
Political Methodology	When is it appropriate to measure whether adaptation objectives have been met? What is the proper unit of measurement for successful adaptation -money saved, lives saved, quality of life preserved, or some other metric? Is it possible to compare adaptation effectiveness across sectors in order to facilitate decision making?

Table 1 (Continued). Political Science Research Questions on Climate Change Adaptation

Public Opinion and Behavior

Opinion research on public concern about climate change is reasonably available and shows that most people know that the climate is changing (Egan and Mullin 2012, 799; Davenport 2013), but they perceive climate change as a spatially and temporally remote risk: "It will affect future generations and other countries, but not me personally, my generation, or my locale" (Whitmarsh, Seyfang, and O'Neill 2011, 57; Bichard and Kazmierczak 2012). Opinion research on adaptation, however, is extraordinarily rare, even in the face of recent disasters such as Hurricane Sandy, which have communities and their leaders scrambling to decide how to rebuild.

Such research by scholars of public opinion, political behavior, and political psychology is urgently needed, because public opinion on adaptation matters. Adaptations are expensive and may require raising taxes or other forms of public finance that could be the subject of electoral debate, and adaptations sometimes involve direct changes in individual behavior such as preventive maintenance on homes, purchasing insurance coverage, relocating, responding to early warning systems, changing agricultural practices, or supporting legal measures to protect climate-threatened species, behaviors which could be influenced by opinions (Hunter 2007, 1358; Bichard and Kazmierczak 2012). The limited research to date suggests that awareness of climate change impacts is somewhat correlated with adaptation action. For example, awareness of flood risks associated with climate change leads to a greater willingness to pay for flood-protection measures, such as raising electrical fixtures, putting in door guards, and replacing wood staircases with concrete (Bichard and Kazmierczak 2012). However, I am not aware of any research that investigates adaptation awareness and opinions on a larger scale and asks, for example, whether New Yorkers are prepared to spend billions on a flood protection barrier and, if so, who they believe should foot the bill. Such studies would amount to much more than opinion polling; they could contribute to research on collective action, social choice, public choice, and other fields.

Public opinion and behavior studies could also help illuminate the barriers to adaptation on the public side—barriers that are hypothesized in the grey literature and the much smaller scholarly literature but that are currently untested. These hypothesized barriers include poor communication, poor transportation, illiteracy, and other factors that limit information and knowledge about adaptation and how to reduce vulnerability (Whitmarsh 2008; "Decision Making" 2010–2011; National Research Council 2010, 127–8); feeling powerless, overwhelmed, in denial, apathetic, or fatalistic (Moser 2009a, 288); competition with other values, emotions, and priorities such as fear of change or love for one's hometown and lifestyle (Adger et al. 2007, 735); differing perceptions of risk (Adger et al. 2007, 735; National Research Council 2010, 127–8); differing perceptions of public versus private responsibility for adaptation (Bichard and Kazmierczak 2012, 638); poverty, the inability to borrow, inconvenience, the unavailability of technological alternatives, and other structural limitations to adaptive behavior (Maddison 2007; Moser 2009a, 289; Whitmarsh and O'Neill 2010); and basic civic disengagement and disinterest in politics (Moser 2009a, 287). Mechanisms for increasing public motivation to adapt are hypothesized to include the media, social networks, civil society organizations, educational programs, outreach campaigns such as agricultural extension services, and public awareness campaigns about threats to wildlife (Maddison 2007; Mandleni and Anim 2010; National Research Council 2010, 127–8; "National Fish, Wildlife and Plants" 2012). Both the hypothesized barriers and the hypothesized mechanisms to overcome the barriers could be systematically tested by political scientists specializing in various dimensions of mass politics.

Political Parties

Specialists in political parties could contribute to understanding the extent to which partisanship drives decision making on adaptation. On the one hand, adaptation leaders in the United States can be found not just among Democrats and liberals but among prominent Republicans such as California Governor Arnold Schwarzenegger, extreme conservatives like Alaska Governor Sarah Palin, and independents such as New York City Mayor Michael Bloomberg, suggesting that there are few meaningful partisan differences on adaptation. On the other hand, US political parties are quite polarized about climate change itself and mitigation (Dunlap and McCright 2008), and it is plausible that this polarization extends to adaptation.

Party polarization is a subject for cross-national study as well. Like in the United States, parties in Australia reduce climate science to an ideological debate, whereas climate science in Germany receives bipartisan acceptance and respect (Christoff and Eckersley 2011, 442). Again, whether party polarization about mitigation extends to adaptation is currently in need of research. Other potentially fruitful areas for cross-national research include the influence on adaptation of a viable green party or other minority party; a strong or weak left wing party; the rules of the electoral system; two-party versus multi-party systems; and presidential versus parliamentary systems. While to my knowledge no literature exists on these topics in reference to adaptation, specialists in political parties could look to the more general literature on parties and the environment (Dolsak 2001; Blackburn and Stone 2003; Neumayer 2003; Spoon 2009).

Political Conflict and National Security

Many specialists in political conflict predict that climate change and its accompanying drought, food insecurity, and stress on state capacity will increase the likelihood of communal violence, ethnic violence, rebellion against the state, internal or civil war, and interstate conflict (Brown, Hammill, and McLeman 2007; Busby 2007, 2008; Brown and Crawford 2009; Burke et al. 2009; Habib 2010; Hsiang, Burke, and Miguel 2013; but see Salehyan 2008; Gleditsch 2012). The conflicts themselves, as well as the diversion of military forces from external defense to domestic disasters and the direct threats to military bases from rising seas and extreme weather events, lead many to suggest that climate change poses a national security risk (Busby 2007, 2008; Broder 2009; de Brito 2010). Moreover, conflict can erode the capacity to adapt to climate change. It can deplete human resources, destroy infrastructure, exhaust natural resources, undermine social networks, weaken government institutions, shift resources to military use, stifle economic development and innovation, and prevent collaboration and information-sharing on climate change (Adger et al. 2007, 730; Brown, Hammill, and McLeman 2007, 1150; Brown and Crawford 2009).

Conflict therefore diminishes the likelihood of adaptation. The pressing question for scholars of political and violent conflict is just the reverse: Can adaptation diminish the likelihood of conflict and increase national security? Two types of adaptations are at issue. One involves non-military adaptations in a variety of economic sectors, with the question being whether the reduction in vulnerability to climate change also reduces the potential for conflict. Does the protection of livelihoods and natural resources from the impacts of climate change preserve peace (Brown, Hammill, and McLeman 2007, 1152; Busby 2007, 20)? Or could adaptations that influence contiguous locations, such as coastal protection, irrigation, or river diversion, actually create or enhance conflict (Goulden, Conway, and Persechino 2009; Lewis 2009, 1207)? A second type of adaptation is specifically related to security: security adaptations, or reductions in the vulnerability of military or domestic police forces to climate change. The question here is whether reducing the military's vulnerability to climate change by, for example, weatherproofing military installations or incorporating climate modeling into military preparations reduces the potential for conflict and enhances security.

Specialists in conflict and national security could make very constructive contributions to adaptation studies by investigating which adaptations hold the greatest promise of reducing or resolving conflict and which hold the greatest promise of causing or enhancing conflict. They might also investigate the possible conditionality of adaptation impacts. Are there circumstances where adaptation provokes conflict and other circumstances where the same adaptation does not provoke conflict (Brown, Hammill, and McLeman 2007, 1152; Goulden, Conway, and Persechino 2009, 822)? Finally, specialists might identify the barriers to military adaptations, as well as barriers to those non-military adaptations that have implications for conflict-resolution and national security.

Conclusion

Adaptation studies sorely need the contributions of political scientists from almost every subfield. Political scientists do not need to gain much additional expertise to make these contributions. Plenty of ecologists, geologists, engineers, and other non-political scientists are working on climate change adaptation and drawing on their expertise in relevant ways, and there is no need to duplicate that expertise. Instead, we need to fill a huge gap. It is our own expertise in politics that is lacking and should be applied to the many critically important and unanswered political questions about adaptation.

Mitigation studies too could benefit tremendously from the involvement of political scientists with relevant expertise. The argument here is that political scientists who do not see the relevance of their expertise to mitigation can still make important contributions to solving problems associated with global climate change by conducting much needed research on adaptation, the other half of the climate puzzle.

Some adaptation-relevant research is already being conducted in regard to individual disasters and recovery efforts, such as Daniel Aldrich's *Building Resilience* and articles in the *Perspectives on Politics'* special issue, "Post-Katrina New Orleans and the Politics of Reconstruction." And of course our discipline has established bodies of work on public choice, governing the commons (e.g., see Ostrom 1990), and environmental politics that are also relevant. The next steps in the adaptation research agenda are to integrate these seemingly discrete topics into a cohesive literature on the politics of adaptation and to expand the number of political scientists who apply their expertise to studying the climate crisis. The latter goal could be facilitated by additional government or foundation funding, new journals or task forces, decisions by the editorial boards of existing journals to solicit climate-relevant articles, and most importantly, decisions by individual political scientists to incorporate climate change into their personal research agendas. Given the urgency, we need not wait for financial or other career incentives to ponder whether we can share our knowledge of politics with the larger community of scholars and policymakers trying to address the climate crisis. We are all relevant to the climate change discussion and all have something to contribute, and we arguably have responsibilities to make those contributions.

Reprinted from Debra Javeline. 2014. "The Most Important Topic Political Scientists Are Not Study-ing: Adapting to Climate Change." Perspectives on Politics 12 (2). Cambridge University Press: 420–34. doi:10.1017/S1537592714000784.

Notes

1. Of climate researchers most actively publishing in the field, 97 to 98 percent agree with the primary conclusions of the Intergovernmental Panel on Climate Change that the Earth's average temperature has warmed and that most warming is caused by anthropogenic greenhouse gases. The remaining tiny minority of climate change skeptics have the least expertise and scientific prominence (Anderegg et al. 2010). There is no meaningful scientific debate occurring about the existence of climate change. The discussion and urgent need for research concern mitigation and adaptation.

2. More specifically, adaptation is the "adjustment in natural or human systems in response to actual or expected climatic stimuli or their effects, which moderates harm or exploits beneficial opportunities" (IPCC 2007c).

3.

Number of Articles	Publication
7	Economic and Political Weekly
5	Policy Sciences
4	Development in Practice American Journal of International Law
3	Environmental Values
2	Journal of Peace Research International Affairs Global Governance
1	Perspectives on Politics International Studies Quarterly Foreign Affairs International Studies Review The World Today World Policy Journal The Modern Law Review Review of International Studies Asian Survey India International Centre Quarterly Journal of Palestine Studies The American Journal of Comparative Law

Table N1. Articles per Publication

4. Information about the IPCC Fifth Assessment Report (AR5) can be found at http://www.ipcc.ch/. The draft of the US National Climate Assessment Report can be found at http://ncadac.globalchange.gov/.

5. Thanks to monetary incentives provided by the United Nations Framework Convention on Climate Change (UNFCCC), most least-developed nations have NAPAs designed for specific adaptation projects; several projects have been funded by the Adaptation Fund (www.adaptation-fund.org); and international support is also available from the Global Environment Facility (GEF), the Least Developed Countries Fund (LDCF), the Special Climate Change Fund (SCCF) and the Green Climate Fund (https://unfccc.int/). However, adaptation needs far exceed the projects proposed or the funding available. Many European countries have National Adaptation Strategies (http://climate-adapt.eea.europa.eu/web/guest/adaptation-strategies), and many US states and cities have

climate action plans that incorporate adaptation or are devoted exclusively to adaptation (e.g., http://www.climatechange.ca.gov/adaptation/). However, it is a grand leap from assessing and planning to implementation, and even the developed world has few funds allocated for adaptation and little evidence of climate preparedness.

6. PlaNYC can be found at http://www.nyc.gov/html/planyc2030/html/theplan/the-plan.shtml.

7. National Adaptation Strategies are available at http://climate-adapt.eea.europa.eu/countries.

8. National Adaptation Programmes of Action are available at https://unfccc.int/index.php/topics/ resilience/workstreams/national-adaptation-programmes-of-action/introduction.

References

Adger, W. Neil, Jouni Paavola, Saleemul Huq, and M.J. Mace, eds. 2006. *Fairness in Adaptation to Climate Change*. Cambridge, MA: MIT Press.

Adger, W. Neil, S. Agrawala, M.M.Q. Mirza, C. Conde, K. O'Brien, J. Pulhin, R. Pulwarty, B. Smit and K. Takahashi. 2007. "Assessment of Adaptation Practices, Options, Constraints and Capacity." In *Climate Change 2007: Impacts, Adaptation and Vulnerability. Contribution of Working Group II to the Fourth Assessment Report of the Intergovernmental Panel on Climate Change*. Edited by M.L. Parry, O.F. Canziani, J.P. Palutikof, P.J. van der Linden and C.E. Hanson. Cambridge, UK: Cambridge University Press. 717–743. http://www.ipcc.ch/pdf/assessment-report/ar4/wg2/ar4-wg2-chapter17.pdf.

Aldrich, Daniel P. 2012. *Building Resilience: Social Capital in Post-Disaster Recovery*. Chicago: University of Chicago Press.

Aldy, Joseph E. and Robert N. Stavins, eds. 2009. *Post-Kyoto International Climate Policy: Summary for Policymakers*. New York: Cambridge University Press.

Anderegg, William R.L., James W. Prall, Jacob Harold, and Stephen H. Schneider. 2010. "Expert Credibility in Climate Change." *Proceedings of the National Academy of Sciences* 107 (27): 12107–9.

Baer, Paul. 2011. "International Justice." In *The Oxford Handbook of Climate Change and Society*. Edited by John S. Dryzek, Richard B. Norgaard, and David Schlosberg. New York: Oxford University Press.

Bättig, Michèle B. and Thomas Bernauer. 2009. "National Institutions and Global Public Goods: Are Democracies More Cooperative in Climate Change Policy?" *International Organization* 63 (2): 281–305.

Berrang-Ford, Lea, James D. Ford, and Jaclyn Paterson. 2011. "Are We Adapting to Climate Change?" *Global Environmental Change* 21: 25–33.

Bichard, Erik and Aleksandra Kazmierczak. 2012. "Are Homeowners Willing to Adapt to and Mitigate the Effects of Climate Change?" *Climatic Change* 112: 633–52.

Bicknell, Jane David Dodman, and David Satterthwaite. 2009. *Adapting Cities to Climate Change: Understanding and Addressing the Development Challenges*. London: Earthscan.

Blackburn, Amanda and Bruce Stone. 2003. "The Environment and Minor-party Insurgency in Australian Politics: The Case of Logging and the 'Liberals for Forests.'" *Australian Journal of Political Science* 38(3): 293–509.

Boin, Arjen, Allan McConnell, and Paul 'T Hart, eds. 2008. *Governing after Crisis: The Politics of Investigation, Accountability, and Learning*. New York: Cambridge University Press.

Bradbury, Roger. 2012. "A World without Coral Reefs." *New York Times*, July 13.

Broder, John M. 2009. "Climate Change Seen as Threat to US Security." *New York Times*, August 9.

Brooks, Thom. 2013. "Climate Change Justice." *PS: Political Science & Politics* 46 (1): 9–12.

Brown, Oli, and Alec Crawford. 2009. "Rising Temperatures, Rising Tensions: Climate Change and the Risk of Violent Conflict in the Middle East." *International Institute for Sustainable Development*, 1–36, http://www.iisd.org/pdf/2009/rising_temps_middle_east.pdf.

Brown, Oli, Anne Hammill, and Robert McLeman. 2007. "Climate Change as the 'New' Security Threat: Implications for Africa." *International Affairs* 83 (6): 1141–54.

Brysse, Keynyn, Naomi Oreskes, Jessica O'Reilly, and Michael Oppenheimer. 2013. "Climate Change Prediction: Erring on the Side of Least Drama?" *Global Environmental Change* 23 (1): 327–37.

Burke, Marshall, Edward Miguel, Shanker Satyanath, John Dykema, David Lobell. 2009. "Warming

Increases Risk of Civil War in Africa." *Proceedings of the National Academy of Sciences* 106 (49): 20670–74.

Busby, John W. 2007. "Climate Change and National Security: An Agenda for Action." Council on Foreign Relations, CSR No.32, November.

Busby, John W. 2008. "Who Cares about the Weather? Climate Change and US National Security." *Security Studies* 17 (3): 468–504.

Caldeira, K. and M.E. Wickett. 2003. "Anthropogenic Carbon and Ocean pH." *Nature* 425 (Sept.): 365–65.

Christoff, Peter and Robyn Eckersley. 2011. "Comparing State Responses." In *The Oxford Handbook of Climate Change and Society*. Edited by John S. Dryzek, Richard B. Norgaard, and David Schlosberg. New York: Oxford University Press.

Dalby, Simon. 2009. *Security and Environmental Change*. Cambridge, UK: Polity.

Davenport, Coral. 2013. "Why It Finally Makes Political Sense to Talk about Climate Change." *National Journal*.

de Brito, Rafaela. 2010 "Climate Change as a Security Issue in the European Union." *Portuguese Journal of International Affairs* 3: 41–50.

Dean, Cornelia. 2012. "With Warming, Peril Underlies Road to Alaska." *New York Times*, July 23.

Dietz, Simon. 2011. "From Efficiency to Justice: Utility as the Informational Basis of Climate Strategies, and Some Alernatives." In *The Oxford Handbook of Climate Change and Society*. Edited by John S. Dryzek, Richard B. Norgaard, and David Schlosberg. New York: Oxford University Press.

Dolsak, Nives. 2001. "Mitigating Global Climate Change: Why Are Some Countries More Committed Than Others." *Policy Studies Journal* 29 (3): 414–36.

Dunlap, Riley E. and Aaron M. McCright. 2008. "A Widening Gap: Republican and Democratic Views on Climate Change." *Environment* 50 (5): 26–34.

Duus-Otterstrom, Goran and Sverker C. Jagers. 2012. "Identifying Burdens of Coping with Climate Change: A Typology of the Duties of Climate Justice." *Global Environmental Change* 22 (3): 746–753.

Ebi, Kristie L. 2010. "ABCD of Adaptation." Congressional Briefing, January 8. http://www.ametsoc.org/atmospolicy/climatebriefing/jan2010.html.

Egan, Patrick J. and Megan Mullin. 2012. "Turning Personal Experience into Political Attitudes: The Effect of Local Weather on Americans' Perceptions about Global Warming." *Journal of Politics* 74 (3): 796–809.

Farber, Daniel A. 2011. "The Challenge of Climate Change Adaptation: Learning from National Planning Efforts in Britain, China, and the USA." *Journal of Environmental Law* 23 (3): 359–82.

Fischlin, A., G.F. Midgley, J.T. Price, R. Leemans, B. Gopal, C. Turley, M.D.A. Rounsevell, O.P. Dube, J. Tarazona, A.A. Velichko. 2007. "Ecosystems, Their Properties, Goods, and Services." In *Climate Change 2007: Impacts, Adaptation and Vulnerability. Contribution of Working Group II to the Fourth Assessment Report of the Intergovernmental Panel on Climate Change*. Edited by M.L. Parry, O.F. Canziani, J.P. Palutikof, P.J. van der Linden and C.E. Hanson.,. Cambridge, UK: Cambridge University Press.

Ford, James D., Lea Berrang-Ford, and Jaclyn Paterson. 2011. "A Systematic Review of Observed Climate Change Adaptation in Developed Nations." *Climatic Change* 106: 327–36.

Gardiner, Stephen M. 2011. "Climate Justice." In *The Oxford Handbook of Climate Change and Society*. Edited by John S. Dryzek, Richard B. Norgaard, and David Schlosberg. New York: Oxford University Press.

Gardiner, Stephen M., Simon Caney, Dale Jamieson, and Henry Shue. 2010. *Climate Ethics: Essential Reading*. New York: Oxford University Press.

Giddens, Anthony. 2009. *The Politics of Climate Change*. Malden, MA: Polity Press.

Gillis, Justin. 2013. "Heat-Trapping Gas Passes Milestone, Raising Fears." *New York Times*, May 10.

Gleditsch, Nils Petter. 2012. "Whither the Weather? Climate Change and Conflict." *Journal of Peace Research* 49 (1): 3–9.

Goulden, Marisa, Declan Conway, and Aurelie Persechino. 2009. "Adaptation to Climate Change in International River Basins: A Case Study of the River Nile." *Hydrological Sciences Journal* 54 (5): 805–28.

Habib, Benjamin. 2010. "Climate Change and Regime Perpetuation in North Korea." *Asia Survey* 50 (2): 378–401.

L.J. Hansen, J.L. Biringer, and J.R. Hoffmann. 2003. *Buying Time: A User's Manual for Building Resistance and Resilience to Climate Change in Natural Systems*. WWF Climate Change Program, Berlin.

Harrison, Kathryn, and Lisa McIntosh Sundstrom, eds. 2010. *Global Commons, Domestic Decisions: The Comparative Politics of Climate Change*. Cambridge, MA: MIT Press.

Hiskes, Richard P. 2009. *The Human Right to a Green Future: Environmental Rights and Intergenerational Justice*. New York: Cambridge University Press.

Howarth, Richard B. 2011. "Intergenerational Justice." In *The Oxford Handbook of Climate Change and Society*. Edited by John S. Dryzek, Richard B. Norgaard, and David Schlosberg. New York: Oxford University Press.

Hsiang, Solomon M., Marshall Burke, and Edward Miguel. 2013. "Quantifying the Influence of Climate on Human Conflict." *Science* DOI: 10.1126/science.1235367.

Hunter Jr., Malcolm L. 2007. "Climate Change and Moving Species: Furthering the Debate on Assisted Colonization." *Conservation Biology* 21 (5): 1356–58.

Intergovernmental Panel on Climate Change (IPCC). 2007a. "Summary for Policymakers." In *Climate Change 2007: The Physical Science Basis. Contribution of Working Group I to the Fourth Assessment Report of the Intergovernmental Panel on Climate Change*. Edited by S. Solomon, D. Qin, M. Manning, Z. Chen, M. Marquis, K.B. Averyt, M. Tignor and H.L. Miller. Cambridge, UK: Cambridge University Press.

Intergovernmental Panel on Climate Change (IPCC). 2007b. "Summary for Policymakers." In *Climate Change 2007: Impacts, Adaptation and Vulnerability. Contribution of Working Group II to the Fourth Assessment Report of the Intergovernmental Panel on Climate Change*. Edited by M.L. Parry, O.F. Canziani, J.P. Palutikof, P.J. van der Linden and C.E. Hanson.. Cambridge, UK: Cambridge University Press.

Intergovernmental Panel on Climate Change (IPCC). 2007c. "Appendix 1: Glossary." In *Climate Change 2007: Impacts, Adaptation and Vulnerability. Contribution of Working Group II to the Fourth Assessment Report of the Intergovernmental Panel on Climate Change*. Cambridge, UK: Cambridge University Press.

Javeline, Debra, Jessica J. Hellmann, Rodrigo Castro Cornejo, and Gregory Shufeldt. 2013. "Expert Opinion on Climate Change and Threats to Biodiversity." *Bioscience* 63 (8): 666–73.

Jones, Nicola. 2011. "Climate Change Curbs Crops." *Nature*, May 5.

Jordan, Andrew, ed. 2010. *Climate Change Policy in the European Union: Confronting the Dilemmas of Mitigation and Adaptation*. New York: Cambridge University Press.

Karl, Thomas R., Jerry M. Melillo, and Thomas C. Peterson, eds. 2009. "Global Climate Change Impacts in the United States." *A State of Knowledge Report from the US Global Change Research Program*. New York: Cambridge University Press.

Keller, Ann Campbell. 2009. *Science in Environmental Policy: The Politics of Objective Advice*. Cambridge, MA: MIT Press.

Keohane, Robert O. and David G. Victor. 2011. "The Regime Complex for Climate Change." *Perspectives on Politics* 9 (1): 7–23.

Krosnick, Jon A. 2010. "The Climate Majority." *New York Times*, June 8.

Kunreuther, Howard and Michael Useem, eds. 2010. *Learning from Catastrophes: Strategies for Reaction and Response*. Upper Saddle River, NJ: Wharton School Publishing.

Lewis, Joanna I. 2009. "Climate Change and Security: Examining China's Challenges in a Warming World." *International Affairs* 85 (6): 1195–213.

Mace, G., H. Masundire, and J. Baillie. 2005. "Biodiversity." In *Ecosystems and Human Well-Being: Current States and Trends*, vol. 1. Edited by R. Hassan, R. Scholes, and N. Ash. Washington, DC: Island Press.

MacLean, I. M. D. and R. J. Wilson. 2012. "Recent Ecological Responses to Climate Change Support Predictions of High Extinction Risk." *Proceedings of the National Academy of Sciences* 108 (30): 12337–42.

Maddison, David. 2007. "The Perception of and Adaptation to Climate Change in Africa." World Bank, policy research working paper 4308.

Mandleni, B. and F.D.K. Anim. 2010. "Climate Change Awareness and Decision on Adaptation Measures by Livestock Farmers in South Africa." *Journal of Agricultural Science* 3 (3): 258–68.

Matthew, Richard A., Jon Barnett, Bryan McDonald, and Karen L. O'Brien, eds. 2011. *Global Environmental Change and Human Security*. Cambridge, MA: MIT Press.

Moser, Susanne C. 2009a. "Communicating Climate Change and Motivating Civic Action: Renewing, Activating, and Building Democracies." In *Changing Climates in North American Politics*. Edited by Henrik Selin and Stacy D. VanDeveer. Cambridge: MIT Press.

Moser, Susanne C. 2009b. "Good morning, America! The explosive US awakening to the need for adaptation." NOAA, CEC, http://www.csc.noaa.gov/publications/need-for-adaptation.pdf.

Mullin, Megan. 2009. *Governing the Tap: Special District Governance and the New Local Politics of Water*. Cambridge: MIT Press.

"National Fish, Wildlife and Plants Climate Adaptation Strategy." 2012. http://www.wildlifeadaptationstrategy.gov/pdf/NFWPCAS-Final.pdf.

National Research Council. 2010. "Adapting to the Impacts of Climate Change: America's Climate Choices." Panel on Adapting to the Impacts of Climate Change. Washington, DC: National Academies Press.

Neumayer, Eric. 2003. "Are Left-wing Party Strength and Corporatism Good for the Environment? Evidence from Panel Analysis of Air Pollution in OECD Countries." *Ecological Economics* 45: 203–20.

Orr, J.C., V.J. Fabry, O. Aumont, L. Bopp, S.C. Doney, R.A. Feely, A. Gnanadesikan, N. Gruber, A. Ishida, F. Joos, R.M. Key, K. Lindsay, E. Maier-Reimer, R. Matear, P. Monfray, A. Mouchet, R.G. Najjar, G.K. Plattner, K.B. Rodgers, C.L. Sabine, J.L. Sarmiento, R. Schlitzer, R.D. Slater, I.J. Totterdell, M.F. Weirig, Y. Yamanaka, and A. Yool. 2005. "Anthropogenic Ocean Acidification over the Twenty-first Century and Its Impact on Calcifying Organisms." *Nature* 437 :681–86.

Ostrom, Elinor. 1990. *Governing the Commons: The Evolution of Institutions for Collective Action*. New York: Cambridge University Press.

Perrow, Charles. 2007. *The Next Catastrophe: Reducing Our Vulnerabilities to Natural, Industrial, and Terrorist Disasters*. Princeton: Princeton University Press.

Pittock, A. Barrie, and Roger N. Jones. 2009. "Adaptation to What and Why?" In *The Earthscan Reader on Adaptation to Climate Change*. Edited by E. Lisa F. Schipper and Ian Burton. London: Earthscan.

Reardon, Sara. 2011. "Climate Change Already Hurting Agriculture." *Science*, 5 May.

Richardson, Anthony J. and David S. Schoeman. 2004. "Climate Impact on Plankton Ecosystems in the Northeast Atlantic." *Science* 305 (5690): 1609–12.

Roberts, Dexter. 2010. "Drought in China Hits the Energy Sector." *Bloomberg Business Week*, April 22.

Roberts, J. Timmons and Bradley C. Parks. 2007. *A Climate of Injustice: Global Inequality, North–South Politics, and Climate Policy*. Cambridge, MA: MIT Press.

Salehyan, Idean. 2008. "From Climate Change to Conflict? No Consensus Yet." *Journal of Peace Research* 45 (3): 315–26.

Schipper, E. Lisa F. 2009. "Conceptual History of Adaptation in the UNFCCC Process." In *The Earthscan Reader on Adaptation to Climate Change*. Edited by E. Lisa F. Schipper and Ian Burton. London: Earthscan.

Schreurs, Miranda A. 2011. "Climate Change Politics in an Authoritarian State: The Ambivalent Case of China." In *The Oxford Handbook of Climate Change and Society*. Edited by John S. Dryzek, Richard B. Norgaard, and David Schlosberg. New York: Oxford University Press.

Selin, Henrik. 2010. *Global Governance of Hazardous Chemicals: Challenges of Multilevel Management*. Cambridge: MIT Press.

Spoon, Jae-Jae. 2009. "Holding Their Own: Explaining the Persistence of Green Parties in France and the UK." *Party Politics* 15: 613–34.

Tryhorn, Lee M. and Amanda H. Lynch. 2010. "Climate Change Adaptation in the Alpine Shire of Australia: A Decision Process Appraisal." *Policy Sciences* 43 (2): 105–27.

United Nations Framework Convention on Climate Change (UNFCCC). 2009. "An Overview of Investment and Financial Flows Needed for Adaptation." In *The Earthscan Reader on Adaptation to Climate Change*. Edited by E. Lisa F. Schipper and Ian Burton. London: Earthscan.

Vanderheiden, Steve. ed. 2008. *Political Theory and Global Climate Change*. Cambridge: MIT Press.

Wald, Matthew L. and John Schwartz. 2012. "Weather Extremes Leave Parts of US Grid Buckling." *New York Times*, July 25.

Webber, Michael E. 2012. "Will Drought Cause the Next Blackout?" *New York Times*, July 23.

Western Governors' Association. 2010. "Climate Adaptation Priorities for the Western States: Scoping Report." http://www.westgov.org/index.php?option=com_content&view=article&id=128&Itemid=62.

Whitmarsh, Lorraine and Saffron O'Neill. 2010. "Green Identity, Green Living? The Role of Pro-Environmental Self-Identity in Determining Consistency across Diverse Pro-Environmental Behaviours." *Journal of Environmental Psychology* 30 (3): 305–14.

Whitmarsh, Lorraine, Gill Seyfang, and Saffron O'Neill. 2011. "Public Engagement with Carbon and Climate Change: To What Extent Is the Public 'Carbon Capable'?" *Global Environmental Change* 21: 56–65.

World Resources Institute. 2011. "Decision Making in a Changing Climate—Adaptation Challenges and Choices." World Resources Report. http://pdf.wri.org/world_resources_report_2010-2011.pdf.

Young, Oran R., Leslie A. King, and Heike Schroeder. 2008. *Institutions and Environmental Change: Principal Findings, Applications, and Research Frontiers*. Cambridge, MA: MIT Press.

An Interesting Bias: Lessons from an Academic's Year as a Reporter

21

DAVID NIVEN

In most any endeavor, it is difficult to be fair. For journalists, the challenge is both profound and public. A journalist's work product inherently depends on a series of subjective judgments. In short order, that work is scrutinized by leaders and readers and often by the very people mentioned in the story. In this article, reflecting on one year spent reporting the news, I make the case that partisan and ideological balance predominate in the mainstream media not because of exceptional training or perpetual hand-wringing over objectivity. Rather, balance is an accidental consequence of the journalist's true quest: to be interesting.

Dating back at least to the 1930s academics have shown that journalists tend to support liberal and Democratic causes (Lichter, Rothman, and Lichter 1986; Patterson and Donsbach 1996; Rosten 1937). Nevertheless, the preponderance of available scholarly evidence from large-scale studies of political news coverage suggests no consistent ideological or partisan bias in the American news media (for example, Eisinger, Veenstra, and Koehn 2007; Niven 2002). That meta-analysis does not find bias (D'Alessio and Allen 2000) adds further credence to this conclusion, as does the recent work of researchers who have peered into the construction of news coverage with innovative techniques. Clayman and his coauthors (2010), for example, scrutinized five decades of presidential press conferences. They found no partisan or ideological pattern in the aggressiveness of reporters' questions. Groeling and Baum (2009) considered which of the numerous statements uttered by members of Congress on televised Sunday morning political talk shows were chosen by reporters as sound bites to be repeated in other venues. Over a two-decade period, they too found no partisan or ideological pattern. When belief in a biased media is nearly an article of faith (for example, Eveland and Shah 2003; Morris 2007), how can that be true?

One explanation for this lack of bias is that the preponderance of the evidence, nevertheless, is wrong. To be sure, a handful of broad-based studies consider multiple media sources over many years and find evidence of partisan or ideological bias. One prominent example is Groseclose and Milyo (2005).

The authors use the citation of think tanks and political advocacy organizations as a barometer of ideology. A news source that predominantly cites the conclusions of liberal groups is considered a liberal news source, whereas the predominant citation of conservative sources earns a conservative label.

When they tally the tendencies of various print and electronic outlets, Groseclose and Milyo "find a systematic tendency for the United States media outlets to slant the news to the left" (2005, 1226). Although they boast that their method "does not require us to make a subjective assessment" (1192), that hardly assures the reader that their process was logical. Indeed, a curious aspect of their scoring system leaves them assigning approximately the same ideological value to the American Civil Liberties Union and the National Rifle Association. Furthermore, their "systematic" bias is typified not by NPR, CBS, the *New York Times*, or any of the usual suspects. Rather, according to their data, the most liberal major news outlet in the United States is the *Wall*

Street Journal. Logical incongruity aside, by failing to establish a meaningful baseline for comparison, this study and others that find a pronounced partisan or ideological bias have difficulty demonstrating what balance would look like, much less measuring its presence (Niven 2002).

Another possible explanation for the pattern of partisan balance is that the training of journalists successfully inculcates a commitment to objectivity. Reading the work of academics who have watched the news being made (for example, Gans 1979; Tuchman 1978), however, leaves one to question the practical applica-bility of an objectivity code applied to an endless series of subjective judgments.

Balance as a By-Product

After first writing academic papers on media coverage of politics (Niven 1999; 2001; 2003; 2004; 2005), I had the opportunity to examine journalism not just as an observer but as a participant. In the midterm election year of 2006 I was a reporter for a Columbus, Ohio, newspaper. I covered a wide array of political topics including office-holders and candidates at the county, state, and federal levels.

In the main, what I saw during my year in journalism was comforting. My colleagues took their work seriously and held themselves to a high standard of fairness and accuracy. Editors were ever vigilant for any kind of skewed information or reportage. Nevertheless, I found that it is not a commitment to professionalism, nor any exceptional journalistic ability to identify and erase personal bias, that keeps a journalist's work balanced. Instead, balance is a by-product of the fact that the first question journalists ask is not "How can I serve a political position?" but "How can I make this interesting?"

Interesting means getting a better position in the paper, perhaps the front page. Interesting means getting more column inches for your article. Interesting means the editor down the hall, who issues a series of audible exclamations when he reads, will put forth a few "humphs" and perhaps a chuckle. Interesting means people will start reading your piece and might even finish it. Interesting means walking into a coffee shop and overhearing someone discussing your article and seeing bloggers praise or attack you. Without interesting, you're not in the paper. You're not read. Nothing you write matters.

This is not to say that trying to be interesting makes the process inherently fair. Rather, the process is skewed in ways that are not constrained by partisanship or ideology. Because interesting is found on both the left and the right, any journalist who values what all journalists value makes a poor vessel for ideological or partisan bias. As I found the job of reporting, the task at hand was to find interesting sources, or alternatively, to get the sources you had to say interesting things.

The fact that the default position for any political actor is to be uninteresting is hardly in dispute. As numerous academic studies make clear, most of what is said and done in politics is not news, regardless of who is saying or doing it. Barrett (2007) points out that most presidential appeals for legislative action fail to make news; nine out of 10 fall short of attracting full articles in the *Washington Post* and *New York Times.* In Groeling and Baum's (2009) examination of members of Congress on Sunday morning talk shows, they calculate that 99% of what is said does not make news. Across several European parliaments (Van Aelst, Sehata, and Van Dalen 2010) and the US House of Representatives (Niven and Zilber 1998), studies find that most members are seldom of interest to journalists.

Interesting Sources

At the beginning of the reporting process, the pages of your spiral notebook are blank. The computer screen on your desk is an open white space. Filling that space, and ultimately filling the assigned column inches on deadline, concentrates the mind on sources. "Who has something interesting to say about this topic?" was the first question I asked myself every time I worked on a story.

Scholars, including Sigal (1973), have suggested that the role of sources tends to limit the significance of a journalist's personal views in their published work. "Even when a journalist is in a position to observe an event directly, he remains reluctant to offer interpretations of his own," Sigal (1973, 69) wrote, "preferring instead to rely on his news sources. For the reporter, in short, most news is not what has happened, but what someone says has happened."

Superficially, such a source-driven process would limit or eliminate the effects of a reporter's personal bias. However, the choice and use of sources still could be heavily slanted to benefit the left or right in support of a reporter's politics. That is, the use of sources could be slanted if reporters were in the business of advocacy. In the business of being interesting, by contrast, whether I agreed with a source or not was irrelevant.

Protecting English Speakers

State Representative Courtney Combs, a Republican from the Cincinnati area, introduced legislation in the Ohio House to establish English as the official language of Ohio and limit the ability of state and local governments to use any other language. Although similar legislation had been introduced unsuccessfully in previous legislative sessions, a unique provision of the new proposal caught my attention and made the bill more newsworthy. Combs' bill was the first in the nation to include explicit protection from discrimination for those who speak English.

If I were assembling an opinion piece to put forth my thoughts on the legislation, I would have spent my time talking to liberal groups and even several business groups that came out against the bill. As a reporter, however, what I wanted most was an authoritative and opinionated voice who could explain the premise of the bill. My first call was to Representative Combs. I suspect that, regardless of one's personal opinion, all journalists would have started their reporting process with the same call.

I left a message (in English, I might add) seeking Combs' comments on the bill. I wanted to know the purpose and effects of the bill. More than anything, I wanted to know about the English speakers who were being discriminated against and needed this protection.

Had Combs responded to any of my messages, his words and perspective would have likely formed the foundation of the article. When he didn't respond, however, the space his comments would have otherwise received still had to be filled. Without Combs, I needed some other voice to provide some perspective on what this type of legislation is meant to accomplish. I turned to two advocacy groups that support "English Only" efforts.

The executive director of ProEnglish, K.C. McAlpin, was effusive in his praise of Combs' bill and particularly impressed with the discrimination provision. He said that most states' English Only legislation lacked discrimination protection because "the laws were enacted before people realized the scope of this problem." McAlpin added that victims of anti-English speaker discrimination were suffering outside the spotlight because, "thus far it's been a beneath the headlines kind of problem."

Tim Schultz, director of government relations for US English, echoed McAlpin's perspective, calling discrimination against those who speak English a problem "equally pernicious as any racist policy of the 1960s."

Depending on the reader, these comments could be taken as establishing the moral imperative to pass Combs' bill or, perhaps, as a demonstration of the paranoid hyperbole of these activists. Yet as a journalist, leaders of these two groups were enormously attractive sources who were both extensively quoted in the final published article because they were interesting.

Indeed, a distinctive response jumps out when you are conducting an interview. Generally I could pinpoint the quotes that were likely to make my final article even as the words were being spoken by the source. Such was the case when I asked Schulz whether angry, anti-immigrant sentiment was what fueled his group. He responded with this gem: "A lot of our members have a lot of vowels in their names," he said. "That's something we're proud of."

Other than a brief quote from a state civil rights commission spokesperson saying that Ohio had yet to receive its first complaint about English-speaker discrimination, contrary voices were limited in the article. This focus on proponents was sufficient for the article because the editor and I thought that the advocates for the bill were not only interesting, they were simultaneously supporting their position and making the case against it with their hysteria.

Although this was a story on a very ideologically charged subject, ideology did not guide the reporting process. The story began because Representative Combs committed news, some-thing any member of the legislature of any ideology could have done.

The story was shaped by who decided to speak on the issue and what they had to say. Combs' refusal to talk meant that his personal perspective would be missing and that advocates who may or may not have been as effective as Combs were given the opportunity to make the case. Again, willingness and effective-ness with the media are not bound by ideology. This is not to say the article was inherently fair, whatever that might entail. When sources are given wide berth to make their case, however, it certainly looks, and in fact may be, fair.

In reporting on the English Only legislation, the bill's sponsor was an obvious first choice for an interview. Indeed, the sponsor would have been the first person I turned to even if this legislation had exactly the opposite intent (say, for example, if it was a bill establishing Que-bec-style official bilingualism).

To be sure, the source selection process is subjective. Nevertheless, to a large extent, the best and most interesting sources seemed obvious and inevitable. For stories about campaign finance and campaign laws, I immediately called the very conservative local law professor who at one time headed the Federal Election Commission. For a story about an Ohio law that requires state employees to affirm that they are not personally a terrorist and do not associate with terrorists, I immediately called the very liberal local law professor known nationally for his First Amendment expertise.

Although collectively this process may provide an outlet for voices from the left and right, individual stories obviously can skew to one side. Hewitt (1996) criticized media coverage of homelessness for relying on liberal homeless advocates to provide estimates of the number of homeless. Of course, it would be the rare political group uninterested in homelessness that spent its resources counting the homeless and providing population estimates to the media.

Scholars have noted, sometimes with concern, the outsize attention paid to experts, insiders, and elites in much of the contemporary media (for example, Steele 1995; Sumpter and Garner 2007). Yet the reality from a journalist's perspective is that regular people with mild views don't have very much to say. And they're boring. And they're hard to find. And, they don't want to talk to you.

With the liberal Jim Wallis, author of *God's Politics*, coming to Columbus to debate a prom-inent local Christian conservative leader—and with a group of area liberal pastors bringing federal tax evasion charges against a group of area conservative pastors—my editor was interested in what life was like in the midst of all this conflict for religious leaders who avoided politics altogether. My task then was to find people who had something interesting to say about some-thing they did not do. It turned out, those were people who were very hard to find. Everyone I spoke to was either political or so nonpolitical that talking about being nonpolitical struck them as being a little too political.

With a deadline looming and endless calls leading nowhere, I was staring at total journalistic failure when a Methodist minister returned my call and started saying things like, "Take the fight over intelligent design versus evolution. The God I serve doesn't care." With that, I had a front-page story.

Ultimately, the availability of interesting Republican sources and interesting Democratic sources, interesting liberal sources and interesting conservative sources, allows a reporter, a news outlet, or the media at-large to create balanced coverage. However, the absence of an aggregate slant does not mean the absence of strong personal slants. There is no doubt that accessible and interesting sources are easier to cover and get more engaging portrayals. Barker and Lawrence (2006) found that John McCain received more favorable coverage than George W. Bush in the 2000 Republican presidential primary. McCain's willingness to bring reporters on his bus and speak candidly no doubt fueled that imbalance.

In my case, coverage of county issues led me to call the three county commissioners in Columbus. The two Democrats generally dodged my calls. The one Republican answered all my calls, spoke directly to the questions asked, and had a folksiness that came through well in print. Although I voted against him, the Republican was a highly valued source who received more attention in my articles than his colleagues. Before I submitted an article to my editor, I asked myself whether anything in my writing might cause the Republican commissioner to stop answering my calls. This was a question I never asked when writing about his Democratic colleagues on the board. Of course, deference to a source can produce not only favoritism but shallow reporting. Pfau and his colleagues (2004) find that journalists embedded in military units can grow so close to their sources that their willingness or ability to provide context about the war they are covering suffers.

Getting Sources to Say Interesting Things

Although the inherently interesting source is a highly valued entity, much of the task of interviewing sources is trying to coax "interesting" out of them. Some individuals are highly resistant to the effort.

For a story on Senator Mike DeWine's campaign advertising, I called, among many others, the spokesperson for DeWine's opponent, then-Representative Sherrod Brown. Brown's spokesperson had message discipline to a degree that rendered him useless to me. Regardless of the question I asked, Brown's spokesperson told me how Brown fights for the middle class, and how DeWine was out of touch with the middle class.

Brown's spokesperson was speaking from a basic script, repeating one and only one talking point. If I wanted to include a Brown comment, which I obviously did or I wouldn't have called him, then effectively the spokesperson had picked the comment for me. Instead, I did not use a word of the 20-minute interview in my article.

What's in a Name

Sources who speak from a script, whose comments could have been anticipated word for word before the interview, are, at best, boring and, at worst, useless. By contrast, sources who say something unexpected, something that perhaps they would later wish they hadn't, can count on their words showing up in print. In pursuit of the quote that will render serious damage to the speaker, one can't help but worry that Janet Malcolm (1990, 3) was right when she wrote of the profession: "Every journalist who is not too stupid or too full of himself to notice what is going on knows that what he does is morally indefensible."

With a number of Ohio cities having passed limitations on smoking in restaurants, a coalition of tobacco companies, tobacco trade associations, and the restaurant industry joined together to fund an effort to place a constitutional amendment on the Ohio ballot. If passed by the voters, the amendment would nullify any local smoking limits. In making their pitch to voters, the coalition named itself "Smoke Less Ohio."

It was a curious name for a group that wanted to expand smok-ing. It struck me as even more curious given that funding for the group was coming from tobacco companies.

I knew that typical questions about the issue itself would produce rote answers. But what, I wondered, would the backers of the group say if I just asked about their group's name?

A call to coalition member Lorillard Tobacco resulted in me being connected to one of the company's senior vice presidents. Asked about the name of this group his company was helping to pay for, he said incredulously, "I don't know why they call themselves *that*."

A spokesman for a tobacco trade association in the coalition was similarly at a loss to explain the Smoke Less Ohio name. "I'd hate to say 'no comment,'" he said, "That would make it look like we couldn't defend our own name."

These two men had no incentive to say these things. It wasn't in the interest of their campaign, and that's what made it great. In contrast to Brown's spokesperson saying Brown was for the middle class, these comments came close to what I would consider the very definition of news. Here we have the backers of a group with a misleading name saying, in effect, that they can't support their own group's name. (The ballot issue was ultimately rejected by Ohio voters.)

Shoot First

The more typical path to eliciting interesting responses, however, is simply to give sources a chance to speak to each other. Get a statement from one side. Get a response. Get a counter to that. And so on. This technique takes longer, but it has the benefit of potentially producing copy that is interesting and inherently balanced.

Such was my strategy in covering a bill in the Ohio legislature that would dramatically expand the ability of Ohioans to use deadly force without fear of prosecution or civil penalty. In essence, the bill established that anyone who entered a home or vehicle without permission could be presumed to intend bodily harm. Anyone using force against such a person would now enjoy legal immunity. The bill would also eliminate the duty to retreat, permitting the use of force even if the threat could be neutralized by merely walking away.

Although I have a very strong personal opinion on the legislation, the resulting article gave both sides a chance to speak quite powerfully to their position. By engaging each other's arguments, I thought the individual comments were not only interesting in isolation, but combined to form a cohesive and interesting whole.

"It's a public safety kind of bill," said state rep. Stephen Buehrer, the primary sponsor of the legislation.

"It's a very ancient premise in human history that a man's house is his castle," the Delta Republican added. "If an intruder or an invader enters your castle you've got the right to repulse that intruder from your home. My bill returns us to what the law has been, probably since the Middle Ages."

But John Murphy, executive director of the Ohio Prosecuting Attorneys Association, sees the legislation as Medieval.

"It's a license to blast away," he said. "You could have a neighbor who thinks he has an informal privilege to enter your home. He takes one step inside, and you blow him away," Murphy said. "Under the bill, you're immune from murder charges."

... For state rep. Keith Faber, a co-sponsor of the bill, eliminating the duty to retreat is crucial.

"If there's a home invasion, what are my obligations? Do I have to run to my safe room, and cower behind the door?" asked Faber, a Republican from Celina. "Do I have a right to defend myself? Some would say 'No. Wait until they break in, rape and molest your children, and then ask them to stop.'"

But opponents of the bill question when, if ever, a homeowner has been prosecuted in the kind of scenario Faber envisions.

"There's nothing here, no case, no story that would justify this bill," said Zack Ragbourn, spokesman for the Brady Campaign to Prevent Gun Violence. "We don't have people lined up to go to prison for defending their home. And if there aren't any now, it's hard to see how there will be any less if the bill passes."

It is difficult to imagine a more stark contrast of views. For the advocates of the bill, this is about a fundamental right of self-defense. For the opponents, the bill creates a lawless and deadly free-for-all.

For the last word in the article, I turned to a pro-gun voice who offered one of the most memorable quotes of my year in reporting.

When I was working on the story, a recent incident occurred in the Columbus area that might have altered debate on the issue. A high school cheerleader, dared by friends to walk through a spooky, overgrown yard leading to a dark, dilapidated house, had been shot in the head by the home's reclusive owner.

Asked if he was concerned that this shooting might dampen support for the bill, Ken Hanson, legislative chair of the Buckeye Firearms Association, spoke with disdain.

"We have to manage the public relations, so the anti's don't get to run away with every single incident," he said. "The anti's are never squeamish about dancing in a pool of blood."

To my personal politics, that quote is repulsive. But the quote struck me as very interesting, and interesting does not have anything to do with which side you're on.

Interesting, Unbiased, and Still Skewed

A year as a reporter renewed the conclusion I had made as an academic (Niven 2002) that mainstream journalism is not a bastion of partisan or ideological bias. That year, however, changed my understanding of why there isn't more bias. In my own reporting I found fairness was less the result of my effort to be fair than the result of my effort to be interesting.

All this should not be read as a character defense of the media or an argument that all is well. Although the search for interesting tends to balance coverage of the left and right, coverage is by no means fair to all (see, for example, Entman and Gross 2008). If your perspective is too far outside the mainstream, nothing you say is interesting (even if, as a rule, you say interesting things) because you will be viewed as lacking credibility. In a year of political reporting, not a single third-party candidate or distinctly nonmainstream political voice wound up quoted in my writing. Van Aelst, Sehata, and Van Dalen (2010) confirm that trend as they show extremity of political views is associated with less media attention among members of parliament.

Meanwhile, the pursuit of interesting carries with it the tendency to inflate aspects of a story that are surprising, new, or edgy. It was surprising when the leaders of the Smoke Less Ohio team could not defend their own name, and that immediately became the central narrative of my story. (It is surprising when members of the president's party criticize him, and consequently those hand-ful of critics are wildly over-represented in news coverage [Groeling and Baum 2009]). The English Only legislation had numerous sections and subsections that had been introduced before, but the discrimination clause was new in Ohio, and new nationally, and a central reason why I was reporting on the bill. (Barrett [2007] found new presidential appeals are more likely to be covered regardless of the significance of the policy.) In seeking the edge that comes with conflicts and disappointments, a year covering politics resulted in not a single hagiographic piece celebrating a political figure's achievements or, frankly, anything. (Indeed, a slant toward negative news pervades in coverage of politics, as Farnsworth and Lichter (2005) and others have found.)

Clearly, interesting is the not the same as important and the resulting coverage leaves out too much of what citizens should know. But it was this reporter's fear, and I suspect every reporter's fear, that a newspaper exclusively built to cover the important might well be the most important thing no one reads.[1]

Of course, my conclusions are just one journalist's perspective (and a temporary journalist at that). But, to ever be a reporter is to want to see your byline. To ever be a reporter is to want to be read. To be a reporter is to want to be on the front page. To be a reporter is to want to hear those audible sounds of interest from your editor, the only person you can actually watch while he reads your article. To be a reporter is to want to have your articles talked and blogged about. To be a reporter is to want to be interesting, because from that flows everything a reporter wants in the job.

In the academic world, calling work "interesting" might be seen as an insult, akin to calling it trivial. To a reporter, however, interesting is the currency of the realm.

Even as I posit that the desire to be interesting is universal among reporters, I readily admit that no other reporter would have produced any of my articles exactly as I reported and wrote them. Nevertheless, all journalists would have faced a similar set of real world constraints that would guide their coverage (Schiffer 2008). Indeed, virtually any reporter would have spoken to the sponsors of the bills I covered. They would have interviewed the leaders who were speaking out for or against these proposals. And they would have put a star next to quotes about how many vowels the US English membership has in their names and the pro-gun lobbyist's belief that his opponents love to dance in a pool of blood. In so doing, the powerful, magnetic pull of what's interesting would have once again overwhelmed the writer's politics and contributed to the balance in American media coverage.

Reprinted from David Niven. 2012. "An Interesting Bias: Lessons from an Academic's Year as a Reporter." PS: Political Science & Politics *45 (2). Cambridge University Press: 259–64. doi:10.1017/ S1049096511002071.*

Acknowledgement

The author appreciates the insightful feedback provided by Adam Schiffer on a previous version of this paper.

Notes

1. As Lippmann (1922, 365) famously put it, the "preference for the curious trivial as against the dull important" is a most powerful force guiding the press.

References

Barker, David, and Adam Lawrence. 2006. "Media Favoritism and Presidential Nominations: Reviving the Direct Effects Model." *Political Communication* 23 (1): 41–59.

Barrett, Andrew. 2007. "Press Coverage of Legislative Appeals by the President." *Political Research Quarterly* 60 (4): 655–68.

Clayman, Steven, Marc Elliott, John Heritage, and Megan Beckett. 2010. "A Watershed in White House Journalism: Explaining the Post-1968 Rise of Aggressive Presidential News." *Political Communication* 27 (3): 229–47.

D'Alessio, Dave, and Mike Allen. 2000. "Media Bias in Presidential Elections: A Meta-Analysis." *Journal of Communication* 50 (4): 133–56.

Eisinger, Robert, Loring Veenstra, and John Koehn. 2007. "What Media Bias? Conservative and Liberal Labeling in Major US Newspapers." *Harvard International Journal of Press/Politics* 12 (1): 17–36.

Entman, Robert, and Kimberly Gross. 2008. "Race to Judgment: Stereotyping Media and Criminal Defendants." *Law and Contemporary Problems* 71 (4): 93–133.

Eveland, William, and Dhavan Shah. 2003. "The Impact of Individual and Interpersonal Factors on Perceived News Media Bias." *Political Psychology* 24 (1): 101–17.

Farnsworth, Stephen, and S. Robert Lichter. 2005. "The Mediated Congress: Coverage of Capitol Hill in the *New York Times* and the Washington Post." *Harvard International Journal of Press/Politics* 10 (2): 94–107.

Gans, Herbert. 1979. *Deciding What's News*. New York: Random House.

Groeling, Tim, and Matthew Baum. 2009. "Journalists Incentives and Media Coverage of Elite Foreign Policy Evaluations." *Conflict Management and Peace Science* 26 (5): 437–70.

Groseclose, Tim, and Jeffrey Milyo. 2005. "A Measure of Media Bias." *Quarterly Journal of Economics* 120 (4): 1191–1237.

Hewitt, Christopher. 1996. "Estimating the Number of Homeless: Media Misrepresentation of an Urban Problem." *Journal of Urban Affairs* 18 (4): 431–47.

Lichter, S. Robert, Stanley Rothman, and Linda Lichter. 1986. *The Media Elite*. Bethesda, MD: Rowman and Littlefield.

Lippmann, Walter. 1922. *Public Opinion*. New York: Harcourt, Brace, and Company.

Malcolm, Janet. 1990. *The Journalist and the Murderer*. New York: Vintage.

Morris, Jonathan. 2007. "Slanted Objectivity? Perceived Media Bias, Cable News Exposure, and Political Attitudes." *Social Science Quarterly* 88 (3): 707–28.

Niven, David. 1999. "Partisan Bias in the Media? A New Test." *Social Science Quarterly* 80 (4): 847–58.

Niven, David. 2001. "Bias in the News: Partisanship and Negativity in Coverage of Presidents George Bush and Bill Clinton." *Harvard International Journal of Press/Politics* 6 (3): 31–46.

Niven, David. 2002. *Tilt? The Search for Media Bias*. Westport, CT: Praeger.

Niven, David. 2003. "Objective Evidence on Media Bias: Coverage of Congressional Party Switchers." *Journalism and Mass Communication Quarterly* 80 (2): 311–26.

Niven, David. 2004. "A Fair Test of Media Bias: Party, Race, and Gender in Coverage of the 1992 House Banking Scandal." *Polity* 36 (4): 637–49.

Niven, David. 2005. "An Economic Theory of Political Journalism." *Journalism and Mass Communication Quarterly* 82 (2): 247–63.

Niven, David, and Jeremy Zilber. 1998. "What's Newt Doing in People Magazine? The Changing Effect of National Prominence in Congressional Elections." *Political Behavior* 20 (3): 213–24.

Patterson, Thomas, and Wolfgang Donsbach. 1996. "News Decisions: Journalists as Partisan Actors." *Political Communication* 13 (4): 453–68.

Pfau, Michael, Michel Haigh, Mitchell Gettle, Michael Donnelly, Gregory Scott, Dana Warr, and Elaine Wittenberg. 2004. "Embedding Journalists in Military Combat Units: Impact on Newspaper Story Frames and Tone." *Journalism and Mass Communication Quarterly* 81 (1): 74–88.

Rosten, Leo. 1937. *The Washington Correspondents*. New York: Harcourt, Brace.

Schiffer, Adam. 2008. *Conditional Press Influence in Politics*. Lanham, MD: Lexington Books.

Sigal, Leon. 1973. *Reporters and Officials*. Lexington, MA: DC Heath.

Steele, Janet. 1995. "Experts and the Operational Bias of Television News: The Case of the Persian Gulf War." *Journalism and Mass Communication Quarterly* 72 (4): 799–812.

Sumpter, Randall, and Johny Garner. 2007. "Telling the Columbia Story: Source Selection in News Accounts of a Shuttle Accident." *Science Communication* 28 (4): 455–75.

Tuchman, Gaye. 1978. *Making News: A Study in the Construction of Reality*. New York: The Free Press.

Van Aelst, Peter, Adam Sehata, and Arjen Van Dalen. 2010. "Members of Parliament: Equal Competitors for Media Attention? An Analysis of Personal Contacts between MPs and Political Journalists in Five European Countries." *Political Communication* 27 (3): 310–25.

The Political Scientist as a Blogger

22

JOHN SIDES

I n November 2007, I helped found a blog, *The Monkey Cage*, with two of my colleagues, David Park and Lee Sigelman. This site joined a nascent political science blogosphere that is now composed of at least 80 blogs (Farrell and Sides 2010). The goals of *The Monkey Cage* are to publicize political science research and use this research to comment on current events. Although blogging is a promising way for scholars to promote their work to a larger audience, political scientists have been slow to take up this medium. To be sure, blogging is not without its challenges, particularly in terms of the time and energy needed to maintain a site. But blogging can also have its benefits by not only helping polit-ical science reach a broader audience, but also aiding individual scholars' research, teaching, and service goals.

How to Blog

Becoming a blogger is easy. Platforms such as blogspot.com provide hosting space and design templates, with no money and little specialized expertise required. Once the blog is created, the central task is producing content in the form of blog posts. Few blogs are successful if they are not updated frequently—ideally, more than once a day. At *The Monkey Cage*, we average about 2.5 posts per day. A post may take anywhere between five minutes and two hours to write, depending on its content. Other avenues to blogging entail affiliating with websites that regularly publish academic perspectives. For example, *Pollster.com*, which is now a part of the *Huffington Post*, features several political scientists among its contributors. The difference, of course, is that a personal blog allows the blogger greater opportunities and freedom than may be available at established blogs.[1]

What should a blog post address? Writing regular blog posts is not necessarily easy. It takes time to find a voice and learn the kinds of topics and ideas that will appeal to a broader audience. One guideline should be obvious: avoid personal complaints about your life, commute, colleagues, discipline, and so on—topics that are perilous from a professional perspective anyway (Tribble 2005). Choose topics to which you can add value as a political scientist. This approach will distinguish your blog from other blogs about politics and from most pundits' commentary. You can summarize your research or the work of other scholars, analyze data, and make simple graphs that are understandable to a lay audience. Ideally, your posts should be pegged to current events, but topical commentary is not always necessary. Even when political science research is months (if not years) behind the news cycle, its findings can still be relevant. For example, although few pundits are still analyzing the 2008 election, their potted histories and stylized impressions of that time drive their present thinking about current events, making new research about the election topical. If your post disagrees with a pundit, all the better: nothing attracts readers' attention like a little conflict.

If producing a regular flow of posts is too time-consuming, consider recruiting other authors for your blog. *The Monkey Cage* has always been a group blog, which ensures fresh content as well as diverse perspectives and expertise that may even lead to debates within the group that we subsequently publish as well. Our current roster of regular bloggers has expanded to five—Henry Farrell, Andrew Gelman, Joshua Tucker, Erik Voeten, and me—and includes scholars of

American politics, comparative politics, and international relations. Many other scholars have served as guest-bloggers at our site—which is a good way to get one's feet wet. Although is possible to maintain a blog single-handedly, we have found that a group format eases the task of producing a continuous stream of new posts.

Blogging also necessitates certain administrative chores: registering and maintaining a domain name (if necessary), designing the site's appearance, reviewing and publishing readers' comments, and deleting the inevitable spam from such interested readers as "Fat Loss 4 Idiots." These are very manageable tasks. Determining the name and appearance of the site can be a one-time decision. Managing the flow of comments takes only a small amount of time each day, especially if you are content to allow real comments to intermingle with spam.

Finally, every blog encourages attention to other blogs and websites that discuss related content and, hopefully, your posts. It is easy to be drawn in by what other people write, especially if they take issue with your perspective. Conversation that results from these disputes can actually be an asset: attention from online conversations among bloggers will usually help to build an audience. For lesser-known blogs, taking issue with an established blogger and thereby drawing a response will often help expand the pool of readers.

This sort of attention is largely how *The Monkey Cage* built its audience over time. Between November 2007 and December 2010, *The Monkey Cage* was visited by about 719,000 people and viewed over 2 million times. Approximately 1,500 people visit the site on any given weekday, 2,700 people sub-scribe to our RSS feed, and over 600 follow us on Twitter. The blog's content has been cited by *Newsweek*, the *New Yorker*, the *New York Times*, *Salon*, the *Economist*, the *American Prospect*, the *Washington Post*, and the *Financial Times*, among others—although, relatively speaking, *The Monkey Cage* remains a niche blog.

But Do I Really Want To Be a Nazi Scumbag Moron?

The ease with which one can begin blogging conceals the pitfalls that a blogger may encounter. First, blogging takes time. Many scholars feel burdened by their teaching, research, and administrative responsibilities and frequently lament a lack of time for research and writing. Clearly, maintaining a blog entails effort that could be spent on other pursuits. As a blog becomes more successful, it will naturally demand more time.

Second, although scholars typically want to publicize their ideas in books and journals, daily publication can be treacherous. The average blog post reflects quicker and more haphazard thinking, simpler (and even simplistic) analyses, and more ill-advised dudgeon than the typical academic article. There is no peer review to save you from mistakes, and once your mistakes are published, they cannot easily be removed from the public domain. Political scientist bloggers can be spectacularly wrong, as I was in predicting a 2008 presidential race between Mitt Romney and Hillary Clinton (Sides 2008a).

Third, if the purpose of the blog is to discuss academic research, scholars may soon learn that readers outside of the academy or the discipline do not understand and sometimes willfully misunderstand findings. A discipline's theoretical perspectives and methodologies will often strike individuals outside of the field as wrong or even worthless, which can be surprising to scholars trained to believe that their methods are normal, even if problematic in certain ways. A colleague and I once wrote a blog post and then an op-ed (Sides and Lawrence 2008) to discuss some research in which we combined a set of survey questions about respondents' positions on political issues to create a left-right ideological scale and then described the behavior of respondents in different ideological camps (e.g., the "far left," the "far right"). We encountered strong objections from individuals who believed that we were characterizing respondents in some absolute sense and thus implying that people on the "far left" were extremists (Morill 2008). When my coauthor and coblogger Henry Farrell defended the research on *The Monkey Cage*, most commenters were not persuaded (Farrell 2008).

Fourth, readers' reactions can be vitriolic. Although scholarly discourse allows for strong disagreement, rarely are these differences expressed as bluntly or even profanely as they are on blogs, particularly in the comments that readers can leave, often anonymously. For example, I once wrote a short post (Sides 2008b) about an article by Michael Ross (2008), who argues that dependency on oil production, not Islam per se, restricts gender equality in the Middle East. Thanks in part to links from other blogs with larger audiences, the post attracted such comments as:

Systematically removing women's genatilia [sic] and imprisoning them for getting raped isn't obvious enough for Ross?

It is not serious that a professional review lends its pages to this statistical nonsense. Have they lost their common sense? I wish Ross a sex change and moving [sic] to Saudi Arabia. He will be able to check his/her [sic] statistical associations in situ.

I find it amazing that this was published in a peer-reviewed journal. Does Ross have tenure at UCLA?

At my instigation, Ross kindly replied to these and other comments. None of the people who made the original com-ments chose to engage him on the actual substance of his research.

In other cases, readers' responses are even more *ad hominem*. Henry Farrell once wrote what seemed an innocuous post on public opinion about health care reform, leading one reader to deduce his Irish ancestry and then email him the following message, under the subject line "Nazi Scumbag Moron":

Henry,

Can a Mick be convicted of treason or just espionage? I'd play it safe and skedaddle back to Dublin. Who knows, if the Jacobins take DC, you might find yourself tarred and feathered or drawn and quartered.

Love, Stan

Comments like these are, to be sure, the exception rather than the rule. If you have a thick enough skin, they are easy to ignore. A blogger can also take the time to moderate comments and enforce norms of civility. Regardless of how you react, it is important to be prepared for the occasional Stan.

A final pitfall is potentially worse than criticism: being ignored. Unless you are content to treat your blog as a diary, you will inevitably want someone to read your posts. But because there are many blogs—probably too many, with hundreds of millions by some estimates—it is difficult for any one blog to gain much prominence. The challenge of broad exposure is even greater for a political science blog, which will never dish out the fare that many readers want from blogs about politics: Talmudic parsing of the horse race during election season or red meat for their preferred partisan or ideological faction.

Even if academic bloggers target a more "professional" audience—for political science, this group might consist of politicos and journalists—they may again find themselves dismissed. Many of these professionals have succeeded without paying much attention to political science but nevertheless believe they possess considerable expertise in the area. Some of these individuals are actively hostile to political science, such as *New York Times* writer Matt Bai:

Generally speaking, political writers don't think so much of political scientists, either, mostly because anyone who has ever actually worked in or covered politics can tell you that, whatever else it may be, a science isn't one of them. Politics is, after all, the business of humans attempting to triumph over their own disorder, insecurity, competitiveness, arrogance, and infidelity; make all the equations you want, but a lot of politics is simply tactile and visual, rather than empirical. My dinnertime conver-sation with three Iowans may not add up to a reliable portrait of the national consensus, but it's often more illu-minating than the dissertations of academics whose idea of seeing America is a trip to the local Bed, Bath & Beyond. (2009)

Being misunderstood, criticized, or ignored may sound like nothing new for the average academic. At times, criticism or inattention is entirely warranted: every utterance that a political scientist makes is not transcendental wisdom. However, it is sometimes easier to countenance a critical reaction from peers than one from a lay audience. Even well-regarded scholars who devote significant time to crafting accessible blog posts may find that they receive little to no attention or deference because of their training and expertise.

Why Blog?

Despite the occasional frustration, blogging can be fun—in fact, this is probably the first and best reason to do it. Once blogging starts to feel like work, you are probably not long for the blogo-sphere. A second reason is that blogging can help scholars become better teachers and researchers.

At a minimum, content produced for a blog can often be incorporated into teaching. I illustrate many blog posts with graphs of data that I later paste into a PowerPoint presentation for the classroom. Readers who are academics can and do use these materials for their own teaching. Furthermore, students often want to connect class material to real-life politics, and blogging can help articulate these connections, since the nature of the medium tempts the blogger into addressing current events. For example, media coverage of health care reform, like coverage of many policy debates, often focused on what Barack Obama did or did not do, should or should not have done, and so on. Treating Obama as the focal point of the issue gave short shrift to a lot of political science, which emphasizes the limited powers of the presidency (e.g., Edwards 2003; Neustadt 1990) and the importance of multiple veto points within the separation of powers system (e.g., Krehbiel 1998). When I eventually complained about this reification of presidential power on *The Monkey Cage* (Sides 2009), I was able to later insert this complaint into a lecture to provoke a broader discussion about the presidency.

The temptation to blog about current events also encourages scholars to become generalists, an orientation that is useful for teaching. Doctoral training pushes scholars into subfields within subfields, but undergraduate and graduate teaching demand familiarity with diverse topics and literatures. Scholars of political behavior have to explain how a bill becomes a law. Scholars of nuclear disarmament have to explain counterinsurgency. This is where blogging comes in. Every political scientist is familiar with versions of these queries from friends and relatives: "Well, you're a political scientist. Tell me who's going to win the election." Or "Tell me how we're going to win this war." Or "Tell me why those jerks in Washington can't get anything done." These queries do not respect subfield boundaries, and neither do the questions frequently posed by students. Dimly remembered graduate courses may offer little help in answering these questions. Blogging, though hardly a ticket to deep knowledge and expertise, can force scholars to canvass relevant literature, formulate thoughts, articulate them in accessible language, and add any necessary caveats.

The aspects of blogging described thus far—daily posts on a wide array of topics, debates with truculent commenters, and so on—may seem anathema to conducting research. However, blogging can easily facilitate research. One challenge of scholarly work is finding the time to both do the research and write about the findings. Conference paper deadlines are helpful but occur too infrequently. Maintaining a blog essentially creates a daily deadline.

The key is to use the blog as a long-running test-drive of a research project. Blogging forces you to write, and writing, for better or for worse, is often synonymous with thinking. A blog is thus a convenient repository for half-baked notions and tid-bits of analysis. Blogging may provide a reality check as commenters chime in with questions, objections, and suggestions, thereby leading you to refine a project further. Much of *Red State, Blue State, Rich State, Poor State* (Gelman et al. 2008) was previewed on Andrew Gelman's personal blog. John Quiggin, an economist and blogger at *Crooked Timber*, "book-blogged" his way to the entire manuscript for *Zombie Economics* (2010) by posting regularly on the ideas in each chapter and soliciting feedback from readers.

Allowing readers to peek at the seamy underbelly of research—hypotheses constructed and abandoned, clerical errors in data analyses, and so on—may seem ill-advised. The question is whether these costs are outweighed by the pay-offs. Often, they will be. Moreover, other modes of developing research, such as the public presentation and posting of conference papers, have not only their own costs, but also, if anecdotes are to be believed, few payoffs in terms of helpful feedback. Blogs, if not an ideal forum for incubating research, may still prove more useful than any other existing approach.

Should Junior Faculty Blog?

Is blogging for the untenured? By dint of their relative youth, untenured faculty are often those most disposed to read and produce content online, but they may perceive blogging as professionally risky. One political scientist and prominent blogger, Daniel Drezner, did not receive tenure at the University of Chicago—a fact that cannot be directly attributed to his blogging but nonetheless may make junior faculty anxious (see Drezner 2005).

At one level, skepticism about the time you spend blogging has an arbitrary quality. Because blogging is public, some may consider it a direct threat to research productivity. But why focus on the opportunity cost of blogging? This activity is far from the only thing that detracts from time devoted to research. Political scientist and blogger Chris Blattman makes this point well:

> I average under 30 minutes a day blogging—less than most peo-ple would take to commute (I don't), practice an instrument (nope), or watch a TV show (don't even own one). Has anyone ever reflected, "A pity Bob didn't get tenure. It's a shame he lives in the suburbs and plays the piano. But it's that fourth season of 'Lost' that really screwed him"? (2009)

Nevertheless, it does not hurt to minimize the professional risks of blogging. Blogging will not substitute for good research or teaching in the minds of promotion and tenure committees, and untenured scholars are unwise to let blogging prevent them from completing necessary work. It may also be valuable to consult with senior colleagues before starting to blog. I followed this strategy, and the blessings of my senior colleagues were perhaps most evident in the decision of one, Lee Sigelman, to co-found *The Monkey Cage* and the willingness of several others to guest-blog from time to time.

Let us suppose that colleagues have given the blog the green light. Why do it? First, all of the benefits for teaching and research noted previously apply doubly to untenured faculty, who are not as experienced as senior faculty at developing course content and an active research agenda.

A second benefit for untenured faculty is publicity. Naturally, the mere existence of your blog does not mean that anyone will read it. If the blog is something that you want to gain attention, you will need to mention it to friends and colleagues, as well as email other political science bloggers. It cannot hurt to add the blog to your CV under the heading of "other writing" or something similar. As long as your blogging is supported by your colleagues, you should promote your blog.

Once your blog has gained an audience, it will help make your name more familiar—a simple but important outcome in a growing field in which individual recognition, especially outside of your chosen subfield, can be elusive. Moreover, if you blog about your research, you will expand its impact. Too much research is currently being produced for even the most diligent scholars to consume it all. Blogging about your research raises its visibility, which is a valuable result, given that your promotion depends upon your being well-situated in the discipline and enmeshed in a network of scholars who know you and your work.

The publicity that a blog produces may lead people outside of academia to perceive you as an expert. This awareness may spark requests for media interviews or solicitations from the popular press for pieces of writing. Although op-eds cannot take the place of peer-reviewed research or effective teaching, some departments and universities consider activities that reach a broader audience to be a service to the university.

Blogging can be a valuable service to the discipline as well. The easiest way to provide such a service is to publicize the work of other political scientists on your blog. Because the average scholarly article reaches only a small audience of aca demics, even a single blog post may increase this audience severalfold. In my experience, no scholar has objected to this kind of attention on *The Monkey Cage*—their work is already in the public domain, in any case, and so blog posts are not revealing state secrets. (However, it is always courteous to let someone know that you are blogging about him or her.) Thus, blogging can accrue goodwill for you within the scholarly community, which certainly cannot hurt when some of these people will be writing tenure letters on your behalf.

Blogging about others' research also builds another useful skill: appreciative thinking. Appreciative thinking means identifying and emphasizing the positive, which can be difficult. Graduate training is centered on critical thinking; after all, most dissertations are motivated by the belief that previous work is either wrong or incomplete. Academia is competitive, has too many scholars and too few faculty positions, and offers only occasional accolades at best. Academics can easily fall prey to jealousy, status anxiety, and resentment. When you regularly publicize others' research, blogging can serve as an antidote to these maladies. In the years since *The Monkey Cage* was founded, my attitude has changed. When I receive a scholarly journal and skim abstracts in search of blogging material, naturally, some articles interest me, while others do not. But now, I dwell much less on the latter and much more on the articles I do like and how they can be effectively summarized in a blog post.

Of course, any increased visibility or attention that a blog brings you is no ticket to tenure, lucrative job offers, or other glories. It may be difficult to prove that the blog has had any positive professional impact, just as it is difficult to prove that it has had any negative impact. This ambiguity is why the key to successful blogging is enjoying the time you spend on it. The expressive benefits will often outweigh the instrumental benefits. But these gains can be enough, especially if Conway's (2010) description of the prototypical academic blogger applies to you: "You are a nerd. You enjoy writing."

Tearing Down Paywalls

Academic knowledge is traditionally generated and disseminated in ways guaranteed to reduce its impact. Academics are given specialized training and learn to produce research that few others can understand. This research is then discussed at conferences attended only by other academics. The work is published, if at all, in journals available only to subscribers or in books that are rarely promoted widely. Even intrepid outsiders will stumble across it only infrequently.

This state of affairs should not satisfy us as political scientists. Interesting and important findings are gathering dust. Although not everyone who might benefit from reading political science will do so if given the opportunity, we should make our research available to people who want to read it and promote it vigorously so that some will discover that they want to read it. Political science needs public forums beyond the classroom that are readily available and accessible. Blogs are one such forum. If more political scientists turn to blogging, the discipline can become even more intellectually effervescent and pertinent to current political debates.

This argument is not simply naive and eager cheerleading, as the traffic statistics for *The Monkey Cage* attest. Even a niche blog like ours can attract enough attention—from more prominent bloggers, mainstream media outlets, and interested readers—to push political science into the spotlight and change public perspectives of how politics works. This aim is perhaps the most satisfying part of blogging: not merely convincing people that political science is relevant, but convincing people that its insights are valuable.

Reprinted from David Niven. 2012. "An Interesting Bias: Lessons from an Academic's Year as a Reporter." PS: Political Science & Politics *45 (2). Cambridge University Press: 259–64. doi:10.1017/ S1049096511002071.*

Notes

I thank Henry Farrell, Seth Masket, Michael McDonald, and Brendan Nyhan for helpful comments.

1. Of course, scholars can maintain a public presence in other ways, such as providing important data via their websites—e.g., the NOMINATE scores available at Keith Poole's website (http://voteview. com) or the turnout statistics available at Michael McDonald's website (http://elections.gmu.edu/).

References

Bai, Matt. 2009. "Bloggers at the Gate." *Democracy* 12: 108–14.

Blattman, Chris. 2009. "Should Junior Faculty Blog?" *Chris Blattman.* January 4. http://chrisblattman. com/2009/01/04/should-junior-facultyblog/.

Conway, Drew. 2010. "Ten Reasons Why Grad Students Should Blog." *Zero Intelligence Agents.* June 8. http://www.drewconway.com/zia/?p2174.

Drezner, Daniel. 2005. "So FridayWas a Pretty Bad Day." *Daniel Drezner.* October 8. http://www.danieldrezner.com/archives/002353.html.

Edwards, George C., III. 2003. *On Deaf Ears: The Limits of the Bully Pulpit.* New Haven: Yale University Press.

Farrell, Henry. 2008. "The Netroots and the Far Left." *The Monkey Cage.* July 20. http://www.themonkeycage.org/2008/07/the_far_left_and_the_netroots.html.

Farrell, Henry, and John Sides. 2010. "Building a Political Science Public Sphere with Blogs." *Forum* 8 (3): article 10.

Gelman, Andrew, David Park, Boris Shot, Joseph Bafumi, and Jeronimo Cortina. 2008. *Red State, Blue State, Rich State, Poor State: Why Americans Vote the Way They Do.* Princeton, NJ: Princeton University Press.

Krehbiel, Keith. 1998. *Pivotal Politics: A Theory of US Lawmaking.* Chicago: University of Chicago Press.

Morill, Barbara. 2008. "The 'Far Left' is the Mainstream." *Daily Kos.* July 17. http://www.dailykos.com/ storyonly/2008/7/17/12526/4386/984/551257.

Neustadt, Richard E. 1990. *Presidential Power and the Modern Presidents: The Politics of Leadership from Roosevelt to Reagan.* NewYork: Free Press.

Quiggin, John. 2010. *Zombie Economics.* Princeton, NJ: Princeton University Press.

Ross, Michael L. 2008. "Oil, Islam, andWomen." *American Political Science Review* 102 (1): 107–23.

Sides, John. 2008a "Who Will Win the Nominations?" *The Monkey Cage.* January 3. http://www.themonkeycage.org/2008/01/who_will_win_the_nominations.html.

Sides, John. 2008b. "Does Oil HurtWomen's Rights?" *The Monkey Cage.* June 10. http://www.themonkeycage.org/2008/06/does_oil_hurt_womens_rights.html.

Sides, John. 2009. "WhatWe Have Learned from the Health Care Debate." *The Monkey Cage.* December 16. http://www.themonkeycage.org/2009/12/what_we_have_learned_from_the.html.

Sides, John, and Eric Lawrence. 2008. "Who Listens to Bloggingheads?" *Los Angeles Times,* July 13.

Tribble, Ivan. 2005. "Bloggers Need Not Apply." *Chronicle of Higher Education,* July 8. http://chronicle. com/article/Bloggers-Need-Not-Apply/45022/.

Complicating the Political Scientist as Blogger

23

ROBERT FARLEY

John Sides "The Political Scientist as Blogger," on the developing relationship between blogging and the discipline of political science, was published in *PS* shortly before Sides' blog, *The Monkey Cage*, won "Blog of the Year" from *This Week* magazine (Sides 2011, 267; *The Week* Editorial Staff 2011). The richly deserved award reflected the spotlight that *The Monkey Cage* has brought on the discipline of political science, and the degree to which the blog has served as a bridge between the discipline and the policy and journalistic communities. In the last decade numerous political scientists have taken to blogging in several venues, each with a slightly different approach to the relationship between discipline and medium. The success of *The Monkey Cage* indicates that traditional political science research has an important role to play even in the wild-and-woolly world of the blogosphere.

Sides' article also contributes on the critically important question of the role that blogging can play in an academic career, arguing that having a blog need not weigh down a tenure or promotion case. Successful blogging requires developing a breadth of knowledge that can strengthen teaching and advisory roles. Blogging also creates a habit of writing that can persist during conventional research projects. Blog posts can undoubtedly serve as trial balloons for ideas not quite ready for the light of day, as blog posts create instant (by academic standards) feedback from multiple sources, including commenters and other bloggers. Although this feedback can often be useless and annoying, separating the wheat from the chaff can reveal some excellent critiques and good advice for the future of any research project. The blogosphere is sufficiently diverse that even relatively obscure discussions can find a community of sufficient size and expertise to offer good comments.

Still, Sides' article left me with a sense of disquiet. Although I appreciate the effort to "just add blogging" to the discipline of political science, I worry that in making blogging safe, Sides gives away too much of what makes it interesting, influential, and fun. Specifically, I have two major objections to Sides' characterization of blogging in political science. First, the article heralds an effort to discipline the political science blogosphere, establishing metrics for differentiating between "good" blogs that can contribute to (or at least should not be held against) a political science career, and "bad" blogs that do no one any good. In short, Sides's article served both prescriptive and proscriptive purposes. Second, by emphasizing the "safe" elements of blogging, Sides has left winnings on the table; blogging could play a larger role in political science than he suggests.

Disciplining the Undisciplined

Certainly, Sides wants more political scientists to blog. Laying out the basics of how to create and maintain a blog is an important contribution, as is the advice about how to react to the inevitable comments that any semisuccessful blog attracts. Sides also hopes to erode the idea that political scientists should be "punished" for producing work of interest to policymakers and journalists (Yglesias 2010). Recently, "Bridging the Divide" is a much discussed topic among policy oriented political scientists (Drezner 2011). *The Monkey Cage* has played an important role in this endeavor, mostly by bringing the fruit of political science research to bear on major policy questions.

But here is the problem:

> Writing regular blog posts is not necessarily easy. It takes time to find a voice and learn the kinds of topics and ideas that will appeal to a broader audience. One guideline should be obvious: avoid personal complaints about your life, commute, colleagues, discipline, and so on—topics that are perilous from a professional perspective anyway. Choose topics to which you can add value as a political scientist. This approach will distinguish your blog from other blogs about politics and from most pundits' commentary. You can summarize your research or the work of other scholars, analyze data, and make simple graphs that are understandable to a lay audience. (Sides 2011, 267).

This passage has the whiff of an effort at discipline. Wheras the sources of "professional peril" are left anonymous, the inevitable implication is that some blogs are good, appropriate, and should not blot the tenure and promotion cases of their authors; other blogs are inappropriate and not quite "political science." The question now invariably is to distinguish between the appropriate and inappropriate blogs. Appropriate blogs tackle topics that add value from political science training. Inappropriate blogs address such perilous concerns as personal complaints about children, cats, cars, and (oddly enough) the discipline of political science. The last is particularly problematic, as Sides seems to be suggesting that political scientists ought not comment about the state of the political science discipline on their political science blogs.

Given the attacks that some critics have leveled against academic bloggers, a defensive effort at disciplining the political science blogosphere is understandable (Tribble 2005). We should appreciate that Sides' approach amounts to an effort to defuse certain lines of critique by distinguishing between safe and unsafe forms of blogging. In effect, this burns half of the blogosphere to save the other half. I have a personal interest in this question because I worry that my own blogging falls on the wrong side. *Lawyers, Guns and Money* was founded in 2004 by three political science graduate students at the University ofWashington (Farley 2012). Although additional members have been added since 2004, five political scientists have written roughly 83% of 12,000 or so posts at *Lawyers, Guns and Money*. Traffic to the site reached one million visitors per year sometime around 2006 and last year exceeded two million. *Lawyers, Guns and Money* currently has between 5,000 and 8,000 subscribers (actual numbers are difficult to determine because of different counting methodology). These numbers are very roughly double those reported by Sides for *The Monkey Cage* (Sides 2011, 267) during a similar time period. Yet when he lists the major political science blogs, Sides made no mention of *Lawyers, Guns and Money* in "The Political Scientist as Blogger."

To be sure, it is difficult to criticize Sides on this omission without seeming petty and bitter, and "How could you possibly have ignored my blog?!?" is a silly and unproductive question. An article titled "The Political Scientist as Blogger" surely cannot productively mention every political science blog. The exclusion of *Lawyers, Guns and Money* makes sense, however, if we understand Sides' effort as both prescriptive and proscriptive; including some blogs as decent and appropriate political science while implicitly excluding others as professionally problematic. Indeed, *Lawyers, Guns and Money* does not fit many of the criteria that Professor Sides sets forth for "political science blogging." Posts that synthesize the latest work in political theory and international relations are followed by posts that lament John Lackey's earned run average, or disparage Michael Bay's aptitude for film-making. Moreover, the approach to politics at *Lawyers, Guns and Money* is explicitly partisan. While the authors are trained political scientists, they use their training in service of charged, highly partisan arguments that are often frowned on in traditional political science. *Lawyers, Guns and Money* concentrates less on the transmission of academic research into the policy sphere and more on the direct application of research knowledge and skills to political and policy questions.

Thus, the exclusion of *Lawyers, Guns and Money* was tactful rather than accidental; a blog like *Lawyers, Guns and Money* is not discussed as a political science blog (although its authors clearly think of it as political science) because it is embarrassing to the kind of argument that Sides makes. What constitutes the difference between a political science blog and a blog about politics written by political scientists? Is this is a distinction without a helpful difference? Jonathan Bernstein, unaffiliated scholar and author of a "Plain Blog about Politics" is oft-cited by *The Monkey Cage*, but he frequently writes about culture and baseball in addition to American electoral politics (Bernstein 2012).

Surely, lines must be drawn. A blog by a political scientist that focused solely on baseball statistics, or that is preoccupied with photographs of cats in amusing predicaments, should probably be excluded from the genus "political science blog." If we include or exclude blogs based on particular criteria, we need to be explicit about what are those criteria; what blogging is considered good for the discipline (and presumably good for the careers of the authors), and what blogging is considered embarrassing, problematic, and not the sort of thing you want to include in a tenure file. The cat and baseball blogs listed are easy cases; *Lawyers, Guns and Money*, *American Power* (Douglas 2012), and other highly partisan blogs are more difficult to categorize and threaten to test the boundaries (Douglas 2012). Unfortunately, Sides gives little insight as to where the boundary between "a political science blog" and "a blog about politics written by political scientists" lies.

What the Medium Means for the Profession

Professor Sides ably discusses the professional positives of blogging for junior and senior faculty members. Blogging improves teaching, gives scholars the chance to test-drive research ideas, encourages a habit of writing, and publicizes both the scholar and the scholar's research. All of these activities enhance tenure and promotion cases, although Sides also notes that blogging can irritate senior colleagues and consume valuable writing and research time. Again, Sides promotes blogging, however, in an essentially defensive fashion; blogging can help improve earning tenure and promotion, but it is unlikely to have an independent positive impact on a blogger's career. In short, the blog itself is a means to multiple ends, and not an end in itself.

Sides' article surely represents a useful contribution to warn young (and not so young) scholars of the dangers of blogging. However, if the medium of blogging does all that Sides attributes to it, not to mention granting a higher profile to a department and helping "bridge the gap" between policymakers and the academy, then why is blogging not counted in the context of tenure and promotion decisions? A genuine appreciation of the role that blogging plays in an academic career would consider the merits of the medium, and in particular what the medium can offer than alternative venues cannot. Sides suggests a political science blog community that acts in *support of* the traditional pillars of an academic career, including teaching, but especially research. This idea is fine, but a different approach might examine how blogging might *replace* some of those traditional elements.

Here is an example: if you are reading this article in *PS*, the article has gone through a vetting and editing process that has probably lasted at least 18 months. This process undoubtedly improved the quality of the article, but it also substantially delayed its entry into the debate. Had I simply posted this discussion as a blog response to Sides, it probably would have taken me three or four days to write and edit it. I would have included multiple hyperlinks, effectively "citing" not only Sides article but a plethora of different pieces on blogging and the academy. The article could have been viewed by some 4,000 regular visitors to *Lawyers, Guns and Money*, plus another 8,000 or so subscribers. Any one of these subscribers could have responded (helpfully or unhelpfully) in our comments section, likely generating a long debate both on the mer-its of the article and on the merits of the author. Sides could have responded within a day, and a multitude of other political science bloggers might have chimed in during the ensuing weeks.

Instead, I published the article here in *PS*, giving up all of that in return for a line on my CV with the "peer review" annotation. The delay of this article, the loss of all of the interactivity that the Internet provides, and the substantial reduction in the number of people likely to read the piece buy me a slightly improved chance at tenure and promotion. It is true, readers of this article will not be forced to skip over a long debate about the relative merit of Ivan Rodriguez' defense versus Mike Piazza's offense, but then the number of people who read *PS* cover-to-cover is likely small.

To say that this makes little sense is an understatement.

And so, rather than think in terms of how blogging, tweeting, and other forms of social media could accommodate themselves to the traditional profile of an academic career, let me suggest that we should, as a discipline, think in more radical terms. Effectively, our tenure and promotion system is built around an obsolete social and technological foundation, with career success built around posting a few articles in a few journals subscribed to by a few libraries and read by few people (Cosgrove 2011; Healy 2011). Rather than take the apologetic line that Sides advocates, we should think about blogging as a crowbar to pry open the tenure and promotion process. As Stephen Walt has argued,

> What is also needed is a change in academic practice, including the criteria that are used to make key hiring and promotion decisions. The standards by which we assess scholarly value are not divinely ordained or established by natural law; they are in fact "socially constructed" by the discipline itself. In other words, we collectively decide what sorts of work to valorize and what sorts of achievement to reward. If university departments placed greater weight on teaching, on contributions to applied public policy, on public outreach, and on a more diverse range of publishing venues—including journals of opinion, trade publishers and maybe even blogs—then individual scholars would quickly adapt to these new incentives and we would attract a somewhat different group of scholars over time (Walt 2010).

This is not to say that the peer review system lacks merit, because it remains a relevant and important element of the academic project. *The Monkey Cage* has successfully exploited a hunger in the blogospheric and journalistic communities for good, traditional political science research. A replacement of the peer review system with some sort of "open blog" format would hardly solve all problems. For example, the authors of popular blogs such as *Lawyers, Guns and Money* and *The Monkey Cage* have the luxury of receiving feedback from many potential commenters, while excellent work at smaller blogs unfortunately may escape notice. But the peer-review system is hardly the only means to either (a) say something interesting or (b) influence the public policy debate.

To be sure, the metrics for evaluating the contribution that blogging could make to a tenure or promotion case remain murky. Measures such as traffic, links, and comments are all problematic often to the point of uselessness. The best we can offer, perhaps, is that each blog can be evaluated as part of an academic career, and no clear template for how blogging should fit into career progress exists. This proposal sounds frustratingly amorphous, but in most cases the arguments for and against tenure and promotion rely on fuzzy distinction between journals, publishers, and course evaluations, not to mention the always-important-but-never-concrete quality "will this person make a good colleague?" A more holistic approach to tenure and promotion (Young 2010) would remedy some of the problems of relying on the peer-review system, while also encouraging young scholars to "bridge the gap" by writing articles that people will actually read (Young 2010). An American Historical Association working group report on the field of public history suggested the adjustment of tenure standards to take into account public engagement (Working Group on Evaluating Pub-lic History Scholarship 2010).

Conclusion

With state legislatures displaying an increasing reluctance to underwrite political science research that their constituents neither understand nor care about, blogging could become an important avenue for public engagement. Thus, the practice of blogging touches on a core interest of the discipline of political science, even if we have not quite recognized that it is a core interest.

What we have not yet seen, but what I suspect may be coming, is the infection of the political science blogosphere with all of the dysfunction that marks the typical political science department. We should prepare for all of the endless skirmishes that characterize the borders between subdisciplines and methodologies to play out in the blogosphere. Such a development is probably inevitable, but is more likely when we define the contribution of political science blogging in terms of increasing the visibility of extant political science literature.

This is why I find Sides' article so personally depressing. Blogging was a way out of the dysfunction of political science, and particularly of the ongoing and utterly unproductive methodological war between "quals" and "quants." In a blog posts, political scientists could use their training to write something interesting without worrying about the crushing expectations of methodological conformity. As *The Monkey Cage* brings political science to the blogosphere and helps build another bridge over the gap, it also brings all of the debates, arguments, and disputes of graduate school.

Blogging needs to come out of its defensive crouch. Professor Sides appreciates this, but he still concedes too much. Moreover, at the very least, an effort at prescription and proscription should make the line between acceptable and unacceptable clear. As a discipline, political science needs to ask whether there is any value to blogging, specifically, and to public engagement, more generally. If there is value, then we need to create career incentives for junior faculty to engage. A world in which only senior faculty feel safe blogging is necessarily impoverished. Similarly, we need to accept that the technological and social transformations that have accompanied the development of the Internet have the potential to revolutionize not just political science, but the entire academy. Pretending that nothing has changed does no one any good.

Reprinted from Robert Farley. 2013. "Complicating the Political Scientist as Blogger." PS: Political Science & Politics *46 (2). Cambridge University Press: 383–86. doi:10.1017/S1049096513000061.*

References

Bernstein, Jonathan. 2012. *A Plain Blog about Politics.* http://plainblogaboutpolitics.blogspot.com/.

Cosgrove, Mike. 2011. "Academic Publishing Rip-Offs, Part XVII?" *Mike Cosgrove: Life, the Universe and Everything.* http://www.mikecosgrave.com/blog2006/?p708.

Douglas, Donald. 2012. *American Power.* http://americanpowerblog.blogspot.com/.

Drezner, Daniel. 2011. "Pssst.... wanna read about bridging the gap between theory and policy?" *Foreign Policy.* http://drezner.foreignpolicy.com/posts/2011/03/10/pssst_wanna_read_about_bridging_the_gap_between_theor_and_policy.

Farley, Robert. 2012. *Lawyers, Guns and Money.* http://lawyersgunsmoneyblog.com.

Healy, Kieran. 2011. "Academic Journals and Copyright Control." Orgtheory.net. http://orgtheory.wordpress.com/2011/05/19/academic-journals-and-copyrightcontrol/.

Sides, John. 2011. "The Political Scientist as Blogger." *PS: Political Science & Politics* 44 (2): 267–71.

Tribble, Ivan. 2005. "Bloggers Need Not Apply." *Chronicle of Higher Education.* http://chronicle.com/article/Bloggers-Need-Not-Apply/45022.

Walt, Stephen. 2010. "What to Do on Your Summer Vacation." *Foreign Policy*. http://walt.foreignpolicy.
com/posts/2010/12/07/what_to_do_on_your_summer_vacation.

The Week Editorial Staff. 2011. "John Sides and The Monkey Cage: Blogger of the Year." *The Week*. http://
theweek.com/article/index/215150/john-sides-and-themonkey-cage-blogger-of-the-year.

Working Group on Evaluating Public History Scholarship. 2010. "Tenure, Promotion, and the Publicly
Engaged Academic Historian." http://ncph.org/cms/wpcontent/uploads/2010/06/Engaged-Histo-
rian-Report-FINAL1.pdf.

Yglesias, Matthew. 2010. "If a Working Paper Falls in the Wilderness and a Journalist Hears About It,
Is that Worse?" Thinkprogress: Yglesias. http://thinkprogress.org/yglesias/2010/09/03/198419/if-a-
working-paper-falls-in-thewilderness-and-a-journalist-hears-about-it-is-that-worse/.

Young, Jeremy C. 2010. "Blogging and Peer Review Revisited." *The Crolian Progressive*. http://herbertcroly.
wordpress.com/2010/04/30/blogging-and-peer-reviewrevisited/.

Part Five

Self-Conceptions

Political Science as a Vocation

24

ROBERT O. KEOHANE

About 90 years ago, at the end of World War I, Max Weber gave two now-famous lectures, published in English as "Science as a Vocation" and "Politics as a Vocation." They well repay reading and re-reading. Thinking of those lectures, it seemed appropriate, on this occasion, to reflect on "Political Science as a Vocation." As the title of my lecture indicates, I am directing my comments principally to the graduate students in attendance here, who are beginning careers in our field. After the lecture, I want to hear about your reasons for becoming political scientists, and your aspirations. In the lecture, I will reflect on our vocation from the vantage point of someone who has been a practicing political scientist—teaching, reflecting, and writing about politics—for 43 years.

I begin by pointing out that, viewed historically, you are in distinguished company. Aristotle was probably the first systematic Western political scientist, theorizing the relationship of politics to other spheres of life and creating a typology of regimes—what we would now call comparative politics. Machiavelli not only advised the prince but sought to analyze the nature of leadership, the characteristic hypocrisy of political speech, and the sources of republican greatness. Hobbes provided what is still one of the most compelling discussions of the causes of political violence and the sources of, and justification for, the state. Montesquieu and Madison developed a durable theory of constitutionalism, and Toqueville put forward insights into the nature of democracy that remain vibrant today—for example, in the work of Robert Putnam. I have already mentioned Max Weber. In the generation of political scientists born in the first three decades of this century I would list, somewhat arbitrarily, Gabriel Almond, Robert Dahl, Judith Shklar, and Kenneth Waltz—all of whom profoundly affected our knowledge of politics. Today, there are so many fine colleagues doing insightful work that to mention a few would be to risk slighting others whose work is equally important. The point is that you are joining a vibrant profession with a rich history. If I were conversant with classical Chinese and Indian sources, I could probably add to this list and extend this history even further into the past.

Following Virginia Woolf, many of you probably noticed that except for Judith Shklar, this is a "procession" of men. Fortunately, however, this lamentable situation has changed. Had I listed contemporary political scientists of note I would have had to include Elinor Ostrom, Theda Skocpol, Margaret Levi, and Suzanne Rudolph, as well as many younger women who are now leaders in our profession. Although exclusion on gender and racial lines was long a reality, our profession is now increasingly open to talented people from a wide variety of backgrounds.

What, then, is "political science"? I have an economist colleague who likes to say that any discipline with "science" in its name is not really a science—that it protests too much. Were one to adopt a narrow view of science, as requiring mathematical formulations of its propositions, precise quantitative testing, or even experimental validation, *political science* would indeed be an oxymoron. But today I will defend our nomenclature by taking a broader view.

I define *politics* as involving attempts to organize human groups to determine internal rules and, externally, to compete and cooperate with other organized groups; and reactions to such attempts. This definition is meant to encompass a range of activities from the governance of a democracy such as Great Britain to warfare, from corporate takeovers to decisions made in the UN Security Council. It includes acts of leadership and resistance to leadership, behavior resulting from deference and from defiance. I define *science* as a *publicly known* set of procedures designed to make and evaluate *descriptive and causal inferences* on the basis of the self-conscious application of *methods* that are themselves subject to public evaluation. All science is carried out with the understanding that any conclusions are *uncertain* and subject to revision or refutation (King, Keohane, and Verba 1994, 7–9). Political science is the study of politics through the procedures of science.

Teaching

Most of this lecture will be devoted to an explication of how, in my view, political science should be carried out: that is, the processes of thinking and research that yield insights about politics. But I want to begin by talking about *teaching*. Teaching is sometimes disparaged. Colleagues bargain to reduce their "teaching loads." The language is revealing, since we speak of "research opportunities" but of "teaching loads." National and global reputations are built principally on written work, not on teaching. But when we look around, we see that virtually all top-ranked political scientists in the world today are active teachers. Few of them have spent their careers at research institutes or think tanks. In my view, there is a reason for this. Teaching undergraduates compels one to put arguments into ordinary language, accessible to undergraduates—and therefore to people who have not absorbed the arcane language of social science. Teaching graduate students exposes one to new ideas from younger and more supple minds—as long as the students are sufficiently critical of the professor's views.

I want to emphasize this point about criticism, because in my experience, most students—but rarely the best—are too deferential. In 1927, so the story goes, the chief justice of the United States, former president William Howard Taft, came to Yale Law School, where his host was the chancellor of Yale Law School, Robert Maynard Hutchins, who was only 28 years old. Yale was then seen as a radical place; Taft was a conservative. So the chief justice said to Chancellor Hutchins, "Well, I understand that at Yale you teach your students that judges are fools." To which Robert Maynard Hutchins replied, "No, Mr. Chief Justice, at Yale we teach our students to find *that* out for themselves." Like the Yale students, you need to discover for yourself which senior political scientists are wise, and which are fools—by using your own critical faculties.

Teaching is rewarding in other ways. I have learned a lot from my colleagues indirectly through students, who come to me with insights, or works to read, suggested by other faculty members. And over the long run, one may see former undergraduate students become politicians or even rise to high positions. A former student of mine just entered the United States Senate, and another one is president of the World Bank. With former PhD students ties are much stronger, since they remain in the profession. Two of my most valued colleagues and best friends at Princeton are former students, including the chair of politics, Helen Milner, and the eminent student of the European Union, Andrew Moravcsik. Former students of mine are scattered at colleges and universities around the United States, with some in Europe or Japan. In my office I keep a shelf of books that began as PhD dissertations under my supervision. Paraphrasing Mark Twain: "It is good to do research. It is also good to advise others on how to do research—and a lot less trouble."

Never disparage teaching. It is an intrinsic part of political science as a vocation. Furthermore, it provides much more immediate gratification than research. When I am working on a major project, I never know whether the results will be worthwhile. I have left unpublished quite a bit of work, when I realized that the premises or methods that I used were flawed. Sometimes even one's published work will be ignored. Like politics for Weber, research can seem like the "long, hard boring of hard boards." The eventual rewards may be substantial or they may be meager; you never know until quite a bit later. If you give a good lecture or teach a lively, thoughtful seminar, however, the gratification is immediate: you know you accomplished something that day. During periods of self-doubt, teaching can keep you going.

The Science in Political Science

I now turn to research, asking: what do political *scientists* do? What are the processes they go through in the search for knowledge? I will focus on four activities: *puzzling, conceptualizing, describing, and making causal inferences.*

Puzzles

Interesting work begins not just with a problem—how democracy works in the United States, for instance—but with a puzzle. Puzzles are anomalies: what we observe does not fit with our preconceptions based on established theory. Hobbes sought to make sense of civil war and regicide. Toqueville wanted to understand how a decentralized, individualistic society as the United States in the 1830s could exhibit such overall cohesion, and even suffer from oppressive public opinion. Barrington Moore and a line of successors have sought to explain why some societies develop stable democracies while others do not; Theda Skocpol and others seek to account for great revolutions—and their absence. Great leaps forward in political science often take place when someone sees puzzles, where others have only seen facts. The great philosopher of science, Imre Lakatos, says that "science proceeds on a sea of anomalies," which certainly applies to political science.

There is an implication for graduate students, and teachers, of the importance of puzzles: never dismiss what appears to be a naïve question. This point was brought home to me when I was at Stanford in the 1970s, trying to understand economics better. I was not trained in economics but sought to pick it up on the fly, partly by attending economics seminars. I remember one such seminar, by an eminent student of multinational corporations who spoke very well, in a highly organized way. After about three minutes a young bearded man raised his hand to ask a question, which the speaker answered to my satisfaction. After three or four minutes the same hand went up, then again a few minutes later with a different question, each seeming rather obvious to me. After three or four questions, I was getting annoyed: can't you please let the speaker proceed? But after five or six questions it dawned on me that the questioner was the *only* person in the room who really understood the topic: his apparently naïve questions had dismantled the premises of the talk. I have forgotten everything else about the seminar, but I vividly remember the questions from the back of the room and the lesson: apparently naïve questions are often the most fundamental. So if you are puzzled, ask. In our field, there are no dumb questions. If you ask a naïve question, 90% of the time you may just have missed the point, and you will get the benefit of being corrected. But 10% of the time, you may be the only person in the room to see the anomaly—to sense, like a good detective, that there is something wrong about the story you are being told. The rewards of identifying major puzzles, for the profession and for yourself, are very large indeed.

Conceptualization

The next step is conceptualization: being clear about the meaning of concepts. As Giovanni Sartori pointed out long ago, concepts get "stretched" out of shape by political scientists seeking to do too much with too little (1970). And much often depends on definitions. How we think about the relationship between democracy and liberty, for example, depends on how we conceptualize both key terms. Likewise, whether democracies ever fight one another, or whether international institutions degrade or enhance democracy, depends heavily on how we define democracy. Whether civil wars are becoming more or less frequent may turn on how we conceptualize what is a civil "war" rather than a lesser form of civil conflict. And whether peace requires justice or is often in conflict with it depends on how we define both of those contested terms.

There are, in my view, no right or wrong definitions. But there are explicit and implicit definitions, those consistent with ordinary usage and those that are not. And authors can be consistent or inconsistent in their use of terms. At the conceptualization stage, it is our obligation to put forward explicit definitions and to seek to operationalize them consistently. The more our definitions conform to ordinary usage, furthermore, the less confusion is likely to result.

Description and Interpretation

The core of what most political scientists do, most of the time, is *descriptive inference*. Inference means drawing more general conclusions from established premises plus a particular set of facts. For example, from known facts—such as that each of 150 countries has a particular form of government and particular economic characteristics—we may infer that there is a correlation between wealth and democracy. Properly speaking, such a conclusion rests on a chain of inferences—for instance, we may have inferred from a sample survey of tax returns what per capita GDP is for the country and from observation of three elections whether the country is democratically governed. These inferences are subject to error: people might systematically falsify their tax returns and the incumbent government might conceal decisive manipulations from election monitors. Other examples of descriptive inferences in political science are the generalization that democracies do not fight one another, the claim that international institutions typically provide information to governments about other governments' compliance with rules, and Moravcsik's claim that the European Union was formed by leaders concerned more about economic gains than security benefits (1998). As the examples indicate, descriptive inferences can be generalizations about a wide set of cases, or statements about events at a particular time and place. We can make inferences about individuals—for instance, the sincerity or hypocrisy of leaders or their perceptions of other leaders' behavior. We can also make inferences about the behavior of collective actors that may have subunits pulling in different directions: what "the United Kingdom" or "China" did in a particular situation, or whether "the United States," or unauthorized individuals, engaged in torture at Abu Graib or Guantanamo. And we can make inferences about relationships. Were there back-channel communications during the Cuban missile crisis between the Soviet ambassador and Robert M. Kennedy, and if so, what were they about? Did NGOs and state representatives collaborate in leaking information about the OECD negotiations 10 years ago about multilateral rules for investments?

Often political scientists seek to make their descriptive inferences more precise by attaching numbers to whatever process they are seeking to understand. Precision is certainly enhanced by numbers that are both reliable and valid, so such activities are to be encouraged. But it is important to understand the importance of both reliability and validity. Reliability essentially means that, using the criteria publicly employed, the number could be replicated by an independent observer. If, by criteria defining wars as organized violence involving 1,000 or more deaths, one team of observers finds 50 wars in a given period of time, another team, using the same criteria, should also find 50 wars. Validity is different: it refers to whether the measurement used—in this case, 1,000 battle casualties—fairly reflects the underlying phenomenon being discussed: that is, war. Are all conflicts involving 1,000 deaths wars, even if some take place in small societies, so that 1,000 deaths is a large proportion of the active population, while others are undertaken by very large societies that suffer many times more deaths in traffic accidents? Should all wars—from the skirmish that took 1,100 lives to World War II—be counted equally? These are questions of validity that cannot be solved by quantification, but for which one has to think hard about how one's conceptualization relates to the phenomena that can be measured. Before we accept a descriptive inference, we need to have asked questions about validity as well as reliability.

The issue of validity is highlighted by the famous philosophical distinction between a wink and a twitch. As Clifford Geertz writes, "the difference between a wink and a twitch is vast, as anyone unfortunate enough to have taken the first for the second knows" (1973). And, one might add, *vice versa*. If you see someone who is attractive to you moving her eyelids rapidly, you need to engage in interpretation before moving to a descriptive inference. If you interpret the eye movement as a wink, you may infer: "she loves me, too." But woe to you if you act on that interpretation and it was only a twitch!

Political scientists engage in interpretation all the time. When states "reject" a public offer, as China and India were reported as rejecting last summer's recent G8 proposal on climate change, are they really rejecting it, or simply establishing a bargaining position? When the International Criminal Court indicts the president of Sudan, is it seeking to bring him to justice or making a symbolic statement about Sudan's behavior toward its own people? When Bill Clinton pointed out during the US primaries last spring that many white people were hesitant to vote for a black man, was he simply reporting an unpleasant reality or appealing to racism?

My point about descriptive inference is twofold. Descriptive inference is not the same as simple description: it involves an inference, from known to unknown, that can be incorrect or otherwise flawed. And both description and descriptive inference often rest on the interpretation of inherently—sometimes deliberately—ambiguous actions.

Causal Inference

Causality necessarily involves consideration of a counterfactual situation. If Charles II had not been executed in 1649, would Great Britain have a different political system now? If nuclear weapons had not been invented, would the United States and the Soviet Union have fought World War III? If Hillary Rodham Clinton had planned beyond Super Tuesday, February 5, would she have won the Democratic nomination for president? If the United States and Great Britain had occupied Iraq with twice as many troops, would the insurgency have been prevented? Since we cannot observe what actually happened and what didn't happen at the same time, making causal inferences is extremely difficult.

In experimental science the answer is to conduct experiments in which only one feature is different—for instance, adding or not adding a chemical to a solution—and observing how outcomes differ. Experiments are the best way to make valid causal inferences, and some of the most exciting work in political science now involves experimentation, sometimes in conjunction with surveys. I expect the domains in which experiments yield new causal knowledge to expand as imaginative political scientists explore the possibilities as well as the limitations of experimental methods.

Unfortunately for science but perhaps fortunately for the human race, political scientists cannot manipulate large-scale political phenomena, such as the outcomes of elections or the incidence of war, for their convenience—not that human subjects committees would let us even if we could do so! If we can find and measure many highly similar instances of the same action—for example, votes for Parliament or expressions of party preference in surveys—we may be able to make quite good causal inferences through the use of statistics. But even then, our procedures may contaminate our findings—for instance, people often make up answers to public opinion polls because they do not want to seem ignorant, and they deliberately recall having voted for winning candidates more than can actually have been the case.

More seriously, our inferences may be flawed because of omitted variables—something else changed that we failed to measure, and this change, rather than the one on which we focused, may explain what we want to understand. Or we can confront endogeneity: what we stipulate as the effect is actually, in whole or part, the cause rather than vice versa. A recent article in the *American Economic Review* disputes even the long-held view of political scientists and economists that increasing wealth promotes democracy. Daron Acemoglu and his colleagues believe that the correlation between wealth and democracy—which is very strong—does not suggest causality, because of omitted variables: other factors correlated with wealth that are also correlated with democracy (Acemoglu et al. 2008). None of our sacred cows is immune to criticism!

Furthermore, anticipation of consequences may create false impressions of causality. States may comply with international law not because they have incentives to follow it, or believe they are obliged to do so, but because they have carefully agreed only to rules with which they intended in any event to comply. Conversely, real causality may be obscured. Political scientists seeking to determine the effect of deterrence threats in international crises did not find any significant effects. Critics, however, pointed out that states that would submit to deterrent threats should have anticipated the threats, and their submission, and therefore not have stimulated crises in the first place. The difficulties of causal inference seem endless. As many of you know, social scientists have worked out ingenious responses to all of these problems, and continue to do so; but all of these responses are imperfect, relying on uncertain inferences. They are responses, not solutions.

Making causal inferences is the "Holy Grail" of political science, but with respect to large-scale events involving strategic interactions we are not very good at it—not because we are stupid, but because of inherent difficulties. Causal inferences are particularly difficult in international politics, where each major event seems to have multiple contributing causes and to be sufficiently different from other events of the same name that aggregation is problematic. There was only one French Revolution and only one World War I. However important it may have been, the Orange Revolution in the Ukraine was not very similar to the French Revolution, nor can the Iraq War be closely matched with World War I. Furthermore, events separated in historical time not only have different contexts—technological, political, social, economic, and ecological—they are affected by knowledge of earlier events. So any methods that require independence are jeopardized.

Aspirations to causal inference are often linked to hopes for prediction. Our causal knowledge of gravity helps us to predict the movement of planets and other celestial objects, and our causal knowledge of biology and, increasingly, genetics helps us to predict the incidence of disease. Sometimes we can make predictions—for instance, of election outcomes on the basis of economic conditions—but even our best predictions are imperfect. For my own subject of international politics the situation is even worse, because it revolves around conscious strategies of reflective actors. I act as I do because I anticipate what you will do, but you, knowing this, act differently than I expect, and I, in turn anticipating this, change my behavior. This is an infinite regress about which no prediction can be made: one would have to know how many cycles the players would go through, but if this could be ascertained, smart players would learn it and go one step further.

Why Choose Political Science as a Vocation?

If causal inferences in our field, and prediction, are so intractable, why choose political science as a vocation? My short answer is that we study politics not because it is beautiful or easy to understand, but because it is so important to all fields of human endeavor. I readily admit that I cannot prove that politics is important. Weber, in "Science as a Vocation," says that the presupposition that something is "worth knowing" "cannot be proved by scientific methods. It can only be *interpreted* with reference to its ultimate meaning" (2004, 18).

Without governance, as Hobbes said, life is "poor, nasty, brutish and short." Democracy is in my view immensely better than autocracy, much less tyranny; but "making democracy work" is hard and imposing it from the outside seems close to impossible (Putnam 1993). Peace, economic development, health, and ecological sustainability all depend on political institutions and on political decisions, and often on leadership. If the state fails or gets involved in wars that involve high levels of violence on its own territory, creative activity in virtually every field except weapons development is likely to be stymied. Without a vibrant political science, leaders would be guided only by their limited personal experiences, historical analogies, and folk wisdom—all highly unreliable as a basis for inference.

We should therefore judge our work, in my view, not according to some idealization of science, or by the standards of the physical and biological sciences. Unlike Newtonian physics, we cannot properly aspire to knowledge of grand covering laws that explain a myriad of disparate events. Instead, we should ask whether knowing the political science literature on a given topic has prepared us better to anticipate what could happen and assign probabilities to these various scenarios. Are the results superior to historical analogies, extrapolation from the very recent past, and common sense? The answer is not always affirmative, but there are enough phenomena that we understand better because of the work of political scientists—from the operation of democracies to the operation of international institutions, from the exercise of various forms of power to the incidence of civil war—that we can be proud, within limits, of our profession.

But I said at the outset of this lecture that my audience is principally the graduate students assembled here, and that you should be critical of your elders. Although you are learning to build on previous work, I hope you are dissatisfied with the accomplishments of earlier generations, and skeptical about many of their inferences. I also hope that you see puzzling anomalies in some of the conventional wisdom—issues that need to be unpacked. And I hope that you have objections to express to what I have said here today.

Many of you will have noticed that my sources and examples come almost entirely from Europe and the United States, and from international politics, which has been dominated for five centuries by Europe and its offshoots. There is a sort of parochialism, therefore, about the way I have presented this subject. This parochialism is presumably due in some measure to my own limitations, but it also reflects the discipline, which is heavily American and to some extent European, with relatively few genuinely important independent contributions from scholars on other continents. As the economic and political centers of gravity shift away from Europe and the United States—as we move into the "post-American era" as Fareed Zakaria calls it—this is bound to change. Political science will become a global discipline. It will, however, only prosper if liberal democracy thrives. If we do our job, we political scientists will be irritating to political leaders, since we illuminate their deliberate obscurities and deceptions, we point to alternative policies that could be followed, we question their motivations and dissect the operations of organizations that support them and governments over which they preside. They will try to buy us off or, failing that, if not prevented from doing so, to shut us up. As a result, we have a symbiotic relationship with democracy. We can only thrive when democracy flourishes, and democracy—in a smaller way—needs us, if only as a small voice of dispassionate reason.

Our symbiotic relationship to democracy means that political science cannot be value-neutral. Nor can we be neutral with respect to order vs. chaos, war vs. peace. In our particular investigations we need to seek objectivity—a goal that is never realized but that we should strive for—because otherwise people with other preferences, or who do not know what our values are, will have no reason to take our findings seriously. In the absence of a serious culture of objectivity, no cumulative increases in knowledge can take place. But the overall enterprise should never be value-neutral. We should choose normatively important problems because we care about improving human behavior, we should explain these choices to our students and readers, and we should not apologize for making value-laden choices even as we seek to search unflinchingly for the truth, as unpleasant or unpopular as that may be. So I hope you will consult your values, as well as the literature, in deciding what to work on.

In conclusion, let me express the hope that you—the new generation of political scientists—will see openings where we see closure, and that you will have ideas about how to move through those openings to the insights that lie behind them. There are surely productive new interpretations to offer, and new descriptive and causal discoveries to be made. You may already be formulating some of these new views. The continuing vitality of our discipline depends, as it always has, on the critical imagination, conceptual boldness, and intellectual rigor of successive cohorts of newly trained scientists. The best of these political scientists will have learned theory, method, and much empirical knowledge from their predecessors—but will also have learned to question what they have learned.

Reprinted from Robert O. Keohane. 2009. "Political Science as a Vocation." PS: Political Science & Politics *42 (2). Cambridge University Press: 359–63. doi:10.1017/S1049096509090489.*

References

Acemoglu, Daron, Simon Johnson, James A. Robinson, and Pierre Yared. 2008. "Income and Democracy." *American Economic Review* 98 (3): 808–42.

Geertz, Clifford. 1973. *An Interpretation of Cultures*. New York: Basic Books.

King, Gary, Robert O. Keohane, and Sidney Verba. 1994. *Designing Social Inquiry*. Princeton: Princeton University Press.

Moravcsik, Andrew M. 1998. *The Choice for Europe: Social Purpose and State Power from Messina to Maastricht*. Ithaca: Cornell University Press.

Putnam, Robert D. 1993. *Making Democracy Work*. Princeton: Princeton University Press.

Sartori, Giovanni. 1970. "Concept Misformation in Comparative Politics." *American Political Science Review* 64 (4): 1033–53.

Weber, Max. 2004. *Science as a Vocation*. Translated by Rodney Livingstone. Indianapolis: Hackett Publishing Co.

American Politics and Political Science in an Era of Growing Racial Diversity and Economy Disparity

25

Rodney E. Hero

We meet at this conference in a year which is a special anniversary of various landmark events in US political history. Of course, that can be said regarding almost *any* year because of the pervasive and profound significance of politics, which is amplified by the special importance which we as political scientists attach to "*the political.*" Momentarily, I will cite some landmark events from particular years—years which, like this year, end in the number five or zero, as is our wont when considering the anniversaries of those major historical moments. I mean those events to serve as a backdrop for observations regarding American/ US politics, and political science more broadly, particularly in an era of growing racial diversity and economic disparity,

Let me state my core points and make a plea at the very outset: the levels and unique configurations of class inequality and racial diversity that have characterized the last several decades of US history—and there is much evidence for this—raise big questions for political science and political scientists to study. And understanding *the nexus between* differences or hierarchies associated with class dynamics and race/ethnicity, and gender, is immensely important. Yet—with some notable exceptions—they are too often examined entirely separately, overlooked, or not sufficiently engaged by research in our discipline. Standard political science perspectives certainly have had something substantial to say about these. But rather more can be done in terms of theory and empirical analysis to capture the breadth and depth of the large and significant issues present when economic inequality is linked to racial disparity present.

Alternative perspectives, or other states of mind, can conceptualize and consider the issues differently and be more analytically open and disposed to considering different dimensions of inequality, as well as connections between them. (I would also hope for and look forward to newly developed theories, evidentiary bases, and methods that could be brought to bear on these issues as well.)

Now, I certainly recognize that the nature and magnitude of the issues I will identify present difficult intellectual challenges (which I, myself, have not entirely thought through, but I will explore today). Nevertheless, I'm convinced that political science should, and I'm entirely confident that we can, play a larger and more integral role in grappling with the political roots, meanings, and implications of these and other dimensions of inequality. I offer some observations about the research, or lack thereof, and indicate suggestions about how we might think about and do more in these respects.

I will come at these concerns as follows: (1) noting some developments that influenced the present in social and political terms, and other events in political science; (2) identifying intellectual guideposts that may help how we think about research issues of our day; (3) considering why race and class are not studied (more); (4) acknowledging that to be the case and how the questions *have* been studied, as well as noting some reservations about these; (5) providing several examples from research in which I have been involved, both directly and indirectly, which suggest how we might or can study these questions; (6) then concluding. I begin with reference to a number of landmark events in American history and in the history of our discipline to foreground and serve as a segue to broader points.

Developments

This year, 2015, marks 150 years since the end of the Civil War and ratification that same year of the Thirtenth Amendment to the US Constitution, which ended slavery; ratification of the Fifteenth Amendment, regarding right to vote for former slaves, occurred in 1870 (and the fundamentally important Fourteenth Amendment was ratified in between, in 1868). These pre-date the establishment of the American Political Science Association by thirty years or more. The Nineteenth Amendment, regarding women's suffrage, was ratified 95 years ago. It has been 80 years since the passage of the Social Security Act and of major labor legislation, as well the enactment of laws, leading to major infrastructure throughout the United States, including here in the San Francisco Bay area, which we use to this day.

It is fifty years since the passage of the Voting Rights Act (VRA) and of major Immigration legislation, which alone and in combination transformed the social composition of the United States and of its electorate. The Elementary and Secondary Education Act, Pell Grants, the Head Start program, and Medicare and Medicaid also emerged in 1965—as did the Watts riots in Los Angeles. It is forty years since the 1975 extension of the VRA to "language minorities," and twenty-five years since the passage of the Americans with Disabilities Act (ADA). Hurricane Katrina devastated New Orleans ten years ago. Just five years ago, in 2010, the Affordable Care Act (ACA, often referred to as Obamacare) became law, and its signature importance was described in lively, expletive-deleted, terms by Vice President Joe Biden at the time.

To note but a few important developments in international relations—it has been seventy years since the first use of the atomic bomb, the end of World War II and the creation of the United Nations, first headquartered here in San Francisco. It has been 55 years now since the Cuban Embargo Act (October 1960), which was situated in the context of the Cold War United States. Regular US combat troops were deployed in Vietnam in 1965 (fifty years ago); the United States completed its pullout from Viet Nam in 1975.

And we meet here in this place, California, which became a state 165 years ago in 1850, as part of the treaty ending the Mexican-American War, an event of tremendous importance in American history. California's vast population (about 38 million) is by a large margin the biggest in the country, and comprises about ten percent of the nation's population. It is also one of several "majority-minority" states in terms of its demographic profile.

One could easily go on and on, and I'm certain others could identify many other, and different, events but I leave it at that for now.

We can also identify a few landmarks *within* the American Political Science Association and our discipline and contemplate their significance, as well as how and how much they may or may not parallel the broader changes just noted. Founded in 1903, the association grew incrementally until after World War II, and its membership expanded dramatically in the 1960s and 1970s. In 1950 (65 years ago) Ralph Bunche received the Nobel Peace prize; he became the APSA's first black president (in 1953–54). A major book award given by our association and

Figure 1. Street sign in Nairobi, Kenya
Source: Hero and Levy 2015.

a summer program for young aspiring political scientists came to bear his name, and his name has been recognized elsewhere in the world.

The first woman president of the APSA, Judith Sklar, gave her Presidential Address just a quarter century ago, in 1990. A decade ago in 2005, Margaret Levi, gave her presidential address, and Levi's two immediate predecessors were Theda Skocpol and Suzanne Rudolph. This marked the first (and only) time the APSA has had three women presidents in succession. Tomorrow [September 4, 2015] the association will formally install its ninth (but *only* its ninth) woman president.

Also within our association, the Race, Ethnicity and Politics (REP) Organized Section was established 20 years ago. And the Perestroika movement emerged in 2000, 15 years ago. Formed within five years of each other, the REP section and Perestroika had some ostensibly convergent interests. But they also diverged, to some degree, in their intellectual orientations, in their social composition, and in other important ways (Monroe 2005; Warren 2005; Scott 2005). We can also ponder what the emergence other formal entities such as additional Organized Sections might mean. One section to quickly note here is a new[er] one focusing on "Class Inequality," which, along with the now-longstanding REP section, engages concerns about inequality, and at the same time brings some similar—yet also divergent—perspectives to bear on those and related questions. Whether, and if, these sections will intersect and interact remains to be seen, but their very co-existence in certain ways is consistent with some of my points about the frequent separation of race and class in the study of American politics; that separation may well be justified in many circumstances but the potential connections should not be overlooked.

The events highlighted here are obviously but a tiny, tiny slice, and touch upon only certain types of political phenomena and developments. But as we think about these, they begin to suggest the relation of political science to its subject matter and its relation to larger society—i.e., they raise questions about what we study, and why, as well as how we do and how we think we should study politics. Further, and in a related vein, as we bring critical lenses to that which we study, we also mirror the dispositions, attributes, and strengths or deficits of the socio-political and intellectual milieu of which we are a part and in which we are imbedded. Accordingly, this should lead us to be constantly mindful of what we assume or take to be "normal" or "natural" or "neutral" (or all of these) in the world of politics and in our scholarship.

How might we think about and approach these concerns? These types of concerns surface in various venues, including previous APSA presidential addresses, a few of which I will touch upon here. While these addresses are different they share important attributes: they are characterized by erudition and subtle passion and they affirm—and at the same time vigorously challenge—us as scholars and teachers of political science. My later comments are informed by the spirit of these perspectives.

Precedents and Guidance

Margaret Levi's presidential address ten years ago thoughtfully revisited and rearticulated "why we need(ed) a '[new] theory of government,'" engaging issues of how to make governments more representative and effective (Levi 2006). I suggest we need to reconsider or create new (empirical) theories of race and class, and their intersection.

Two years ago, Jane Mansbridge implored us to join her in reflecting upon "what is political science for," i.e., the basic purpose(s) of political science (Mansbridge 2014). I suggest that studying issues such as race and economic inequality is a worthy goal, having the kind of substantive purposes and normative underpinnings that Mansbridge suggests.

On the other hand, several presidential addresses have called on us to be self-aware and self-critical as a discipline. In his 1981 presidential address, Charles Lindblom cautioned scholars of American politics against accepting, indeed perhaps creating, overly facile assessments of the American political system, and declared the need to adopt "another state of mind," i.e., to take seriously alternative interpretations to the dominant, and what he saw as overly simplistic, characterizations of American politics (Lindblom 1982).

And in one of the most provocative presidential addresses ever, in the early 1990s Theodore Lowi contended that we should be cognizant of and concerned that we could, and had actually, "become what we study." Lowi posited that "US political science is itself a political phenomenon." And further, that "every [political] regime tends to produce a politics consonant with itself; therefore, every regime tends to produce a political science consonant with itself. Consonance between the state and political science is a problem worthy of the attention of every political scientist" (Lowi 1992).[1] I will explore partially the consonance of political science views and understandings of race and of class that mirror even as they may also seek to critically assess "real world" politics and "the state."

Other Presidential Addresses focused on distinct features of American history and their implications for the substance of and the discipline's approach to studying the political system. For example, Lucius Barker (1994) in 1993 and Dianne Pinderhughes (2009) in 2008, with different emphases, stressed the enduring and contemporary relevance of race as an element of American political history. In that spirit, I continue to seriously focus on race, but also extend to and grapple with its increased complexity, associated with Latinos, and Asians, and immigration, and other developments, and more directly bring class, and gender into account.

I note one more Presidential Address. Robert Putnam's 2002 address spoke eloquently about pressing issues of social justice and said that "perhaps the most fundamental problem facing America, and most other advanced countries." will be to reconcile "the demands of diversity, equality, and community." He added that "this is a quintessential *big issue*" and "political scientists have a professional responsibility to contribute to this nascent debate" (Putnam 2003, italics original).

There is so much to agree with in the comments Putnam's made at the time, and he was correct in suggesting that the issues would become more pressing. These thirteen years later affirm that the issues are indeed bigger ones—and this is so despite or perhaps because of the election of the first African American president in 2008, something that few, if any, would have anticipated in 2002.

At the same time, I would contend that issues regarding diversity and inequality were not then, in 2002, necessarily "nascent." A considerable number of political scholars, particularly those studying race/ethnicity in American politics, had been examining the structures and the concentration of political and economic inequality among certain groups—racial minority groups—in the society for years. Attention to racial diversity and economic (in)equality had been examined and had been the staple of a larger body of research for a long time, and the interconnection between race and economic status was, of necessity, a central feature given the historical patterns. For example, arguments about "multiple theoretical traditions" (Smith 1993), "*faces* of inequality" (Hero 1998), *two-tiered* pluralism (Hero 1992) and neo-liberal (economic) orientations and (racial) paternalism in 1996 welfare policy "reform," and also links to criminal justice policy (Soss, Fording, and Schram 2011; Branton and Jones 2005) had been made some years before. But much of this research had somehow escaped attention, was overlooked or ignored, or the focus on a range of inter-related inequalities was not recognized. Most pointedly here, however, political science needs to theorize and examine the dynamics of racial/ethnic, class, and gender inequality much further.

Theoretical Context and Framing

The critical policy junctures spotlighted earlier have mostly to do with civil rights and formal racial/ethnic equality on the one hand, but also to policies pertaining to economic opportunity and security and equality on the other hand. Those two are also deeply affected and mediated by gender and vice versa (Penner and Saperstien 2013). The rise in inequality in the United States (and elsewhere) challenges democratic governance. Better addressing this requires more and more nuanced attention that instills, but also goes beyond, the important goals of "accuracy" in our research endeavors regarding some aspects of the inequalities, and suggests that we think further in terms of the adequacy, i.e., fuller and more complete assessments and appropriateness of research, that it betters suits or fits the complex nature of the politics of class and race in our studies of these matters.

Other disciplines, particularly sociology, history, and economics, have extensively explored various aspects of these issues. But the distinctive and comprehensive analytical lenses that only political science is uniquely suited to bring have not been as prominent as they should and could be. Robert Reich gave a lively presentation at a Plenary session earlier today [September 3, 2015] titled "Why Economics [Policy] Is Too Important to Be Left to Economists." My plea is that racial and class inequality is too important for political scientists to not do and to not have done more—and for so much of the study of these concerns to have been conducted in other fields. This raises the question of why there is often inattention or disconnect of race and class in political science research, and in public discourse as well. Several possible explanations, which are not mutually exclusive, come to mind.

Maybe it is simply that each phenomenon—class and race—is just not seen as being as important or prominent or as legitimate a *political* phenomenon or they are not seen being as consistently or deeply connected as I'm claiming or assuming. Alternatively, some might say these issues have in fact been studied quite a lot (and appropriately and effectively). If either of these is mostly or entirely the case, then my basic premise is called into question. But I think not, and will thus set those views aside.

More generally, they may not be studied more, or more directly, because race as well as class may be underspecified and underappreciated in common research approaches. Most pointedly, a number of major studies omit attention to race altogether—quite some number of analyses—including some which purport to assess inequality broadly or "general theories" of American politics. Also, some prominent research approaches tend to (unconsciously) "de-racialize" politics, while others de-politicize race; this may also occur in "real world" politics).

De-racialization of politics often occurs in (standard) "pluralist" renderings of politics and studies oriented around *competitive* (Hero 1998, 1992), or what I've come to think of as liberal, pluralism. Racial groups are not "really" fundamentally different substantively, in kind (qualitatively), than other groups, but only or mostly differ in degree (quantitatively, in the amount of resources, prestige, etc.). In a related vein, standard pluralism takes as *given*, as some of its basic tenets—such as fair "rules of the game," multiple access points, dispersed/non-cumulative resources, etc.—that scholars of race believe need to be investigated in the first place. Even studies which, very appropriately, examine "biased pluralism" typically confine their analysis of bias to economic resource differentials, overlooking or understating (the potential impact of) race (Hero 1992, 1998).

On the other hand, research perspectives may de-politicize race by overly emphasizing that the nature and workings of "civil society" is the primary—virtually sole—issue in democratic polities rather than politics, as such, including interest groups or state institutions and hence, muffles an understanding of race as a political phenomenon. Thus, studies with an emphasis on "civic association," social networks, and communitarian-type underpinnings (or which also suggest a consensual, perhaps communitarian, pluralism) sometimes seem to assume away race as "political" (Hero 2007, 1998). In a different way, this may also occur when class and/ or racial inequality is seen as largely a matter of "market" forces or of an "invisible [ostensibly non-political] hand."[2]

Other plausible explanations as to why race and class are not studied together as might be anticipated—and, I would suggest, than is desirable (and that if and when studied, they are approached separately)—may include normative, conceptual, and empirical reasons, and some combinations of these. Normatively, race has been fundamental, salient, and deeply troublesome, the "original sin," because the specific form of inequality departs from—is the *most* fundamentally inconsistent with—American core values. While certainly disconcerting, economic inequality may be seen as the lesser evil, grounded in claims of achievement (rather than ascription, as is race) and thus in some ways is more legitimate to address in research. Also, race has been legally/formally addressed in civil rights legislation and is a protected category, which, to some, implies a degree of resolution in ways that arguably is not the case regarding class and rising economic inequality. Further attention to how race and class have been juxtaposed normatively (and in other ways) is revisited extensively in later sections of this essay.

From a conceptual standpoint, each notion—race and class—is complex, frequently ambiguous, fluid, having different meanings across time and by place, and are blurred in practical politics as well as in scholarly conceptualization and research. There is a great deal of differentiation within as well as between the political science research literatures, as well as in the "real world" as to how these phenomena are or can and should be understood, how to measure them and, more broadly, what they mean to begin with. For example, if we assume for the sake of argument that broad agreement on definitions can be achieved, other issues such as whether objective or subjective indicators of class should be used, and, if *objective* indicators, which one[s], if *subjective* ones, which ones? And there are many other such debates about these matters.

There are also (empirical) questions of "*where* to look for" these, which has differed a great deal. For example, within the literature on race there is a vast body of research unto itself on individual-level attitudes; there are debates about old-style racism and racial resentment, symbolic racism versus principled conservatism, explicit and implicit (racial) bias, and so on. Beyond these micro-level analyses, other research focuses on the macro- or meso-levels, typically posing somewhat different questions and reaching different answers. Cumulatively, over all conclusions are unclear or highly conditional, and there is little attention to matters of economic class and inequality.

I conclude this section by noting two observations from recent years which capture some of the dilemmas in our understanding and assessments of these issues.

"Many decades after the achievements of the civil rights movement, our society is still plagued by inequality. To some extent, inequality is the *enduring legacy* of the age of Jim Crow, red-lining, and other once-legal practices. The *more proximate cause*, however, is the enormous rise in *economic inequality* in the last three decades, *trends that have transformed our social structure and, tragically, reinforced in many ways the racial stratification of the past.* (Mettler 2008, 533, emphasis added)

Reducing [formal/legal racial] discrimination made it easier to justify rewarding the/an [economic] elite." (Stille 2011)

These comments are but some of many examples showing that issues of race and class inequality have in fact been acknowledged and engaged in recent years. An enduring legacy, the past versus the proximate, and the rationalization and juxtaposition of the two social phenomena have been debated not just recently but more or less intensely from time to time and is still important to consider. A sampling of how these have been addressed in American previous scholarship is useful.

Sampling Political Science Thinking about Race and Class in American Politics

To some degree the simultaneous consideration of race and class and of racial groups and social classes has (at least implicitly) been a staple in American political science assessments of the nature and orientations of the American regime. At the Founding, the presence of slavery was central to debates about and became imbedded in the representational structure of the US Congress and other constitutional provisions. At the same time, Madison (*Federalist No. 10*) claimed that the "most common and durable sources of factions" had been differences in economic standing—those "with and without property, creditors vs debtors, a manufacturing interest, a mercantile interest ... divide [nations] into different *classes*" (Madison [1788], emphasis added). Explanations for "American exceptionalism," i.e., its ostensibly smallish or minimalist welfare state and the forms it has taken, is often attributed to the difficulty historically of creating class-based political coalitions because of racial animus. Similarly, analyses on issues of race, and certain policies, by scholars of American political development (APD) have documented the impact of racial considerations on the formulation of policies regarding basic economic security, such as social security (Lieberman 1998), and other policies adopted during the eras "when affirmative action was white" (Katznelson 2005).

In the aftermath of the civil rights legislation, race has been used to explain "why Americans hate welfare" (Gilens 1999) and the connections are also apparent in analyses of "how the poor became black" (Gilens 2003), linking race and redistributive or economic security-related policies. The evolution of race as an issue was seen as integral to the "transformation" of American politics in the 1950s–1960s and beyond (Carmines and Stimson 1989). The broad and deep impact of race in the public policies and politics of the American states has been shown as well (Hero 1998). Also research on blacks and Hispanics regarding education policies demonstrated the importance of race as well as class factors (Meier, Stewart, and England 1989; Meier and Stewart 1991).

Analyses concerning "disciplining the poor" make such connections as well. The convergence of *racial* "paternalism" and "neo-liberal" (economic) policies in the adoption and implementation of the 1996 "welfare reform" legislation has been powerfully demonstrated (Soss, Fording, and Schram 2011). Furthermore, the importance of race, the implications of America's broad racial dispositions, have been relevant beyond domestic politics as well, influencing US foreign policy decisions, along with military, political economy, and other considerations (Katzenstein 2010). Yet many such issues are under-explored in historical/institutional or in more contemporary contexts.

How race and class have played out in "actual politics" has been debated for many years. In 1974, Wolfinger, discussing *"ethnic* succession" in northeastern US cities (particularly New Haven, Connecticut) argued that "irrespective of the lines of coincidence between ethnicity and class, ethnic consciousness retards political expression of class-based interests" (Wolfinger 1974, 63–64).

On the other hand, Wolfinger characterized Glazer and Moynihan's arguments in *Beyond the Melting Pot* (1963) as a school of thought that "race allows us to talk about class," i.e., ethnic politics is a way of having class politics "without offending egalitarian myths" (Wolfinger 1974, 63). In Glazer and Moynihan's words, which drew inferences about racial/ethnic politics and class by studying early twentieth-century politics in immigrant-heavy New York City: "In a democratic culture that has never much liked to identify individuals in terms of social classes... the ethnic shorthand is a considerable advantage" (Glazer and Moynihan 1963, 301–302, emphasis added).

An analysis which brings further breadth and more completeness to these questions assessed relief (or welfare) policies of the early decades of the twentieth century (before the New Deal) in various US localities found there were "*three* worlds of relief." These worlds were shaped by race *and* class or economic forces, as well as by local institutions. That is, different racial/ethnic groups, different political economies, as well as different local political institutions—white ethnics in the industrialized northeast (who were included through "machine politics"), black sharecroppers in the south (excluded through Jim Crow and various other social mechanisms), Mexican fieldworkers in the southwest (constrained by deportation and other threats)—were relevant for local welfare policy (non)decisions (Fox 2012).

In stark contrast, several major latter-day political science studies on inequality gave virtually no attention to race at all. A widely noted recent (2014) article tested four "theories of American democracy": majoritarian electoral democracy, economic-elite domination, majoritarian pluralism, and biased pluralism. Economic inequality is at the center of the analysis and is accordingly considered carefully—particularly in the economic elite domination, and biased pluralism (meaning economically biased) theories. The article's general finding that oligarchy as much (or more) than democracy accurately describes American politics is powerful and deeply sobering. But the word "race" is not mentioned at all in this article (Gilens and Page 2014).[3] While one might thus accept the essential accuracy of the findings, one wonders if there can be an adequate assessment, particularly of a (purported) "theory[ies] of 'American politics'" and equality—in which groups are a central component—which does not at least reference, much less examine, racial and minority groups as part of the analysis in some (significant) way.

Keith Banting and Will Kymlicka's (2006, 10–22) considerations of "multiculturalism and the welfare state" may be instructive for present purposes. Their assessments of nations' recognition of groups through "multicultural" policies and how this may affect levels of support for redistributive (welfare) policies is revealing. I draw on and seek to adapt their theoretical framing to inform understanding of political discourse and the politics of race and class issues I have been discussing. Banting and Kymlicka contend that those policy debates can be analyzed as to whether policies (multicultural, and welfare) are seen as "crowd[ing] out" each other in terms of public debates and public support for policies in that only finite time and attention and resources are available to address each (or both). Or, when the substance of one policy (multiculturalism) might undercut support for the other (welfare), "erosion" of a political coalition in support of the latter can occur. There can also be a "misdiagnosis," where one set of observers perceive that others (are purported to) incorrectly diagnose the bases of inequality as to what is the "real problem," leading the presumed "correct" perspective to dismiss the other. To give attention to one in actual policy leads to dismissal of the other. Banting and Kymlicka put forth evidence that supports, but also considerable evidence that refutes, the claims about crowding out, erosion, and misdiagnosis (2006). The understandings—the perceptions, and the realities—of the relation of race-based (or multiculturalism) and economic-based (welfare) policies is complex and requires careful theoretical, substantive, and normative reflection; by extension, that can also be said about race and class inequality more directly.

The issues seem yet more complex in the context of American politics debates and in political science research, given the country's unique racial history. Not only are the two factors sometimes viewed as in tension or competition with one another as explanations. One may be seen to "absorb" the other, they may also obscure one another, and there are different views as to which is a legacy or proximate cause, which is primary or secondary, whether one affects (certain aspects of) inequality more, whether impacts are direct or indirect, whether they are viewed as compartmentalized or combined, whether they are assessed in absolute or aggregate versus relative terms, and on and on. We need to be attentive to the possibility that political discussions, and research, treat race and class in ways that conflates, confuses or offsets them, through commission or omission. At the same time, we need to recognize that is it frequently not "either/or," but "both/and," and that these are mediated by other factors such as gender, institutions, and so on.

The importance and breadth and depth of interactions and political implications of these social forces clearly present formidable challenges, but—or, therefore—ones we should take up. I give some examples of how this has been done and how more might be done.

Race and Class in American Politics and Political Science

The Great Divergence and Class—and Racial—Inequality

Economic inequality has, of course, received a tremendous attention associated with the great divergence of America's rich from its middle class, which thrust it to the center of American politics, punctuated by the "great recession" beginning in 2007. To many observers, the income (and wealth) divide has supplanted race as the country's primary political fault line. However, such a conclusion potentially overlooks or understates the persistent "racial structuring" of economic inequality and that race should be considered in relation to economic forces. The two may (perversely) supplement each other, but sometimes to a degree and in ways that are not altogether obvious.

With that possibility in mind, a study of the US states was undertaken which disaggregated or "decomposed" income inequality into "between-race" and "between-class" components (using the Theil Index), which facilitates understanding the breadth and depth or the structure of inequality. Drawing on data from three decades, 1980 to 2010, evidence (summarized in figure 2) shows—or simply, pointedly reaffirms—that economic inequality has, indeed, increased dramatically over that period. At the same time, the evidence indicates that inequality between races remained a steady share of total income inequality over this period nationally, and in most states. That between-race inequality has changed little (perhaps even gotten worse) is especially striking these many years after the Civil Rights or other legislation (Hero and Levy 2015).

Beyond this powerful descriptive evidence, however, analysis *also* shows that between-race inequality influences state welfare-policy (measured several ways) decisions—substantially, and negatively so—whereas between-class and total levels of inequality (as well as the racial composition of the population itself) has *not* (refer to figure 3). Clearly, the upsurge in economic inequality is staggering, yet it is striking that it apparently has had essentially no impact on welfare policy in the states. On the other hand, (ongoing) between-race inequality does have major impacts (Hero and Levy 2015). (Other research on related issues and policies is less clear.) These findings underscore the importance of careful attention to race and class inequality in our analyses, as well as their implications for public polices.

President Obama's 2015 State of the Union Address

Another piece of evidence I note is President Barack Obama's [January 20] 2015 State of the Union (SOTU) address.[4] Examining this speech is useful, at least for the illustrative purposes I intend here; though my observations are admittedly selective and suggestive, I think they help illuminate the parameters or the (acceptable) bounds of contemporary public discourse on these significant issues of class and race. SOTUs are one of the most visible, institutionalized events and rituals in American politics. In those speeches, a president identifies pressing contemporary concerns (as s/he sees them) in relation, at least implicitly, to larger values, goals, and policy agenda, and places them in a larger historical and political context.[5]

Two aspects of the speech that I would bring attention to are, first, the organization or placement of issues and topics, i.e., *where*, at what point(s) in the speech, they are raised and,

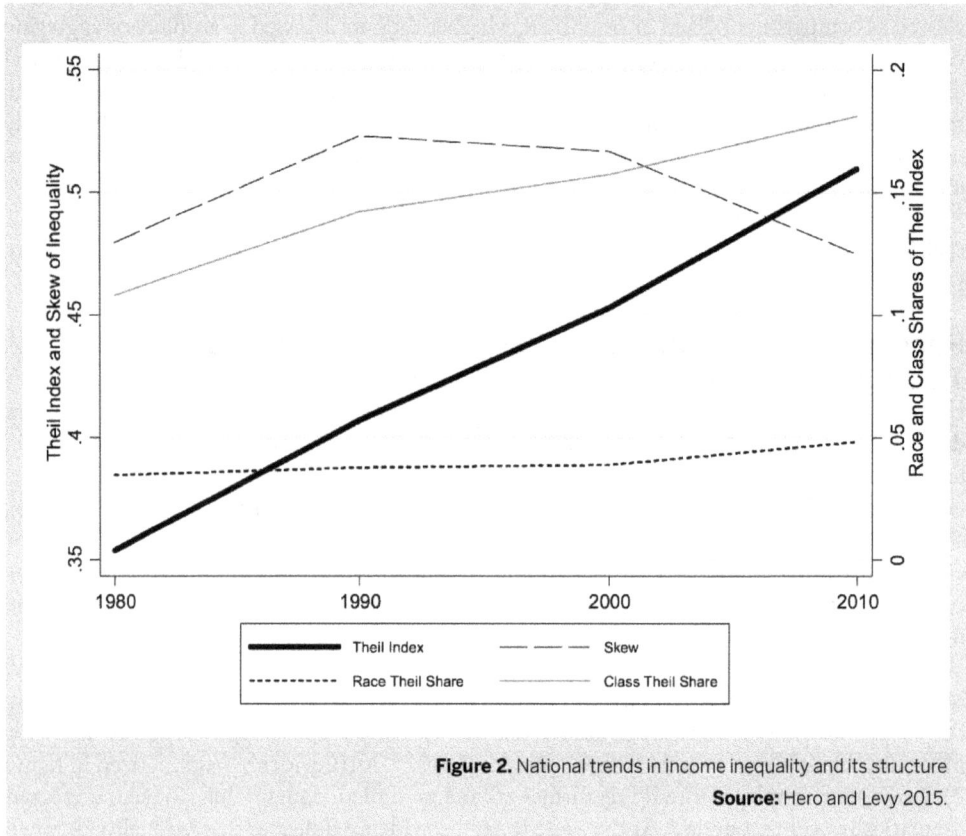

Figure 2. National trends in income inequality and its structure
Source: Hero and Levy 2015.

second, *how* issues associated with class or race are talked about, as well as whether race and class are discussed in some way that connects them to each other. In the case of President Obama, I recognize that these issues are yet more complex in that the message is presented by a unique and particular messenger, i.e., the first African American president.[6]

It is not uncommon for SOTUs to be structured into sections on domestic policy on the one hand, and foreign policy on the other hand, and economic issues may be considered separately as well. A prominent theme in the 2015 SOTU address, one which was introduced not long after the first few pages of the speech, was middle-class economics. My very rough estimate is that about twenty percent of the address gave attention to such ostensible concerns, with an emphasis on economic *opportunity*. The day after the speech, media commentaries emphasized that theme as well. At the same time, some observers talked about the speech in terms of economic "inequality." Notably, however, the word "inequality" appeared only once in the speech.[7] On the other hand, there were numerous mentions of "hard work[ing]," "effort," and that one must "earn" and make oneself deserving. Also, equality of opportunity (not equality of condition or outcome) was said to be the appropriate goal. Interestingly, along with numerous mentions of middle class not once was the phrase "working *class*" mentioned; instead, middle class was juxtaposed to "lower *income*," or "working *families*," and other terms. (While the phrase "underclass" was once prominent in American political discourse, and suggested a combination of [lower] class and race, it is seldom heard these days. At the same time the now infrequent use of "working class" by politicians is interesting.)

Other words, having to do with "fair(ness)," a "fair shot," and "fair share" were also frequently invoked. References to child care, sick leave, maternity leave, health care, etc. to support workers were also interspersed. A belief in the need for equality and fairness of opportunity, as well as

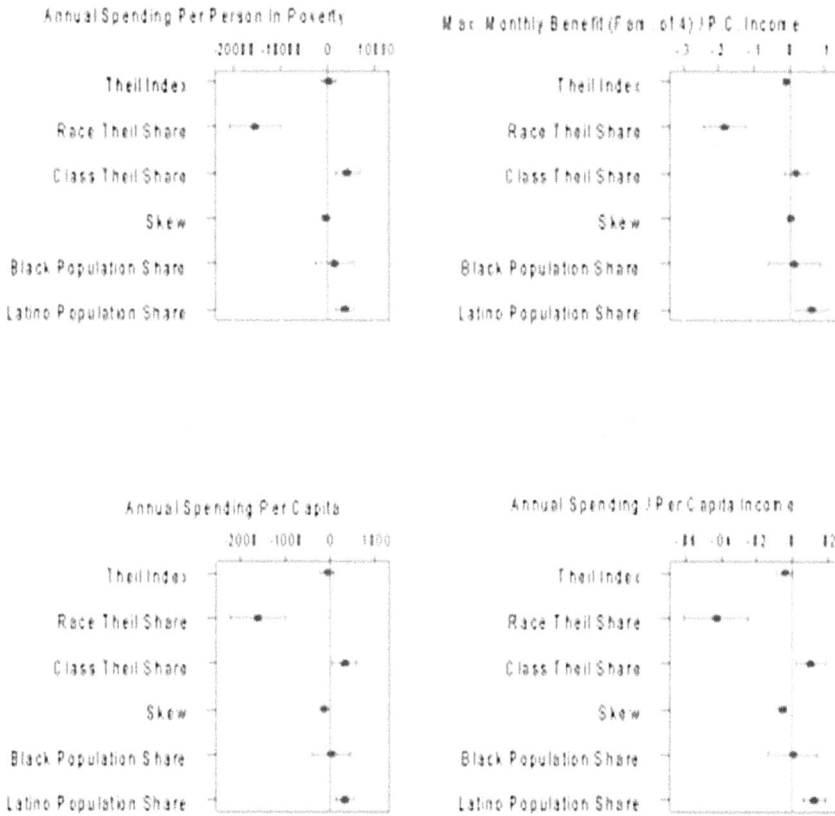

Figure 3. Relationships of racial and class inequality, and demography on welfare policy in the US states

mentions of wages—minimum wage (two mentions); high(er) wages (five mentions), as was "equal pay for women." For the most part, issues relevant to economic well-being (or inequality per se) were not linked to racial factors (or racial inequality) at all.

Obama noted that "40% of our students *choose* community college" (emphasis added); this seems to assume or imply, perhaps too readily, a degree of free choice or agency, rather than possibly necessity, particularly if an individual might actually prefer other (higher, or better) alternatives.[8] Obama added that students must "earn it" [free community college tuition] with "grades and graduation." Regarding unions, he said that "we still need laws that strengthen rather than weaken unions, and give American workers a voice," and nothing more.

These broad comments about class issues, middle-class economics, etc. are "color blind," and many observers, especially critics of race-conscious policies, would say they *should* be. But it is not inconceivable that they might have been raised at least somewhat differently, noting some disproportionate patterns. Finally, comments of an economic populism flavor—such as the super-rich, lobbyists, loopholes, bailouts—sprinkled the speech but were hardly prominent.

The second point I raise has to do with *where* and *how* issues associated with race are talked about, as well as whether race and class are discussed in some way that connects them to each other. It was not until toward the end of the SOTU speech (around pages 15–17 of a 17 page speech) that a set of domestic issues pertaining to certain social groups often having some gender or some racial/ethnic dimension, were discussed (again, recall that economic issues were posed ear-

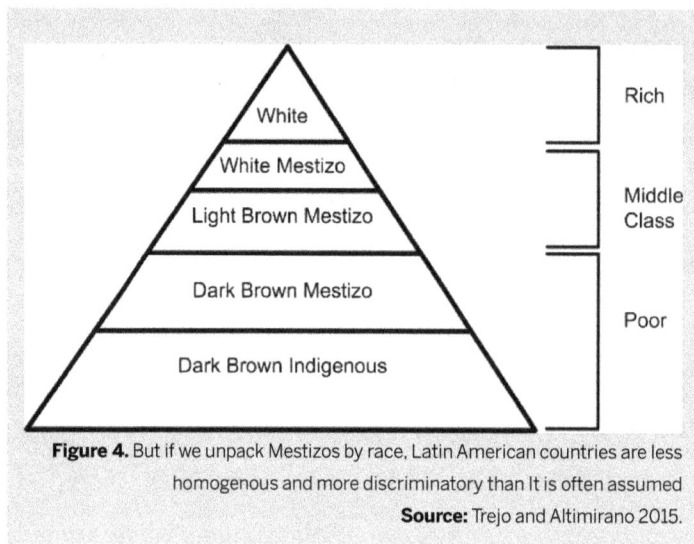

Figure 4. But if we unpack Mestizos by race, Latin American countries are less homogenous and more discriminatory than It is often assumed
Source: Trejo and Altimirano 2015.

ly in the address). It seems fair to say these were discussed in tempered fashion and indirectly, and that racially-relevant issues were discussed in color-blind ways. This occurred in rapid succession and in a couple of pages, in something like the order I present here. The only time the word "race" is used in the entire speech (as a social trait or factor) is when Obama says (around page 15) that he "grew up in Hawaii, a melting pot of races and customs." The allusion to an older narrative of race/ethnicity in the United States—a "melting pot"—is itself intriguing, as is the general tenor of his remarks on such concerns.

Obama makes a number of broadly and ostensibly group- and policy-related references, stressing commonalities or common ground, though difference is also part of the narrative. How he talks about, or does not talk about, the issues is notable. The "social construction of target populations" as developed by Ingram and Schneider (1993)—in terms of groups being "(re) constructed" positively or negatively, and as weak or strong—comes to mind here, reframing so as to soften negative perceptions and making certain groups or behaviors seem less "deviant."

To wit:

Passions still fly on immigration, but surely we can all see something of ourselves in the *striving young student*, and agree that no one benefits when a *hardworking mom* is snatched from her child, and that it's possible to shape a law that upholds our tradition as a nation of laws and a nation of immigrants.

We may have different *takes on the events of Ferguson and New York*. But surely we can understand a *father* who fears his *son* can't walk home without being harassed. And surely we can understand the *wife* who won't rest until *the police officer she married* walks through the front door at the end of his shift.

This framing may be understandable and I am not necessarily criticizing this phrasing in the address, but emphasize its nature or content, which avoids any (direct) references to race (or racial), or class dimensions or to (in)equality. In both these instances, some notion of family (relations) and to certain virtues is invoked—the mom, who is hardworking, and her child, and the striving young student; the father and the son; the wife whose husband is a police officer. And what transpired in Ferguson and New York are "events" which we can "take" or view differently. This is not to say these descriptions are necessarily wrong, but the word choices and phrasing are interesting, I think. It is also stated that

We still may not agree on *a woman's right to choose*, but surely, we can agree it's a good thing that teen pregnancies and abortions are nearing all-time lows, and that every woman *should have access to* the health care that she needs.

The emphasis is on "access;" the actual ability to receive "health care that she needs" is less clear.

A paragraph toward the very end of the address again stresses commonality and unity, and here we do see broad allusion to economic well-being—improving life chances—*and* to race, in naming several groups, as well as to gender and sexual orientation:

> [To] every child, in every neighborhood: your life matters, and we are as committed to improving your life chances as committed as we are to working on behalf of our own kids. … we are a people who see our differences as a great gift …a people who value the dignity and worth of every citizen: man and woman, young and old, black and white, Latino and Asian, immigrant and Native American, gay and straight, Americans with mental illness or physical disability. Everybody matters.

A couple of points about this last paragraph occur to me. The breadth and inclusiveness of groups noted is striking. The (broad) framing of economic well-being, in terms of *"improving. … life chances,"* though without specific reference to economic class or to economic (in)equality, is intriguing; e.g., there is no mention of other possible groupings such as "rich and poor," or "middle class and working class," or some such wording. Also interesting are the groupings and juxtapositions of social group dyads (as suggested by the placement of the commas) and the particular dyads selected, which don't suggest an "intersectionality" (or, on the other hand, "cross-cutting cleavages") of the various dyads, and is further interesting in how some of the dyads are presented. That is, racial groupings are "black and white"/"Latino Asian"—rather than, say, black, white, Latino, Asian (—i.e., all together). Whether this is accurate, or "correct," or (un)desirable is open to debate, but we can at least take note of this and consider what to make of it.

To be sure, and to be fair, President Obama has discussed these and related issues in other, different venues and has spoken about them rather differently, and often more forcefully. On the other hand, where and how race and class are discussed in this 2015 SOTU—i.e., by and large separately, and each arguably in very muted ways—probably obscures more than articulates any links between these social forces in contemporary political discourse(s). Recognizing and seeking to understand this as part of understanding racial and class inequalities in contemporary society is worthy of further scholarly attention.

Task Force on Race and Class Inequalities in the Americas

Finally, I bring attention to the APSA Task Force on "Racial and Class Inequalities in the Americas" which, as its name suggests, has engaged said issues directly. One of the papers for the Task Force (Hajnal and Trounstine 2015) assesses the effect of race and class on the urban (cities) political arena in the United States with an array of data regarding the role of these, and a number of other factors. It finds that both factors significantly affect political behavior and policy outcomes, but that "race is the primary driver of urban politics across most contexts." The impact of racial differences typically exceeds that of other factors frequently found to be powerful in politics, such as partisanship and ideology. "Minorities are grossly underrepresented among elected office and are more apt than whites to end up on the losing side of the vote, policy outcomes Local politics is "more likely to represent the interests of whites and the wealthy than the interests of minorities and the poor" (Hajnal and Trounstine 2015); refer to table 1.

Another paper from the Task Force, by Paul Pierson (2015), contends that race has (likely) played an important role in the extreme and "asymmetric" political and policy polarization, and policy "drift," in the American party system in recent years. He also points to the essentially unprecedented decisions of some of the US states to not accept federal funds to expand Medicaid or to refrain from involving themselves with federal health care programs, and suggests racial and associated considerations may play a role in this (at least indirectly.)

Race	38.3 (22.1)
Class	
Income	19.6 (12.8)
Education	18.2 (10.4)
Employment status	8.3 (3.7)
Other Demographics	
Age	21.4 (11.8)
Gender	5.8 (5.0)
Religion	29.9 (16.0)
Sexuality	14.9 (7.3)
Marital status	6.4 (6.9)
Union membership	7.1 (3.1)
Children	5.1 (3.6)
Political Orientation	
Liberal-Conservative ideology	27.4 (13.8)
Party identification	33.0 (18.7)

Table 1. Racial, demographic, and political divisions in urban elections: Average divide in vote for winning candidate in a group of US cities, Hajnal and Trounstine (2015). **Source:** Elections for mayor, council, advocate, comptroller, clerk, city attorney, and ballot propositions in New York, Los Angeles, Chicago, Houston, and Detroit. **Note:** (Standard Deviation in Parentheses).

An assessment of Mexico, a self-perceived "mestizo" nation, shows distinct patterns of economic status associated with race and skin color in that country; refer to figure 4 (Trejo and Altamirano 2015). On the other hand, Banting and Thompson argue that because of the timing of the formation of the Canadian welfare state, racial factors (has) had little impact on its policies. However, the "powerful persistence" of economic inequality, which is disproportionately found among indigenous populations, is "puzzling" (Banting and Thompson 2015). Other papers explore various other dimensions and venues and in other (Latin American) countries regarding class and racial inequality, and demonstrate their commonly deep and complex interrelations. The Task Force papers inform our understanding of fundamental questions of race and class in various contexts and with regard to an array of political dimensions in the United States and elsewhere.

Conclusion

The distinct and increasingly complicated constellations of racial diversity and large economic disparities of recent decades represents a unique—and disconcerting—period in American political history. It beckons us to engage questions regarding what about the political system(s)—its ideas, institutions, interests, and other elements—are and have been implicated in or may be related to the causes and consequences of these developments. Political science research has had a good deal to say about all this already—and that is as it should be, because this is part of the purpose of political science, "what political science is for," as Mansbridge might say. These reside squarely within our disciplinary domain. Accordingly, there is a vast amount more to be analyzed and much more that we, with our distinct critical theoretical perspectives, substantive foci, and varied approaches, can (and should) contribute to understanding these issues.

Considering and juxtaposing race and class, and bringing in assessments of gender as well, as regular practices in new theorizing and novel analyses of social and political factors germane to (in)equality spur us to vigorously engage major issues of our time, to pursue fundamental values which undergird political science inquiry. Beyond prominent mainstream theories, there are other rich analytical perspectives which have been developed that directly acknowledge racial legacies as well as class and its implications. A host of related questions that I have posed are but some of the pressing concerns which I hope—and urge—scholars of American politics—and throughout political science—to continue to or begin to address—indeed to embrace—such challenges in our studies. Yes, doing so is immensely challenging, and in various ways. But doing so reflects, (re)affirms, and furthers some of the most compelling purposes and aspirations of our discipline.

Reprinted from Rodney E. Hero. 2016. "American Politics and Political Science in an Era of Growing Racial Diversity and Economic Disparity." Perspectives on Politics *14 (1). Cambridge University Press: 7–20. doi:10.1017/S1537592715003199.*

Notes

1. I'm not necessarily arguing that the specific criticisms or challenges raised by Lindblom or by Lowi remain accurate today (and, I suspect, one could challenge how accurate they were when written). However, their concerns are probably still relevant, though in different ways, to different degrees, and so on. One might thus think of their perspectives as general "cautionary tales" that encourage us to look critically at ourselves as a discipline.

2. Perhaps there is also "class without politics" in that relations between different individuals and groups, or classes, in the economic sphere (e.g., owners versus workers) are seen as (almost entirely) determined by the "invisible hand of the market." Classes exist but politics (of inequality) rooted in class is thereby obscured in this scenario. And, finally, a "politics without class" might exist, which would imply an aggregation of individuals aspiring to or perceiving themselves as part of a broad "middle-class."

3. But these scholars are hardly alone. I wish not to single out individual scholars, but I do wish to stress how striking I find this, and that I think it rather powerfully demonstrates the points I wish to make about inattention to race, and, to a lesser degree to class. In addition to several other recent works, we find puzzling inattention to race (and class) even in the scholarship of some of the most eminent political scientists in the history of the discipline. An article in 1977 by Robert Dahl, "On Removing Certain Impediments to Democracy in the United States," indicates this. There he discusses major developments in American political history, which are, he said, commitments to (1) a liberal political and constitutional order that gave primacy to the protection of certain political and civil rights among citizens [the Founding]; (2) about 1800–1836 [Jacksonian era]—commitment to belief that only proper constitutional and pol systems comprised democracy; (3) corporate capitalism from the late 1800s to the early 1900s; (4) emergence of the welfare state beginning with the New Deal; and (5) commitment to play an international role as a world power in the aftermath of World War II. One could readily agree on the importance of the events and periods noted and find them accurate depictions. But many analysts, myself included, see a glaring inadequacy owing to the neglect of race by not mentioning the Civil War and Reconstruction and the Civil Rights movement, which are conspicuous and surprising. In effect, though presumably not intentionally, landmark events regarding formal procedural quality are absent. Also, note that this article was published in years well after the publication of Dahl's seminal book, *Who Governs?*.

4. All my discussion here about President Obama's comments draw directly from his State of the Union Message, delivered January 15, 2015.

5. On the other hand, some of the very attributes that make such a speech worthy of attention might also be reasons why *not* to attach too much significance to them. Such speeches are carefully crafted, and vetted, to communicate with a wide (the widest) audience and appeal to core American values, though giving specific emphasis to or understandings of issues and values. The limitations of examining a SOTU speech notwithstanding, they are still a leading expression of contemporary ideas and issues by the US president.

6. Let me make clear what I *am* trying to do here, and what I am *not* doing. I am *not* directly passing normative judgments on Obama's points. Rather, I am exploring the parameters of race and class discourse in this period of diversity and racial and economic inequality and how I interpret how they are talked about, particularly through a lens of social relations suggested by economic or social and racial group (non)references, and whether and how they are presented in this SOTU address.

7. There were 106 articles in the *New York Times* (58) and *Washington Post* (48) newspaper editions in the week following that included the phrase "State of the Union." Of those 106, 59 articles

included the terms "class" or "income" or "inequality," and 13 included the terms "race" or "African American" in a non-trivial way (i.e., not "race" in the sense of an election campaign).

8. More than half of all Hispanic undergraduate students attended a community college in 2010. That may be viewed "positively" or not so positively depending on whether we think about these issues in relative terms (i.e., Hispanics relative to non-Hispanics) or in absolute terms (i.e., the within-group increase or trajectory of educational attainment over time).

References

Banting, Keith and Will Kymlicka. 2006. "Multiculturalism and the Welfare State: Setting the Context." In *Multiculturalism and the Welfare State: Recognition and Redistribution in Contemporary Democracies.* Edited by Keith Banting and Will Kymlicka. Oxford: Oxford University Press.

Banting, Keith and Debra Thompson. 2015. "The Puzzling Persistence of Racial Inequality in Canada." Paper for Task Force on "Racial and Class Inequalities in the Americas." Washington, DC: American Political Science Association.

Barker, Lucius J. 1994. "Limits of Political Strategy: A Systemic View of the African American Experience." Presidential Address to the American Political Science Association, 1993. *American Political Science Review* 88 (1): 1–13.

Branton, Regina P. and Bradford S. Jones. 2005. "Reexamining Racial Attitudes: The Conditional Relationship between Diversity and Socioeconomic Environment." *American Journal of Political Science* 49 (2): 359–72.

Carmines, Edward G. and James A. Stimson. 1989. *Race and the Transformation of American Politics.* Princeton, NJ: Princeton University Press.

Dahl, Robert A. 1961. *Who Governs? Democracy and Power in an American City.* New Haven: Yale University Press.

Dahl, Robert A. 1977. "On Removing Certain Impediments to Democracy in the United States." *Political Science Quarterly* 92 (1): 1–20.

Fox, Cybelle. 2012. *Three Worlds of Relief: Race, Immigration, and the American Welfare State from the Progressive Era to the New Deal.* Princeton, NJ: Princeton University Press.

Gilens, Martin. 1999. *Why Americans Hate Welfare: Race, Media and the Politics of Antipoverty Policy.* Chicago, IL: University of Chicago Press.

Gilens, Martin. 2003. "How the Poor Became Black." In *Race and the Politics of Welfare Reform.* Edited by Sanford F. Schram, Joe Soss and Richard C. Fording. Ann Arbor: University of Michigan Press.

Gilens, Martin and Benjamin I. Page. 2014. "Testing Theories of American Politics: Elites, Interest Groups, and Average Citizens." *Perspectives on Politics* 12 (3): 564–81.

Glazer, Nathan and Daniel P. Moynihan. 1963. *Beyond the Melting Pot: The Negroes, Puerto Rican, Jews, Italians, and Irish of New York City.* Cambridge: MIT Press.

Hajnal, Zoltan and Jessica Trounstine. 2015. "Race and Class Inequality in Local Politics" Paper for Task Force on "Racial and Class Inequalities in the Americas." Washington, DC: American Political Science Association.

Hero, Rodney E. 1992. *Latinos and the US Political System: Two-tiered Pluralism.* Philadelphia, PA: Temple University Press.

Hero, Rodney E. 1998. *Faces of Inequality: Social Diversity in American Politics.* New York: Oxford University Press.

Hero, Rodney E. 2007. *Racial Diversity and Social Capital: Equality and Community in America.* New York: Cambridge University Press.

Hero, Rodney E. and Morris Levy. 2015. "The Racial Structure of Inequality and Redistribution in the US States." Unpublished.

Katzenstein, Peter J. 2010. "'Walls' between 'Those People': Contrasting Perspectives on World Politics." Presidential Address to the American Political Science Association, 2009. *Perspectives on Politics* 8 (1): 11–25.

Katznelson, Ira. 2005. *When Affirmative Action was White: An Untold History of Racial Inequality in America.* New York, NY: W.W. Norton.

Levi, Margaret. 2006. "Why We Need a New Theory of Government." Presidential Address to the American Political Science Association, 2005. *Perspectives on Politics* 4 (1): 1–19.

Lieberman, Robert C. 1998. *Shifting the Color Line: Race and the American Welfare State.* Cambridge, MA: Harvard University Press.

Lindblom, Charles. 1982. "Another State of Mind." Presidential Address to the American Political Science Association, 1981. *American Political Science Review* 76 (1): 9–21.

Lowi, Theodore J. 1992. "The State in Political Science: How We Become What We Study." Presidential Address to the American Political Science Association, 1991. *American Political Science Review* 86 (1): 1–7.

Madison, James. [1788]. *Federalist No. 10.*

Mansbridge, Jane. 2014. "What Is Political Science For?" Presidential Address to the American Political Science Association, 2013. *Perspectives on Politics* 12 (1): 8–17.

Meier, Kenneth and Joseph Stewart Jr. 1991. *The Politics of Hispanic Education.* Albany: State University of New York Press.

Meier, Kenneth, Joseph Stewart Jr., and Robert England. 1989. *Race, Class and Education: The Politics of Second Generation Discrimination.* Madison: University of Wisconsin Press.

Mettler, Suzanne. 2008. "Suzanne Mettler: Reply to Ira Katznelson." In "On Race and Policy History: A Dialogue about the G.I. Bill." *Perspectives on Politics* 6 (3): 519–37.

Monroe, Kristen Renwick, ed. 2005. *Perestroika! The Raucous Rebellion in Political Science.* New Haven, CT: Yale University Press.

Obama, Barack. Presidential State of the Union Address [to the US Congress]. January 20, 2015. Washington, DC.

Penner, Andrew M. and Aliya Saperstein. 2013. "Engendering Racial Perceptions: An Intersectional Analysis of How Social Status Shapes Race." *Gender & Society* 27 (3): 319–44.

Pierson, Paul. 2015. "Race, Partisanship, and the Rise of Income Inequality in the United States." Paper for Task Force on "Racial and Class Inequalities in the Americas." Washington, DC: American Political Science Association.

Pinderhughes, Dianne. 2009. "The Challenge of Democracy: Explorations in American Racial Politics." Presidential Address to the American Political Science Association, 2008. *Perspectives on Politics* 7 (1): 3–11.

Putnam, Robert D. 2003. "APSA Presidential Address: The Public Role of Political Science." *Perspectives on Politics* 1 (2): 249–55.

Schmidt Sr., Ronald, Andrew Aoki, Yvette Alex-Assensoh, and Rodney E. Hero. 2002. "Political Science—The New Immigration and Racial Politics in the United States: What Do We Know? What Do We Need to Know?" Presented at the American Political Science Association Annual Meeting, August 29–September 1, Boston, MA.

Schneider, Anne and Helen Ingram. 1993. "Social Construction of Target Populations: Implications for Politics and Policy." *American Political Science Review* 87 (2): 334–47.

Scott, Joanna Vecchiarelli. 2005. "Ironic Representation." In *Perestroika! The Raucous Rebellion in Political Science.* Edited by Kristen Renwick Monroe. New Haven, CT: Yale University Press.

Soss, Joe, Richard C. Fording, and Sanford S. Schram. 2011. *Disciplining the Poor: Neoliberal Paternalism and the Persistent Power of Race.* Chicago, IL: University of Chicago Press.

Smith, Rogers M. 1993. "Beyond Tocqueville, Myrdal, and Hartz: The Multiple Traditions in America." *American Political Science Review* 87 (3): 549–66.

Stille, Alexander. 2011. "The Paradox of the New Elite." *New York Times*, Sunday Review. October 23, 1.

Trejo, Guillermo and Melina Altamirano. 2015. "Race and Redistribution in Latin America: Why Societies Discriminate against Individuals with Indigenous Phenotypical Features." Paper for Task Force on "Racial and Class Inequalities in the Americas." Washington, DC: American Political Science Association.

Warren, Dorian T. 2005. "Will the Real Perestroikans Please Stand Up? Race and Methodological Reform in the Study of Politics." In *Perestroika! The Raucous Rebellion in Political Science*. Edited by Kristen Renwick Monroe. New Haven, CT: Yale University Press.
Wolfinger, Raymond E. 1974. *The Politics of Progress*. Englewood Cliffs, NJ: Prentice Hall.

Left Pessimism and Political Science

<big>**26**</big>

JENNIFER L. HOCHSCHILD

> If you had to choose a moment in human history to live—even if you didn't know what gender or race, what nationality or sexual orientation you'd be—you'd choose now. There's power in nostalgia, but the fact is the world is wealthier, healthier, better educated, less violent, more tolerant, more socially conscious and more attentive to the vulnerable than it has ever been. Now there's also enormous cruelty and tragedy and stupidity and pain. But we tend to forget what the world was like.
>
> —*President Barack Obama* (Galanes 2016, 14)

My father died in June 2016, aged 98 and a half. His passing was peaceful, and he was lucid and making bad puns almost to the end, so his death was sad rather than a tragedy. But this transition focused my thinking on what "the Greatest Generation" (Brokaw 2004) lived through during the last century—the Great Depression, World War II, and the Holocaust; fascism in Paris, Rome, Berlin, Tokyo, Addis Ababa; mass starvation, the Great Leap Forward, Siberian exile and gulags; lynchings and Jim Crow. Up to eighty million people died in World War II alone, across forty countries.

My father was in military intelligence behind German lines; he was among the first Allied soldiers into Dachau and tracked down the head of Hitler Youth. He would not talk about his war experience and it scarred him irrevocably, but like millions of others, he somehow came home and went on with his life (see figures 1 and 2).

My generation and its successors have had our own horrors—the war in Vietnam and Cambodia, 9/11, the 2008 Great Recession, massacres of Kurds and Rwandans, Palestine, Ferguson, MO—but they have not matched the sheer scale and scope of earlier catastrophes. Nonetheless we are arguably more pessimistic than is the Greatest Generation. The 2008 American National Election Study (ANES) asked respondents, "When you think about the future of the United States as a whole, are you generally optimistic, pessimistic, or neither optimistic nor pessimistic?" More people over age 65 than under age 50 chose optimism (58 percent to 54 percent). Respondents over 80 were (marginally) the most optimistic, at 59 percent. The survey results showed a greater disparity among self-identified liberals: 61 percent of those under 50, compared with 71 percent of those over 65 described themselves as optimistic.

My reflections on the passage of the World War II generation merge with Obama's buoyancy in the epigraph and the ANES results to solidify into this question: *Why are contemporary social scientists on the political left relatively pessimistic about the public arena and its trajectory?* Answers emerge from two distinct sources: the trajectory of social science research since the 1960s, and the reverberation of world-wide shocks in 1989.

I approach my central question through several more particular questions: What is the evidence of left pessimism among social scientists? Why is left pessimism not the only plausible stance? Why is left pessimism problematic, and surprising? Why does it nonetheless occur? How can social scientists counter left pessimism? I address these questions with illustrative, not definitive, evidence; I believe it to be convincing, but a full research project would need to provide greater breadth and depth. My evidence mainly draws from two arenas of my own research and teaching, but my thinking was invaluably enriched by comments from almost forty colleagues who responded generously to my emailed versions of the questions just enumerated.[1]

Almost every substantive statement could plausibly be festooned with caveats and conditions; I will mostly spare the reader (and myself) those shadings, but I am all too aware of the many nuances I am striding past.

Legion of Merit

Figure 1. Reinhard George Hochschild, 1949

Defining Terms

What do I mean by "relative pessimism among contemporary social scientists on the political left?" First, optimism and pessimism: The optimist "is centered on advancement concerns …. [He or she is driven] by motivations for attaining growth and supports eager strategies of seeking possible gains even at the risk of committing errors or accepting some loss" (Hazlett et al. 2011, 77) My interlocutors characterized optimistic political actors as those who "believed they were changing history, History was on their side, they have at their full disposal the instruments of the state." Optimistic scholars engage in "a political science that is founded on an intrinsic idealism and desire for/almost faith in progress." Such scholars believe that "through careful study, seeking to explain, and leading to understanding, things will somehow be better in some broad sense." For optimistic social critics, "exposure always carries the connotation, often against likelihood, of pleasing counterfactual states of affairs being attainable "

A pessimist, in contrast, "is centered on security concerns … [and] supports vigilant strategies of protecting against possible losses even at the risk of missing opportunities of potential gains." As interlocutors put it, pessimism in this context is an "attack on the very idea that progress is being made." Or, "programs have reached the limit of their achievement and their proponents have not come up with anything new." Most broadly, "many relevant aspirations have been butting up against either a) nature or b) democracy—and nature and democracy have been winning."

I define social scientists on the political left in two ways. The first is self-identification. The broadest and most recent survey of scholars, conducted in 2006, included a stratified sample yielding 1,416 full-time faculty respondents in almost all disciplines and type of institution (Gross 2013). Overall, 58 percent of social scientists, 52 percent of humanists, and 45 percent of biological and physical scientists identified as liberal (Gross and Simmons 2014). Almost no biologists, but 38 percent of sociologists and 15 percent of political scientists and historians are self-identified radicals or on the far left (Gross 2013, 46–47).

A second way to identify social scientists on the political left is through a set of shared substantive concerns. The Social Science Research Council's Anxieties of Democracy program nicely encapsulates the institutional face of leftist social science: its investigation "is motivated by a concern about whether the core institutions of established democracies—elections, mass media, political parties, interest groups, social movements, and, especially, legislatures—can capably address large problems in the public interest."[2] An interlocutor nicely summarized the distributive face: left social scientists share the commitment "that advances in equality, in the redistribution of power, would occur along class, gender, and racial lines, and international lines—that somehow the whole thing would move together."

My time period for "contemporary" is expansive—from 1776 to the present. Although I focus much more on the last half-century than on the two centuries before that, the time scale is such that I have little to say about current political phenomena such as the United States' presidential election of 2016, Great Britain's Brexit vote of June 2016, or war in Syria.

Evidence of Left Pessimism among Social Scientists

Racial and Ethnic Politics

Illustrative evidence for my examination of left pessimism and social science comes mainly from the study of racial and ethnic politics in the United States—my chief research arena for the past few decades. An only slightly simplistic summary of that field is that pointing to socioeconomic or political gains made by disadvantaged minority groups, or to policy initiatives that have substantially diminished group-based hierarchy, is perceived by many scholars to be a conservative stance. Conversely,

Figure 2. Reinhard George Hochschild, Honor Flight Network, 2010

pointing to deep and unchanging racism or white supremacy, the overweening carceral state, the racialization of immigrants, or other failures to erode group-based hierarchy is largely the purview of people who see themselves as being on the left. I discuss why that is a surprising and troubling pattern below—but first some evidence on the point.

Consider the following observations from eminent experts on American racial and ethnic politics:

the [fiscal] crisis has made Obama … a 'hollow prize' for black America …. [Racial] recognition without a commitment to eradicating racial inequality may actually end up further perpetuating inequality; (Harris 2014, 186, 187)

beyond the increase in explicit racism, … black people have suffered tremendously on Obama's watch …. Black communities have been devastated …. In 2008 and again in 2012, Obama sold black America the snake oil of hope and change …. Maybe black people believed he represented real change. Maybe we didn't. Maybe we needed the illusion of hope. It doesn't matter. The reality, among the thick fog of unmet expectations, is that very little has changed in this country. In fact, things have gotten worse; (Glaude 2016, 7–8)

over roughly the last half-century we have moved from an era of black insurgency in this country to … a period of black nihilism …. For many years now, the capacity of African Americans' ability to mobilize, influence policy, demand accountability from government officials, and contribute to and influence American political discourse … has been extremely weak, and it remains so; (Dawson 2011, viii, ix)

the election of President Obama helped usher in a *most-racial political era* where racially liberal and racially conservative Americans were more divided over a whole host of political positions than they had been in modern times; (Tesler 2016, 193, emphasis original)

> US policies are moving Mexican Americans steadily away from their middle position in the economic hierarchy and toward formation as an underclass. Segregation levels are rising, discrimination is increasing, poverty is deepening, educational levels are stagnating, and the social safety net has been deliberately poked full of holes to allow immigrants to fall through; (Massey 2007, 157) and

> [the United States risks subjecting undocumented Mexican immigrants] to the harshest, most exploitive, and cruelest treatment that human beings are capable of inflicting on one another. (Massey 2007, 150)

These are, of course, selected quotations out of a river of writing on American racial and ethnic dynamics over the past few decades, so I cannot prove that they are representative. They are, nonetheless, exemplary; the authors quoted here are among the most widely read and respected political scientists or sociologists teaching and publishing today. I could have added many other similar depictions of America's failure to reduce, or even its tendency to expand, racial hierarchy or ethnic exclusion since the civil rights era.

Some survey data support the claim that these quotations are representative of left social scientists' views on group-based hierarchy in the United States. The General Social Survey (GSS) asked respondents five times from 1994 through 2002: "In the past few years, do you think conditions for black people have improved, gotten worse, or stayed the same?" Given 7,770 respondents, we can do fairly fine-grained tabulations. Combining all of the surveys, among respondents with postgraduate degrees, 55 percent of self-identified liberals, compared with only 32 percent of conservatives, responded "worse" or "stayed the same." Among liberals, again 55 percent of postgraduates, but only 43 percent of those with a high school degree or less schooling, responded "worse" or "stayed the same." In short, the best-educated liberals are the most pessimistic category of Americans about our country's racial dynamics.

Genomics

My other arena for illustrative evidence is the ideology around genomic science; I use it partly because it is another of my own research fields and partly because genomics is crucial to my argument in ways that I will explain below. Here too, a broad summary of social scientists' positions points to a paradox, or at least a puzzle.

Evidence from public opinion, public officials' stances, and policy initiators shows liberals to be more likely than conservatives to endorse scientific research and its societal use. Prominent examples are the politics surrounding stem cell research, evolutionary theory, and climate change (Gauchat 2012; Mooney 2005; Hochschild and Einstein 2015). However, social scientists' views on genomic science show the opposite pattern. Many scholars on the left reject any suggestion of a genetic component to most behaviors, diseases, or physical features—or if they accept the legitimacy of genomic science, they "question the purpose to which that science will be put," as one of my interlocutors put it. Again I offer a few illustrative quotations, backed by some systematic evidence:

> Forensic DNA repositories are gathered by the state without consent and are maintained for the purpose of implicating people in crimes. They signal the potential use of genetic technologies to reinforce the racial order not only by incorporating a biological definition of race but also by imposing genetic regulation on the basis of race. ... Databanks no longer detect suspects—they create suspects from an ever-growing list of categories. (Roberts 2011, 264–65)

The direct route to eugenics [as in Nazi Germany] is not the issue [with regard to genetic screening for disease] .... It is a more insidious situation about which I would issue a warning and venture a prediction .... With this machinery [genetic sequencing] developing and expanding ... it is only a matter of time before elliptical eugenic uses are made of these new technologies .... The hour is late, the technology is closer, and the public debate has not been vigorous. (Duster 2003, 129, 130–131)

[Biogenetic explanations of disease are misguided, since] we literally biologically embody exposures arising from our societal and ecological context, thereby producing population rates and distributions of health. [Explanations for and treatment of disease should focus on] socially patterned exposure-induced pathogenic pathways ... that affect the development, growth, regulation, and death of our body's biological systems, organs, and cells, culminating in disease, disability, and death. (Krieger 2014, 645, 653).

In order to determine ideological valences of varying views on genomic science, graduate student research assistants hand-coded the relevant highest-impact articles in the highest-impact journals in thirteen disciplines (ten social sciences, law, biology, and biological anthropology) from January 2002 through May 2016. Keywords were "genetic(s)," "genomic(s)," and "DNA," and the articles were coded for "the author(s)' overall valence and intensity with regard to the actual or likely effect of genetics or genomics on society, or in medicine, law, racial definition, etc." The coders were cautious, classifying most articles in most disciplines as lacking a clear valence as I defined it. Setting aside biology, 72 percent of the 1,046 coded social science or law articles were deemed "neutral." Nonetheless, the remaining three-tenths showed clear differences. Roughly 30 percent of the articles in Ethics and in Law argued that genomics would have a positive societal impact, compared with fewer than 10 percent in Cultural Anthropology and Racial and Ethnic Studies. No article in the field of Cultural Studies offered a positive view of genomic science or its impact; scholars in Cultural Studies and Racial and Ethnic Studies were much more likely to see harmful or, at best, mixed impacts of the new science.

In short, the more leftist or liberal a social science discipline is, the more pessimism or concern its experts express about genomic science. That conclusion holds for both the studies' initial queries and their conclusions; as one interlocutor put it, "I conjecture that biologists, psychologists and economists are asking questions about how genetic manipulation can advance, while the humanists, including some political scientists, are asking about the (very substantial) ethical and other dilemmas genetic manipulation poses." Exactly so.

Is Pessimism the Only Sensible or Empirically Warranted Response in these Two Arenas?

It is easy to find evidence to support pessimism about American racial dynamics or the societal deployment of genomic science. The United States is notorious for its racially- and ethnically-inflected poverty and excessive levels of incarceration; undocumented migrants live in legal limbo; new genomics techniques such as CRISPR-Cas9 tempt humankind into hubristic manipulation of nature, and scientists' promises to cure cancer through genetics knowledge ring hollow to many. The question for this article is whether there are also strong grounds for optimism in my two illustrative realms, such that one could plausibly and persuasively choose to be "centered on advancement concerns" rather than "centered on security concerns."

The answer is yes. Again I can point only to illustrative, suggestive evidence. First, the gap between blacks' and whites' life expectancy declined from seven years in 1990 to 3.4 years in 2014. That is an astonishing, perhaps unprecedented, rate of change given the usual slow pace of demographic transformation. It is important in itself, of course, and also as a summary statement about an array of other social phenomena in which racial disparities are declining.

Blacks are living longer mainly because of declining rates of homicides, HIV mortality, infant mortality, cancer and heart disease, and suicide among black men (Tavernise 2016; "Looking Up" 2016; Sanger-Katz 2016; Firebaugh et al. 2014). A lot of things have to go right for a group's life expectancy to rise rapidly.

Second, applications for US citizenship rose from the previous year in ten of the fifteen years from 2000 to 2015, while declining in four (and remaining stable in one). That is an important indicator of immigrant incorporation, and especially relevant to political scientists because "Hispanics and Asians who are naturalized citizens tend to have *higher* voter turnout rates than their US-born counterparts" (Krogstad 2016, emphasis in original).

Third, non-white Americans themselves tend to feel pretty good about their lives. Gallup Poll asked in 2016, "Where do you expect your life satisfaction to be in five years?" If whites' response is standardized at 1, then blacks are at 2.97, and Hispanics at 1.29. Only Asian Americans, at 0.97, were less optimistic than whites. Gallup also asked about one's level of stress in the previous day. If whites are again standardized at 1, then blacks are at 0.48; Hispanics at 0.53; and Asian Americans at 0.75. Middle-class blacks were half as likely as middle class whites to report stress during the previous day (Graham 2016).

In the arena of genomics also, one can point to grounds for optimism rather than pessimism. The Innocence Project, "dedicated to exonerating wrongfully convicted individuals through DNA testing and reforming the criminal justice system to prevent future injustice," has enabled about 350 people to be released from prison. (Not so parenthetically, seven out of ten are African American or Latino, mostly poor men.) More extensive DNA testing might lead to many more exonerations; one careful analysis of serious crime convictions found that "in five percent of homicide and sexual assault cases DNA testing eliminated the convicted offender as the source of incriminating physical evidence." Previous estimates had pegged the share of wrongful convictions at no more than one to two percent (Roman et al. 2012). More generally, "DNA profiling [of convicted felons] reduces the probability of future convictions by 17% for serious violent offenders and by 6% for serious property offenders .... These are likely underestimates of the true deterrent effect of DNA profiling" (Doleac 2017).

Genomic scientists can point to impressive successes with regard to Mendelian (single-gene) diseases, and they focus even more on diagnoses and cures yet to come. Eric Lander, director of the Broad Institute, likens the trajectory of genomic medicine to the development of medicine based on the germ theory of disease, which "took about 75 years. With genomics, we're maybe halfway through that cycle." In his view, "the rate of progress is just stunning. As costs continue to come down, we are entering a period where we are going to be able to get the complete catalogue of disease genes." Cancer is a prime target, almost in sight: "If you understand that this is a game of probability, and there is only a finite number of cancer cells and each has only a certain chance of mutating, and if we can put together two or three independent attacks on the cancer cell, we win. If we invest vigorously in this and we attract the best young people into this field, we get it done in a generation. If we don't, it takes two generations." Lander is "not Pollyanna .... [I]t's not for next year. We play for the long game. I don't want to overpromise in the short term, but it is incredibly exciting if you take the 25-year view" (Fallows 2014).

This is a classic statement of optimism, or being centered on advancement concerns. It begins with expertise and perspective, sees dangers and weaknesses, and nonetheless asserts empirical grounds for faith. President Obama's insistence that "if you had to choose a moment in human history to live ... you'd choose now" has the same quality. My point is not that left pessimism is wrong—only that there are grounds, perhaps equally strong, for left optimism. One can choose either, and then find good evidence for that choice.

Why Is Left Pessimism Problematic?

That wily politician, Barney Frank, offers the best answer from the vantage point of the public arena: "When you tell your supporters that nothing has gotten better, and that any concessions you've received are mere tokenism, you take away their incentive to stay mobilized. As for those you're negotiating with, if you denigrate anything they concede as worthless, they will soon realize they can obtain the same response by giving nothing at all" (Frank 2015).

One can offer the same type of answer from the vantage point of a teacher. Many of us have had the experience of teaching a course—about civil war, inequality and politics, environmental policy, or the meaning of liberty—only to have our students politely request on the last day of class some idea or piece of information about which they can feel good or which they can use in their public engagement. We need to offer answers. Optimism may also be associated with academic success; one careful study found that "although achievement in mathematics was most strongly related to prior achievement and grade level, optimism and pessimism were significant factors. In particular, students with a more generally pessimistic outlook on life had a lower level of achievement in mathematics over time" (Yates 2002). A study of college students similarly found that "dispositional and academic optimism were associated with less chance of dropping out of college, as well as better motivation and adjustment. Academic optimism was also associated with higher grade point average" (Nes, Evans, and Segerstrom 2009, 1887).

And for those of us of a certain age, it is heartening to discover that "after adjusting for covariates, the results suggested that greater optimism [among middle-aged, predominantly white Americans] was associated with greater high-density lipoprotein cholesterol and lower triglycerides .... In conclusion, ... optimism is associated with a healthy lipid profile; moreover, these associations can be explained, in part, by the presence of healthier behaviors and a lower body mass index" (Boehm et al. 2013, 1425).

Why Should We Be Surprised at Left Pessimism?

For at least the past few hundred years, scholars and activists on the left have been associated with optimism. In fact, the left—understood as progressivism, American-style liberalism, or radicalism—has often been partly defined in terms of optimism. Yuval Levin, in *The Great Debate: Edmund Burke, Thomas Paine, and the Birth of Right and Left* (2014), argues that the long decades of disagreement between Edmund Burke and Thomas Paine with regard to the American and French revolutions "still describe two broad and fundamental dispositions toward political life and political change in our ... age" (2014, 225) Levin's analysis of the two thinkers is dense and complex but perhaps can be encapsulated, once again, in a few illustrative quotations. From Paine:

We have it in our power to begin the world over again; (2014, 34)

From what we now see, nothing of reform in the political world ought to be held improbable; (2014, 201) and

Every generation is, and must be, competent to all the purposes which its occasions require. (2014, 209)

Burke, in contrast, feared revolution on the grounds that "a spirit of innovation is generally the result of a selfish temper and confined views. People will not look forward to posterity who never look backward to their ancestors" (2014, 215). He confessed to the British House of Commons that "I advance to it [his proposed financial reforms] with a tremor that shakes me to the inmost fiber of my frame" (2014, 9).

Analytic philosophy concurs with and provides a framework for understanding Levin's discursive history of political ideas. In fact, Albert Hirschman's *The Rhetoric of Reaction: Perversity, Futility, Jeopardy* inspired my thinking on the subject of left pessimism and continues to shape my analysis (1991). Hirschman argues that conservative thinkers, historically and currently, tend to react to proposals for change in three ways. First, they offer the perversity thesis: "any purposive action to improve some feature of the political, social, or economic order only serves to exacerbate the condition one wishes to remedy." More pointedly, "the attempt to push society in a certain direction will result in its moving ... in the opposite direction" (1991, 11). Alternatively, conservatives offer the futility thesis: "attempts at social transformation will be unavailing, that they will simply fail to 'make a dent'." More expansively, "any alleged change is, was, or will be largely surface, facade, cosmetic, hence illusory, as the 'deep' structures of society remain wholly untouched." Finally, conservatives offer the jeopardy thesis: "the cost of the proposed change or reform is too high as it endangers some previous, precious accomplishment," or "the proposed change, though perhaps desirable in itself, involves unacceptable costs or consequences" (1991, 18). These theses may seem to contradict one another, but opponents of political or societal change frequently offer them in combination.

Liberals, in Hirschman's analysis, offer countervailing rhetorical tropes. Instead of the jeopardy thesis, they promote the synergy illusion: "progressive observers will focus on reasons why a new and an older reform will interact positively .... Progressives are eternally convinced that 'all good things go together'" (1991, 151–2). Instead of the futility thesis, progressives insist that "the world is 'irrevocably' moving in some direction they advocate." Leftists "enjoy and feel empowered by the confidence ... that they *have history on their side*" (1991, 155, 158). Finally, instead of the perversity thesis, "the progressive counterpart ... is to throw caution to the wind .... Progressives are forever ready to mold and remold society at will and have no doubt about their ability to control events" (1991, 159–60).

Hirschman may be historically or empirically mistaken—indeed, my argument is that he *is* mistaken about many contemporary social scientists. But he has captured in a typology what Levin and others have claimed through narrative: part of what it has historically meant be on the right is pessimism about societal reform or scientific innovation, whereas part of what it has historically meant to be on the left is optimism about societal reform or scientific innovation.[3]

How Do I Explain Left Pessimism?
The Trajectory of Social Science Research

The first of my two proffered explanations for left pessimism among social scientists addresses the social sciences themselves. Again I focus on illustrative themes, four in this case, rather than attempting a complete analysis. The 1960s provided vivid examples of all three Hirschmanian liberal tropes. Theorists of modernization of "underdeveloped countries," including Talcott Parsons, Edward Shils, Gabriel Almond, Walt Rostow, and Lucian Pye, among others, were one cluster. David Potter provided the vision of historical progress: "the United States is presiding at a general reorganization of the ways of living throughout the world" (Gilman 2007, 1). Daniel Lerner provided the synergy: "modernity is felt as a *consistent whole* among people who live by its rules." All features of modernization "went together so regularly because, in some historical sense, they *had* to go together" (Gilman 2007, 5). These scholars also exhibited little doubt about their country's "ability to control events"—hence the involvement of Walt Rostow, for example, at the highest level of the Kennedy administration. "Armed with the tools of social science and confident in their rational, analytic powers, representative thinkers ... define[d] the requirements for movement" from "traditional" to "modern" societies (Latham 2000, 3). As Nils Gilman summarizes, "the ideal terminus of development ... was an abstract version of what postwar American liberals wished their country to be. ... Modernization theory was the fruit of American social scientists' effort to build a comprehensive theory ... for promoting change that would make these regions become more like 'us'" (2007, 3).

I conducted a JSTOR word search for the term "modernization" in articles, books, or review titles, in English, in political science, from 1950 through 2000. Figure 3 displays the number of appearances of "modernization" that resulted from the search, and shows its rising, then declining, popularity during and after the 1960s. The trajectory is clear and unambiguous: the study of, and commitment to, modernization theory rose through the 1960s, then fell almost as precipitously in the 1970s never to rise again. In its heyday, it provided a rich and intricate theory from which many scholars developed research agendas, deep and powerful empirical results—and a level of optimism that came to be seen as both naïve and imperialistic.

A second strand of theory and research enabled similar optimism with regard to western, already "modern" nations. T. H. Marshall's 1950 classic statement in *Citizenship and Social Class*, "achieve[d] its full impact in 1963" and thereafter (Rees 1996). Marshall portrayed the progress of rights revolutions in western states, from civil ("rights necessary for personal freedom"), to political ("right to participate in an exercise of political power"), to social ("right to a modicum of economic welfare and security to share to the full in the social heritage and to live the life of a civilized being"). Achievement of these rights roughly corresponded to the eighteenth, nineteenth, and twentieth centuries respectively, in a teleology from which there was no going back.

Marshall and his successors provide, in short, a second example of Hirschman's synergy illusion and liberal confidence that "history was on their side." Ralf Dahrendorf captured the essential optimism of this analysis: "In the early centuries of the modern age ... legally entrenched differences in entitlements ... had to be broken and the principle of citizenship established. Then the struggle for giving this principle civil, political, and social substance began. From the point of view of the 1950s, it was quite successful .... It might indeed have seemed for a while that the battle was almost over" (Dahrendorf 1996, 40). This was the path to which modernizing nations could, should, and indeed did aspire.

A third strand of 1960s social science was more methodological, but shared the normative and empirical optimism of the first two. What came to be known as the behavioral revolution, with its claim to "scientific empiricism," swept through much of American social science, encouraging "a mood of optimism about the possibilities of improving the study of politics." As Robert Dahl continued, "the evidence of the voting studies tends to pile up in a single direction .... There has been a steady and obvious improvement in quality, range, and depth" (1961, 763, 766, 769). Even earlier, John Gaus had used his own 1946 APSA presidential address to lay out the "job analysis of political science" (1946). Confronted as the world is with "the atomic bomb problem," his listeners have an urgent responsibility. "For those committed to reason, as our very title commits us, we cannot retreat; we must push the application of science further into the analysis of human behavior and institutions." After all, "a science of materials ... is incomplete to man ... if he does not complete it with a science of the institutions of the community whereby man may live at peace in that community and realize more nearly what he is capable of being as a man" (Gaus 1946, 225). Alongside Dahl and Gaus, eminent scholars such as Philip Converse, Donald Stokes, Sidney Verba, Gabriel Almond, James Coleman, Arthur Miller, and many others embraced behavioral methods; their compelling findings and even more powerful mode of research still form the substrate for a great deal of excellent political science, even as their optimism about behavioral science's capacity to enable people to live better has lost adherents.

A final strand of social science research in the 1950s and 1960s speaks directly to the issue of American racial and ethnic dynamics. In the era of *Brown v. Board of Education* and burgeoning civil rights activism, optimistic theories about the promotion of racial justice dominated the academy. Gunnar Myrdal's canonical *An American Dilemma* set the tone in 1944. Dozens of chapters and a thousand pages of text developed the theme of the American dilemma, "the ever-raging conflict between ... the American Creed ... of high national and Chris-

tian precepts and … group prejudice against particular persons or types of people." The dilemma is deep, broad, and devastating. Nonetheless, Americans "are all good people; … America is constantly reaching for … democracy at home and abroad. The main trend in its history is the gradual realization of the American Creed ….
America can demonstrate

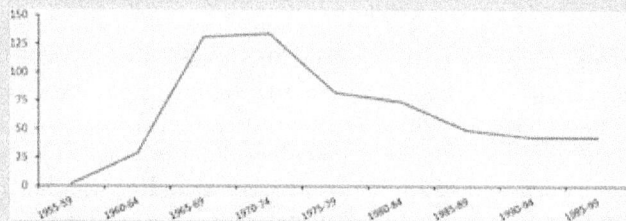

Figure 3. The rise and decline of "modernization" in political science scholarship, in 5-year increments, 1955–2000
Data from JSTOR keyword search; refer to the text for explanation.

that justice, equality, and cooperation are possible between white and colored people" (Myrdal 1944, xlvii, 1021–1022).

A decade later, social scientists spelled out one crucial mechanism for promoting the American Creed. Gordon Allport's contact theory was a subtle and conditional argument about the circumstances under which direct connections across racial lines could lead to genuine interaction and more equal relations (Allport 1981). Its argument was careful, but it rested on a strong ideological assumption: "most Americans have a deep inner conviction that discrimination is wrong and unpatriotic …. They may …sigh with relief if the law, in accord with their 'better natures,' is passed—and enforced. People want and need their consciences bolstered by law, and this is nowhere more true than in the area of group relations" (Allport 1981, 471). Allport's argument that well-designed intergroup contact would yield better and fairer relations became the model, at least in principle, for school desegregation and other institutional efforts to overcome Myrdal's dilemma.

Milton Gordon extended social scientists' optimism about American racial dynamics to American ethnic dynamics (1964). His model of the seven stages of assimilation aimed to refute early twentieth-century fears about hordes of indigestible semi-white southern and eastern Europeans who were ruining our democracy and culture. Starting with acculturation to the language and values of the host country, an immigrant (or more likely, several generations of a family of immigrants) became successively incorporated into institutions, marriage, national identity, attitudes, behavior, and finally the full polity. Gordon was acutely aware of "the deeper roots of the problem" (Gordon 1964, 4) manifested through ethnic discrimination or violence, and he almost despaired of solving the problem of race in the United States. But he remained optimistic about full ethnic incorporation, even to the point of worrying instead about the "intellectual subsociety … who, because of wide-ranging interest in ideas, the arts, and people, find ethnic communality personally uncongenial" (Gordon 1964, 256).

By the early 1960s, social scientists found evidence that the United States' new political commitment to racial justice was having the desired impact. Herbert Hyman and Paul Sheatsley's renowned article in *Scientific American* demonstrated, at least to the authors' satisfaction, that behavior change leads to attitude change (Hyman and Sheatsley 1964). They recognized resistance and hostility, of course, as well as the flaws of survey research. They nonetheless provided evidence to show that "the overall picture is … one of a massive trend …. Official action [to desegregate schools] has *preceded* public sentiment, and public sentiment has then attempted to accommodate itself to the new situation …. Public acceptance of integration increases because opinions are readjusted to the inevitable reality …. In the hearts and minds of the majority of Americans the principle of integration seems already to have been won" (Hyman and Sheatsley 1964, 17, 20, 21, 23).

These were powerful arguments, powerfully theorized and supported, and they resonated across the social sciences. Linking them with other strands of social science research enabled a vision of robust rights in modern polities, strong forces working to grant rights to those previously excluded, equally strong forces moving nonwestern polities into the modern era, and a new set of methodological tools to document, analyze, and encourage all of these forces. Social scientists had, it seemed, persuasive grounds for Hirschmanian optimism; history was on their side.

Then came the long 1960s. In quick succession, African Americans' anger erupted into violence and rejection of white liberals; the Vietnam war escalated; the Watergate scandal unspooled; white backlash - or frontlash? (Weaver 2007) - sponsored racial surveillance and incarceration; former colonial states rejected western liberal modes of governance and understandings of rights. Perhaps inevitably, the research of a new generation of scholars responded to these domestic and international disasters.[4]

I have no room to detail the history of social scientists' reaction against the optimism of the early 1960s; I will simply point to some of the results. First, theories of modernization came to appear simplistic, imperialistic, or merely wrong. In their place arose an array of analytic frameworks, almost all much more pessimistic: dependency theory, theories of the rise or persistence of religious or ethnic nationalism, post-colonialism, neoliberalism, theories about state failure and stateless warfare, governmental overload, and more.

T.H. Marshall's progression of rights came similarly to seem simplistic, imperialistic, or merely wrong. Scholars increasingly argued that the language of universal rights is itself profoundly parochial or domineering, that even western polities were built on a gendered social contract or a white supremacist racial contract, that economic inequality is rising to the point that it will overwhelm political rights and societal opportunities. By now, say some scholars, "political systems that had seemed very stable a few short years ago suddenly appear to be under great strain …. [T]he fate of liberal democracy hangs in the balance" (Mounk 2016, B7–B8).

At the same time, the shiny promise of the behavioral revolution got tarnished, even among empirical researchers. Even while celebrating its promise, Dahl pointed out that behavioralism is poor at systemic analyses: "analysis of individual preferences cannot fully explain collective decisions …, yet one classic concern of students of politics has been the analysis of *systems* of individuals and groups" (Dahl 1961, 770). In response, another array of analytic frameworks, almost all much more pessimistic, arose: Foucauldian genealogies, historical institutionalism, critical race theory, feminist and queer frameworks, rational choice institutionalism, path dependency, motivated reasoning, and more.

Proponents of these frameworks disagree, sometimes vituperatively, with one another. Nonetheless, they share the assumption that individual agency is constrained, distorted, partial, perhaps even impossible. Scholarship abounds on the tragedy of the commons, prisoner's dilemmas, Arrow's impossibility theorem, structural constraints. Two of my interlocutors captured this point well: "one of the things that leads to pessimism … is the influence of Foucault—there is no way out of the box; even when you try to implement reforms, you end up supporting the system of oppression …. [Also] at their worst, discussions of neoliberalism can be all-encompassing (like the Foucault approach)—a tight interlocked system that is hard to break through. Focusing on neoliberalism, and especially focusing on it with such an approach, is likely to reinforce pessimism." Or, "structural and critical approaches tend to assume human domination …. Whereas structuralism and critical theory were once used to identify counterfactuals to hegemony, today many counterfactuals (e.g., instances of progress) are now considered manifestations of oppression. There is no change: only stability." This is a far cry from Paine's commitment to remaking the world, or the Hirschmanian conviction that "history is on their side."

We see the same move toward less volitional and more pessimistic analyses in the arena of racial and ethnic politics. Myrdal, Allport, Gordon, Hyman and Sheatsley, and their ilk came to seem at best naïve, at worst white supremacist. New analyses moved in two distinct though not necessarily incompatible directions. The first probed the psychological, perhaps unconscious, individual impulses that contribute to hierarchy. This line of argument has developed under various labels—implicit racism, the need for covering, social dominance orientation, or dog whistle politics. Figure 4 captures this line of argument.

Alternatively, post-1960s analyses of racial dynamics focus on structures that created or sustain white supremacy. Scholars point to constitutive features of the United States such as federalism, the two houses of Congress, or whites' settlement of western territories and laws for the creation of new states. Both in and outside the United States, they identify racial domination in economic structures including taxes and tariffs, financial systems and the international market economy, transportation networks, and the role of undocumented or enslaved workers in creating national wealth. Policies that, intentionally or not, sustain white supremacy include wealth-creating subsidies in the American housing market, social welfare policies tied to employment in the primary labor market, and immigration and naturalization policies.

Most broadly and amorphously, left social scientists felt increasingly betrayed in the twenty-first century by governmental forces that they had perceived as allies in the 1960s. American leftists of my generation imprinted on the positive role of the federal government at same time that political science was maturing and becoming much more empirical. E.E. Schattschneider's observations about "expand[ing] the scope of the conflict" made a great deal of sense in the era of Sheriff Bull Connor and state's rights on the one hand, and the 1964 Civil Rights Act, Medicare, Hart-Celler Immigration Act, and the Warren Court on the other.[5] The emergence of the European Union from a myriad of small polities, with its commitment to internal free trade and open borders, seemed similarly to be an almost miraculous response to the horrors of internecine destruction in World Wars I and II.

But then came the Reagan and Thatcher administrations, the Burger, Rehnquist, and Roberts Courts, bureaucratic sclerosis in Brussels, and the USSR's repression of religious freedom and nationalist sentiment. Perhaps we should not have been surprised; over the past two centuries, American elected officials and courts more often sustained white supremacy and opposed downwardly redistributive policies than their opposites. Nonetheless, my interlocutors captured the sense of intellectual as well as moral betrayal: "critical race theory and the republican tradition in black political thought … turn to pessimism in moments where the state abrogates its responsibility to enforce the rule of law due to institutional inertia or is captured by conservative forces …. Left pessimism is a cyclical response to real periods of retrenchment." Or, "the discipline has become considerably more skeptical about what 'government' can accomplish. Under the influence of economics, states were more often seen as entities that extracted rents (Bates, Levi, etc.) or at a minimum introduced inefficiencies into a market economy. Development agencies, conscious of corruption now a major issue in the discipline, began to sidestep states to deliver aid via NGOs. So the government/state—the vehicle for collective agency—has been delegitimized."

One line of research exemplifies social scientists' decades-long move from excitement about the possibilities of human agency and government reform to the unreachable depths of psychological irrationality and structural rigidity. I teach this trajectory in my course on "Power in American Society" (with "American" stretched to include Virginia Woolf, Foucault, Franz Fanon, and other demonstrably non-Americans). The first face of power is a classic instance of Dahlian behavioralism: a count of explicit actions in which A gets B to do something that B would not otherwise have done (Dahl 1957). So the Council on Foreign Relations persuaded Congress and the president that South Vietnam must be defended "at all costs" (Domhoff 2005, 87); Miss Grava and her neighbors pressured the New Haven city council into rejecting a developer's plan to build cheap metal houses in their neighborhood (Dahl 2005, ch. 16).

Scholars responded to this argument by pointing to the second face of power, involving anticipated reactions, hidden agendas, the dog that doesn't bark. The real power is wielded by those who can keep people from even trying to achieve their interests in the political arena because they know they will lose (Bachrach and Baratz 1962; Crenson 1971). Thus New Haven's bankers need not take an active role in city governance; Mayor Lee does not bother to propose policies or reforms that they would successfully oppose.

Next came the third face of power: false consciousness, constrained imagination, linguistic and conceptual narrowing. In this view, the exercise of power prevents citizens from even knowing, much less pursuing, their own interests (Gaventa 1980; Lukes 2004). Thus the overwhelming presence of coal companies ensures that Appalachian miners oppose unionization or taxation of corporate coal wealth.

Scholars next came to perceive a further face of power: a Foucauldian total disciplinary and surveillance system in which power creates the categories of knowledge that we use to

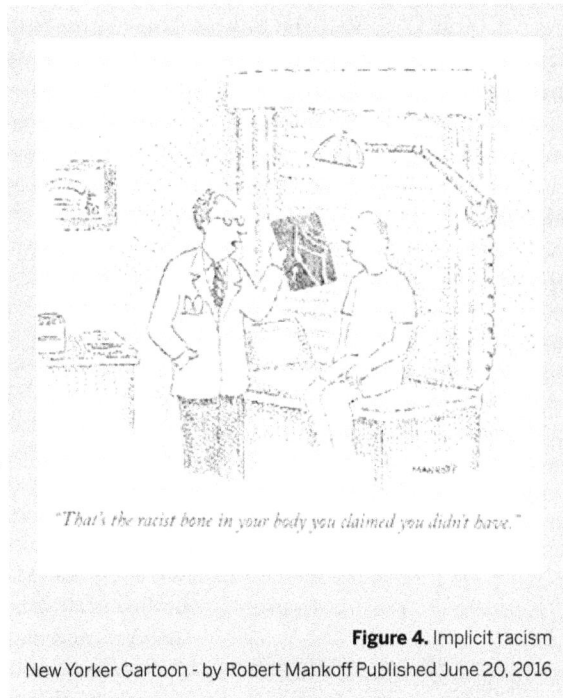

"That's the racist bone in your body you claimed you didn't have."

Figure 4. Implicit racism
New Yorker Cartoon - by Robert Mankoff Published June 20, 2016

understand power (Foucault 1979; Isaac 1987; Digiser 1992). This is truly Sartre's *No Exit*; the very words in which we think, want, or act are constructed by and reinforce the exercise of state control, down to the capillaries. Perhaps this intellectual trajectory ends in postmodernism, which depicts even Foucauldian structures and disciplines as linguistic inventions, no less ephemeral than a thought or perception. If "there is no text in this class," then each interpretive community, or perhaps each person, participates in defining or creating power. Any given understanding of power is only as powerful as the interpretive community permits it to be (Fish 1982). There is no there there.

My point is not that the increasingly structural arguments, or even the radically deconstructionist viewpoint, are wrong; any or all may capture some crucial facet of that mysterious core of political science, the study of power. My point instead is that, as political scientists pursue ever-deeper understanding of structural constraints, multiple forms of domination, or manipulated micro-foundations of political thought and action, the role of agency—of individual, group, social movement, or political party—recedes from plausibility or even visibility. Here is where genomic science is reinserted into my analysis: genetic explanations for phenotypes appear to threaten the last hope of claiming intentional action. They must, therefore, be denied, perhaps especially by those who are most persuaded of societal, cultural, political, or group domination.

How Do I Explain Left Pessimism?
The Trajectory of Revolutionary Movements

The second of my two proffered explanations for left pessimism among social scientists addresses the external world rather than disciplinary activities. The key term is 1989, the year in which the hope for world-historical revolutionary change ended.

Through the nineteenth and twentieth centuries, leftists had always lived no more than a generation away from a revolutionary movement aimed at radical structural and personal transformation. Even if the movement failed, as many did, leftists could recall or hear from their parents about efforts to make the world anew. The American revolution, the French revolution, the American Civil War, the Bolshevik revolution, and the Chinese revolution provided vivid demonstrations of what might be possible when individuals commit themselves to transformation through faith, action, and solidarity.

There were also a plethora of intermediate movements, not quite on the scale of the Big 5 but exhilarating and inspiring nonetheless. They occurred, among other times and places, in Haiti in 1791, France in 1848; Paris in 1871; India in the 1920s; Spain in 1938; Israel in 1948; Algeria in the 1950s, and Vietnam in 1973. As one of my interlocutors put it, "many of those movements drew on utopian visions whose proper starting point was the Atlantic Revolutions of the late eighteenth century, visions then refueled by the socialist and communist imaginings and revolutions of the twentieth century. All shared a belief in worlds transformed by revolution, and the implementation of regimes of liberty and equality for all." Another personalized the same vision: "We believed that progress (as we defined it) was possible and would happen (sooner or later). I think that for everyone who was significantly influenced by Marxism (myself included), this type of optimism was somewhat present: Marxism was a scathing indictment of capitalism but promised light at the end of the tunnel."

The 1989 fall of the Berlin wall and occupation of Tiananmen Square both seemed momentarily to be additional movements drawing on the utopian visions of earlier revolutions. Chinese art students created a 10-meter-tall Goddess of Democracy, who appears in figure 5. Berlin's protesters wrote "FREEDOM" in huge letters on the Wall, and danced on its top the day it was breached.

Figure 5. The Goddess of Democracy, Tiananmen Square, 1989

But massacre soon followed in Beijing, with hundreds, or perhaps thousands, of student demonstrators killed by the tanks of the purportedly revolutionary People's Republic of China. Workers who had demonstrated were tried and executed later. The image seared in our minds of Tiananmen is not the Goddess of Democracy, but "tank man," shown in figure 6. I do not know his fate. East Germans were not killed in the act of tearing down the Berlin Wall, but their desperate eagerness to do so was another deeply disillusioning moment, showing the destruction of the communist dream of an egalitarian socialist republic.

Since 1989, we have witnessed a few additional moments of revolutionary fervor—the end of South African apartheid in 1992, Arab Spring in 2010, perhaps Black Lives Matter. But the first of these moments is mired in difficulties, the second was swamped by ruthless authoritarians, and the third has not yet caught fire with a broad swath of American youth. In short, as an interlocutor put it, after the failure of the communist vision and the winding down of liberalism as a revolutionary liberating force, "the belief in big-H history has declined, [and] hasn't been accompanied by an increasing faith in human agency, the belief that we make our own world through concerted human action, cunning strategy, etc. So what's left is a belief that inequality has deep structural sources that we can do little

Figure 6. "Tank man," Tiananmen Square, 1989

about." Or, "I don't think that same belief [in worlds transformed by revolution] has animated liberals and leftists since 1989. Some of that [loss of belief] is good; a lot of revolutions turned out badly. But something has been lost too." The vacuum left by the collapse of Hirschman's liberal optimism seems to have been filled by the rhetoric of reaction, now espoused by self-pro-claimed progressives.[6]

How Can Social Scientists Counter Left Pessimism?

Let me repeat once more: I do not think pessimism about the state of American politics, or the politics of other nations, is necessarily wrong. I do think it is a choice, as optimism would be, since there are good empirical grounds for both views.[7] I also think left pessimism is an unfortunate choice, for reasons ranging from Barney Frank's political calculation to the risk of dreariness in a research and teaching arena that gives up on human agency, never mind revolutionary fervor. So I close with a few (optimistic?) suggestions.

I begin by pointing to exciting work in our discipline that focuses precisely on what I have noted as missing, systematic attention to human action and agency. Examples include David Mayhew's articles on contingency and the importance of proper nouns in the study of leadership; Nan Keohane's and Ian Shapiro's (separate) analyses of leadership;[8] Nancy Rosenblum's and Danielle Allen's (separate) explorations of how small interactions between neighbors cumulate to reinforce or undermine democracy; Steven Teles' book on conservatives' new stance with regard to incarceration; Hahrie Han's analysis of the making of policy activists, and more.

Second, political scientists are ourselves becoming more visible and energizing actors in the public arena, as evidenced by blogs such as the Monkey Cage or Crooked Timber, or public engagement through the Scholars' Strategy Network, Tobin Project, Project on Middle East Political Science, Latino Decisions, or the Black Youth Project.

Third, political scientists' teaching increasingly revolves around encouraging students to be politically engaged and efficacious. Examples include the blog, http://activelearningps.com/, re-enactments of the March on Washington at the University of Louisville, the volume on *Teaching Civic Education: From Student to Active Citizen*, the APSA Taskforce report on *Let's Be Heard: How to Better Communicate Political Science's Public Value*, and the Consortium for Intercampus Research on the Science of Teaching and Learning. These and other examples manifest the wisdom articulated by one final interlocutor: "Political scientists should look for ways in which critique is not surrender, but the handmaiden of positive changes."

Reprinted from Jennifer L. Hochschild. 2017. "Left Pessimism and Political Science." Perspectives on Politics 15 (1). Cambridge University Press: 6–19. doi:10.1017/S1537592716004102.

Supplementary Materials

To view Appendix A: Interlocutors' Reflections on Left Pessimism and Political Science, visit doi:10.1017/S1537592716004102.

Notes

1. The biggest "nuance," of course, is the presidential election of November 2016 (which occurred after this article was written). The outcome was deeply troubling to me, but arguably it reveals the even greater importance now of maintaining an optimistic vision for human societies and polities. See online appendix, "Interlocutors' Reflections on Left Pessimism and Political Science."
2. http://www.ssrc.org/programs/view/anxieties-of-democracy/
3. As a partial confirmation of the historical component of Hirschman's argument, note that Wikipedia presents a "dynamic list," that it agrees may never be complete, of roughly 100 publicly visible and reasonably well-established utopian communities in the United States in the nineteenth century. Some, such as the Owenite, Shaker, Icarian, and Oneidan sites, included several or many local

instances of a broader utopian vision. The Wikipedia article identifies four such communities in the twentieth century. These are clearly soft counts so I relegate them to a note; the scale of difference is nonetheless illuminating.

4. The puzzle of left pessimism persists even for that era, however. The 1960s were also a period of (white) women's liberation, rising incomes for poor Americans, economic growth and improved standards of living in many countries, expansion of social welfare policies, gains in health and life expectancy, robust assertions of rights in the United States for everything from free speech on campuses to non-whites' movement into all-white neighborhoods and jobs, the creation of new nation-states and the independence of older ones, the consolidation of the European Community. So why did the undoubted traumas of the long 1960s have so much more impact on the lines of scholarship that I am tracing than did the successes of the same decade?

5. Again, this broad generalization has important exceptions. Leftist scholars and activists also promoted school choice, "maximum feasible participation," community empowerment, and grassroots social movements in the United States during the long 1960s, with comparable views in Europe and elsewhere.

6. A few questions that would need to be answered to fully decide if my argument in here is persuasive: What about left optimism among social scientists? An answer would enable one to determine if my illustrative examples are generalizable. What about right pessimism? An answer would enable one to determine whether I have been examining left pessimism, or pessimism, among social scientists? Does left pessimism among social scientists extend beyond the United States, and if so, are the reasons the same? An answer would enable one to determine if I am analyzing American political science, or political science more broadly. What about the relationship between left pessimism of academics and of political activists? An answer would enable one to determine if I am talking about scholars or politically engaged liberals/progressives more generally.

7. As yet another interlocutor put it, "Pessimism perhaps made us miss real change on issues like sexuality and gender and race (especially in the past ten years or so). A lot of rules and alliances have changed and our methods and theories haven't."

8. Shapiro's main article on this topic is co-authored with James Read.

References

Allport, Gordon. 1981. *The Nature of Prejudice.* Reading, MA: Addison-Wesley.

Bachrach, Peter and Morton Baratz. 1962. "Two Faces of Power." *American Political Science Review* 56 (4): 947–52.

Boehm, Julia, D. R. Williams, E. B. Rimm, C. Ryff, and L. D. Kubzansky. 2013. "Relation between Optimism and Lipids in Midlife." *American Journal of Cardiology* 111 (10): 1425–31.

Brokaw, Tom. 2004. *The Greatest Generation.* New York: Random House.

Crenson, Matthew. 1971. *The Un-Politics of Air Polution: A Study of Non-Decisionmaking in the Cities.* Baltimore, MD: Johns Hopkins Press.

Dahl, Robert. 1957. "The Concept of Power." *Behavioral Science* 2 (3): 201–15.

Dahl, Robert. 1961. "The Behavioral Approach in Political Science: Epitaph for a Monument to a Successful Protest." *American Political Science Review* 55 (4): 763–72.

Dahl, Robert. 2005. *Who Governs? Democracy and Power in an American City.* 2d ed. New Haven, CT: Yale University Press.

Dahrendorf, Ralf. 1996. "Citizenship and Social Class." In *Citizenship Today: The Contemporary Relevance of T.H. Marshall.* Edited by Martin Bulmer and Anthony Rees. London: Routledge.

Dawson, Michael. 2011. *Not in Our Lifetimes: The Future of Black Politics.* Chicago, IL: University of Chicago Press.

Digiser, Peter. 1992. "The Fourth Face of Power." *Journal of Politics* 54 (4): 977–1007.

Doleac, Jennifer. 2017. "The Effect of DNA Databases on Crime." *American Economic Journal: Applied Economics* 9 (1): 165–201.

Domhoff, G. William. 2005. *Who Rules America? Power, Politics, and Social Change.* 5th ed. New York: McGraw Hill.

Duster, Troy. 2003. *Backdoor to Eugenics*, 2d ed. New York: Routledge.

Fallows, James. 2014. "When Will Genomics Cure Cancer?" *The Atlantic*, January/February.

Firebaugh, Glenn, Francesco Acciai, Aggie Noah, Christopher J Prather, Claudia Nau. 2014. "Why the Racial Gap in Life Expectancy Is Declining in the United States." *Demographic Research* 31 (32): 975–1006.

Fish, Stanley. 1982. *Is There a Text in This Class? The Authority of Interpretive Communities.* Cambridge, MA: Harvard University Press.

Foucault, Michel. 1979. *Discipline and Punish.* New York: Vintage Books.

Frank, Barney. 2015. *Frank: A Life in Politics from the Great Society to Same-Sex Marriage.* New York: Farrar, Straus and Giroux.

Galanes, Philip. 2016. "The Roles of a Lifetime." *New York Times*, May 8.

Gauchat, Gordon. 2012. "Politicization of Science in the Public Sphere: A Study of Public Trust in the United States, 1974 to 2010." *American Sociological Review* 77 (2): 167–87.

Gaus, John. 1946. "A Job Analysis of Political Science." *American Political Science Review* 40 (2): 217–30.

Gaventa, John. 1980. *Power and Powerlessness: Quiescence and Rebellion in an Appalachian Valley.* Urbana, IL: University of Illinois Press.

Gilman, Nils. 2007. *Mandarins of the Future: Modernization Theory in Cold War America.* Baltimore, MD: Johns Hopkins University Press.

Glaude Jr., Eddie. 2016. *Democracy in Black: How Race Still Enslaves the American Soul.* New York: Crown.

Gordon, Milton. 1964. *Assimilation in American Life: The Role of Race, Religion and National Origins.* New York: Oxford University Press.

Graham, Carol. 2016. *Unhappiness in America.* Washington, DC: Brookings Institution.

Gross, Neil. 2013. *Why Are Professors Liberal and Why Do Conservatives Care?* Cambridge, MA: Harvard University Press.

Gross, Neil and Solon Simmons. 2014. "The Social and Political Views of American College and University Professors." In *Professors and Their Politics.* Edited by Neil Gross and Solon Simmons. Baltimore, MD: Johns Hopkins University Press.

Harris, Fredrick. 2014. *The Price of the Ticket: Barack Obama and Rise and Decline of Black Politics.* New York: Oxford University Press.

Hazlett, Abigail, Daniel C. Molden, and Aaron M. Sackett. 2011. "Hoping for the Best or Preparing for the Worst: Regulatory Focus and Preferences for Optimism and Pessimism in Predicting Personal Outcomes." *Social Cognition* 29 (1): 74–96.

Hirschman, Albert. 1991. *The Rhetoric of Reaction: Perversity, Futility, Jeopardy.* Cambridge, MA: Harvard University Press.

Hochschild, Jennifer and Katherine Levine Einstein, 2015. "'It Isn't What We Don't Know That Gives Us Trouble, It's What We Know That Ain't So': Misinformation and Democratic Politics " *British Journal of Political Science.* 45 (3): 467–75.

Hyman, Herbert and Paul Sheatsley. 1964. "Attitudes toward Desegregation " *Scientific American* 211 (1): 16–23.

Isaac, Jeffrey. 1987. *Power and Marxist Theory: A Realist View.* Ithaca, NY: Cornell University Press.

Krieger, Nancy. 2014. "Discrimination and Health Inequities." *International Journal of Health Services* 44 (4): 643–710.

Krogstad, Jens. 2016. "Immigrant Naturalization Applications Climb, but Not as Much as Past Years." Pew Research Center. http://www.pewresearch.org/fact-tank/2016/09/15/immigrant-naturalization-applications-up-since-october-but-past-years-saw-larger-increases/.

Latham, Michael. 2000. *Modernization as Ideology: American Social Science and "Nation Building" in the Kennedy Era.* Chapel Hill, NC: University of North Carolina Press.

Levin, Yuval. 2014. *The Great Debate: Edmund Burke, Thomas Paine, and the Birth of Right and Left.* New York: Basic Books.

"Looking Up." 2016. The Economist, May 14, 19–20.

Lukes, Steven. 2004. *Power: A Radical View*. 2d ed. London: Palgrave Macmillan.

Massey, Douglas. 2007. *Categorically Unequal: The American Stratification System*. New York: Russell Sage Foundation.

Mooney, Chris. 2005. *The Republican War on Science*. New York: Basic Books.

Mounk, Yascha. 2016. "How Political Science Gets Politics Wrong." *Chronicle of Higher Education*, November 4.

Myrdal, Gunnar. 1944. *An American Dilemma*. New York: Harper & Brothers.

Nes, Lise, Daniel R. Evans, and Suzanne C. Segerstrom. 2009. "Optimism and College Retention: Mediation by Motivation, Performance, and Adjustment." *Journal of Applied Social Psychology* 39 (8): 1887–912.

Rees, Anthony. 1996. "T.H. Marshall and the Progress of Citizenship." In *Citizenship Today: The Contemporary Relevance of T.H. Marshall*. Edited by Martin Bulmer and Anthony Rees. London: Routledge.

Roberts, Dorothy. 2011. *Fatal Invention: How Science, Politics, and Big Business Re-Create Race in the Twenty-First Century*. New York: New Press.

Roman, John, Kelly Walsh, Pamela Lachman, and Jennifer Yahner. 2012. "Post-Conviction DNA Testing and Wrongful Conviction." Washington, DC: Urban Institute. http://www.urban.org/research/publication/post-conviction-dna-testing-and-wrongful-conviction/view/full_report.

Sanger-Katz, Margot. 2016. "Bucking a Health Trend, Fewer Kids Are Dying." *New York Times*, June 19.

Tavernise, Sabrina. 2016. "Black Americans See Gains in Life Expectancy." *New York Times*, May 8.

Tesler, Michael. 2016. *Post-Racial or Most-Racial? Race and Politics in the Obama Era*. Chicago, IL: University of Chicago Press.

Weaver, Vesla. 2007. "Frontlash: Race and the Development of Punitive Crime Policy." *Studies in American Political Development* 21 (2): 230–65.

Yates, Shirley. 2002. "The Influence of Optimism and Pessimism on Student Achievement in Mathematics." *Mathematics Education Research Journal* 14 (1): 4–15.

Restructuring the Social Sciences: Reflections from Harvard's Institute for Quantitative Social Science

27

GARY KING

The social sciences are in the midst of an historic change, with large parts moving from the humanities to the sciences in terms of research style, infrastructural needs, data availability, empirical methods, substantive understanding, and the ability to make swift and dramatic progress. The changes have consequences for everything social scientists do and all that we plan as members of university communities.

Universities, foundations, funding agencies, nonprofits, governments, and others have been building social science research infrastructure for many years and in many forms, but recently a growing number of research universities have been organizing their response to the new challenges with versions of a new type of institution we created at Harvard, the Institute for Quantitative Social Science (IQSS; see http://iq.harvard.edu). As representatives from many universities have contacted or visited us to learn about how we built IQSS, and an increasing number have started their own related centers, we offer here some thoughts on our experiences to help distribute the same information more widely.

In the sections that follow, we offer a summary of the changes remaking the social sciences, a brief overview of IQSS, and some suggestions for universities and their local academic entrepreneurs attempting to improve their social science infrastructure. Ultimately, universities build locally and cooperate internationally; as a result, the social sciences, each of the disciplines within it, what we all learn, and our impact on the world are all greatly improved as a result.

The State of Social Science
Recent Progress
The influence of quantitative social science (including the related technologies, methodologies, and data) on the world in the last decade has been unprecedented and is growing fast. Defined by the subset of "big data" (as it is now understood in the popular media) that has something to do with people, it is something every social scientist should feel proud to have contributed to. Indeed, few areas of university research approach the impact of quantitative social science. It had a part in remaking most Fortune 500 companies; establishing new industries; hugely increasing the expressive capacity of human beings; and reinventing medicine, friendship networks, political campaigns, public health, legal analysis, policing, economics, sports, public policy, commerce, and program evaluation, among many others areas. The social sciences have amassed enough information, infrastructure, methods, and theories to be making important

293

progress in understanding and even ameliorating some of the most important, but previously intractable, problems that affect human societies. Popular books and movies, such as *Moneyball*, *SuperCrunchers*, and *The Numerati*, have even gotten the word out.

An important driver of the change sweeping the field is the enormous quantities of highly informative data inundating almost every area we study. In the last half-century, the information base of social science research has primarily come from three sources: survey research, end-of-period government statistics, and one-off studies of particular people, places, or events. In the next half-century, these sources will still be used and improved, but the number and diversity of other sources of information are increasing exponentially and are already many orders of magnitude more informative than ever before. However, big data is not only about the data; what made it all possible are the remarkable concomitant advances in the methods of extracting information from, and creating, preserving, and analyzing those data and the resulting theoretical and empirical understanding of how individuals, groups, and societies think and behave. See King (2009, 2011).

Although the immediate and future consequences of these developments for the world seem monumental, our narrower focus here is on the important consequences of these changes for the day-to-day lives of the social science faculty and students who support these efforts, and for the universities and centers that facilitate them. Social scientists are now transitioning from working primarily on their own, alone in their offices—a style that dates back to when the offices were in monasteries—to working in highly collaborative, interdisciplinary, larger scale, lab-style research teams. The knowledge and skills necessary to access and use these new data sources and methods often do not exist within any one of the traditionally defined social science disciplines and are too complicated for any one scholar to accomplish alone. Through collaboration across fields, however, we can begin to address the interdisciplinary substantive knowledge needed, along with the engineering, computational, ethical, and informatics challenges before us.

Many examples of the types of research that improved social science infrastructure makes possible are given in King (2009, 2011), but consider three that have been conducted with IQSS infrastructure in recent years.

First, for almost a century scholars have been studying what newspaper advertisements convey about social attitudes, purchasing patterns, and economic history (Salmon 1923). Until recently, the largest collection included a data set with only about 200 ads per year (Schultz 1992). Today, traditional newspapers, now operating online, display dynamic advertisements where ad content is highly personalized. No two experiences on a newspaper website are likely to generate the same ad. With the resources available at IQSS, a faculty member archived more than 120,000 advertisements and documented how ad content changes as readers search for different first and last names. She found clear evidence of racial discrimination in ad delivery, with searches of names with a first name given primarily to black babies, such as Tyrone, Darnell, Ebony, and Latisha, generating ads suggestive of an arrest 75%–96% of the time. Names with first names given at birth primarily to whites, such as Geoffrey, Brett, Kristen, and Anne, generated more neutral copy: the word "arrest" appeared 0%–9% of the time, regardless of whether the actual subjects actually had an arrest record (Sweeney 2013).

Second, the quality of US state voter registration lists, from which the eligibility of voters is determined, has long been an issue in American politics. Yet, the data requirements meant that previous systematic analyses of this have been one-off studies of small numbers of people or places. More recently, two faculty members and a team of five graduate students from IQSS tackled this problem by studying all 187 million registered voters from every US state (Ansolabehere et al. 2013). They found that *one third* of those listed by states as "inactive" actually cast ballots, and the problem is not politically neutral. The researchers have gone on to suggest productive solutions to the problem.

And finally, fewer than two decades ago, Verba, Scholzman, and Brady (1995) amassed the most extensive data set to date on the voices of political activists, including 15,000 screener questions and 2,500 detailed personal interviews, and they wrote a landmark book on the subject. Shift forward in time and, with new data collection procedures, statistical methods, and changes in the world, an IQSS team composed of a graduate student, a faculty member, and eight undergraduate research assistants were able to download, understand, and analyze all English language blog posts by political activists during the 2008 presidential election and develop methods capable of extracting the meaning from them (Hopkins and King 2010). The methods were patented by the university and licensed to a startup, and now mid-sized, company (Crimson Hexagon, Inc.). Even more recently, a team of two graduate students, a faculty member, and five undergraduates downloaded 11 million social media posts from China before the Chinese government was able to read and censor (i.e., remove from the Internet) a subset; they then went back to each post (from thousands of computers all over the world, including inside China) to check at each time point whether it was censored. Contrary to prior understandings, they found that criticisms of the Chinese government were not censored but attempts at collective action, whether for or against the government, were censored (King, Pan, and Roberts 2013).

In these and many other projects, IQSS scholars built methods and procedures that made it feasible to understand much larger quantities of information than could possibly have been accessed by earlier researchers. These research projects depended on IQSS infrastructure, including access to experts in statistics, the social sciences, engineering, computer science, and American and Chinese area studies. Having this extensive infrastructure and expertise frees researchers associated with IQSS, and affiliated scholars, to think more expansively and to take on projects that would not merely have been impossible otherwise, but which we would have likely not even imagined.

The Coming End of the Quantitative-Qualitative Divide

A promising side effect of this change in research style is that the most significant division within the social sciences, that between quantitative and qualitative researchers, is showing signs of breaking down. You can almost hear the quantitative researchers—who have spent decades analyzing time series cross-national data sets with only a few impoverished variables—saying "OK, we give! So much is left out of our models that qualitative researchers include. Can't someone systematize that information so we can include it?" And at the same time, you can just about hear the qualitative researchers complaining "We are overwhelmed by all the information we are gathering, and more is coming in every day; we can't read, much less understand, more than a tiny fraction of it all. Can't you quantitative researchers do something to help?" In fact, versions of both are commonplace within the context of numerous individual research projects.

Fortunately, social scientists from both traditions are working together more often than ever before, because many of the new data sources meaningfully represent the focus and interests of both groups. The information collected by qualitative researchers, in the form of large quantities of field notes, video, audio, unstructured text, and many other sources, is now being recognized as valuable and actionable data sources for which new quantitative approaches are being developed and can be applied. At the same time, quantitative researchers are realizing that their approaches can be viewed or adapted to assist, rather than replace, the deep knowledge of qualitative researchers, and they are taking up the challenge of adding value to these additional richer data types.

The divergent interests of the two camps also converge as the need for tools to cope with, organize, preserve, and share this onslaught of data, the search for new understandings of where meaning exists in the world and how it can be represented systematically, and the rise of inherently collaborative projects where researchers bring their own knowledge and skills to attack common goals. Instead of quantitative researchers trying to build fully automated methods and qualitative researchers trying to make do with traditional human-only methods, now both are heading toward using or developing computer-assisted methods that empower both groups. This development has the potential to end the divide, to get us working together to solve common problems, and to greatly strengthen the research output of social science as a whole.

The Boundaries of "Social Science"

As social science has become increasingly interdisciplinary and collaborative, so too has the de facto definition of the field broadened. The result is that the historical or institutional definitions of "social science," based only on what work is being done in specific departments (sociology, economics, political science, anthropology, psychology, and sometimes others), is unhelpful as it excludes numerous social scientists elsewhere in most universities. We instead use the term "social science" more generally to refer to areas of scholarship dedicated to understanding, or improving the well-being of, human populations, using data at the level of (or informative about) individual people or groups of people.

This definition covers the traditional social science departments in faculties of schools of arts and science, but it also includes most research conducted at schools of public policy, business, and education. Social science is referred to by other names in other areas but the definition is wider than use of the term. It includes what law school faculty call "empirical research," and many aspects of research in other areas, such as health policy at schools of medicine. It also includes research conducted by faculty in schools of public health, although they have different names for these activities, such as epidemiology, demography, and outcomes research.[1]

The breadth of the field also covers many of those with whom we collaborate when they spread social science to their fields. To take one such example, over the last 20 years, political methodology has built a bridge to the discipline of statistics and the methodological subfields of the other social sciences (such as econometrics, sociological methodology, and psychometrics). Scholars, who began by importing methods from those fields, now also regularly make contributions used in those fields as well. Political science graduate students are now trained at a high enough level in political methodology so that they can move from the end of a sequence in political science directly into advanced courses in these other fields. Students in these other fields also do the same in our courses. The resulting vibrant interdisciplinary collaborations have resulted in statisticians and others becoming participants in the enterprise of social science.

Another version of the same pattern is now beginning to emerge between several traditional social science disciplines and computer science. Graduate students in economics, political science, and sociology now regularly learn computer languages and computer science concepts, and they are even beginning to include formal training in computer science as part of their graduate degrees. Associated with this development are computer scientists doing research in what is effectively social science. Indeed, this activity is being formalized in new departments at some universities, often under the banners "computational social science," "applied computational science," or "data science."

Any scholar doing research in the area, regardless of their home department, should be included in a proper definition of social science. In fact, strictly speaking, parts of the biological sciences are effectively becoming social sciences, as genomics, proteomics, metabolomics, and brain imaging produce huge numbers of person-level variables, and researchers in these fields join social scientists in the hunt for measures and causes of behavioral phenotypes. These fields developed very differently from the social sciences, but they now use many of the same survey instruments, statistical methods, substantive questions, and even data sets. When methods, data, procedures, theories, and institutions can help research in other areas, the more inclusive we are and the more we will all benefit.

What Type of Centers to Build

In this section, we describe the key elements behind IQSS and related social science research centers. We describe how community is the fundamental driver behind successful centers; how to build such a community even though individual faculty members may well be pursuing their own divergent self-interests most of the time; and the standard elements of successful centers. We focus on how turning the insights of social science research on ourselves can greatly increase the chances of success. Ultimately, social science centers, run by social scientists who are familiar with the social science literature, have tremendous advantages not usually available to those building other types of university centers.

The Goal

We began IQSS with a research project, asking a wide range of academic leaders what distinguished the world's most renowned academic research centers—in their heyday, the Cavendish, Bell Labs, ISR, some of the Population Centers, and so on—from others, and what was the key ingredient for their success. Most said more or less the same thing in different ways: yes, you need the obvious components such as space, money, staff, colleagues, and projects, and of course the end product in terms of the creation, preservation, and distribution of knowledge is the ultimate measure of success. However, by common assent (although often in very different languages), by far the most important component leading to success identified was *community*. The world's best research centers each had an enviable research community that caused individual scientists to want to join in and contribute. Members of the community joined for either the self-centered reasons of maximizing the quality of their own research, or because (as social science teaches) social connections provide independent motivation. Either way, the quality of the community is fundamental.

Adjusting Individual Incentives to Build Community

How do we create a community out of large numbers of ambitious, hard driving, often single-minded, researchers pursuing their own separate, and often competitive, research goals? Our answer, and our operating theory, is, at the first instant, to make IQSS attractive to individual researchers by ensuring that the specific services, products, and programs they can access make their research better and the research process faster and more efficient. Faculty and students often *come* to IQSS as individuals to solve their own highly specific problems holding back their research; they then *stay* for the research community. The advantages of the community then feeds back on itself, improving IQSS for those already participating, and then providing independent motivation for them to stay and others to join.

The services, products, and programs that IQSS offers researchers fall on a continuum from academic to administrative. At one extreme, we developed a convening power that attracts some of the world's best social scientists from Harvard and elsewhere to spend time here and interact at a very high level about their research. At the other extreme, IQSS provides what is sometimes thought of as "mere" administrative or infrastructural services, such as grant support that enables scholars to focus only on the intellectual component of proposals (leaving the rest to our expert staff); help fixing computer code, desktop computers, cell phones, or survey questions; or assistance incubating, administering, and hosting centers, labs, research groups, student and scholarly activities, and technology platforms. Although the former extreme may sometimes be more fun than the latter, activities all along this continuum are valuable. They all attract scholars to IQSS who might not otherwise have come, leading to synergies we would not otherwise have been able to realize. Plumbing may not be the most intellectually stimulating activity, but if the sewage pipes in your house break, the plumber becomes the most important person around. We are proud to provide "plumbing services" right next to someone who can help you prove the theoretical properties of a new statistical estimator, because they will each get you to visit IQSS, to interact with others, and to give back.

We therefore aim in the first instance to help individual faculty and students get their work done better, faster, and more efficiently on their own terms. Then, while individual scholars are receiving these individual services for their narrow self-interests, they cross paths with other researchers often from apparently distant areas, find collaborative opportunities, and eventually make substantial contributions to building our research community. Every path that is crossed increases the probability of an intellectual connection, even if each path had nothing to do with the reason for the connection. Individual scholars are not always focused on, or even aware of, their important contribution to the collective, but the research community is much stronger as a consequence of these interactions. The result is that the community here, and in similar organizations, seems to be flourishing and is now filled with social scientists from disciplines representing the many departments and schools at Harvard and beyond.

Organizing the Institute

We organize IQSS activities into what we offer scholars: *research programs, services, and products*. Our research programs include the Program on Quantitative Methods, Program on Survey Research, Program on Text Research, Experience Based Learning in the Social Sciences, the Data Privacy Lab, undergraduate and graduate scholars programs, the NASA Tournament Lab, the Global History of Elections Program, among others. Larger entities under the IQSS umbrella also include the Center for Geographic Analysis, the Murray Research Archive, and the Harvard-MIT Data Center.[2] These centers and programs offer numerous weekly seminars, regular workshops, and one-off or recurring research conferences. Hundreds of people come and go on a regular basis.

Services involve common administrative management for all the separate research groups, such as financial management and transaction approvals, strategic advice, human resources, and technology infrastructure, including support for acquiring, storing, and analyzing data on our high-performance computing cluster; research technology consulting, technical training classes, desktop support, public labs, and the like. We also prepare pre- and post-award sponsored research administration, following the theory that the only part of grants faculty should have to write is the intellectual justification. The key to gaining the considerable economies of scale possible from this activity is pairing common administration and management with intellectual leadership left entirely in the hands of separate faculty leaders in charge of each program. The faculty members get to focus on what they are good at and benefit from staff focusing on what they are good at. And all the while the institute benefits by the economic efficiencies gained and the community that is fostered.

Our products include services that we packaged and made self-service. These include the Dataverse Network, OpenScholar, Zelig, a research computing environment, and others, some of which we discuss below.

Applying Social Science Research Findings to Ourselves

To best facilitate the types of researcher connections that foster community, we founded IQSS as an unusual *hybrid organization*, both a research center and an integral part of the university administration. We often do both together by taking routine activities of the administration and turning those into quasi-research projects. Good social science research centers are not merely generic research centers, functionally equivalent to those in other fields save only for the subject area. The fact that we are behavioral scientists gives us an inherent advantage in understanding, building, and running organizations, in designing policies that build off individual incentives, and in fostering intellectual communities. And the fact that we have technical computer and statistical skills means we also have an advantage in automating routine tasks. Together these advantages extend the impact, efficiency, creativity, and productivity of the overall effort.

For example, by applying quantitative social science research techniques and cutting edge computer science to our own activities, we can sometimes make products that scale to many more faculty members and students at far lower cost—improving the research lives of those associated with IQSS and freeing up funding for "higher level" research activities. For example, we automated, through our Dataverse Network® software project (see http://TheData.org; Crosas 2011, 2013; King 2007), most of the activities of the Murray Research Center (previously at the Radcliffe Institute and now at IQSS). For more than three decades, the Murray was widely known for carefully and lovingly collecting and curating a small group of data sets. By automating the operations of the Murray, the staff became far more efficient.

In addition, the Murray's previously traditional model of data collection was similar to many other archives, but not well aligned with the incentives of researchers. Researchers who wanted to make data available had to choose between putting it in a professional archive like the Murray—which ensured long-term preservation, but often resulted in citations thanking the Murray rather than the researcher—or distributing it themselves—which would keep credit with the researcher but would likely flout professional archiving standards and so usually give up long-term preservation. The Dataverse Network project breaks this tension by using better technology and aligning it properly with incentives gleaned from social science research: we do this by adding an extra page to any researcher's website with a virtual archive, called a "dataverse." The dataverse includes a list of the researcher's data sets, along with a vast array of services, including archiving, distribution, on-line analysis, citation, preservation, backups, disaster recovery, among others. The researcher's dataverse page devolves all credit to the researcher by being branded entirely as the researcher's (with the look and feel of the rest of the researcher's website) but the page is virtual and so installation takes a few minutes, and it is served out by a central archive and managed by others following professional archiving standards. We also researched citation standards and developed a standard for data, so that the researcher who makes data available through dataverse gets more web visibility and more academic credit (Altman and King, 2007).

In the first year after the Murray moved to IQSS, it collected more than 10 times the number of data sets as had been collected in the previous 30 years at Radcliffe, at lower cost, and with vastly increased access to data for our researchers and others. At the same time, we directed some of the archive's financial resources to more productive research activities. The synergies from this activity are apparent in the ecosystem of research projects from around the world that have grown up around dataverse, the many scholars who contribute to and work collaboratively with this open source software project instead of building their own solutions from scratch, and the millions of dollars in federal and other grants that have supported these activities. The Dataverse Network now offers access to more social science research data than any other system in the world. The Harvard University library system has also formally adopted the Dataverse Network and is using it to provide archiving services to astronomers, biologists, medical researchers, humanists, and others. The open source software is also installed at a variety of other universities around the world.

We have also repeated this model several times in other areas. In each, we find a piece of the administration, a center, or an activity, and we apply social science methods, theories, technologies, evaluation procedures, and insights about human behavior to improve the resulting services or activities.

Because we are emphasizing the advantages of "plumbing," consider an example near this end of the continuum—desktop computer support, an essential but thankless activity, typically engendering many complaints, flames, and turmoil. We fixed these problems by setting up a system that encouraged the staff to "teach to the test." To be more specific, we customized (through considerable experimentation) an automated ticketing system, and tuned the incentives with what we know from social science research. Thus, when faculty, students, or staff have a desktop support issue, they email the support group and receive an automated response immediately and a promise of a human contact shortly. If a member of the team does not make contact within that time period, they get prompted automatically. Because their manager would get prompted too, users rarely have to wait long. If during the interaction, the staff member is waiting for information from the user or the user is waiting for something from the staff member, the ticketing system gently prompts the right person to make sure progress is made. When the staff member thinks the issue has been resolved, the system administers a fast three-question "how did we do" survey. If a user does not mark "extremely satisfied" for all three questions, then staff, their supervisors, and top management are notified immediately. Staff closely monitor how they do on these brief surveys and try to satisfy users as indicated by the questions; by constantly evaluating and tweaking the survey questions, the staff, management, and users understand each other much better. And, after some years of learning, and randomized experiments, it now seems to work well. In the last 18 months, the number of tickets marked "dissatisfied" or "extremely dissatisfied" (of more than 7,000 filed) is exactly zero. Users are never left wondering what is happening, and staff know exactly what the community regards as good service. With the management of desktop support thus effectively automated, the rest of us can turn from firing off angry memos about customer service to writing more scholarly articles.

When possible, we emphasize *infrastructure that scales*, so that spending is highly leveraged. We do this by our focus on research computing infrastructure that is naturally amenable to use by large numbers; by our day-to-day emphasis on creating synergies among the different parts of the institute; with the help from faculty and students from all over the university who interact here; and by marshaling the efforts of several open source communities in contributing software and other assistance from inside and outside of Harvard. Other examples of these activities include OpenScholar (http://openscholar.harvard.edu), a single open source (software as a service) web software installation that creates thousands of highly professional and custom-ized websites for faculty, projects, and academic departments, saving $6000–$25,000 per site (as of this writing, about 3,000 scholars and departments have OpenScholar sites at Harvard, and about 150 other universities have their own installations); "Zelig: Everyone's Statistical Software" (http://projects.iq.harvard.edu/zelig), an all-purpose statistical package built on the R Project for Statistical Computing, now used by hundreds of thousands researchers worldwide; our "Research Computing Environment," which is an infrastructure to make high-performance research computing straightforward to run, and easier to scale; among others.

Other Models
Centers elsewhere may choose to work on software infrastructure, like IQSS, and if so can work collaboratively with us on these projects, as some do now. As the social sciences branch out, get connected to other fields, and draw in new forms of data, they need many different types of infrastructure. Any of these approaches will likely benefit by applying social science principles and research to our own activities in these and many other ways.

Suggestions for Academic Entrepreneurs
Don't Try to Replicate the Sciences
As parts of the social sciences move from the humanities to the sciences, we might wish to receive the level of support from our universities that our colleagues do in the natural and physical sciences. Social science research would certainly be massively better off if we outfitted all social science faculty members with their own lab on the scale of those in, say, chemistry or biology, with $2–3 million of startup money, 3,500 square feet of lab space, and a dozen full-time employees. This is, of course, wildly unrealistic in the short term (and insisting your university administration instantly impose this notion of equity would likely get your more reasonable requests ignored), but we ought to be able to make such an expectation unnecessary as well.

That is, instead of attempting to replicate the physical and natural science model within the social sciences today, we can take a far more efficient approach that involves building *common infrastructure* to solve problems across the labs and research programs. The fast emerging models of collaboration and cooperation make this both possible and much more likely to be productive.

Don't Try to Build it from Scratch

Handing a copy of the IQSS budget to your university's administration as your budget request to start your own center is highly unlikely to work. The dollar amounts are just too big for them to take you seriously, or for your administration to come up with the money to pay for it even if they want to. If we had sent what is now our budget as a proposal to the Harvard administration to form IQSS, they would have thought we were crazy, politically naive, or both.[3] The point, however, is that we did not build IQSS from scratch; we built it from components that existed—largely unconnected—around the university. In our case, these included the Murray Research Center, the Harvard-MIT Data Center, the Center for Geographic Analysis, and some others. In most universities, a good deal is spent on social science infrastructure, but the parts are scattered under different administrative units, not working together, without any faculty direction, and each working less efficiently than they could together. Look for such units in the obvious places, but do not overlook the library, the information technology infrastructure, academic computing groups, and elsewhere in your administration.

A good approach is to carefully map out the local political landscape and find existing units that already have some type of financial support. Then talk to those individuals who are in charge of each unit and find out what they need, how to empower them, how they can accomplish *their* goals by working together with you. Radical decentralization is often the best politically achievable path to centralization. Build from the ground up and the specific request to the administration can be more reasonable and easier to accomplish; instead of something they cannot approve, you can make it almost impossible to turn down.

Build Adaptable Infrastructure

The infrastructure we need in the social sciences must be reliable and flexible. Our field, and the technologies we use, is changing fast, as are, therefore, our infrastructural needs and research opportunities. For example, as technology changes, we adapt IQSS along with it. We change the organization charts regularly. In only the last few years, we have built large open source computer programs, started new seminar series, run international conferences, brought together scholars from disciplines who have rarely collaborated, taken over and built quasi-research projects that make our university administration more efficient, started new programs, closed down completed programs and projects, spawned commercial firms and nonprofit startups, given services we developed to other parts of the university to run, educated students and faculty in new technologies, data, methods, and theories, and led many other activities. We build, but we also continually rebuild.

Build Incentive Compatible Administration at Scale

Research institutes like IQSS, and its various component centers and programs, require substantial faculty time and effort. Faculty members may love to teach, but running the university, and especially research are also an essential part of their mission. So the only way to build infrastructure sustainably is to make it incentive compatible. Buying off faculty with time off or extra compensation can work, but is not efficient and probably not sustainable. A better approach is to align the public spirited interests of the center with the private interests of the faculty leadership.

I have always been closely involved in computer operations because I teach methods and need my students to have the best possible computer technology. Leaving computer technology to the university IT department does not work, no matter how qualified they are because their incentives are first to satisfy the 95% with vanilla services, whereas cutting-edge methods researchers are usually in the remaining 5%. But the same holds true for many other areas: university bureaucracies are appropriately designed for the many people they serve, whereas researchers are by definition at the cutting edge and therefore need more finely tuned or different services.

Faculty involved in administration are at first fearful (for their time, research careers, etc.) of hiring staff and building administrative structures, but the economies of scale are valuable and when done properly incentive compatible, too. I think I got this point the first time I noticed two of my staff members going out to lunch to solve a problem without me. At that time, we had only two staff; now we have 50–100 (depending on how you count), but the economies of scale continue way beyond where we are now. With more staff, you can hire better people, build career paths, and so hire even more qualified people, and so on. Undoubtedly, economies of scale will eventually turn into diseconomies of scale, but as long as the staff is properly hired, managed, and organized, few social science centers are near that point. Managing a large staff may require different skills than managing only two, but with a proper hierarchical organization, the task need not be more difficult or time consuming.

Emphasize Extreme Cooperation
Tremendous progress can be made merely by cooperating with other units. This does not mean acquiescing to every request from the outside, because most other units will not make requests and collaboration needs to be incentive compatible on both sides. Instead, find other units and do whatever it takes to establish connections, collaborations, and joint activities that make sense. If academic research became part of the X-games, our competitive event would be "extreme cooperation"; administrative units within universities do best when they follow that lead, especially because so few do. A key to remember is that influence is more important than control. If you give up the idea of being the sole supplier and producer of every activity, you can have far more influence intellectually, educationally, socially, and politically. It is also generally worth cooperating for its own sake in the short run, even if it for a while it takes considerably more effort than the benefits received.

You Don't Want Overhead from Grants
Early in the negotiations to create many centers is a often a discussion about whether it can be funded with overhead from federal grants. My advice is to not raise the issue and to turn it down if offered. The goal is to build durable infrastructure, not meet a payroll and have to fire people with every grant you happen to lose. The library and student health services also do not pay permanent staff from overhead on grants they bring in. A much better setup is for the administration to make whatever commitment they desire. If you do bring in a lot of money in grants, some level of trust will mean that you can count on them being somewhat more generous the next time you have a request. This need not be set down in writing, or even said, but it will happen. As congressional scholars have discovered, it is better to shoot for favor not favors.

Keep a Role for Theorists
Because most of the advances in the social sciences have been based on improvements in empirical data and methods of data analysis, some argue that the theorists (economic theorists, formal theorists, statistical theorists, philosophers, etc.) have no part in this type of center. This makes no sense. In every social science field, and most academic fields, a friendly division exists between theorists and empiricists. They compete with each other for faculty positions and on many research issues, but all know that both are essential. The empiricists in your center will need to interact with theorists at some point, and the theorists will benefit by conditioning their theories on better empirical evidence. The fact that the big data revolution has enabled more progress on the empirical front does not reduce what theorists can contribute.[4]

Concluding Remarks: Federal Funding Priorities

The social sciences are undergoing a renaissance, and the infrastructure making it possible is growing, adapting, and greatly furthering our collective goals. As we all separately nurture and build this infrastructure within our own universities, we should not lose sight of a set of logical national and international goals that are even broader. Toward this end, we should cooperate and further build connections across centers within different universities. Then at the right time, we should set a collective goal to work together to change federal funding priorities. (And I'm not talking about the short-sighted recent change which effectively allows the National Science Foundation to fund any political science research except that about members of Congress or the public policies they write.)

Instead, we should think broader, and bigger. Most federal research funding comes from the $31 billion National Institutes of Health (NIH) and $7 billion National Science Foundation (NSF) budgets; in this, the social sciences are relegated to merely 4.4% of the smaller NSF budget. Although portions of NIH and other NSF programs contribute to the broader social science research enterprise, the disparity between these federal spending patterns and congressional priorities is enormous. Although members of Congress are clearly interested in many areas of health, science, and technology, they must be focused on issues their constituents want or they will lose their jobs. The issues that concern Americans the most have long been those directly addressed by social scientists, including the economic, political, cultural, and social well being of themselves, their communities, and the country. Of course, Washington is not in the business of funding researchers because they study interesting topics. Only when we can demonstrate that we can make a real difference will the funds flow. As our impact on solving problems becomes more and more obvious, changing federal priorities to more seriously fund social science research will be easier to see as in everyone's interest. At the right point, we should all consider a road trip to Washington.

Reprinted from Gary King. 2014. "Restructuring the Social Sciences: Reflections from Harvard's Institute for Quantitative Social Science." PS: Political Science & Politics *47 (1). Cambridge University Press: 165–72. doi:10.1017/S1049096513001534.*

Acknowledgements

Thanks to Neal Beck, Kate Chen, Mercè Crosas, Phil Durbin, and Mitch Duneier for many helpful comments and suggestions.

Notes

1. Among public health scholars, the term social science is sometimes confused with, and so must be carefully distinguished from "social epidemiology," which is one of many subfields of our broader definition of the social sciences.
2. We also included the now defunct Center for Basic Research in the Social Sciences.
3. By all means use whatever success we have had as evidence that your university needs to invest more to compete. And since the rules of our industry are symmetric, we hope you succeed!
4. Moreover, theorists don't cost anything! They require some seminars, maybe a pencil and pad, and some computer assistance. There is no reason to exclude them, and every intellectual (and political) reason to include them.

References

Ansolabehere, Stephen, Adam Cox, James Snyder, Anthony Fowler, Marshall Miller, Jordan Rasmusson, Benjamin Schneer. 2013. "Inactive and Dropped Records on State Voter Registration Lists." working paper.

Altman, Micah, and Gary King. 2007. "A Proposed Standard for the Scholarly Citation of Quantitative Data." *D-Lib Magazine* 13 (3-4).

Crosas, Mercè. 2013. "A Data Sharing Story." Journal of eScience Librarianship 1 (3): 173–79.

Crosas, Mercè. 2011. "The Dataverse Network: An Open-Source Application for Sharing, Discovering and Preserving Data." *D-Lib Magazine* 17 (1-2).

Hopkins, Daniel, and Gary King. 2010. "A Method of Automated Nonparametric Content Analysis for Social Science." *American Journal of Political Science* 54 (1): 229–47.

King, Gary. 2007. "An Introduction to the Dataverse Network as an Infrastructure for Data Sharing." *Sociological Methods and Research* 36 (2): 173–99.

King, Gary. 2011. "Ensuring the Data Rich Future of the Social Sciences." *Science* 331 (11): 719–21.

King, Gary. 2009. "The Changing Evidence Base of Social Science Research." In *The Future of Political Science: 100 Perspectives*. Edited by Gary King, Kay Schlozman, and Norman Nie. 91–93. New York: Routledge.

King, Gary, Jennifer Pan, and Molly Roberts. 2013. "How Censorship in China Allows Government Criticism but Silences Collective Expression." *American Political Science Review* 107 (2): 1–18.

Salmon, Lucy. 1923. *The Newspaper and the Historian*. New York: Oxford University Press.

Schultz, M. 1992. "Occupational Pursuits of Free American Women: An Analysis of Newspaper Ads, 1800–1849." *Sociological Forum* 7 (4): 587–607.

Sweeney, Latanya. 2013, "A Closer Examination of Racial Discrimination in Online Ad Delivery." Working paper. Data archived at http://foreverdata.org/onlineads.

Verba, Sidney, Kay Scholzman, and Henry Brady. 1995. *Voice and Equality: Civic Voluntarism in American Politics*. Cambridge, MA: Harvard University Press.

Restructuring the Social Sciences? A Reflection from the Editor of Perspectives on Politics

28

Jeffrey C. Isaac

Gary King's "Restructuring Social Science: Reflections from Harvard's Institute for Quantitative Social Science" (King) is an honest reflection on King's experience as founder of a successful research institute. Our discipline needs more serious reflection about how we work and what we can learn from each other. In the spirit of such reflexivity I am moved to reflect on King's piece, and to offer an alternative account. My account is also based on extensive experience, as the longtime editor in chief of *Perspectives on Politics* (going on six years) and the even longer time editor of the *Perspectives* Book Review (going on 10 years). This experience leads me to support an emphatically humanistic and pluralistic conception of political science.

Reflections on King's Reflection

King begins straightforwardly: "The social sciences are in the midst of an historic change, with large parts moving from the humanities to the sciences in terms of research style, infrastructural needs, data availability, empirical methods, substantive understanding, and the ability to make swift and dramatic progress. The changes have consequences for everything social scientists do and all that we plan as members of university communities." King outlines this change and indicates how the Institute represents an exemplary way of embracing it. His piece is clear and easy to summarize. It centers on the recent progress of quantitative social science, which he defines as "the subset of 'big data' (as it is now understood in the popular media) that has something to do with people." One sign of this progress is the impact of this science on many areas of social life, from medicine to social networks to sports (King waxes enthusiastic here); another is the diffusion of its insights to "popular books and movies such as *Moneyball*, *Supercrunchers*, and *The Numerati*." But the main sign of progress is the proliferation of quantitative research itself.

Driven by intellectual ingenuity and "the enormous quantities of highly informative data inundating almost every area we study," quantitative social science is growing intellectually—in terms of the capacity of scholars to analyze vast quantities of data in innovative ways—and institutionally—in terms of the development of new research communities centering on this progress. This is transforming, *modernizing*, the sociology of knowledge: "Social scientists are now transitioning from working primarily on their own, alone in their offices—a style that dates back to when the offices were in monasteries—to working in much more highly collaborative, interdisciplinary, larger scale, lab-style research teams."

It also portends the "end of the quantitative/qualitative divide" in social science. King writes: "The information collected by qualitative researchers, in the form of large quantities of field notes, video, audio, unstructured text, and many other sources, is now being recognized as valuable and actionable data sources for which new quantitative approaches are being developed and can be applied. At the same time, quantitative researchers are realizing that their approaches can be viewed or adapted to assist, rather than replace, the deep knowledge of qualitative researchers, and they are taking up the challenge of adding value to these additional richer data types." King's observations articulate not simply an *institutional* but an *intellectual* vision—*his* take on the influential approach outlined in King, Robert Keohane, and Sidney Verba's *Designing Social Inquiry* (1994), one of the most important books of political science methodology to be published in the past twenty years. "KKV" generated much debate about whether the "methods of scientific inference" valorized in that volume represented the tolerance toward or rather the *subsumption* of qualitative by quantitative research. King believes there *has* been a subsumption and this is a good thing. He suggests that this new model of scientific inquiry not simply effaces methodological divides within disciplines; it also effaces scholarly boundaries between social science disciplines and between the social and the natural sciences. If the new social science centers on "the subset of 'big data'...that has something to do with people," then it is easy to see how all kinds of inquiries—into physics, chemistry, genetics, neurobiology, sociobiology, computer science and "informatics," etc.—contribute to social science by analyzing data about people.

King proceeds to offer practical lessons to "academic entrepreneurs" about how to build research centers designed to promote this vision by providing institutional public goods and services; furnishing administrative management and promoting research efficiency; and "scaling up" organizational innovations from micro- to macro-settings.

King's essay lucidly outlines an approach to scholarship that is growing in influence and momentum and plays an increasingly important role in funding, recruitment, and programmatic decisions at research universities.

But unless our discipline has suddenly become a bastion of Hegelian metaphysics, it does not follow from the fact that something is emergent that it will become hegemonic, nor does it follow from the fact that something is real that it is rational and ought to become hegemonic.

King's essay is *partial*. It articulates *one* perspective on the discipline, and King is admirably frank about this. Instead of arguing with this view, I would like to note some of its elisions or silences, which suggest that it is less ecumenical than it purports to be.

Science

King sincerely wishes to include a range of scientific approaches (to the extent consistent with the logic of "KKV"). Toward his conclusion he warns academic entrepreneurs: "don't try to replicate the sciences," that is, "the physical and natural science model." But what he really means here is to avoid trying to replicate the proliferation of individual *labs*. King's entire piece treats "the sciences" as exemplary and holds that social science will progress by mimicking the nonsocial sciences. ("The social sciences are in the midst of an historic change, with large parts moving from the humanities to the sciences in terms of research style...") King relies on a conception of science with strong positivistic roots that is heavily contested in political science. King simply sidesteps all such discussion. In fairness, he would likely respond that he has already coauthored a book on this topic, and he is now doing something different—drawing lessons from the success of the Institute. Apparently he believes that this is possible without attending to knotty issues in the philosophy of science, for these presumably have been settled. Yet for many, they have not been settled.

Social Science

By construing quantitative social science as "big data" that "has something to do with people," King implies that *social* means "something to do with people." On this view most things having to do with people are central to social science, from their genetics to their brain chemistry to the epidemiology of their diseases to their climatological determinants to their responses to all manner of small group experiments. But there is a *different* view of "the social" as developed by such classical social theorists as Marx, Durkheim, Simmel, and Weber. On this view, social science is inquiry into the historically evolved understandings, institutions, and relations of power that enable and constrain what people can do as members of different kinds of societies. A classic statement of *this* view is C. Wright Mills's 1959 *The Sociological Imagination*. But it is a conception developed in different ways by a range of contemporary social scientists, from social theorists like Anthony Giddens, Jeffrey Alexander, and Michael Burawoy to "historical institutionalists" like Charles Tilly, Theda Skocpol, Ira Katznelson, and Peter Hall. This view of social science implies different attitudes about a range of things that figure heavily in King's account, from the exemplary status of quantitative styles of scientific inference to the desirability of effacing the boundaries between the social sciences and the natural sciences. To note this is not to refute King, merely to observe that his perspective on "the social" is selective, and that it bleaches out most of what would be regarded as distinctively social by adherents of a more richly sociological perspective.

Theory

King advises leaders of social scientific institutes to "keep a role for theorists." He writes: "Since most of the advances in the social sciences have been based on improvements in empirical data and methods of data analysis, some argue that the theorists (economic theorists, formal theorists, statistical theorists, philosophers, etc.) have no part in the type of center we are talking about. This makes no sense." King insists that such theorists play *some* role in contributing to the development of social scientific knowledge. Exactly *what* role is unclear. If you re-read his list, you will note that it includes mainly what might be considered "high tech" kinds of "theory," and does *not* include the kinds of theory that comprise a bona fide subfield of political science—*political* theory, that is, *historical and normative* theory. Such theory might be included under his conception of "philosophers." But this is unlikely. Given his list and its broader context, it seems likely that by "philosophers" he means the kinds of scholars of language, cognitive science, and logic that increasingly dominate academic philosophy departments. Because he has chosen to publish the piece in *PS*, and made a sincere show of ecumenicism, he could have said "*political theory*" if he intended to. King maintains that social science contributes to "understanding or improving the well-being of human populations." Yet ironically his account includes no clear place for the kinds of historical and normative inquiries about human well-being, freedom, and justice that have been central to much recent social scientific inquiry.

A Case in Point

King offers the following anecdote: "Fewer than two decades ago, Verba, Scholzman, and Brady (1995) amassed the most extensive data set to date on the voices of political activists, including 15,000 screener questions and 2,500 detailed personal interviews, and wrote a landmark book on the subject. Shift forward in time and, with new data collection procedures, statistical methods, and changes in the world, a team composed of a graduate student, a faculty member, and eight undergraduate research assistants were able to download, understand, and analyze all English language blog posts by political activists during the 2008 presidential election, and develop methods capable of extracting the meaning we needed from them (Hopkins and King 2010)." King references here his coauthored *AJPS* article, "A Method of Nonparametric Automated Content Analysis for Social Science." I am sure this is a fine article. But it is worth slowing down to analyze this passage. King is talking about scientific progress. His "evidence" for this progress is quantitative *efficiency*. While three senior professors were able to write a "landmark book" based on what was then considered extensive data, today a team consisting of only one professor, one graduate student, and eight undergraduate assistants can process vastly greater amounts of data to "extract the meaning" needed, and to present this "meaning" in an 18-page journal article.

I respect the prowess that is being described. But a question presents itself: what exactly do we mean here in talking about "extracting meaning," and does the move from *Voice and Equality: Civic Voluntarism in American Politics* to "A Method of Nonparametric Automatic Content Analysis for Social Science" really represent unambiguous intellectual progress?

Verba, Schlozman, and Brady's Voice and Equality, and their recently published sequel, *The Unheavenly Chorus: Unequal Political Voice and the Broken Promise of American Democracy*, are book-length treatments of one of the perennial questions of political science, traceable to Aristotle: what forms of civic participation do and should constitute a well-functioning democracy? Verba et al. are methodologically sophisticated. But their research agenda centers on big political questions and draws from a tradition of thinking about these questions that is historical and humanistic as well as empirical and "scientific." This tradition, linked to Almond and Verba's *The Civic Culture*, and to the work of Dahl, Lipset, Tocqueville, Montesquieu, and Aristotle, is nicely summarized in this passage by Almond: "There is a political sociological tradition going all the way back to Plato and Aristotle, continuing through Polybius, Cicero, Machiavelli, Hobbes, Locke, Montesquieu, Hume, Rousseau, Tocqueville, Comte, Marx, Pareto, Durkheim, Weber and continuing up to Dahl, Lipset, Rokkan, Sartori, Moore, and Lijphart, which sought, and seeks, to relate socioeconomic conditions to political constitutions and institutional arrangements, and to relate these structural characteristics to policy propensities in war and peace… This broad tradition of political science beginning with the Greeks and continuing up to the creative scholars of our own generation, is the historically correct version of our disciplinary history." Almond's 1988 "Separate Tables"—from which the above passage was quoted—was the *crie de coeur* of a behavioralist revolutionary confronting a "revolution betrayed." An eloquent statement of the discipline's rich history of intellectual breadth and methodological pluralism, "Separate Tables" outlined a conception of social scientific research different from the vision extolled by King. Back in 1988 Almond bemoaned the fact that what he and his generation had accomplished had become *passé*. One can only imagine what he would think about the modernizing aspirations of today's cutting edge "quantitative social science."

Perspectives on Politics: A Different Experience, A Different Vision

Almond's essay helped lay the groundwork for a broad questioning of whether political science had become too specialized and method-driven, and whether a more capacious, comprehensible, and civically engaged political science ought to be encouraged. One consequence of this questioning was the founding of *Perspectives on Politics* by the American Political Science Association in 2001–02.

Perspectives is a journal, not a research institute. Its principal purpose is to *publish* and not to generate excellent work. And its "constituency" is the discipline as a whole, and not a "research team" or the specialized audiences to whom such teams speak. It is thus a different sort of enterprise than the Institute for Quantitative Social Science. At the same time, *Perspectives* too is a political science institution that is run collaboratively according to a vision of social science. And the experience of leading such an institution can underwrite a future vision of social science inquiry.

Certain features of *Perspectives* exemplify its integrative mission:

Broadly Interesting Research Articles

We are explicit about publishing articles that tackle big questions, bridge conventional subfield and methodological divides, and are well written and readable. We have a growing queue of excellent articles. In market terms, there is a strong "supply" of research that fits our journal's distinctive profile. There is also a strong supply of reviewers willing to review manuscripts according to our specific and demanding criteria.

Our peer-review process involves many hundreds of reviewers and is designed to counter disciplinary tendencies toward specialization. The reviewer pool for every article sent out for external review includes experts in the submission's topic and approach; at least one expert on the topic who has published from a different approach and is likely to be critical; and one or two scholars who work on broadly connected topics and who "ought" to be interested in the paper if it is interesting and well written. Every article is thus critically subjected to a *range* of perspectives. We assume that reviewers will disagree. My job as editor is to read every paper in light of the reviews, to balance the reviews against each other in terms of biases, expertise, and credibility, and then to use my scholarly judgment about the promise of a piece and explain that judgment to the author in a careful, constructive, fair, and kind way. Sometimes reviewers will politely decline to review a piece. A political theorist writing about Mill, for example, might say: "I'm sorry, but I'm not a specialist on parliaments," and then recommend a colleague who publishes in *Legislative Studies Quarterly*. And I will write back, and say: "I know your work, and that is exactly why I asked you to read the paper. This paper is about representation. You write about theories of representation. *Perspectives* is not *Legislative Studies Quarterly*, and if we are to publish a piece like this, it has to speak to legislative politics experts but also to people like you. Will you please evaluate the piece from your perspective and in terms of your knowledge and interests?" Almost always, the response is "yes." A few things are notable about such transactions: (1) they are outside of the disciplinary norm and they require colleagues to go a bit beyond their comfort zones; (2) they are not automated nor do they involve esoteric methods of calculation or judgment; they involve personal contact, actual correspondence, and human dialogue; and (3) they combine editorial judgment and prompt, intellectually serious, and collegial communication with authors and reviewers. I have found that a great many of our colleagues are hungry for this kind of editing, reviewing, writing, and reading, and are happy to participate in the journal.

While some of these colleagues are connected to research institutes, most are housed in conventional political science departments responsible for teaching a wide variety of nonspecialist undergraduates. Most of them do "expert" research and value this work. But they also value a more dialogic approach to scholarly excellence and a broader style of communication; they know that political science is inherently pluralistic, and that this is what makes it *interesting*.

Books

Perspectives houses the APSA official Book Review. Last year we published reviews of approximately *400* books. Books are a distinctively valuable part of scholarly writing, reading, and discussion. They are more than containers of information and data analysis or vehicles for parsimoniously presenting expert findings. Books offer authors the chance to develop sustained and discursive arguments. They are the means whereby scholars—individual scholars or small groups of *coauthors* (which is not the same thing as "research team collaborators")—develop and express their ideas for others whom they regard as *readers* (something different than being a "consumer" of information). Verba, Schlozman, and Brady's *Voice and Equality* develops a perspective on American democracy in a way that no journal article can express.

The ability to write a sharp account of a book within space constraints, and to balance exposition and constructive criticism, involves skills and *dispositions* that are central to political science. Our journal helps to nurture these skills and dispositions. Neither books nor book reviews represent the most parsimonious way to report research findings. But what makes political science a rich, productive and interesting social scientific discipline is less the reporting of findings, however important, than the contest and communication of *ideas* about important political problems.

Political Problems and Themes

The research that King extols involves highly sophisticated research designs and methods. A recent post on *The Political Methodologist* blog went so far as to suggest that the ideal preparation for research in any "substantive area" of political science would include two semesters of calculus, one semester each of matrix linear algebra, econometrics or probability theory, and computer programming, and a "serious research design/epistemology" course (http://thepoliticalmethod-ologist.com/2013/10/13/what-courses-do-i-need-to-prepare-for-a-phd-in-political-science/). There may well be benefits to such training, especially for those inclined to do certain kinds of quantitative or formal research. But the more technical and specialized political science research becomes, the less such research can serve as a common currency of the discipline.

There is another way of thinking about the intellectual requisites of excellent political science, one admittedly more "primitive" and more humanistic than this. It is the notion that political scientists ought to discern and engage *important political problems and themes*. "Nonparametric automated content analysis" is not a political problem or theme; it is a method. Civic participation. Revolution. Political violence. Democracy versus authoritarianism. Gender inequality. *These* are themes. They implicate a range of important questions, and can be analyzed from a variety of perspectives and through a variety of methods. They are the *substance* of political science. When the proponents of quantitative social science privilege math and methods expertise, they imply that the substance can simply be taken for granted, and indeed that the substance is merely an occasion to deploy methods that allow for the "extraction" of maximum quantitative "meaning" about "something having to do with people." This brings to mind an old Steve Martin joke about the steps to becoming a millionaire. "First get a million dollars." The lack of the money is precisely the problem. And when political scientists become methodologists and mathematicians, that is, not simply value a range of methods, but *define* the discipline in terms of the importance of specific methods, and regard the achievement of methodological prowess as more important than learning languages or history, then the *lack of the political* becomes the problem.

These are complicated issues that have been raised many times in our discipline's history. King's way of proceeding is not the only way, and *Perspectives* proceeds in a *very* different way. Our journal's distinctive approach to what constitutes important research has leaned heavily toward work that addresses political problems and themes of broad importance, whatever range of methods is employed. This is a matter of editorial policy and vision. For all scholarship involves judgments of *significance*. And it is deliberate. Our editorial letters press authors to ask themselves how the representatives of other important perspectives might comment on their paper (e.g., "you are writing about Latin American elections. What do you think Guillermo O'Donnell would have said about your argument?" or "your piece as written is primarily as a contribution to the American political development literature; how do you think it speaks to the literatures on parties or political behavior?"). Part of my editorial role is to prompt authors to construct imaginary conversations with their diverse readers as a way of getting them to think harder about explaining and justifying their arguments. This makes their papers broader and *better*.

We also promote broader thinking through the scheduling and packaging of particular issues of the journal. Our March 2013 issue, for example, centered on the theme of "The Politics of Inequality in the Face of Financial Crisis." The issue contained quantitative and qualitative work, and included work in every subfield. It was planned so that this work could be read as part of a common conversation about an important and timely political theme. This is not the way most journals work. The pieces published in most disciplinary journals hardly speak to each other at all. We believe that the ability to discern important research problems, and to think broadly about why they are important, does not come naturally. And it is not cultivated by an approach to disciplinary training focused on methods (whether quantitative or qualitative). It is cultivated by the promotion and publication of work that is, for want of a better phrase, *broad-minded*.

Broad-mindedness is a *humanistic* value par excellence.

The Futures of Political Science

King is correct to observe that "large parts" of the social sciences are "moving from the humanities to the sciences…" But large parts of the political science discipline are not part of this move and do not wish to be part of this move. And the fact that *Perspectives on Politics* exists as the institutional co-equal of the *American Political Science Review* is one important sign of this. In the very heart of institutionalized political science in the United States there exists a successful and arguably popular scholarly journal that promotes, and enacts, a practice of broad-minded, ecumenical, intellectually serious, and politics-centered political science.

Perspectives on Politics is one political science journal among many, and its distinctive editorial philosophy is hardly universally embraced. It represents one possible vision of political science that coexists with, jostles with, and sometimes competes with, other visions. King's social science is surely formidable. But it has not cleared the field, and alternatives are very much alive.

In *The Use and Abuse of History*, Friedrich Nietzsche criticizes a major "progressive": "he has implanted in a generation leavened throughout by him the worship of the 'power of history' that turns practically every moment into a sheer gaping at success, into an idolatry of the actual… the man who has learned to crook the knee and bow the head before the power of history nods 'yes, at last,' like a Chinese doll, to every power, whether it be a government or a public opinion or a numerical majority… If each success has come by a 'rational necessity,' and every event shows the victory of logic…then—down on your knees quickly, and let every step in the ladder of success have its reverence." Nietzsche was attacking the ultimate metaphysician, Hegel. He was also targeting a deeper and more pervasive idea, the idea that the progress of technique and method necessarily means intellectual or ethical progress.

Political science is a science. It thus properly fosters the development of a wide range of techniques, methods, experiments, arguments, and approaches. The dramatic growth in the sophistication, academic cache, and instrumental usefulness of quantitative social science is an accomplished fact of contemporary scholarship. And it represents progress for one conception of social science. But it does not represent the future of political science. For there are alternatives. And the future of political science remains open.

Reprinted from Jeffrey C. Isaac. 2014. "Restructuring the Social Sciences? A Reflection from the Editor of Perspectives on Politics." PS: Political Science & Politics 47 (2). Cambridge University Press: 279–83. doi:10.1017/S1049096514000018.

Acknowledgements

I would like to thank Adrian Florea, Bob Keohane, Rafael Khachaturian, Margot Morgan, James Moskowitz, Sid Tarrow, and Brendon Westler for their comments.

References

Almond, Gabriel. 1988. "Separate Tables: Schools and Sects in Political Science." *PS: Political Science & Politics* 21 (4): 828–42.

King, Gary, Robert O. Keohane, and Sidney Verba. 1994. *Designing Social Inquiry: Scientific Inference in Qualitative Research.* Princeton University Press.

Contributors

Emily Beaulieu is an associate professor of comparative politics at the University of Kentucky. Her book *Electoral Protest and Democracy in the Developing World* was published with Cambridge University Press and her research has appeared in such journals as *Comparative Political Studies*, *International Organization*, *Governance*, and the *Journal of Experimental Political Science*.

Amber E. Boydstun is associate professor of political science at the University of California, Davis. She uses lab experiments, large-scale media studies, and manual and computational text analysis to study how issues make the news, how issues are framed in the news, and how media attention and framing influences public opinion. She is a big fan of giraffes.

Nadia E. Brown is a University Faculty Scholar and associate professor of political science and African American studies at Purdue University. Dr. Brown's research interests lie broadly in identity politics, legislative studies, and Black women's studies.

Peter W. Brusoe is a campaign finance, lobbying, and legislative data analyst for Bloomberg Government. His research currently focuses on organizational interest group behavior around legislation, small donor democracy, and experiential education and learning outcomes.

Christopher Chambers-Ju is a postdoctoral fellow at the Center for Inter-American Policy and Research at Tulane University. His research centers on the politics of education in Latin America.

Wendy N. Whitman Cobb is an associate professor of political science at Cameron University in Lawton, Oklahoma. She is the author of *The Politics of Cancer: Malignant Indifference* and *The CQ Press Career Guide for Political Science Students*.

Kim Yi Dionne is assistant professor of political science at the University of California, Riverside and contributing editor to *The Monkey Cage*, a blog on politics and political science at the *Washington Post*. Her areas of expertise include African politics, public opinion and political behavior, and health and development interventions. She is the author of *Doomed Interventions: The Failure of Global Responses to AIDS in Africa*.

Robert Farley received his PhD from the University of Washington Department of Political Science in 2004. Since 2005, he has worked at the Patterson School of Diplomacy and International Commerce at the University of Kentucky.

Andra Gillespie is associate professor of political science and director of the James Weldon Johnson Institute for the Study of Race and Difference at Emory University. Her research focuses on African American political leadership, campaign strategy, and race and political behavior.

Kerstin Hamann is Pegasus Professor in the Department of Political Science at the University of Central Florida. Her research focuses on politics in Western Europe, Spanish politics, and the Scholarship of Teaching and Learning.

Rodney E. Hero is the Raul Yzaguirre Chair and professor in the School of Politics and Global Studies at Arizona State University. He was previously (2010-17) the Haas Chair in Diversity and Democracy at the University of California, Berkeley, and he served as president of the American Political Science Association in 2014-15.

Jennifer Hochschild is the Henry LaBarre Jayne Professor of Government at Harvard University, professor of African and African American studies, Harvard College Professor, and the chair of the Department of Government. In 2011, she held the John W. Kluge Chair in American Law and Governance at the Library of Congress. She was president of the American Political Science Association in 2015-2016.

Roselyn Hsueh is an associate professor of political science at Temple University and the author of *China's Regulatory State: A New Strategy for Globalization*. She is completing her second book, *Micro-institutional Foundations of Capitalism: National Sectoral Pathways to Development*, which examines the politics of market governance across industrial sectors in the globalization of China, India, and Russia.

Jeffrey C. Isaac is James H. Rudy Professor of Political Science at Indiana University. He is a contributing editor at *Dissent* and *Public Seminar*.

Debra Javeline is associate professor of political science at the University of Notre Dame. She is currently studying coastal homeowner action to reduce the risks to property and human life from rising seas and increased hurricane activity. Other projects focus on adaptation of ecosystems to climate change and civil society and political protest in Russia.

Francesca Refsum Jensenius is associate professor of political science at the University of Oslo and Senior Research Fellow at the Norwegian Institute of International Affairs. She specializes in comparative politics, comparative political economy, and research methods, with a regional focus on South Asia and Latin America.

Timothy Kaufman-Osborn is the Baker Ferguson Professor of Politics and Leadership at Whitman College. Kaufman-Osborn has published on diverse topics including the discipline of political science; torture and the death penalty (*From Noose to Needle: Capital Punishment and the Late Liberal State*); feminist theory and the world of material things (*Creatures of Prometheus: Gender and the Politics of Technology*); and the political theory of John Dewey (*Politics/Sense/Experience: A Pragmatic Inquiry into the Promise of Democracy*).

April Kelly-Woessner is professor of political science and chair of the Department of Politics, Philosophy, and Legal Studies at Elizabethtown College. She conducts research in political psychology with emphasis on political tolerance, civic education, and political discourse.

Robert O. Keohane is professor of public and international affairs in the Woodrow Wilson School at Princeton University. He has served as the president of the International Studies Association and the American Political Science Association, and he is a member of the National Academy of Sciences. He is author or coauthor of *Power and Interdependence* (with Joseph S. Nye, Jr.), *After Hegemony: Cooperation and Discord in the World Political Economy*, and *Designing Social Inquiry* (with Gary King and Sidney Verba).

Gary King is the Weatherhead University Professor at Harvard University. He also serves as director of the Institute for Quantitative Social Science. He and his research group develop and apply empirical methods in many areas of social science research.

Samara Klar is an assistant professor at the University of Arizona School of Government Public Policy. She studies how individual's identities and social surrounding influence their political attitudes and behavior. She lives in Tucson with her husband, two sons, two dogs, and many fish.

Jeffrey W. Knopf is a professor at the Middlebury Institute of International Studies (MIIS) in Monterey, California. At MIIS, he serves as the chair of the MA program in Nonproliferation and Terrorism Studies and a senior research associate at the James Martin Center for Nonproliferation Studies.

Yanna Krupnikov is associate professor of political science at Stony Brook University. Her research focuses on the ways political communication can (and cannot) affect the way people make political decisions.

Jody LaPorte is a Tutorial Fellow at Lincoln College, University of Oxford, where she holds the Gonticas Fellowship in Politics and International Relations. Her research centers on the dynamics of politics and policymaking in non-democratic regimes, with a regional focus on post-Soviet Eurasia.

Gregory B. Lewis is a professor and the chair of the department of public management and policy in the Andrew Young School of Policy Studies at Georgia State University. He has published widely on the career patterns and attitudes of public employees and on public support for lesbian and gay rights.

Linda K. Mancillas is an associate professor of political science at Georgia Gwinnett College. Her book *Presidents and Mass Incarceration: Choices at the Top, Repercussions at the Bottom* was published in 2018.

Michael P. Marks is a professor of politics at Willamette University in Salem, OR, where he teaches in the areas of international relations and comparative politics. Prof. Marks' current research focuses on the role of metaphors in international relations and pedagogical techniques, and is author most recently of *Revisiting Metaphors in International Relations Theory*.

Melissa R. Michelson is professor of political science at Menlo College. Her current research projects explore voter registration and mobilization in minority communities and persuasive communication on LGBT rights. In her spare time, she knits and runs marathons.

Akasemi Newsome is associate director of the Institute of European Studies at the University of California, Berkeley. She is working on a book manuscript titled, *The Color of Solidarity: Explaining Labor Union Support for Immigrants in Western Europe*.

David Niven is an associate professor of political science at the University of Cincinnati and is the author of several books including *The Politics of Injustice: The Kennedys, The Freedom Rides and the Electoral Consequences of a Moral Compromise*. His experience outside academia includes serving as the speechwriter for Ohio Governor Ted Strickland and for Martin O'Malley's presidential campaign.

Jon C.W. Pevehouse is Vilas Distinguished Achievement Professor of Political Science at the University of Wisconsin-Madison. His research interests lie in international relations, international political economy, American foreign policy, international organizations, and political methodology.

Philip H. Pollock III is professor of political science at the University of Central Florida. He teaches courses in quantitative methods and American electoral politics.

Timothy S. Rich is an associate professor of political science at Western Kentucky University. His research focuses on electoral politics and public opinion in East Asian democracies (Taiwan, South Korea, and Japan).

Ron Rogowski is Distinguished Professor and former chair of political science at the University of California, Los Angeles, served from 2007-2012 as lead editor of the *American Political Science Review*, and is a fellow of the American Academy of Arts and Sciences. His principal books are *Rational Legitimacy, Commerce and Coalitions*, and (with Eric Chang, Mark Kayser, and Drew Linzer) *Electoral Systems and the Balance of Consumer-Producer Power*.

Suzanne E. Scoggins is an assistant professor of political science at Clark University who does work on policing and authoritarian control in reform-era China. Her articles have appeared in the China Quarterly and Asian Survey, and she is currently working on a book manuscript entitled *Policing in the Shadow of Protest*.

Kathleen Searles holds a joint appointment in the Louisiana State University Manship School of Mass Communication and the Department of Political Science. Her work draws on psychology and communication to understand politics, and her research interests include news, information communication technology, and campaign advertising.

John Sides is a professor in the Department of Political Science at George Washington University. He helped found *The Monkey Cage* and currently serves as its editor in chief.

Vasundhara Sirnate is the Director of Research of The Polis Project Inc. Her research is on variation in the state's counterinsurgency strategy, sexual violence, and collective public violence in India.

Rogers M. Smith is the Christopher H. Browne Distinguished Professor of Political Science at the University of Pennsylvania. Author or coauthor of seven books and many articles, he is a fellow of the American Academy of Arts and Sciences, the American Academy of Political and Social Science, and the American Philosophical Society, and he was elected to the presidency of the American Political Science Association for 2018-2019.

Dustin Tingley is professor of government at Harvard University. His research interests include international relations, international political economy, statistical methodology, and experimental approaches to political science.

Beth Miller Vonnahme is associate professor and chair of the Department of Political Science at the University of Missouri, Kansas City. Her research focuses on the ways in which psychological processes affect the formation and persistence of political choices. Specifically, her published work and ongoing projects explore how voters process and use certain types of campaign information (e.g., scandal involvement, physical characteristics like weight) to evaluate political candidates.

Bruce Wilson is professor of political science at the University of Central Florida. His research focuses on comparative judicial politics in Latin America and the Scholarship of Teaching and Learning.

Rick Wilson is a political scientist at Rice University interested in human behavior. His current work focuses on human cooperation and conflict. He has served as a program officer at the National Science Foundation and as editor of the *American Journal of Political Science*.

Matthew Woessner, associate professor of political science at Penn State University in Harrisburg, is the coauthor of *The Still Divided Academy: How Competing Visions of Power, Politics, and Diversity Complicate the Mission of Higher Education*. In addition to his scholarship on higher education and shared governance, Woessner served as the 52nd chair of the Penn State University Faculty Senate from 2017-2018.

Christina Wolbrecht is professor of political science at the University of Notre Dame. Her areas of expertise include American political parties, gender and politics, and American political development. She is most recently the coauthor of *Counting Women's Ballots: Female Voters from Suffrage Through the New Deal*.

Kent Worcester is professor of political science at Marymount Manhattan College. His books include *C.L.R. James: A Political Biography*; *The Social Science Research Council, 1923-1998*; *Violence and Politics: Globalization's Paradox* (coedited with Sally Avery Bermanzohn and Mark Ungar); and *A Comics Studies Reader* (coedited with Jeet Heer).

www.ingramcontent.com/pod-product-compliance
Lightning Source LLC
Chambersburg PA
CBHW081412270326
41931CB00015B/3249